LOST SCRIPTURES

BOOKS THAT DID NOT MAKE IT INTO THE NEW TESTAMENT

Bart D. Ehrman

OXFORD
UNIVERSITY PRESS
2003

OXFORD
UNIVERSITY PRESS

Oxford   New York
Auckland   Bangkok   Buenos Aires   Cape Town   Chennai
Dar es Salaam   Delhi   Hong Kong   Istanbul   Karachi   Kolkata
Kuala Lumpur   Madrid   Melbourne   Mexico City   Mumbai
Nairobi   São Paulo   Shanghai   Taipei   Tokyo   Toronto

Copyright © 2003 by Oxford University Press, Inc.

Published by Oxford University Press, Inc.
198 Madison Avenue, New York, New York 10016

www.oup.com

Oxford is a registered trademark of Oxford University Press

Library of Congress Cataloging-in-Publication Data
Lost scriptures : books that did not make it into
    the New Testament / [edited by] Bart D. Ehrman.
      p. cm.   Includes bibliographical references.
    ISBN 0-19-514182-2
    1. Apocryphal books (New Testament)
    I. Ehrman, Bart D.

  BS2832.E37 2003   229'.9205209—dc21   2003045965

9 8 7 6

Printed in the United States of America
on acid-free paper

Contents

NON-CANONICAL APOCALYPSES AND REVELATORY TREATISES   249

CANONICAL LISTS   329

General Introduction

Even though millions of people world-wide read the New Testament—whether from curiosity or religious devotion—very few ask what this collection of books actually is or where it came from, how it came into existence, who decided which books to include, on what grounds, and when.

The New Testament did not emerge as an established and complete set of books immediately after the death of Jesus. Many years passed before Christians agreed concerning which books should comprise their sacred scriptures, with debates over the contour of the "canon" (i.e., the collection of sacred texts) that were long, hard, and sometimes harsh. In part this was because other books were available, also written by Christians, many of their authors claiming to be the original apostles of Jesus, yet advocating points of view quite different from those later embodied in the canon. These differences were not simply over such comparatively minor issues as whether a person should be baptized as an infant or an adult, or whether churches were to be run by a group of lay elders or by ordained priests, bishops, and pope. To be sure, such issues, still controversial among Christian churches today, were at stake then as well. But the alternative forms of Christianity in the early centuries of the church wrestled over much larger doctrinal questions, many of them unthinkable in most modern Christian churches, such as how many gods there are (one? two? twelve? thirty?); whether the true God created the world or whether, instead, it was created by a lower, inferior deity; whether Jesus was divine, or human, or somehow both; whether Jesus' death brought salvation, or was irrelevant for salvation, or whether he ever even died. Christians also debated the relationship of their new faith to the religion from which it came, Judaism. Should Christians continue to be Jews? Or if not already Jews, should they convert to Judaism? What about the Jewish Scriptures? Are they to be part of the Christian Bible, as the "Old Testament"? Or are they the Scriptures of a different religion, inspired perhaps by a different God?

Such fundamental issues are for the most part unproblematic to Christians today, and their solutions, as a result, appear obvious: There is only one God; he created the world; Jesus his Son is both human and divine; his death brought salvation to the world, in fulfillment of the promises made in the Old Testament, which was also inspired by the one true God.

One of the reasons these views now seem obvious, however, is that only one set of early Christian beliefs emerged as victorious in the heated disputes over what to believe and how to live that were raging in the early centuries of the Christian movement. These beliefs, and the group who promoted them, came to be thought of as "orthodox" (literally meaning, "the right belief"), and alternative views—such as the view that there are two gods, or that the true God did not create the world, or that Jesus was not actually human or not actually divine, etc.—came to be labeled "heresy" (= false belief) and were then ruled out of court. Moreover, the victors in the struggles to establish Christian orthodoxy not only won their theological battles, they also rewrote the history of the conflict; later readers, then, naturally assumed that the victorious views had been embraced by the vast majority of Christians from the very beginning, all the way back to Jesus and his closest followers, the apostles.

What then of the other books that claimed to be written by these apostles, the ones that did not come to form part of the New Testament? For the most part they were suppressed, forgotten, or destroyed—in one way or another lost, except insofar as they were mentioned by those who opposed them, who quoted them precisely in order to show how wrong they were. But we should not overlook the circumstance that in some times and places these "other" writings were in fact sacred books, read and revered by devout people who understood themselves to be Christian. Such people believed that they were following the real teachings of Jesus, as found in the authoritative texts that they maintained were written by Jesus' own apostles.

Historians today realize that it is over-simplified to say that these alternative theologies are aberrations because they are not represented in the New Testament. For the New Testament itself is the collection of books that *emerged* from the conflict, the group of books advocated by the side of the disputes that eventually established itself as dominant and handed the books down to posterity as "the" Christian Scriptures.

This triumph did not happen immediately after Jesus' death. Jesus is usually thought to have died around 30 CE.[1] Christians probably began to produce writings shortly afterwards, although our earliest surviving writings, the letters of Paul, were not made for another twenty years or so (around 50–60 CE). Soon the floodgates opened, however, and Christians of varying theological and ecclesiastical persuasion wrote all kinds of books: Gospels recording the words, deeds, and activities of Jesus; accounts of the miraculous lives and teachings of early Christian leaders ("acts of the apostles"); personal letters ("epistles") to and from Christian leaders and communities; prophetic revelations from God concerning how the world came to be or how it was going to end ("revelations" or "apocalypses"), and so on. Some of these writings may well have been produced by the original apostles of Jesus. But already within thirty or forty years books began to appear that *claimed* to be written by apostles, which in fact were forgeries in their names (see, e.g., 2 Thess. 2:2).

---

[1]I.e., 30 of the "Common Era," which is the same as the older designation, AD 30.

The practice of Christian forgery has a long and distinguished history. We know of Gospels and other sacred books forged in the names of the apostles down into the Middle Ages—and on, in fact, to the present day. Some of the more ancient ones have been discovered only in recent times by trained archaeologists or rummaging bedouin, including Gospels allegedly written by Jesus' close disciple Peter, his female companion Mary Magdalene, and his twin brother Didymus Judas Thomas.

The debates over which texts actually were apostolic, and therefore authoritative, lasted many years, decades, even centuries. Eventually—by about the end of the third Christian century—the views of one group emerged as victorious. This group was itself internally diverse, but it agreed on major issues of the faith, including the existence of one God, the creator of all, who was the Father of Jesus Christ, who was both divine and human, who along with the Father and the Holy Spirit together made up the divine godhead. This group promoted its own collection of books as the only true and authentic ones, and urged that some of these books were sacred authorities, the "New" Testament that was to be read alongside of and that was at least as authoritative as the "Old" Testament taken over from the Jews.

When was this New Testament finally collected and authorized? The first instance we have of any Christian author urging that our current twenty-seven books, and only these twenty-seven, should be accepted as Scripture occurred in the year 367 CE, in a letter written by the powerful bishop of Alexandria (Egypt), Athanasius. Even then the matter was not finally resolved, however, as different churches, even within the orthodox form of Christianity, had different ideas—for example, about whether the Apocalypse of John could be accepted as Scripture (it finally was, of course), or whether the Apocalypse of Peter should be (it was not); whether the epistle of Hebrews should be included (it was) or the epistle of Barnabas (it was not); and so on. In other words, the debates lasted over three hundred years.

The issues I have been addressing in the previous paragraphs are highly involved, of course, and require a good deal of discussion and reflection. I have dealt with them at greater length in the book written as a companion to the present collection of texts: *Lost Christianities: The Battles for Scripture and the Faiths We Never Knew* (New York: Oxford University Press, 2003). There I discuss the wide ranging diversity of the early Christian movement of the first three centuries, the battles between "heresies" and "orthodoxy," the production of forged documents in the heat of the battle by all sides, the question of how some of these books came to be included in the canon of Scripture, on what grounds, and when. The present volume is intended to provide easy and ready access to the texts discussed in *Lost Christianities*—that is, revered texts that were *not* included in the canon. Many of these texts were excluded precisely because they were thought to embody heretical concerns and perspectives. Others were accepted as "orthodox," but were not deemed worthy of acceptance in the sacred canon of Scripture, for one reason or another.

I have called this collection of other sacred texts "Lost Scriptures," even though the writings I have included here are obviously no longer lost. But most of them *were* lost, for centuries, until they turned up in modern times in archaeological discoveries or in systematic searches through the monasteries and libraries of the Middle East and Europe. Some of them are known only in part, as fragments of once-entire texts have appeared—for example, a famous Gospel allegedly written by the apostle Peter. Others are cited by ancient opponents of heresy precisely in order to oppose them— for example, Gospels used by different groups of early Jewish Christians. Yet other books have turned up in their entirety—for example, the Gospel allegedly written by Jesus' twin brother Judas Thomas. And yet others have been available for a long time to scholars, but are not widely known outside their ranks—for example, the account of the miraculous life of Paul's female companion Thecla.

Scholars have never devised an adequate term for these "Lost Scriptures." Sometimes they are referred to as the Christian "Pseudepigrapha," based on a Greek term which means "written under a false name." But some of the books are anonymous rather than pseudonymous. Moreover, in the judgment of most New Testament scholars, even some of the books that were eventually included in the canon (e.g., 2 Peter) are pseudonymous.

And so, more often these texts are referred to as the early Christian "Apocrypha," another problematic term, in that it technically refers to "hidden books" (the literal meaning of "apocrypha"), hidden either because they contained secret revelations or because they simply were not meant for general consumption. A number of these books, however, do not fit that designation, as they were written for general audiences. Still, so long as everyone agrees that in the present context, the term "early Christian apocrypha" may designate books that were sometimes thought to be scripture but which were nonetheless finally excluded from the canon, then the term can still serve a useful function.

The present collection of early Christian apocrypha is not meant to be exhaustive, nor is this the only place one can turn now to find some of these texts. Most other collections of the lost Scriptures, however, cover only certain kinds of documents (e.g., non-canonical Gospels)[2] or documents discovered in only one place (e.g., the cache of "gnostic" writings discovered near Nag Hammadi Egypt in 1945).[3] Or they include several of the "other" scriptural texts only as a part of a wider collection of early Christian documents.[4] The major collections that contain all of these early Christian writings—and even more—are written for scholars and embody scholarly concerns.[5] The

---

[2]See, for example, the handy collection by Ron Cameron, *The Other Gospels* (Philadelphia: Westminster Press, 1982) and more recently by Robert Miller, *The Complete Gospels: Annotated Scholars Version* (Sonoma, CA: Polebridge Press, 1994). [3]E.g., James Robinson, ed. *The Nag Hammadi Library in English*, 4th ed. (New York/Leiden: E.J. Brill, 1996). [4]For example, Bart D. Ehrman, *After the New Testament: A Reader in Early Christianity* (New York: Oxford University Press, 1999). [5]Most accessibly, J.K. Elliott, *The Apocryphal New Testament: A Collection of Apocryphal Christian Literature in English Translation* (Oxford: Clarendon Press, 1993), and yet more comprehensively, Wilhelm Schneemelcher, ed. *New Testament Apocrypha*, 2 vols., tr. R. McL. Wilson (Louisville, KY: Westminster/John Knox, 1991).

purpose of the present collection is to provide the non-scholar with easy access to these ancient Christian documents that were sometimes regarded as sacred authorities for Christian faith and practice. I have organized the collection in traditional rubrics, based for the most part on the genres that eventually came to comprise the New Testament: Gospels, Acts, Epistles, and Apocalypses (including in the final two categories related kinds of writings). I have also included several "canonical lists" from the early centuries of Christianity—that is, lists of books that were thought by their authors to be the canon. This final category shows how even within "orthodox" circles there was considerable debate concerning which books to include.

Altogether there are forty-seven different texts here, each provided with a concise introduction. Most of the texts are given in their entirety. For some of the very long ones, I have given sufficiently lengthy extracts to provide a sense of what the books were like. Each is in a modern and highly readable English translation. Nineteen of the translations are my own.

In conclusion I would like to thank those who have made this volume a possibility: my wife, Sarah Beckwith, whose insatiable curiosity and vast knowledge make her, among other things, an extraordinary dialogue partner; my graduate student at the University of North Carolina at Chapel Hill, Carl Cosaert, whose diligence as a research assistant is *sans pareil;* Darryl Gless, my unusually supportive Senior Associate Dean, and the entire dean's office at UNC-Chapel Hill, who provided me with a much needed academic leave from my duties as chair in the Department of Religious Studies, allowing me to complete the project; and especially my editor Robert Miller, who convinced me to produce the book and once more went above and beyond the call of editorial duty in helping me bring it to completion.

NON-CANONICAL GOSPELS

Introduction

There were many Gospels available to early Christians—not just the Matthew, Mark, Luke, and John familiar to readers of the New Testament today. Even though most of these other Gospels have become lost from public view, some were highly influential within orthodox circles throughout the Middle Ages. These would include, for example, the intriguing Infancy Gospel of Thomas, which tells of the miraculous and often mischievous deeds of Jesus as a young boy between the ages of five and twelve, and the so-called Proto-Gospel of James, which records events leading up to (and including) Jesus' birth by recounting the miraculous birth, early life, and betrothal of his mother, the Virgin Mary—an account highly influential on pictorial art in subsequent centuries.

Others of these Gospels played a significant role in one community or another in antiquity, but came to be lost—known to us only by name until modern times, when uncovered by professional archaeologists looking for them or by accident. Of these, some have been uncovered in their entirety, as is the case of the Coptic Gospel of Thomas, a collection of 114 sayings of Jesus, some evidently representing actual teachings of the historical Jesus, but others conveying "gnostic" understandings of Jesus' message. Other Gospels have been recovered only in fragments, including the famous Gospel allegedly written by Peter, Jesus' apostle, which, among other things, records the actual events of the resurrection, in which Jesus is seen emerging from his tomb, tall as a giant. Yet others are known only as they are briefly quoted by church fathers who cite them in order to malign their views, including several Gospels used by various groups of Jewish Christians in the early centuries of the church.

I have included fifteen of our earliest non-canonical Gospels in the collection here. They are of varying theological persuasion: some appear to be perfectly "orthodox" in their views (e.g., Egerton Papyrus 2); others represent a form of Jewish Christianity that later came to be condemned as heretical (e.g., the Gospel of the Nazareans); yet others appear to have been written by early Christian "Gnostics"[1] (e.g., the Gospel of Philip). These texts are not completely representative of the various forms of early Christian belief about Jesus' words, deeds, and activities; but since they derive from a wide range of time and place from within the first three centuries of early Christianity, they give some sense of the rich diversity of Christian views from this early period of the church.

---

[1]For the views of Gnostics, see Ehrman, *Lost Christianities*, 113–34.

The Gospel of the Nazareans

Jewish Christians in the early centuries of the church were widely thought to have preferred the Gospel of Matthew to all others, since it is Matthew that stresses the importance of keeping the Jewish Law down to every jot and tittle (5:17–20) and that emphasizes, more than any other, the Jewishness of Jesus.[1] According to a number of ancient sources, one group of Jewish Christians, sometimes known as the Nazareans, produced their own version of Matthew, translated into Aramaic, the language of Jesus and of Jews living in Palestine.[2] This version would have been produced sometime near the end of the first century or the beginning of the second.

Eventually this "Gospel of the Nazareans" fell into disfavor with the Christian community at large, both because few Christians in later centuries could read Aramaic and because the Gospel's Jewish emphases were considered suspicious. As a result, the Gospel came to be lost. Now we know of it only through quotations of its text by church fathers like Jerome, and by references to it in the margins of several Greek manuscripts of the Gospel according to Matthew.

These quotations reveal clearly the Jewish-Christian concerns of the Gospel and show that the Gospel contained stories of Jesus' baptism, public ministry, death, and resurrection. It evidently did not include, however, the first two chapters of Matthew's Gospel, which record the events surrounding Jesus' miraculous birth. For according to many Jewish Christians, Jesus was not born of a virgin, but was a natural human being who was specially chosen to be the messiah because God considered him to be more righteous than anyone else.

Today scholars debate whether the church fathers were right in thinking that the Gospel of the Nazareans was an Aramaic version of Matthew; it may have instead been an original composition, in Aramaic, based on oral traditions about Jesus that were in wide circulation and available both to this author and the author of Matthew.

---

[1]See Bart D. Ehrman, *The New Testament: A Historical Introduction to the Early Christian Writings*, 3rd ed. (New York: Oxford, 2003), chap. 7.   [2]See Ehrman, *Lost Christianities*, 99–103.

Translation by Bart D. Ehrman, based on the Greek, Latin, and Syriac texts in A. F. J. Klijn, *Jewish-Christian Gospel Tradition* (VCSupp 17; Leiden: E. J. Brill, 1992) 47–115.

The following are the fragments of the Gospel quoted in our surviving sources.

1 It is written in a certain Gospel that is called "according to the Hebrews" (if in any event anyone is inclined to accept it, not as an authority, but to shed some light on the question we have posed) that another rich man asked [Jesus], "Master, what good thing must I do to have life?" He replied to him, "O man, you should keep the law and the prophets." He responded, "I have already done that." Jesus said to him, "Go, sell all that you have and distribute the proceeds to the poor; then come, follow me."

But the rich man began to scratch his head, for he was not pleased. And the Lord said to him, "How can you say, 'I have kept the law and the prophets?' For it is written in the law, 'You shall love your neighbor as yourself.' But look, many of your brothers, sons of Abraham, are clothed in excrement and dying of hunger while your house is filled with many good things, not one of which goes forth to these others." He turned and said to his disciple Simon, sitting beside him, "Simon, son of Jonah, it is easier for a camel to pass through the eye of a needle than for a rich person to enter the kingdom of heaven." (Origen, *Commentary on Matthew*, 15, 14)

2 [Cf. Matt. 25:14–30] For the Gospel that has come down to us in Hebrew letters makes the threat not against the one who hid the (master's) money but against the one who engaged in riotous living. For [the master] had three slaves, one who used up his fortune with whores and flute-players, one who invested the money and increased its value, and one who hid it. The first was welcomed with open arms, the second was blamed, and only the third was locked up in prison. (Eusebius, *Theophania*, 4, 22)

3 But [the Lord] taught about the reason for the division of the souls in the houses, as we have found somewhere in the Gospel used by the Jews and written in Hebrew, where he says "I will choose for myself those who are good— those given to me by my Father in heaven." (Eusebius, *Theophania* 4, 12)

4 In the Gospel that is called "according to the Hebrews," for the words, "bread to sustain our lives" I found the word "mahar," which means "[bread] for tomorrow." (Jerome, *Commentary on Matthew*, 6, 11)

5 In the Gospel that the Nazareans and Ebionites use, which I recently translated from Hebrew into Greek, and which most people consider the authentic version of Matthew, the man with a withered hand is described as a mason, who sought for help in words like these: "I was a mason who made a living with my hands; I beseech you, Jesus, restore my health so I do not have to beg for food shamefully." (Jerome, *Commentary on Matthew*, 12, 13)

6 In the Gospel the Nazareans use, we find "son of Johoiada" instead of "son of Barachia." (Jerome, *Commentary on Matthew* 23, 35)

7 The name of that one (i.e., Barabbas) is interpreted to mean "son of their master" in the Gospel written according to the Hebrews. (Jerome, *Commentary on Matthew* 27, 16)

8 In the Gospel we have often referred to, we read that "the enormous lintel of the temple was broken and split apart." (Jerome, *Commentary on Matthew* 27, 51)

9 In the Gospel according to the Hebrews, which was actually written in the Chaldean or Syriac language but with Hebrew letters, which the Nazareans still use today and which is the Gospel according to the Apostles, or, as most believe, according to Matthew—a Gospel that can also be found in the library of Caesarea—the following story is found: "Behold, the mother of the Lord and his brothers were saying to him, 'John the Baptist is baptizing for the remission of sins. Let us go and be baptized by him.' But he replied to them, 'What sin have I committed that I should go to be baptized by him? Unless possibly what I just said was spoken in ignorance.' " (Jerome, *Against the Pelagians*, 3, 2)

10 And in the same volume the following is found: "[Jesus] said, 'If your brother sins by speaking a word against you, but then makes it up to you, you should accept him seven times a day.' His disciple Simon said to him, 'Seven times in a day?' The Lord responded, 'Yes indeed, I tell you—even up to seventy times seven! For even among the prophets, after they were anointed by the Holy Spirit, a word of sin was found.' " (Jerome, *Against the Pelagians*, 3, 2)

Variant Readings Noted in New Testament Manuscripts

11 • On Matthew 4:5. The Jewish Gospel does not have, "into the holy city," but "in Jerusalem." (MS 566)
• On Matthew 5:22. The words "without cause" are not present in some copies, nor in the Jewish Gospel. (MS 1424)

• On Matthew 7:5. In this place the Jewish Gospel reads: "Even if you are resting on my breast but do not do the will of my Father in heaven, I will cast you away from my breast." (MS 1424)
• On Matthew 10:16. The Jewish Gospel says, "more than serpents." (MS 1424)
• On Matthew 11:12. The Jewish Gospel reads, "plunders." (MS 1424)
• On Matthew 11:25. The Jewish Gospel says, "I give you thanks." (MS 1424)
• On Matthew 12:40. The Jewish Gospel does not read, "Three days and three nights." (MS 899)
• On Matthew 15:5. The Jewish Gospel says, "That which you would have had as a benefit from us is now an offering [to the Temple?]." (MS 1424)
• On Matthew 16:2–3. The passages marked with an asterisk are not set forth in other copies, nor in the Jewish Gospel. (MS 1424)
• On Matthew 16:17. The Jewish Gospel says, "son of John." (MS 566)
• On Matthew 18:22. After the words "seventy times seven" the Jewish Gospel reads: "For even among the prophets, after they were anointed by the Holy Spirit, a word of sin was found." (MSS 566, 899)
• On Matthew 26:74. The Jewish Gospel says, "And he made a denial, and swore, and cursed." (MSS 4, 273, 899, 1414)
• On Matthew 27:65. The Jewish Gospel says, "And he gave them armed men to sit opposite the cave, to keep watch over it day and night." (MS 1424)

The Gospel of
the Ebionites

The Ebionites were a group of Jewish Christians located in different regions
of the Mediterranean from at least the second to the fourth centuries.[1] What
distinguished this group of Christians from many others was their attempt
to combine Jewish views and lifestyles with the belief that Jesus was the
messiah. In particular, they were said to have emphasized belief in only one
God to such an extent that they denied, as a consequence, Jesus' own
divinity. At the same time, the Ebionites differed from non-Christian Jews
in asserting that Jesus was the sacrifice for the sins of the world and that all
other sacrifices had therefore become meaningless. Among other things,
this belief led them to embrace a vegetarian diet, since most meat was
procured, in the ancient world, through the religious act of sacrificing an
animal.

One of the sacred books these Jewish Christians appealed to in support
of their views was known in antiquity as the Gospel of the Ebionites.
Regrettably, the book as whole has been lost; but we are fortunate to have
some quotations of it in the writings of an opponent of the Ebionites, the
fourth-century heresy-hunter, Epiphanius of Salamis. These quotations give
us a good idea of what the entire Gospel must have looked like. It was
written in Greek, and represented a kind of harmony of the Gospels of
Matthew, Mark, and Luke. This can be seen most clearly in the account of
the voice at Jesus' baptism. In the three canonical accounts, the voice says
slightly different things. These differences are harmonized, however, in the
Gospel according to the Ebionites, where the voice comes from heaven
three times, saying something slightly different on each occasion, corresponding to the words found in each of the three earlier Gospels.

Some of the Ebionites' distinctive concerns are embodied in their

---

[1]See Ehrman, *Lost Christianities*, chap. 6.

Translation by Bart D. Ehrman based on the Greek text found in Egbert Schlarb and
Dieter Lührmann, *Fragmente apocryph gewordener Evangelien in griechischer und
lateinischer Sprache* (Marburg: N. G. Elwert, 2000) 35–39.

Gospel. This is shown, for example, in the reference to the diet of John the Baptist, in which the canonical statement that he ate locusts (i.e., meat) and wild honey was modified by the change of simply one letter, so that now the Baptist, in anticipation of the Ebionites themselves, maintains a vegetarian cuisine: here he is said to have eaten pancakes and wild honey.

It is difficult to assign a date to this Gospel, but since it betrays a knowledge of Matthew, Mark, and Luke, and presupposes a thriving community of Jewish Christians, it is perhaps best to locate it sometime early in the second century. The following extracts are all that remain of the Gospel, drawn from Epiphanius's work, the *Panarion* (=*The Medicine Chest*), Book 30.

1 The beginning of the Gospel they use reads as follows: "And so in the days of Herod, King of Judea, John came baptizing a baptism of repentance in the Jordan River. He was said to have come from the tribe of Aaron, the priest, and was the child of Zacharias and Elizabeth. And everyone went out to him." (Epiphanius, *Panarion*, 30, 13, 6)

2 For by chopping off the genealogies of Matthew they make their Gospel begin as we indicated before, with the words: "And so in the days of Herod, King of Judea, when Caiaphas was high priest, a certain one named John came baptizing a baptism of repentance in the Jordan River." (Epiphanius, *Panarion*, 30, 14, 3)

3 And so John was baptizing, and Pharisees came to him and were baptized, as was all of Jerusalem. John wore a garment of camel hair and a leather belt around his waist; and his food was wild honey that tasted like manna, like a cake cooked in oil. (Epiphanius, *Panarion*, 30, 13, 4–5)

4 And after a good deal more, it says: "When the people were baptized, Jesus also came and was baptized by John. When he came up out of the water, the heavens opened and he saw the Holy Spirit in the form of a dove, descending and entering him. And a voice came from heaven, 'You are my beloved Son, in you I am well pleased.' Then it said, 'Today I have given you birth.' Immediately a great light enlightened the place. When John saw this," it says, "he said to him, 'Who are you Lord?' Yet again a voice came from heaven to him, 'This is my beloved Son, with whom I am well pleased.' And then," it says, "John fell before him and said, 'I beg you, Lord— you baptize me!' But Jesus restrained him by saying, 'Let it be, for it is fitting that all things be fulfilled in this way.' " (Epiphanius, *Panarion*, 30, 13, 3–4)

5 In the Gospel that they call "according to Matthew"—which is not at all complete, but is falsified and mutilated—which they refer to as the Hebrew Gospel, the following is found:

"And so there was a certain man named Jesus, who was about thirty years old. He is the one who chose us. When he came to Capernaum he entered the house of Simon, also called Peter, and he opened his mouth to say, 'As I was passing by the lake of Tiberias I chose John and James, the sons of Zebedee, and Simon,

Andrew, Thaddaeus, Simon the Zealot, and Judas Iscariot; and I called you, Matthew, while you were sitting at the tax collector's booth, and you followed me. I want you, therefore, to be the twelve apostles as a witness to Israel." (Epiphanius, *Panarion*, 30, 13, 2–3)

6 Again they deny that he was a man, even basing their view on the word the Savior spoke when it was reported to him, "See, your mother and brothers are standing outside." "Who," he asked, "is my mother and brothers?" Stretching out his hand to his disciples he said, "These are my brothers and mother and sisters— those who do the will of my Father." (Epiphanius, *Panarion*, 30, 14, 5)

7 They do not allege that he was born from God the Father, but that he was created as one of the archangels, yet was made greater than they, since he rules over the angels and all things made by the Almighty. And, as found in their Gospel, they say that when he came he taught, "I have come to destroy the sacrifices. And if you do not stop making sacrifice, God's wrath will not stop afflicting you." (Epiphanius, *Panarion*, 30, 16, 4–5)

8 They have changed the saying and abandoned its true sequence, as is clear to everyone who considers the combination of the words. For they have the disciples say, "Where do you want us to make preparations for you to eat the Passover lamb?" And they indicate that he responded, "I have no desire to eat the meat of this Passover lamb with you." (Epiphanius, *Panarion*, 30, 22, 4)

The Gospel According to the Hebrews

The Gospel according to the Hebrews is quoted by a number of church fathers connected with the city of Alexandria, Egypt—Clement, Origen, Didymus the Blind, and Jerome (who studied with Didymus in Alexandria); for this reason, scholars assume that it was used, and possibly written, there, probably during the first half of the second century. Regrettably, the book no longer survives intact, but only in the scattered references to it in these other authors' writings. Its name probably derives from the circumstance that it was used principally by Jewish-Christians in that large and thriving metropolis—i.e., it was called this by outsiders of that community, not by those who actually used it.

The Gospel according to the Hebrews was written in Greek and narrated important events of Jesus' life, including his baptism, temptation, and resurrection. It appears, however, that these stories were not simply taken over and modified from the Gospels that came to be included in the New Testament. They were instead alternative forms of these traditions that had been passed along orally until the unknown author of this Gospel heard them and wrote them down.

The Jewish emphases of the Gospel are evident in a several of the surviving quotations, such as fragment 5, which presupposes the importance of James, the brother of Jesus, the head of the Jewish-Christian community in Jerusalem after Jesus' death. Yet some of the sayings of the Gospel have a Gnostic tone to them (see fragment 1, which is quite similar to Coptic Gospel of Thomas 2).[1] It may be, then, that this particular Jewish-Christian community was more sympathetic than others to the prominent Gnostic teachers in Alexandria in the second century. In any event, the Gospel evidently contained a number of Jesus' ethical teachings (fragments 4 and 7). And some of its accounts were highly legendary—including the post-

---

[1]On Gnosticism, see Ehrman, *Lost Christianities*, 113–34.

Translation by Bart D. Ehrman, based on the Greek, Latin, and Syriac texts in A. F. J. Klijin, *Jewish-Christian Gospel Tradition* (VC Supp 17; Leiden: E. J. Brill, 1992) 47–115.

resurrection appearance of Jesus to James, who had sworn at the Last Supper (in a story found in this Gospel, but not cited by any other authority) not to eat until he should see Jesus raised from the dead (fragment 5).

The following are the quotations of the Gospel that survive in our ancient sources.

1 As it is also written in the Gospel according to the Hebrews, "The one who is amazed will rule, and the one who rules will find rest." (Clement of Alexandria, *Miscellanies*, 2, 9, 45)

2 If anyone accepts the Gospel according to the Hebrews, there the Savior himself says, "Just now my mother, the Holy Spirit, took me by one of my hairs and carried me up to the great mountain, Tabor." (Origen, *Commentary on John*, 2, 12)

3 It may appear that Matthew is named Levi in the Gospel of Luke. But in fact that is not so; it is Matthias, the one who replaced Judas, who is the same as Levi, known by two names. This is found in the Gospel according the Hebrews. (Didymus the Blind, *Commentary on the Psalms*, 184, 9–10)

4 As we read in the Hebrew Gospel, the Lord said to his disciples: "You should never rejoice except when you look upon your brother in love." (Jerome, *Commentary on Ephesians*, 5:4)

5 The Gospel that is called "according to the Hebrews," which I have recently translated into both Greek and Latin, a Gospel that Origen frequently used, records the following after the Savior's resurrection: "But when the Lord had given the linen cloth to the servant of the priest, he went and appeared to James. For James had taken a vow not to eat bread from the time he drank the cup of the Lord until he should see him raised from among those who sleep." And soon after this it says, "The Lord said, 'Bring a table and bread.' " And immediately it continues, "He took the bread and blessed it, broke it, gave it to James the Just, and said to him, 'My brother, eat your bread. For the Son of Man is risen from among those who sleep.' " (Jerome, *Illustrious Men*, 2)

6 It is stated in the Gospel written in Hebrew, which the Nazareans read: "The entire fountain of the Holy Spirit will descend on him. For the Lord is the Spirit, and where the Spirit of the Lord is, there is liberty." Later in that Gospel that we have mentioned we find the following written: "It came to pass that when the Lord came up from the water, the entire fountain of the Holy Spirit descended and rested on him; and it said to him, 'My Son, in all the prophets I have been expecting you to come, that I might rest on you. For you are my rest, you are my firstborn Son, who rules forever.' " (Jerome, *Commentary on Isaiah* 11:1–3)

7 And in the Gospel according to the Hebrews, which the Nazareans are accustomed to read, the following is described as among the worst offenses: that someone should make the spirit of his brother sad. (Jerome, *Commentary on Ezekiel*, 18:7)

The Gospel of
the Egyptians

The Gospel of the Egyptians is another Gospel that has been lost since the early centuries of Christianity. The only access we have to it is in the quotations of an early church father, the late second-century Clement of Alexandria, who at one point identifies one of his non-canonical quotations of the words of Jesus as having come from this book (fragment 5). Most of Clement's quotations of the Gospel involve conversations between Jesus and a woman named Salome, mentioned in the New Testament as one of the women who discovered Jesus' empty tomb (Mark 15:40; 16:1).

Eventually Salome became a prominent figure in some circles of Christianity, including those that produced this Gospel according to the Egyptians, where her questions and comments lead to important sayings of Jesus. These sayings embody ascetic concerns, in which the desires of the flesh and sexual activity are condemned as being opposed to the will of God. In particular, the Gospel appears originally to have condemned the practices of marriage and procreation. In a number of instances Clement himself interprets these sayings; it is sometimes difficult to know, however, whether Clement's interpretations represent the views of the Gospel's anonymous author, or are instead Clement's own attempts to make sense of the Gospel in light of his own views.

At least one of the sayings stresses a Gnostic notion that the revelation of God will be complete when people trample on the "shameful garment" (= the human body?) and all things are restored to their ultimate unity—including male and female, which will no longer be differentiated but made one (fragment 5). Similar notions can be found in the Coptic Gospel of Thomas, also used in Egypt (see Gospel of Thomas 22, 37, 114).

Some scholars maintain that the Gospel was named "according to the Egyptians" to differentiate it from another Gospel used in Egypt, the Gospel "according to the Hebrews"—the latter in use among Jewish-Christians and the former, therefore, among Gentile Christians. Others find it more likely

Translation by Bart D. Ehrman based on the Greek text found in Egbert Schlarb and Dieter Lührmann, *Fragmente apocryph gewordener Evangelien in griechischer und lateinischer Sprache* (Marburg: N. G. Elwert, 2000) 29–31.

that the book was first given its name by those living outside of Egypt, to identify it as a book in common use there.

Since the Gospel is well-known to Clement and, evidently, his community, it may have been composed already by the first part of the second century.

1 When Salome asked, "How long will death prevail?" the Lord replied, "For as long as you women bear children." But he did not say this because life is evil or creation wicked; instead he was teaching the natural succession of things; for everything degenerates after coming into being. (Clement of Alexandria, *Miscellanies*, 3, 45, 3)

2 Those who oppose God's creation because of self-control—which at least sounds good—quote the words spoken to Salome, the first of which we have already mentioned, found, I think, in the Gospel according to the Egyptians. For they claim that the Savior himself said, "I have come to destroy the works of the female." By "the female" he meant desire and by "works" he meant birth and degeneration. (Clement of Alexandria, *Miscellanies*, 3, 63, 1)

3 When the Word made a reasonable disclosure concerning the consummation of all things, Salome asked, "How long will people continue to die?" Now Scripture refers to people in two ways, as having a visible part and the soul, that is, the part that is saved and the part that is not. And sin is called the death of the soul. For this reason, the Lord replied shrewdly, "For as long as women bear children"—that is to say, for as long as

desires continue to be active. (Clement of Alexandria, *Miscellanies*, 3, 64, 1)

4 Why do those who adhere to everything except the gospel rule of truth not cite the following words spoken to Salome? For when she said, "Then I have done well not to bear children" (supposing that it was not suitable to give birth), the Lord responded, "Eat every herb, but not the one that is bitter." (Clement of Alexandria, *Miscellanies*, 3, 66, 1–2)

5 This is why Cassian indicates that when Salome asked when the things she had asked about would become known, the Lord replied: "When you trample on the shameful garment and when the two become one and the male with the female is neither male nor female." The first thing to note, then, is that we do not find this saying in the four Gospels handed down to us, but in the Gospel according to the Egyptians. (Clement of Alexandria, *Miscellanies*, 3, 92, 2–93, 1)

6 And when the Savior said to Salome, "Death will last as long as women give birth," he was not denigrating birth—since it is, after all, necessary for the salvation of those who believe. (Clement of Alexandria, *Excerpts from Theodotus* 67, 2)

The Coptic Gospel
of Thomas

The Coptic Gospel of Thomas was one of the most sensational archaeological discoveries of the twentieth century.[1] The document was unknown except by name before 1945, when peasants digging for fertilizer near the village of Nag Hammadi, Egypt accidentally uncovered a jar containing thirteen leather-bound manuscripts buried sometime in the late fourth century. When the manuscripts came to the attention of scholars of antiquity, their significance was almost immediately recognized: they contained fifty-two tractates, principally of "heretical" writings of Gnostic Christians.[2] Although originally composed in Greek, the writings were in Coptic (ancient Egyptian) translation. Many of them had been previously known by title only. Today these writings are known as the "Nag Hammadi Library."[3]

None of the fifty-two tractates has attracted more attention than the Gospel of Thomas. For this is a collection of Jesus' sayings that claims to have been written by Didymus Judas Thomas. According to some early Christian legends, Thomas was Jesus' twin brother.

The book records 114 "secret teachings" of Jesus. It includes no other material: no miracles, no passion narrative, no stories of any kind. What ultimately mattered for the author of Thomas was not Jesus' death and resurrection, which he does not narrate or discuss, but the mysterious teachings that he delivered. Indeed, the Gospel begins by stating that anyone who learns the interpretation of these words will have eternal life (saying 1).

Many of the sayings will sound familiar to readers already conversant with the Gospels of Matthew, Mark, and Luke. For example, here one finds, in slightly different wording, the warning against the "blind leading the

---

[1]For a full discussion, see Ehrman, *Lost Christianities*, 44–66.   [2]On what such "Gnostics" believed, see Ehrman, *Lost Christianities*, 122–25.   [3]Full translations of all the writings, with incisive introductions, can be found in James Robinson, *The Nag Hammadi Library in English*, 4th rev. ed. (Leiden: E. J. Brill, 1996).

Translation by Thomas O. Lambdin in James Robinson, *The Nag Hammadi Library in English,* 3rd ed. (Leiden: E. J. Brill, 1988) 126–38; used with permission.

blind" and the parables of the sower and of the mustard seed (sayings 9, 20, 34). Other sayings, however, are quite different and appear to presuppose a Gnostic point of view, in which people are understood to be spirits who have fallen from the divine realm and become entrapped in matter (i.e., in the prisons of their material bodies). Salvation, according to this perspective, comes to those who learn the truth of their plight and so are enabled to escape this impoverished material existence by acquiring the knowledge necessary for salvation (e.g., sayings 11, 22, 29, 37, and 80). Jesus is the one who conveys this knowledge.

Some scholars have maintained that the sayings of Thomas may be closer to what Jesus actually taught than what we find in the New Testament; others, however, have pointed out that the theology implicit in the more Gnostic teachings cannot be dated with confidence prior to the beginning of the second century. Thus, while some of these sayings may be quite old— may, in fact, go back to Jesus himself—the document as a whole probably came to be written sometime after the New Testament Gospels (although perhaps independently of them), possibly in the early second century.

These are the secret sayings which the living Jesus spoke and which Didymos Judas Thomas wrote down.

1 And he said, "Whoever finds the interpretation of these sayings will not experience death."

2 Jesus said, "Let him who seeks continue seeking until he finds. When he finds, he will become troubled. When he becomes troubled, he will be astonished, and he will rule over the all."

3 Jesus said, "If those who lead you say to you, 'See, the kingdom is in the sky,' then the birds of the sky will precede you. If they say to you, 'It is in the sea,' then the fish will precede you. Rather, the kingdom is inside of you, and it is outside of you. When you come to know yourselves, then you will become known, and you will realize that it is you who are the sons of the living father. But if you will not know yourselves you dwell in poverty and it is you who are that poverty."

4 Jesus said, "The man old in days will not hesitate to ask a small child seven days old about the place of life, and he will live. For many who are first will become last, and they will become one and the same."

5 Jesus said, "Recognize what is in your (sg.) sight, and that which is hidden from you (sg.) will become plain to you (sg.). For there is nothing hidden which will not become manifest."

6 His disciples questioned him and said to him, "Do you want us to fast? How shall we pray? Shall we give alms? What diet shall we observe?"

Jesus said, "Do not tell lies, and do not do what you hate, for all things are plain in the sight of heaven. For nothing hidden will not become manifest, and nothing covered will remain without being uncovered."

7 Jesus said, "Blessed is the lion which becomes man when consumed by man; and cursed is the man whom the lion consumes, and the lion becomes man."

8 And he said, "The man is like a wise fisherman who cast his net into the sea

and drew it up from the sea full of small fish. Among them the wise fisherman found a fine large fish. He threw all the small fish back into the sea and chose the large fish without difficulty. Whoever has ears to hear, let him hear."

9 Jesus said, "Now the sower went out, took a handful (of seeds), and scattered them. Some fell on the road; the birds came and gathered them up. Others fell on rock, did not take root in the soil, and did not produce ears. And others fell on thorns; they choked the seed(s) and worms ate them. And others fell on the good soil and it produced good fruit: it bore sixty per measure and a hundred and twenty per measure."

10 Jesus said, "I have cast fire upon the world, and see, I am guarding it until it blazes."

11 Jesus said, "This heaven will pass away, and the one above it will pass away. The dead are not alive, and the living will not die. In the days when you consumed what is dead, you made it what is alive. When you come to dwell in the light, what will you do? On the day when you were one you became two. But when you become two, what will you do?"

12 The disciples said to Jesus, "We know that you will depart from us. Who is to be our leader?"

Jesus said to them "Wherever you are, you are to go to James the righteous, for whose sake heaven and earth came into being."

13 Jesus said to his disciples, "Compare me to someone and tell me whom I am like."

Simon Peter said to him, "You are like a righteous angel."

Matthew said to him, "You are like a wise philosopher."

Thomas said to him, "Master, my mouth is wholly incapable of saying whom you are like."

Jesus said, "I am not your (sg.) master. Because you (sg.) have drunk, you (sg.) have become intoxicated from the bubbling spring which I have measured out."

And he took him and withdrew and told him three things. When Thomas returned to his companions, they asked him, "What did Jesus say to you?"

Thomas said to them, "If I tell you one of the things which he told me, you will pick up stones and throw them at me; a fire will come out of the stones and burn you up."

14 Jesus said to them, "If you fast, you will give rise to sin for yourselves; and if you pray, you will be condemned; and if you give alms, you will do harm to your spirits. When you go into any land and walk about in the districts, if they receive you, eat what they will set before you, and heal the sick among them. For what goes into your mouth will not defile you, but that which issues from your mouth—it is that which will defile you."

15 Jesus said, "When you see one who was not born of woman, prostrate yourselves on your faces and worship him. That one is your father."

16 Jesus said, "Men think, perhaps, that it is peace which I have come to cast upon the world. They do not know that it is dissension which I have come to cast upon the earth: fire, sword, and war. For there will be five in a house: three will be against two, and two against three, the father against the son, and the son against the father. And they will stand solitary."

17 Jesus said, "I shall give you what no eye has seen and what no ear has heard and what no hand has touched and what has never occurred to the human mind."

18 The disciples said to Jesus. "Tell us how our end will be." Jesus said, "Have you discovered, then, the beginning, that you look for the end? For where the beginning is, there will the end be. Blessed is he who will take his place in the beginning; he will know the end and will not experience death."

19 Jesus said, "Blessed is he who came into being before he came into being. If you become my disciples and listen to my words, these stones will minister to you. For there are five trees for you in Paradise which remain undisturbed summer and winter and whose leaves do not fall. Whoever becomes acquainted with them will not experience death."

20 The disciples said to Jesus, "Tell us what the kingdom of heaven is like."

He said to them, "It is like a mustard seed. It is the smallest of all seeds. But when it falls on tilled soil, it produces a great plant and becomes a shelter for birds of the sky."

21 Mary said to Jesus, "Whom are your disciples like?" He said, "They are like children who have settled in a field which is not theirs. When the owners of the field come, they will say, 'Let us have back our field.' They (will) undress in their presence in order to let them have back their field and to give it back to them. Therefore I say, if the owner of a house knows that the thief is coming, he will begin his vigil before he comes and will not let him dig through into his house of his domain to carry away his goods. You (pl.), then, be on your guard against the world. Arm yourselves with great strength lest the robbers find a way to come to you, for the difficulty which you expect will (surely) materialize. Let there be among you a man of understanding. When the grain ripened, he came quickly with his sickle in his hand and reaped it. Whoever has ears to hear let him hear."

22 Jesus saw infants being suckled. He said to his disciples, "These infants being suckled are like those who enter the kingdom."

They said to him, "Shall we then, as children, enter the kingdom?"

Jesus said to them, "When you make the two one, and when you make the inside like the outside and the outside like the inside, and the above like the below, and when you make the male and the female one and the same, so that the male not be male nor the female female; and when you fashion eyes in place of an eye, and a hand in place of a hand, and a foot in place of a foot, and a likeness in place of a likeness; then will you enter [the kingdom]."

23 Jesus said, "I shall choose you, one out of a thousand, and two out of ten thousand, and they shall stand as a single one."

24 His disciples said to him, "Show us the place where you are, since it is necessary for us to seek it."

He said to them, "Whoever has ears, let him hear. There is light within a man of light, and he lights up the whole world. If he does not shine, he is darkness."

25 Jesus said, "Love your (sg.) brother like your soul, guard him like the pupil of your eye."

26 Jesus said, "You (sg.) see the mote in your brother's eye, but you do not see the beam in your own eye. When you cast the beam out of your own eye, then you will see clearly to cast the mote from your brother's eye."

27 <Jesus said,> "If you do not fast as regards the world, you will not find the kingdom. If you do not observe the Sabbath as a Sabbath, you will not see the father."

28 Jesus said, "I took my place in the midst of the world, and I appeared to them in flesh. I found all of them intoxicated; I found none of them thirsty. And my soul became afflicted for the sons of men, because they are blind in their hearts and do not have sight; for empty they came into the world, and empty too they seek to leave the world. But for the moment they are intoxicated. When they

shake off their wine, then they will repent."

29 Jesus said, "If the flesh came into being because of spirit, it is a wonder. But if spirit came into being because of the body, it is a wonder of wonders. Indeed, I am amazed at how this great wealth has made its home in this poverty."

30 Jesus said, "Where there are three gods, they are gods. Where there are two or one, I am with him."

31 Jesus said, "No prophet is accepted in his own village; no physician heals those who know him."

32 Jesus said, "A city being built on a high mountain and fortified cannot fall, nor can it be hidden."

33 Jesus said, "Preach from your (pl.) housetops that which you (sg.) will hear in your (sg.) ear. For no one lights a lamp and puts it under a bushel, nor does he put it in a hidden place, but rather he sets it on a lampstand so that everyone who enters and leaves will see its light."

34 Jesus said, "If a blind man leads a blind man, they will both fall into a pit."

35 Jesus said, "It is not possible for anyone to enter the house of a strong man and take it by force unless he binds his hands; then he will (be able to) ransack his house."

36 Jesus said, "Do not be concerned from morning until evening and from evening until morning about what you will wear."

37 His disciples said, "When will you become revealed to us and when shall we see you?"

Jesus said, "When you disrobe without being ashamed and take up your garments and place them under your feet like little children and tread on them, then [will you see] the son of the living one, and you will not be afraid."

38 Jesus said, "Many times have you desired to hear these words which I am saying to you, and you have no one else to hear them from. There will be days when you will look for me and will not find me."

39 Jesus said, "The pharisees and the scribes have taken the keys of knowledge (gnosis) and hidden them. They themselves have not entered, nor have they allowed to enter those who wish to. You, however, be as wise as serpents and as innocent as doves."

40 Jesus said, "A grapevine has been planted outside of the father, but being unsound, it will be pulled up by its roots and destroyed."

41 Jesus said, "Whoever has something in his hand will receive more, and whoever has nothing will be deprived of even the little he has."

42 Jesus said, "Become passers-by."

43 His disciples said to him, "Who are you, that you should say these things to us?"

<Jesus said to them,> "You do not realize who I am from what I say to you, but you have become like the Jews, for they (either) love the tree and hate its fruit (or) love the fruit and hate the tree."

44 Jesus said, "Whoever blasphemes against the father will be forgiven, and whoever blasphemes against the son will be forgiven, but whoever blasphemes against the holy spirit will not be forgiven either on earth or in heaven."

45 Jesus said, "Grapes are not harvested from thorns, nor are figs gathered from thistles, for they do not produce fruit. A good man brings forth good from his storehouse; an evil man brings forth evil things from his evil storehouse, which is in his heart, and says evil things. For out of the abundance of the heart he brings forth evil things."

46 Jesus said, "Among those born of women, from Adam until John the Baptist, there is no one so superior to John the Baptist that his eyes should not be lowered (before him). Yet I have said, whichever one of you comes to be a child will be acquainted with the kingdom and will become superior to John."

47 Jesus said, "It is impossible for a man to mount two horses or to stretch two bows. And it is impossible for a servant to serve two masters; otherwise, he will honor the one and treat the other contemptuously. No man drinks old wine and immediately desires to drink new wine. And new wine is not put into old wineskins, lest they burst; nor is old wine put into a new wineskin, lest it spoil it. An old patch is not sewn into a new garment, because a tear would result."

48 Jesus said, "If two make peace with each other in this one house, they will say to the mountain, 'Move away,' and it will move away."

49 Jesus said, "Blessed are the solitary and elect, for you will find the kingdom. For you are from it, and to it you will return."

50 Jesus said, "If they say to you, 'Where did you come from?', say to them, 'We came from the light, the place where the light came into being on its own accord and established [itself] and became manifest through their image.' If they say to you, 'Is it you?' say, 'We are its children, and we are the elect of the living father.' If they ask you, 'What is the sign of your father in you?', say to them, 'It is movement and repose.' "

51 His disciples said to him, "When will the repose of the dead come about, and when will the new world come?"

He said to them, "What you look forward to has already come, but you do not recognize it."

52 His disciples said to him, "Twenty-four prophets spoke in Israel, and all of them spoke in you."

He said to them, "You have omitted the one living in your presence and have spoken (only) of the dead."

53 His disciples said to him, "Is circumcision beneficial or not?" He said to them, "If it were beneficial, their father would beget them already circumcised from their mother. Rather, the true circumcision in spirit has become completely profitable."

54 Jesus said, "Blessed are the poor, for yours is the kingdom of heaven."

55 Jesus said, "Whoever does not hate his father and his mother cannot become a disciple to me. And whoever does not hate his brothers and sisters and take up his cross in my way will not be worthy of me."

56 Jesus said, "Whoever has come to understand the world has found (only) a corpse, and whoever has found a corpse is superior to the world."

57 Jesus said, "The kingdom of the father is like a man who had [good] seed. His enemy came by night and sowed weeds among the good seed. The man did not allow them to pull up the weeds; he said to them, 'I am afraid that you will go intending to pull up the weeds and pull up the wheat along with them.' For on the day of the harvest the weeds will be plainly visible, and they will be pulled up and burned."

58 Jesus said, "Blessed is the man who has suffered and found life."

59 Jesus said, "Take heed of the living one while you are alive, lest you die and seek to see him and be unable to do so."

60 <They saw> a Samaritan carrying a lamb on his way to Judea. He said to his disciples, "That man is round about the lamb."

They said to him, "So that he may kill it and eat it."

He said to them, "While it is alive, he will not eat it, but only when he has killed it and it has become a corpse."

They said to him, "He cannot do so otherwise."

He said to them, "You too, look for a

place for yourselves within repose, lest you become a corpse and be eaten."

61 Jesus said, "Two will rest on a bed: the one will die, and the other will live."

Salome said, "Who are you, man, that you . . . have come up on my couch and eaten from my table?"

Jesus said to her, "I am he who exists from the undivided. I was given some of the things of my father."

< . . . > "I am your disciple."

< . . . > "Therefore I say, if he is destroyed he will be filled with light, but if he is divided, he will be filled with darkness."

62 Jesus said, "It is to those [who are worthy of my] mysteries that I tell my mysteries. Do not let your (sg.) left hand know what your (sg.) right hand is doing."

63 Jesus said, "There was a rich man who had much money. He said, 'I shall put my money to use so that I may sow, reap, plant, and fill my storehouse with produce, with the result that I shall lack nothing.' Such were his intentions, but that same night he died. Let him who has ears hear."

64 Jesus said, "A man had received visitors. And when he had prepared the dinner, he sent his servant to invite the guests. He went to the first one and said to him, 'My master invites you.' He said, 'I have claims against some merchants. They are coming to me this evening. I must go and give them my orders. I ask to be excused from the dinner.' He went to another and said to him, 'My master has invited you.' He said to him, 'I have just bought a house and am required for the day. I shall not have any spare time.' He went to another and said to him, 'My master invites you.' He said to him, 'My friend is going to get married, and I am to prepare the banquet. I shall not be able to come. I ask to be excused from the dinner.' He went to another and said to

him, 'My master invites you.' He said to him, 'I have just bought a farm, and I am on my way to collect the rent. I shall not be able to come. I ask to be excused.' The servant returned and said to his master, 'Those whom you invited to the dinner have asked to be excused.' The master said to his servant, 'Go outside to the streets and bring back those whom you happen to meet, so that they may dine.' Businessmen and merchants [will] not enter the places of my father."

65 He said, "There was a good man who owned a vineyard. He leased it to tenant farmers so that they might work it and he might collect the produce from them. He sent his servant so that the tenants might give him the produce of the vineyard. They seized his servant and beat him, all but killing him. The servant went back and told his master. The master said, 'Perhaps he did not recognize them.' He sent another servant. The tenants beat this one as well. Then the owner sent his son and said, 'Perhaps they will show respect to my son.' Because the tenants knew that it was he who was the heir to the vineyard, they seized him and killed him. Let him who has ears hear."

66 Jesus said, "Show me the stone which the builders have rejected. That one is the cornerstone."

67 Jesus said, "If one who knows the all still feels a personal deficiency, he is completely deficient."

68 Jesus said, "Blessed are you when you are hated and persecuted. Wherever you have been persecuted they will find no place."

69 Jesus said, "Blessed are they who have been persecuted within themselves. It is they who have truly come to know the father. Blessed are the hungry, for the belly of him who desires will be filled."

70 Jesus said, "That which you have will save you if you bring it forth from yourselves. That which you do not have within you [will] kill you if you do not have it within you."

71 Jesus said, "I shall [destroy this] house, and no one will be able to build it [. . .]"

72 [A man said] to him, "Tell my brothers to divide my father's possessions with me."

He said to him, "O man, who has made me a divider?"

He turned to his disciples and said to them, "I am not a divider, am I?"

73 Jesus said, "The harvest is great but the laborers are few. Beseech the lord, therefore, to send out laborers to the harvest."

74 He said, "O lord, there are many around the drinking trough, but there is nothing in the cistern."

75 Jesus said, "Many are standing at the door, but it is the solitary who will enter the bridal chamber."

76 Jesus said, "The kingdom of the father is like a merchant who had a consignment of merchandise and who discovered a pearl. That merchant was shrewd. He sold the merchandise and bought the pearl alone for himself. You too, seek his unfailing and enduring treasure where no moth comes near to devour and no worm destroys."

77 Jesus said, "It is I who am the light which is above them all. It is I who am the all. From me did the all come forth, and unto me did the all extend. Split a piece of wood, and I am there. Lift up the stone, and you will find me there."

78 Jesus said, "Why have you come out into the desert? To see a reed shaken by the wind? And to see a man clothed in fine garments [like your] kings and your great men? Upon them are the fine garments, and they are unable to discern the truth."

79 A woman from the crowd said to him, "Blessed are the womb which bore you and the breasts which nourished you."

He said to [her], "Blessed are those who have heard the word of the father and have truly kept it. For there will be days when you (pl.) will say, 'Blessed are the womb which has not conceived and the breasts which have not given milk.' "

80 Jesus said, "He who has recognized the world has found the body, but he who has found the body is superior to the world."

81 Jesus said, "Let him who has grown rich be king, and let him who possesses power renounce it."

82 Jesus said, "He who is near me is near the fire, and he who is far from me is far from the kingdom."

83 Jesus said, "The images are manifest to man, but the light in them remains concealed in the image of the light of the father. He will become manifest, but his image will remain concealed by his light."

84 Jesus said, "When you see your likeness, you rejoice. But when you see your images which came into being before you, and which neither die nor become manifest, how much you will have to bear!"

85 Jesus said, "Adam came into being from a great power and a great wealth, but he did not become worthy of you. For had he been worthy, [he would] not [have experienced] death."

86 Jesus said, "[The foxes have their holes] and the birds have their nests, but the son of man has no place to lay his head and rest."

87 Jesus said, "Wretched is the body that is dependent upon a body, and wretched is the soul that is dependent on these two."

88 Jesus said, "The angels and the prophets will come to you and give to

you those things you (already) have. And you too, give them those things which you have, and say to yourselves, 'When will they come and take what is theirs?' "

89 Jesus said, "Why do you wash the outside of the cup? Do you not realize that he who made the inside is the same one who made the outside?"

90 Jesus said, "Come unto me, for my yoke is easy and my lordship is mild, and you will find repose for yourselves."

91 They said to him, "Tell us who you are so that we may believe in you."

He said to them, "You read the face of the sky and of the earth, but you have not recognized the one who is before you, and you do not know how to read this moment."

92 Jesus said, "Seek and you will find. Yet, what you asked me about in former times and which I did not tell you then, now I do desire to tell, but you do not inquire after it."

93 <Jesus said,> "Do not give what is holy to dogs, lest they throw them on the dung heap. Do not throw the pearls [to] swine, lest they . . . it [. . .]."

94 Jesus [said], "He who seeks will find, and [he who knocks] will be let in."

95 [Jesus said], "If you have money do not lend it at interest, but give [it] to one from whom you will not get it back."

96 Jesus said, "The kingdom of the father is like [a certain] woman. She took a little leaven, [concealed] it in some dough, and made it into large loaves. Let him who has ears hear."

97 Jesus said, "The kingdom of the [father] is like a certain woman who was carrying a [jar] full of meal. While she was walking [on the] road, still some distance from home, the handle of the jar broke and the meal emptied out behind her [on] the road. She did not realize it; she had noticed no accident. When she

reached her house, she set the jar down and found it empty."

98 Jesus said, "The kingdom of the father is like a certain man who wanted to kill a powerful man. In his own house he drew his sword and stuck it into the wall in order to find out whether his hand could carry through. Then he slew the powerful man."

99 The disciples said to him, "Your brothers and your mother are standing outside."

He said to them, "Those here who do the will of my father are my brothers and my mother. It is they who will enter the kingdom of my father."

100 They showed Jesus a gold coin and said to him, "Caesar's men demand taxes from us."

He said to them, "Give Caesar what belongs to Caesar, give God what belongs to God, and give me what is mine."

101 <Jesus said,> "Whoever does not hate his [father] and his mother as I do cannot become a [disciple] to me. And whoever does [not] love his [father and] his mother as I do cannot become a [disciple to] me. For my mother [. . .], but [my] true [mother] gave me life."

102 Jesus said, "Woe to the pharisees, for they are like a dog sleeping in the manger of oxen, for neither does he eat nor does he [let] the oxen eat."

103 Jesus said, "Fortunate is the man who knows where the brigands will enter, so that [he] may get up, muster his domain, and arm himself before they invade."

104 They said to Jesus, "Come, let us pray today and let us fast."

Jesus said, "What is the sin that I have committed, or wherein have I been defeated? But when the bridegroom leaves the bridal chamber, then let them fast and pray."

105 Jesus said, "He who knows the

father and the mother will be called the son of a harlot."

106 Jesus said, "When you make the two one, you will become the sons of man, and when you say, 'Mountain, move away,' it will move away."

107 Jesus said, "The kingdom is like a shepherd who had a hundred sheep. One of them, the largest, went astray. He left the ninety-nine and looked for that one until he found it. When he had gone to such trouble, he said to the sheep, 'I care for you more than the ninety-nine.' "

108 Jesus said, "He who will drink from my mouth will become like me. I myself shall become he, and the things that are hidden will be revealed to him."

109 Jesus said, "The kingdom is like a man who had a [hidden] treasure in his field without knowing it. And [after] he died, he left it to his [son]. The son [did] not know (about the treasure). He inherited the field and sold [it]. And the one who bought it went plowing and [found] the treasure. He began to lend money at interest to whomever he wished."

110 Jesus said, "Whoever finds the world and becomes rich, let him renounce the world."

111 Jesus said, "The heavens and the earth will be rolled up in your presence. And the one who lives from the living one will not see death." Does not Jesus say, "Whoever finds himself is superior to the world"?

112 Jesus said, "Woe to the flesh that depends on the soul; woe to the soul that depends on the flesh."

113 His disciples said to him, "When will the kingdom come?"

<Jesus said,> "It will not come by waiting for it. It will not be a matter of saying 'here it is' or 'there it is.' Rather, the kingdom of the father is spread out upon the earth, and men do not see it."

114 Simon Peter said to them, "Let Mary leave us, for women are not worthy of life."

Jesus said, "I myself shall lead her in order to make her male, so that she too may become a living spirit resembling you males. For every woman who will make herself male will enter the kingdom of heaven."

Papyrus Egerton 2:
The Unknown Gospel

The fragmentary manuscript known as Papyrus Egerton 2 contains a non-canonical Gospel that is never referred to in any ancient source and that was, as a consequence, completely unknown until its publication in 1935.[1] The fragments were discovered among a collection of papyri purchased by the British Museum. They had come from Egypt and are usually dated to around 150 CE. The "Unknown Gospel" narrated in these papyri, however, must have been older than the manuscript fragments that contain it. While some scholars have argued that the Gospel was written before the canonical books of Matthew, Mark, Luke, and John, most have concluded that it was produced somewhat later, during the first half of the second century.

Since the Unknown Gospel is preserved only in fragments, it is impossible to judge its original length and contents. The surviving remains preserve four separate stories: (1) an account of Jesus' controversy with Jewish leaders that is similar to the stories found in John 5:39–47 and 10:31–39; (2) a healing of a leper, reminiscent of Matt 8:1–4; Mark 1:40–45; Luke 5:12–16; and Luke 17:11–14; (3) a controversy over paying tribute to Caesar, comparable to Matt 22:15–22; Mark 12:13–17; and Luke 20:20–26; and (4) a fragmentary account of a miracle of Jesus on the bank of the Jordan River, possibly performed to illustrate his parable about the miraculous growth of seeds. This final story has no parallel in the canonical Gospels.

Scholars continue to debate whether the author of this Gospel (a) used the four canonical Gospels as literary sources for his accounts, (b) quoted from memory stories that he knew from the canonical Gospels (changing them in the process), or (c) acquired his stories not from the canonical Gospels, but from the oral traditions of Jesus in wide circulation in the first and second centuries.

---

[1] See Ehrman, *Lost Christianities*, 49–50.

Translation by Bart D. Ehrman based on the Greek text found in Egbert Schlarb and Dieter Lührmann, *Fragmente apocryph gewordener Evangelien in griechischer und lateinischer Sprache* (Marburg: N. G. Elwert, 2000) 147–53, but I have followed the sequence of the fragments given in H. Idris Bell and T. C. Skeat, *Fragments of an Unknown Gospel and Other Early Christian Papyri* (London: British Museum, 1935).

1 [And Jesus said][2] to the lawyers: "[Punish] every wrong-doer and [transgressor], but not me. [For that one does not consider] how he does what he does."

Then he turned to the rulers of the people and spoke this word: "Search the Scriptures, for you think that in them you have life. They are the ones that testify concerning me. Do not think that I came to accuse you to my Father. The one who accuses you is Moses, in whom you have hoped."

They replied, "We know full well that God spoke to Moses. But we do not know where you have come from."

Jesus answered them, "Now what stands accused is your failure to believe his testimonies. For if you had believed Moses, you would have believed me. For that one wrote to your fathers concerning me. . . ."

2 . . . to the crowd . . . stones together so that they might stone him. And the rulers were trying to lay their hands on him, that they might arrest him and deliver him over to the crowd. And they were unable to arrest him because the hour for him to be delivered over had not yet come. But the Lord himself went out through their midst and left them.

And behold, a leper approached him and said, "Teacher Jesus, while I was traveling with some lepers and eating with them at the inn, I myself contracted leprosy. If, then, you are willing, I will be made clean."

Then the Lord said to him, I am will-ing: Be clean." And immediately the leprosy left him. And Jesus said to him, "Go, show yourself to the priests and make an offering for your cleansing as Moses commanded; and sin no more. . . ."

3 . . . [they came] to him and began rigorously testing him, saying, "Teacher Jesus, we know that you have come from God. For the things you do give a testimony that is beyond all the prophets. And so, tell us: is it right to pay the kings the things that relate to their rule? Shall we pay them or not?"

But when Jesus understood their thought he became incensed and said to them, "Why do you call me teacher with your mouth, when you do not listen to what I say? Well did Isaiah prophecy about you, 'This people honors me with their lips, but their heart is far removed from me. In vain do they worship me, commandments. . . . ' "[3]

4 " . . . hidden away in a secret place . . . placed underneath in secret . . . its weight beyond measure." . . . And while they were puzzling over his strange question, Jesus walked and stood on the banks of the Jordan river; he reached out his right hand, and filled it. . . . And he sowed it on the . . . And then . . . water . . . and . . . before their eyes; and it brought forth fruit . . . many . . . for joy . . .

---

[2]Less certain restorations of the text are enclosed in square brackets. [3]Isa. 29:13.

The Gospel of Peter

The Gospel of Peter was known and used as Scripture in some parts of the Christian church in the second century.[1] Its use was eventually disallowed by church leaders, however, who considered some of its teachings heretical and who claimed, as a consequence, that it could not have been written by its imputed author, Simon Peter. Having fallen out of circulation, it was practically forgotten in all but name until a fragment of its text was discovered near the end of the nineteenth century in the tomb of a Christian monk in Egypt.

The fragment narrates the events of Jesus' passion and resurrection; it begins in mid-sentence with the story of Pilate's washing of his hands at Jesus' trial. The narrative that follows bears a close relationship with the accounts found in the New Testament Gospels, especially Matthew, including descriptions of Jesus' crucifixion, his burial, the posting of a guard, and the events surrounding the resurrection. Some of the details here, however, are strikingly different. During the crucifixion, for example, Jesus is said to have been "silent as if he had no pain" (v. 10). In addition, some of the stories found here occur nowhere else among our early Christian Gospels. Most significantly, the Gospel narrates an account of Jesus' emergence from his tomb. He is supported by two gigantic angels whose heads reach up to heaven; his own head reaches above the heavens. Behind them emerges the cross. A voice then speaks from heaven, "Have you preached to those who are sleeping?" The cross replies, "Yes" (vv. 39–42).

At the conclusion of the narrative the story breaks off in the middle of a sentence in which the author reveals his name: "But I, Simon Peter, and Andrew my brother, took our nets and went off to the sea . . ." (v. 60).

It appears that the complete Gospel of Peter contained a full narrative of Jesus' ministry, not just of his passion, for several other Gospel fragments discovered in Egypt recount conversations between Jesus and Peter, recorded in the first person, plausibly from an earlier portion of the same Gospel.

---

[1]For a full discussion, see Ehrman, *Lost Christianities*, 13–28.

Translation by Bart D. Ehrman, based on the text in M. G. Mara, *Évangile de Pierre: Introduction, texte critique, traduction, commentaire et index* (SC 201; Paris: Cerf, 1973).

One of this Gospel's principal concerns is to incriminate Jews for the death of Jesus. Here, for instance, after Jesus' crucifixion, the Jewish people bewail their guilt and lament the certain fate of their beloved sacred city Jerusalem, which God will now destroy as retribution for their disobedience (v. 25). This anti-Judaic slant can perhaps be used to help date the Gospel in its final form, for such themes became common among Christian authors in the second century. The author was possibly writing at the beginning of the century, utilizing oral and written traditions that were themselves much older. It is not clear whether or not he had access to the accounts now found in the canonical Gospels.

1 . . . but none of the Jews washed his hands, nor did Herod or any of his judges. Since they did not wish to wash, Pilate stood up. 2 The kind Herod ordered the Lord to be taken away and said to them, "Do everything that I ordered you to do to him."

3 Standing there was Joseph, a friend of both Pilate and the Lord; when he knew that they were about to crucify him, he came to Pilate and asked for the Lord's body for burial. 4 Pilate sent word to Herod, asking for the body. 5 Herod said, "Brother Pilate, even if no one had asked for him we would have buried him, since the Sabbath is dawning. For it is written in the Law that the sun must not set on one who has been killed."[2] And he delivered him over to the people the day before their Feast of Unleavened Bread.

6 Those who took the Lord began pushing him about, running up to him and saying, "Let us drag around the Son of God, since we have authority over him." 7 They clothed him in purple and sat him on a judge's seat, saying, "Give a righteous judgment, O King of Israel!" 8 One of them brought a crown made of thorns and placed it on the Lord's head. 9 Others standing there were spitting in his face; some slapped his cheeks; others were beating him with a reed; and some

began to flog him, saying, "This is how we should honor the Son of God!"

10 They brought forward two evildoers and crucified the Lord between them. But he was silent, as if he had no pain. 11 When they had set the cross upright, they wrote an inscription: "This is the King of Israel." 12 Putting his clothes in front of him they divided them up and cast a lot for them. 13 But one of the evildoers reviled them, "We have suffered like this for the evil things we did; but this one, the Savior of the people—what wrong has he done you?" 14 They became angry at him and ordered that his legs not be broken, so that he would die in torment.

15 It was noon and darkness came over all of Judea. They were disturbed and upset that the sun may have already set while he was still alive; for their Scripture says that the sun must not set on one who has been killed.[3] 16 One of them said, "Give him gall mixed with vinegar to drink." And they made the mixture and gave it to him to drink. 17 Thus they brought all things to fulfillment and completed all their sins on their heads.

---

[2]Deut. 21:22–23.   [3]Deut. 21:22–23.

18 But many were wandering around with torches, thinking that it was night; and they stumbled about. **19** And the Lord cried out, "My power, O power, you have left me behind!" When he said this, he[a] was taken up.

20 At that time, the curtain of the Temple in Jerusalem was ripped in half. **21** Then they pulled the nails from the Lord's hands and placed him on the ground. All the ground shook and everyone was terrified. **22** Then the sun shone and it was found to be three in the afternoon.

23 But the Jews were glad and gave his body to Joseph that he might bury him, since he had seen all the good things he did. **24** He took the Lord, washed him, wrapped him in a linen cloth, and brought him into his own tomb, called the Garden of Joseph. **25** Then the Jews, the elders, and the priests realized how much evil they had done to themselves and began beating their breasts, saying "Woe to us because of our sins. The judgment and the end of Jerusalem are near."

26 But I and my companions were grieving and went into hiding, wounded in heart. For we were being sought out by them as if we were evildoers who wanted to burn the Temple. **27** Because of these things we fasted and sat mourning and weeping, night and day, until the Sabbath.

28 The scribes, Pharisees, and elders gathered together and heard all the people murmuring and beating their breasts, saying, "If such great signs happened when he died, you can see how righteous he was!" **29** The elders became fearful and went to Pilate and asked him, **30** "Give us some soldiers to guard his crypt for three days to keep his disciples from coming to steal him. Otherwise the people may assume he has been raised from the dead and then harm us."

31 So Pilate gave them the centurion Petronius and soldiers to guard the tomb. The elders and scribes came with them to the crypt. **32** Everyone who was there, along with the centurion and the soldiers, rolled a great stone and placed it there before the entrance of the crypt. **33** They smeared it with seven seals, pitched a tent there, and stood guard.

34 Early in the morning, as the Sabbath dawned, a crowd came from Jerusalem and the surrounding area to see the sealed crypt. **35** But during the night on which the Lord's day dawned, while the soldiers stood guard two by two on their watch, a great voice came from the sky. **36** They saw the skies open and two men descend from there; they were very bright and drew near to the tomb. **37** The stone cast before the entrance rolled away by itself and moved to one side; the tomb was open and both young men entered.

38 When the solders saw these things, they woke up the centurion and the elders—for they were also there on guard. **39** As they were explaining what they had seen, they saw three men emerge from the tomb, two of them supporting the other, with a cross following behind them. **40** The heads of the two reached up to the sky, but the head of the one they were leading went up above the skies. **41** And they heard a voice from the skies, "Have you preached to those who are asleep?" **42** And a reply came from the cross, "Yes."

43 They then decided among themselves to go off to disclose what had happened to Pilate. **44** While they were still making their plans, the skies were again seen to open, and a person descended and entered the crypt. **45** Those

[a]Or *it*

who were with the centurion saw these things and hurried to Pilate at night, abandoning the tomb they had been guarding, and explained everything they had seen. Greatly agitated, they said, "He actually was the Son of God." 46 Pilate replied, "I am clean of the blood of the Son of God; you decided to do this."

47 Then everyone approached him to ask and urge him to order the centurion and the soldiers to say nothing about what they had seen. 48 "For it is better," they said, "for us to incur a great sin before God than to fall into the hands of the Jewish people and be stoned." 49 And so Pilate ordered the centurion and the soldiers not to say a word.

50 Now Mary Magdalene, a disciple of the Lord, had been afraid of the Jews, since they were inflamed with anger; and so she had not done at the Lord's crypt the things that women customarily do for loved ones who die. But early in the morning of the Lord's day 51 she took some of her women friends with her and came to the crypt where he had been buried. 52 And they were afraid that the Jews might see them, and they said, "Even though we were not able to weep and beat our breasts on the day he was crucified, we should do these things now at his crypt. 53 But who will roll away for us the stone placed before the en-trance of the crypt, that we can go in, sit beside him, and do what we should? 54 For it was a large stone, and we are afraid someone may see us. If we cannot move it, we should at least cast down the things we have brought at the entrance as a memorial to him; and we will weep and beat our breasts until we return home."

55 When they arrived they found the tomb opened. And when they came up to it they stooped down to look in, and they saw a beautiful young man dressed in a very bright garment, sitting in the middle of the tomb. He said to them, 56 "Why have you come? Whom are you seeking? Not the one who was crucified? He has risen and left. But if you do not believe it, stoop down to look, and see the place where he was laid, that he is not there. For he has risen and left for the place from which he was sent." 57 Then the women fled out of fear.

58 But it was the final day of the Feast of Unleavened Bread, and many left to return to their homes, now that the feast had ended. 59 But we, the twelve disciples of the Lord, wept and grieved; and each one returned to his home, grieving for what had happened. 60 But I, Simon Peter, and my brother Andrew, took our nets and went off to the sea. And with us was Levi, the son of Alphaeus, whom the Lord. . . .

The Gospel of Mary

The Gospel of Mary is preserved in two Greek fragments of the third century and a fuller, but still incomplete, Coptic manuscript of the fifth. The book itself was composed sometime during the (late?) second century.

Even though we do not have the complete text, it was clearly an intriguing Gospel, for here, among other things, Mary (Magdalene) is accorded a high status among the apostles of Jesus. In fact, at the end of the text, the apostle Levi acknowledges to his comrades that Jesus "loved her more than us." Mary's special relationship with Jesus is seen above all in the circumstance that he reveals to her alone, in a vision, an explanation of the nature of things hidden from the apostles.

The Gospel divides itself into two parts. In the first, Jesus, after his resurrection, gives a revelation to all his apostles concerning the nature of sin, speaks a final blessing and exhortation, commissions them to preach the gospel, and then leaves. They are saddened by his departure, but Mary consoles them and urges them to reflect on what he has said. She is then asked by Peter to tell them what Jesus had told her directly. In the second part, she proceeds to describe the vision that she had been granted. Unfortunately, four pages are lost from the manuscript, and so we know only the beginning and end of her description. But it appears that the vision involved a conversation she had with Jesus, who described how the human soul could ascend past the four ruling powers of the world in order to find its eternal rest. This description of the fate of the soul is related to salvation narratives found in other Gnostic texts.

The Gospel continues with two of the apostles—Andrew and Peter—challenging Mary's vision and her claim to have experienced it; it ends, though, with Levi pointing out that she was Jesus' favorite, and urging them to go forth to preach the gospel as he commanded. They are said to do so, and there the Gospel ends.

Translation of George MacRae and R McL. Wilson, in James Robinson, *The Nag Hammadi Library in English,* 3rd ed. (Leiden: Brill, 1988) 524–27; used with permission.

[. . .] (pp. 1–6 missing) will matter then be [destroyed] or not?" The Savior said, "All natures, all formations, all creatures exist in and with one another and they will be resolved again into their own roots. For the nature of matter is resolved into the (roots) of its nature alone. He who has ears to hear, let him hear."

Peter said to him, "Since you have explained everything to us, tell us this also: What is the sin of the world?" The Savior said, "There is no sin, but it is you who make sin when you do the things that are like the nature of adultery, which is called 'sin.' That is why the Good came into your midst, to the (essence) of every nature, in order to restore it to its root." Then he continued and said, "That is why you [become sick] and die, for [. . .] of the one who [. . . He who] understands, let him understand. [Matter gave birth to] a passion that has no equal, which proceeded from (something) contrary to nature. Then there arose a disturbance in the whole body. That is why I said to you, 'Be of good courage,' and if you are discouraged (be) encouraged in the presence of the different forms of nature. He who has ears to hear, let him hear."

When the blessed one had said this, he greeted them all, saying, "Peace be with you. Receive my peace to yourselves. Beware that no one lead you astray, saying, 'Lo here!' or 'Lo there!' For the Son of Man is within you. Follow after him! Those who seek him will find him. Go then and preach the gospel of the kingdom. Do not lay down any rules beyond what I appointed for you, and do not give a law like the lawgiver lest you be constrained by it." When he had said this, he departed.

But they were grieved. They wept greatly, saying, "How shall we go to the gentiles and preach the gospel of the kingdom of the Son of Man? If they did not spare him, how will they spare us?"

Then Mary stood up, greeted them all, and said to her brethren, "Do not weep and do not grieve nor be irresolute, for his grace will be entirely with you and will protect you. But rather let us praise his greatness, for he has prepared us and made us into men." When Mary said this, she turned their hearts to the Good, and they began to discuss the words of the [Savior].

Peter said to Mary, "Sister, we know that the Savior loved you more than the rest of women. Tell us the words of the Savior which you remember—which you know (but) we do not, nor have we heard them." Mary answered and said, "What is hidden from you I will proclaim to you." And she began to speak to them these words: "I," she said, "I saw the Lord in a vision and I said to him, 'Lord, I saw you today in a vision.' He answered and said to me, 'Blessed are you, that you did not waver at the sight of me. For where the mind is, there is the treasure.' I said to him, 'Lord, now does he who sees the vision see it <through> the soul <or> through the spirit?' The Savior answered and said. 'He does not see through the soul nor through the spirit, but the mind which [is] between the two—that is [what] sees the vision and it is [. . .].' (pp. 11–14 missing)

"[. . .] it. And desire that, 'I did not see you descending, but now I see you ascending. Why do you lie, since you belong to me?' The soul answered and said, 'I saw you. You did not see me nor recognize me. I served you as a garment, and you did not know me.' When it had said this, it went away rejoicing greatly.

"Again it came to the third power, which is called ignorance. [It (the power)] questioned the soul saying, 'Where are you going? In wickedness are you bound. But you are bound; do not judge!' And the soul said, 'why do you judge me although I have not judged? I was bound though I have not bound. I was not recognized. But I have recognized that the All is being dissolved, both the earthly (things) and the heavenly.'

"When the soul had overcome the third power, it went upwards and saw the fourth power, (which) took seven forms. The first form is darkness, the second desire, the third ignorance, the fourth is the excitement of death, the fifth is the kingdom of the flesh, the sixth is the foolish wisdom of flesh, the seventh is the wrathful wisdom. These are the seven [powers] of wrath. They ask the soul, 'Whence do you come, slayer of men, or where are you going, conqueror of space?' The soul answered and said, 'What binds me has been slain, and what surrounds me has been overcome, and my desire has been ended, and ignorance has died. In a [world] I was released from a world, [and] in a type from a heavenly type, and (from) the fetter of oblivion which is transient. From this time on will I attain to the rest of the time, of the season, of the aeon, in silence.' "

When Mary had said this, she fell silent, since it was to this point that the Savior had spoken with her. But Andrew answered and said to the brethren, "Say what you (wish to) say about what she has said. I at least do not believe that the Savior said this. For certainly these teachings are strange ideas." Peter answered and spoke concerning these same things. He questioned them about the Savior: "Did he really speak with a woman without our knowledge (and) not openly? Are we to turn about and all listen to her? Did he prefer her to us?"

Then Mary wept and said to Peter, "My brother Peter, what do you think? Do you think that I thought this up myself in my heart, or that I am lying about the Savior?" Levi answered and said to Peter, "Peter, you have always been hot-tempered. Now I see you contending against the woman like the adversaries. But if the Savior made her worthy, who are you indeed to reject her? Surely the Savior knows her very well. This is why he loved her more than us. Rather let us be ashamed and put on the perfect man and acquire him for ourselves as he commanded us, and preach the gospel, not laying down any other rule or other law beyond what the Savior said." When [. . .] and they began to go forth [to] proclaim and to preach.

The Gospel of Philip

The Gospel of Philip was almost completely unknown from Late Antiquity, through the Middle Ages, and down to the present day, until it was discovered as one of the documents in the Nag Hammadi Library (see p. 19). Although it is easily recognized as a Gnostic work, the book is notoriously difficult to understand in its details. In part this is due to the form of its composition: it is not a narrative Gospel of the type found in the New Testament nor a group of self-contained sayings like the Coptic Gospel of Thomas. It is instead a collection of mystical reflections that have evidently been excerpted from previously existing sermons, treatises, and theological meditations, brought together here under the name of Jesus' disciple Philip. Since these reflections are given in relative isolation, without any real narrative context, they are difficult to interpret. There are, at any rate, extensive uses of catchwords to organize some of the material, and several of the principal themes emerge upon a careful reading.

One of the clearest emphases is the contrast between those who can understand and those who cannot, between knowledge that is exoteric (available to all) and that which is esoteric (available only to insiders), between the immature outsiders (regular Christians, called "Hebrews") and the mature insiders (Gnostics, called "Gentiles"). Those who do not understand, the outsiders with only exoteric knowledge, err in many of their judgments—for example, in taking such notions as the virgin birth (v. 17) or the resurrection of Jesus (v. 21) as literal statements of historical fact, rather than symbolic expressions of deeper truths.

Throughout much of the work the Christian sacraments figure prominently. Five are explicitly named: baptism, anointing, eucharist, salvation, and bridal chamber (v. 68). It is hard to know what deeper meaning these rituals had for the author (especially the "bridal chamber," which has stirred considerable debate among scholars), or even what he imagined them to entail when practiced literally.

It is difficult to assign a date to this work, but it was probably compiled during the third century, although it draws on earlier sources.

Translation of David Cartlidge and David Dungan, *Documents for the Study of the Gospels*, 2nd ed. (Minneapolis: Fortress Press, 1994) 56–75; used with permission.

1 A Hebrew person makes a Hebrew, and he is called a proselyte. But a proselyte does not make a proselyte . . . there are those who are as they are . . . and they make others . . . it is enough for them that they exist.

2 The slave seeks only to be free. However, he does not seek after his lord's properties. The son, however, is not only a son but writes himself into the inheritance of the father.

3 Those who inherit the dead are dead and inherit the dead. Those who inherit living things are alive, and they inherit the living and the dead. Those who are dead inherit nothing. For how will the one who is dead inherit? If the dead one inherits the living he will not die, but the dead one will live more.

4 A Gentile does not die. He has not lived, so he cannot die. He lives who has believed the truth; and he is in danger that he will die, for he is alive. Now that Christ has come

5 the world is created, the cities are bedecked, the dead are carried out.

6 When we were Hebrews, we were orphans. We had only our mother. But when we became Christians, we gained a father and mother.

7 Those who sow in winter reap in summer. The winter is the world; the summer is the other aeon. Let us sow in the world so that we may reap in the summer. On account of this it is seemly for us not to pray in the winter. That which comes out of the winter is the summer. But if someone reaps in the winter, he really will not be reaping, but he will be tearing things out,

8 since this will not produce . . . not only will it [not] produce . . . but on the Sabbath [his field] is unfruitful.

9 Christ came to ransom some, but others he saved, others he redeemed. Those who were strangers he ransomed and made them his, and he set them apart.

These he made as securities in his will. Not only when he appeared did he lay aside his life as he wished, but at the establishment of the world he laid aside his life. He came to take it when he wished to, because it had been set aside as a pledge. It came under the control of robbers, and it was held prisoner. But he saved it, and he ransomed the good ones and the evil ones who were in the world.

10 Light and darkness, life and death, the right and the left are each other's brothers. They cannot separate from one another. Therefore, the good are not good nor are the evil evil, nor is life life, nor death death. On account of this, each one will dissolve into its beginning origin. But those who are exalted above the world cannot dissolve; they are eternal.

11 The names which are given to the worldly things contain a great occasion for error. For they twist our consideration from the right meaning to the wrong meaning. For whoever hears (the word) "God," does not know the right meaning but the wrong meaning. It is the same way with (such words as) "the Father" and "the Son" and "the Holy Spirit" and "the life" and "the light" and "the resurrection" and "the Church" and all the other names. Folk do not know the right meaning; rather they know the wrong meaning [unless] they have come to know the right meaning . . . they are in the world . . . in the aeon they would never be used as names in the world, nor would they list them under worldly things. They have an end in the aeon.

12 There is only one name which one does not speak out in the world, the name which the Father gave to the Son. It is above everything. It is the name of the Father. For the Son will not become the Father, if he does not put on the name of the Father. Those who have this name truly know it, but they do not speak it. Those who do not have it do not know it.

But the truth engendered names in the world for us, because it is impossible to know it (the truth) without names. The truth is a single thing and is many things. It is this way for our sake, in order to teach us this one thing in love through its many-ness.

13 The archons wanted to deceive the human because they saw that he was kindred to the truly good ones. They took the name of the good ones and gave it to those that are not good, so that by names they could deceive him and bind them to the ones that are not good. If they do them a favor, they are taken away from those who are not good and given their place among those that are good. They knew these things. For they (the archons) wished to take the free person and enslave him forever. . . .

15 Before the Christ came there was no bread in the world. So also in paradise, the place where Adam was, there were many trees as food for the animals, but there was no wheat for human food. The human ate as the animals. But when the Christ, the perfect man came, he brought bread from heaven so that people could eat in a human way.

16 The archons believed that what they did was by their own power and will. However, the Holy Spirit secretly worked all through them as he willed. The truth is sown in every place; she (the truth) was from the beginning, and many see her as she is sown. But only a few see her being gathered in.

17 Some say Mary was impregnated by the Holy Spirit. They err. They do not know what they say. When did a woman become pregnant by a woman? Mary is the virgin whom no power corrupted. She is a great anathema to the Hebrews, who are the apostles and apostolic men. This virgin whom no power defiled . . . the powers defiled them (or, themselves). The Lord (would) not have said, "My [Father who is in] Heaven," if he had not had another Father. But he would have simply said: ["My Father."]

18 The Lord said to the disciples . . . "Enter the Father's house, but do not take anything in the Father's house, nor remove anything."

19 "Jesus" is a secret name; "Christ" is a revealed name. For this reason, "Jesus" does not exist in any (other) language, but his name is always "Jesus," as they say. "Christ" is also his name; in Syriac, it is "Messiah," but, in Greek, it is "Christ." Actually, everyone has it according to his own language. "The Nazarene" is the one who reveals secret things.

20 The Christ has everything in himself: man, angel, mystery, and the Father.

21 They err who say, "The Lord first died and then he arose." First he arose, and then he died. If someone does not first achieve the resurrection, will he not die? So truly as God lives, that one would . . . [text uncertain].

22 No one will hide an extremely valuable thing in something of equal value. However, people often put things worth countless thousands into a thing worth a penny. It is this way with the soul. It is a precious thing which came into a worthless body.

23 Some fear that they will arise naked. Therefore, they wish to arise in the flesh, and they do not know that those who carry the flesh are naked. They who . . . who disrobe themselves are not naked. Flesh [and blood can] not inherit the Kingdom [of God]. What is this which will not inherit? That which is on us. But what is this which will inherit? That which is of Jesus and of his blood. Therefore he said: "The one who does not eat my flesh and drink my blood does not have life in him."[1] What is it? His flesh is the Logos, and his blood is the Holy Spirit. Whoever has received these has food and drink and clothing. I blame those who say it will not rise. Then they are both to blame. You say, "The flesh will not rise." But tell me what will rise, so that we may praise you. You say, "The spirit in the flesh and this light in the flesh." This is also a Logos (or, saying) which is fleshly. Whatever you say, you do not say anything outside the flesh. It is necessary to rise in this flesh; everything is in it.

24 In this world those who put on clothes are worth more than the clothes. In the Kingdom of Heaven the clothes are worth more than those who have put them on. Through water and fire, which purify the whole place,

25 those things which are revealed are revealed by those which are manifest, those which are secret by those which are secret. Some are hidden through those which are manifest. There is water in water; there is fire in anointing.

26 Jesus secretly stole them all. For he showed himself not to be as he really was, but he appeared in a way that they could see him. To those . . . he appeared. [He appeared] to the great as great. [He appeared] to the small as small. [He appeared] to the angels as an angel and to humans as a human. Because of this, his Logos hid from everyone. Some, to be sure, saw him, and they thought that they saw themselves. But, when he appeared in glory to the disciples on the mountain he was not small. He became great; however, he made the disciples great, so that they were able to see him as he was, great.

He said on that day in the thanksgiving, "You who have united with the perfect, the light, the Holy Spirit, have united the angels also with us, with the images."

27 Do not scorn the Lamb. For without it one cannot see the King. No one who is naked will be able to find his way to the King.

28 The heavenly Man has many more children than the earthly man. If the children of Adam are more numerous, and still die, how much more the children of the Perfect One who do not die but are always begotten. . . .

32 There were three who always walked with the Lord: Mary, his mother and her sister and Magdalene, whom they call his lover. A Mary is his sister and his mother and his lover.

33 "The Father" and "the Son" are single names. The "Holy Spirit" is a double name. They are everywhere. They are above; they are below; they are in the secret; they are in the revealed. The Holy Spirit is in the revealed; it is below; it is in the secret; it is above.

34 The saints are ministered to by the evil powers, for the powers are blind because of the Holy Spirit. Therefore, they will believe that they serve a man when they work for the saints. Because of this, one day a disciple sought from the Lord something from the world. He said to him, "Ask your mother, and she will give you from a stranger's (things)." . . .

50 God is a man eater. On account of this the Man [was killed] for him. Before they killed the Man, they killed animals, for those were not Gods for whom they killed.

51 Glass and pottery vessels are both made with fire. But if glass vessels are broken they are made again, for they are created with a breath. But if pottery vessels are broken, they are destroyed, for they are created without a breath.

---

[1]John 6:54.

52 An ass which turns a millstone in a circle went one hundred miles. When he was turned loose he found he was still at the same place. There are people who make many trips and get nowhere. When evening came upon them, they saw no city or town, no creation or nature, no power or angel. The poor fellows labored in vain.

53 The Eucharist is Jesus. For they call him in Syriac *pharisatha*, which is, "the one who is spread out." For Jesus came and he crucified the world.

54 The Lord went into the dye shop of Levi. He took seventy-two colors and threw them into the kettle. He took them all out white, and he said, "Thus the Son of man came, a dyer."

55 Wisdom (*sophia*), whom they call barren, is the mother of the angels, and the consort of Christ is Mary Magdalene. The [Lord loved Mary] more than all the disciples, and he kissed her on the [mouth many times]. The other [women/disciples saw] . . . him. They said to him, "Why do you [love her] more than all of us?" The Savior answered and said to them, "Why do not I love you as I do her?"

56 If a blind person and one who can see are in the dark, there is no difference between them. When the light comes, then the one who sees will see the light, and the one who is blind will stay in the darkness.

57 The Lord said, "Blessed is the one who exists before he came into being. For he who exists was and will be."

58 The greatness of the human being is not revealed, but it is hidden. Because of this he is lord of the animals that are stronger than he and are great according to that which is clear as well as hidden. And this mastery gives to them their stability. But if a person leaves them alone, they kill one another (and) bite one another. And they ate one another because they could find no food. But they have now found food because the person has worked the ground.

59 If anyone goes down into the water and comes up having received nothing and says, "I am a Christian," he has borrowed the name at interest. But if he receives the Holy Spirit, he has taken the name as a gift. If someone has received a gift, it is not taken back. But he who has borrowed something at interest has to meet the payment.

60 It is this way . . . if anyone should be in a mystery. . . .

62 Do not be afraid of the flesh nor love it. If you fear it, then it will be your master. If you love it, it will swallow and strangle you.

63 Either one is in this world, or in the resurrection, or in the places in the middle. God forbid that I be found in them. In this world there is good and evil. Its good is not good, and its evil is not evil. But there is evil after this world, true evil, which they call "the middle." It is death. As long as we are in this world, it is fitting to us to acquire the resurrection, so that when we peel off the flesh we will be found in repose, not making our way in "the middle." For many wander astray off the path. For it is good to come out of the world before one sins. . . .

67 The truth did not come naked into the world, but came in types and images. One will not receive the truth in any other way. There is a being-born-again, and an image of being-born-again. It is truly necessary that they become born again through the image. What else is the resurrection? It is necessary that the image arise through the image. The Bridal Chamber and the image necessarily enters into the truth through the image; this is the recapitulation. It is necessary not only that those who have it received the name of the Father and the Son and the

Holy Spirit, but that they took it themselves. If someone does not take it himself, the name also will be taken away from him. But one receives them in the anointing of the power of [the cross] . . . the apostles call it "the right" and "the left." For this reason one is no longer a Christian, but a Christ.

68 The Lord [did?] all in a Mystery, a Baptism, an Anointing, a Eucharist, a Salvation, and a Bridal Chamber. . . .

82 Is it all right to speak a mystery? The Father of all joined himself with the virgin who came down, and a fire[?] was burned for him that day. He appeared in the great Bridal Chamber. Therefore, his body came into being that day. He came out of the Bridal Chamber as one who came into being from the bridegroom and the bride. Thus, Jesus established all through these. And it is fitting for each of the disciples to enter his repose.

83 Adam came into being from two virgins: from the Spirit and from the virgin earth. Therefore, the Christ was born from a virgin so that he could bring order to the stumbling which occurred in the beginning.

84 There are two trees in paradise. The one engenders a[nimals]; the other engenders people. Adam [ate] from the tree which brought forth animals; [he be]came a beast and he begot beasts. Because of this they worship . . . of Adam. The tree . . . fruit is . . . engenders people . . . the (person) . . . God created the p[erson . . . the perso]n created God.

85 It is like this in the world: people create Gods and they worship those whom they have created. It would be proper if the Gods worshipped people. . . .

99 The world came into being through an error. For he who created it intended to create it imperishable and immortal. He failed to attain his hope. For the world is not imperishable and neither is he who created the world. For there is no imperishability, of things, but there is of sons. And no thing can attain imperishability if it does not become a son. But if someone cannot receive, how much more will he not be able to give?

100 The Cup of Prayer holds wine and it holds water. It serves as a type of the blood for which they give thanks. And it is full of the Holy Spirit and belongs to the completely perfect Man. When we drink this, we will take to ourselves the perfect Man.

101 The living water is a body. It is right that we clothe ourselves with the living Man. Therefore, when he comes to go down to the water, he disrobes in order that he may put this one on. . . .

125 As long as it is hidden, wickedness is really brought to nothing, but it is still not removed from the midst of the seed of the Holy Spirit. They are slaves of evil. When it is revealed, then the perfect light will pour over everyone, all those in it will receive the [anointing]. Then the slaves will become free, and the prisoners will be redeemed.

126 [Every] plant my Father in Heaven does not plant [will be] rooted out. Those who are alienated will be united. They will be filled. Everyone who [will go in] to the Bridal Chamber will [light the light]. For [it shines] as in the marriages which [are seen, although they] are in the night. The fire [burns] in the night, then it is extinguished. But the mysteries of this marriage are fulfilled in the day and the light. That day and its light do not set.

127 If anyone becomes a child of the Bridal Chamber, he will receive the light. If anyone does not receive it while he is in these places (i.e., this world), he will not be able to receive it in the other place. The one who has received light cannot

be seen nor can he be held. And no one can torment him, even while he lives in the world. And further, when he goes out of the world, already he has received the truth in images. The world has become the aeon, for the aeon has become for him the fullness. It is thus; it is revealed only to him. It is not hidden in the darkness and the night, but it is hidden in a perfect day and a holy light.

The Gospel of Truth

A moving expression of Gnostic joy in experiencing enlightenment, the "Gospel of Truth" is one of the real treasures of the Nag Hammadi Library (see p. 19). The book is not a Gospel in the traditional sense—there is no account of the life or teachings of Jesus here. It is called a Gospel because it presents the "good news" of God's gracious revelation of saving knowledge, gnosis, which comes through Jesus Christ. Some scholars believe that it was originally a sermon preached to a Gnostic, or possibly a more broadly Christian, congregation; many are convinced that it was authored by the most famous Gnostic Christian of the second century, Valentinus himself.

The Gospel of Truth presupposes important aspects of Gnostic myth, but it does not explicate them; there are only scattered hints about how the divine realm, the material world, and human beings came into existence. Instead, the book focuses on the truth that brings redemption to an anguished humanity languishing in darkness and ignorance, and especially on the one who brought this revealed truth, Jesus Christ, the Word who comes forth from the Father as his Son. Through Christ's revelation, the fog of error has been dissipated and the illusions of falsehood have been exposed, opening those who receive the truth to understand who they are, allowing them to be reunited with the incomprehensible and inconceivable Father of all.

Whether or not the work actually came from the pen of Valentinus, it was known to the church father and heresy-hunter Irenaeus, and so must have been written sometime before 180 CE.

The gospel of truth is joy for those who have received from the Father of truth the grace of knowing him, through the power of the Word that came forth from the pleroma, the one who is in the thought and the mind of the Father, that is, the one who is addressed as the Savior, (that) being the name of the work he is to

Translation by Harold W. Attridge and George W. MacRae, in Harold W. Attridge, *Nag Hammadi Codex 1 (The Jung Codex)* (Nag Hammadi Studies, 22) (Leiden: E. J. Brill, 1985) 82–117; used with permission.

perform for the redemption of those who were ignorant of the Father, while in the name [of] the gospel is the proclamation of hope, being discovery for those who search for him.

When the totality went about searching for the one from whom they had come forth—and the totality was inside of him, the incomprehensible, inconceivable one who is superior to every thought—ignorance of the Father brought about anguish and terror; and the anguish grew solid like a fog, so that no one was able to see. For this reason error became powerful; it worked on its own matter foolishly, not having known the truth. It set about with a creation, preparing with power and beauty the substitute for the truth.

This was not, then, a humiliation for him, the incomprehensible, inconceivable one, for they were nothing, the anguish and the oblivion and the creature of deceit, while the established truth is immutable, imperturbable, perfect in beauty. For this reason, despise error.

Thus it had no root; it fell into a fog regarding the Father, while it was involved in preparing works and oblivions and terrors, in order that by means of these it might entice those of the middle and capture them.

The oblivion of error was not revealed. It is not a [. . .] from the Father. Oblivion did not come into existence from the Father, although it did indeed come into existence because of him. But what comes into existence in him is knowledge, which appeared in order that oblivion might vanish and the Father might be known. Since oblivion came into existence because the Father was not known, then if the Father comes to be known, oblivion will not exist from that moment on.

Through this, the gospel of the one who is searched for, which <was> revealed to those who are perfect through the mercies of the Father; the hidden mystery, Jesus, the Christ, enlightened those who were in darkness through oblivion. He enlightened them; he showed (them) a way; and the way is the truth which he taught them.

For this reason error grew angry at him, persecuted him, was distressed at him (and) was brought to naught. He was nailed to a tree (and) he became a fruit of the knowledge of the Father. It did not, however, cause destruction because it was eaten, but to those who ate it it gave (cause) to become glad in the discovery, and he discovered them in himself, and they discovered him in themselves.

As for the incomprehensible, inconceivable one, the Father, the perfect one, the one who made the totality, within him is the totality and of him the totality has need. Although he retained their perfection within himself which he did not give to the totality, the Father was not jealous. What jealousy indeed (could there be) between himself and his members? For, if this aeon had thus [received] their [perfection], they could not have come [. . .] the Father. He retains within himself their perfection, granting it to them as a return to him and a perfectly unitary knowledge. It is he who fashioned the totality, and within him is the totality and the totality was in need of him.

As in the case of a person of whom some are ignorant, he wishes to have them know him and love him, so—for what did the totality have need of if not knowledge regarding the Father?—he became a guide, restful and leisurely. In schools he appeared (and) he spoke the word as a teacher. There came the men wise in their own estimation, putting him to the test. But he confounded them because they were foolish. They hated him because they were not really wise.

After all these, there came the little children also, those to whom the knowledge of the Father belongs. Having been strengthened, they learned about the impressions of the Father. They knew, they were known; they were glorified, they glorified. There was manifested in their heart the living book of the living—the one written in the thought and the mind [of the] Father, which from before the foundation of the totality was within his incomprehensibility—that (book) which no one was able to take, since it remains for the one who will take it to be slain. No one could have become manifest from among those who have believed in salvation unless that book had appeared. For this reason the merciful one, the faithful one, Jesus, was patient in accepting sufferings until he took that book, since he knows that his death is life for many.

Just as there lies hidden in a will, before it is opened, the fortune of the deceased master of the house, so (it is) with the totality, which lay hidden while the Father of the totality was invisible, being something which is from him, from whom every space comes forth. For this reason Jesus appeared; he put on that book; he was nailed to a tree; he published the edict of the Father on the cross. O such great teaching! He draws himself down to death though life eternal clothes him. Having stripped himself of the perishable rags, he put on imperishability, which no one can possibly take away from him. Having entered the empty spaces of terrors, he passed through those who were stripped naked by oblivion, being knowledge and perfection, proclaiming the things that are in the heart, [...] teach those who will receive teaching.

But those who are to receive teaching [are] the living who are inscribed in the book of the living. It is about themselves that they receive instruction, receiving it from the Father, turning again to him. Since the perfection of the totality is in the Father, it is necessary for the totality to ascend to him. Then, if one has knowledge, he receives what are his own and draws them to himself. For he who is ignorant is in need, and what he lacks is great, since he lacks that which will make him perfect. Since the perfection of the totality is in the Father and it is necessary for the totality to ascend to him and for each one to receive what are his own, he enrolled them in advance, having prepared them to give to those who came forth from him.

Those whose name he knew in advance were called at the end, so that one who has knowledge is the one whose name the Father has uttered. For he whose name has not been spoken is ignorant. Indeed, how is one to hear if his name has not been called? For he who is ignorant until the end is a creature of oblivion, and he will vanish along with it. If not, how is it that these miserable ones have no name, (how is it that) they do not have the call? Therefore, if one has knowledge, he is from above. If he is called, he hears, he answers, and he turns to him who is calling him, and ascends to him. And he knows in what manner he is called. Having knowledge, he does the will of the one who called him, he wishes to be pleasing to him, he receives rest. Each one's name comes to him. He who is to have knowledge in this manner knows where he comes from and where he is going. He knows as one who having become drunk has turned away from his drunkenness, (and) having returned to himself, has set right what are his own.

He has brought many back from error. He has gone before them to their places, from which they had moved away, since it was on account of the depth that they received error, the depth of the one who encircles all spaces while there is none that encircles him. It was great wonder that they were in the Father, not knowing him, and (that) they were able to come forth by themselves, since they were unable to comprehend or to know the one in whom they were. For if his will had not thus emerged from him—for he revealed it in view of a knowledge in which all its emanations concur.

This is the knowledge of the living book which he revealed to the 23 aeons, at the end, as [his letters], revealing how they are not vowels nor are they consonants, so that one might read them and think of something foolish, but they are letters of the truth which they alone speak who know them. Each letter is a complete <thought> like a complete book, since they are letters written by the Unity, the Father having written them for the aeons in order that by means of his letters they should know the Father.

While his wisdom contemplates the Word, and his teaching utters it, his knowledge has revealed <it>. While forebearance is a crown upon it, and his gladness is in harmony with it, his glory has exalted it, his image has revealed it, his repose has received it into itself, his love has made a body over it, his fidelity has embraced it. In this way the Word of the Father goes forth in the totality, as the fruit [of] his heart and an impression of his will. But it supports the totality; it chooses them and also receives the impression of the totality, purifying them, bringing them back into the Father, into the Mother, Jesus of the infinite sweetness.

The Father reveals his bosom.—Now his bosom is the Holy Spirit.—He reveals what is hidden of him—what is hidden of him is his Son—so that through the mercies of the Father the aeons may know him and cease laboring in search of the Father, resting there in him, knowing that this is the rest. Having filled the deficiency, he abolished the form—the form of it is the world, that in which he

served.—For the place where there is envy and strife is deficient, but the place where (there is) Unity is perfect. Since the deficiency came into being because the Father was not known, therefore, when the Father is known, from that moment on the deficiency will no longer exist. As in the case of the ignorance of a person, when he comes to have knowledge, his ignorance vanishes of itself, as the darkness vanishes when light appears, so also the deficiency vanishes in the perfection. So from that moment on the form is not apparent, but it will vanish in the fusion of Unity, for now their works lie scattered. In time Unity will perfect the spaces. It is within Unity that each one will attain himself; within knowledge he will purify himself from multiplicity into Unity, consuming matter within himself like fire, and darkness by light, death by life.

If indeed these things have happened to each one of us, then we must see to it above all that the house will be holy and silent for the Unity. (It is) as in the case of some people who moved out of dwellings having jars that in spots were not good. They would break them and the master of the house would not suffer loss. Rather <he> is glad because in place of the bad jars (there are) full ones which are made perfect. For such is the judgment which has come from above. It has passed judgment on everyone; it is a drawn sword, with two edges, cutting on either side. When the Word appeared, the one that is within the heart of those who utter it—it is not a sound alone but it became a body—a great disturbance took place among the jars because some had been emptied, others filled; that is, some had been supplied, others poured out, some had been purified, still others broken up. All the spaces were shaken and disturbed because they had no order nor stability. Error was upset, not knowing what to do; it was grieved, in mourning, afflicting itself because it knew nothing. When knowledge drew near it—this is the downfall of (error) and all its emanations—error is empty, having nothing inside.

Truth appeared; all its emanations knew it. They greeted the Father in truth with a perfect power that joins them with the Father. For, as for everyone who loves the truth—because the truth is the mouth of the Father; his tongue is the Holy Spirit—he who is joined to the truth is joined to the Father's mouth by his tongue, whenever he is to receive the Holy Spirit, since this is the manifestation of the Father and his revelation to his aeons.

He manifested what was hidden of him; he explained it. For who contains, if not the Father alone? All the spaces are his emanations. They have known that they came forth from him like children who are from a grown man. They knew that they had not yet received form nor yet received a name, each one of which the Father begets. Then, when they receive form by his knowledge, though truly within him, they do not know him. But the Father is perfect, knowing every space within him. If he wishes, he manifests whomever he wishes by giving him form and giving him a name, and he gives a name to him and brings it about that those come into existence who, before they come into existence, are ignorant of him who fashioned them.

I do not say, then, that they are nothing (at all) who have not yet come into existence, but they are in him who will wish that they come into existence when he wishes, like the time that is to come. Before all things appear, he knows what he will produce. But the fruit which is not yet manifest does not know anything, nor does it do anything. Thus, also, every space which is itself in the Father is from the one who exists, who established it from what does not exist. For he who has no root has no fruit either, but though he thinks to himself, "I have come into being," yet he will perish by himself. For this reason, he who did not exist at all will never come into existence. What, then, did he wish him to think of himself? This: "I have come into being like the shadows and phantoms of the night." When the light shines on the terror which that person had experienced, he knows that it is nothing.

Thus they were ignorant of the Father, he being the one whom they did not see. Since it was terror and disturbance and instability and doubt and division, there were many illusions at work by means of these, and (there were) empty fictions, as if they were sunk in sleep and found themselves in disturbing dreams. Either (there is) a place to which they are fleeing, or without strength they come (from) having chased after others, or they are involved in striking blows, or they are receiving blows themselves, or they have fallen from high places, or they take off into the air though they do not even have wings. Again, sometimes (it is as) if people were murdering them, though there is no one even pursuing them, or they themselves are killing their neighbors, for they have been stained with their blood. When those who are going through all these things wake up, they see nothing, they who were in the midst of all these disturbances, for they are nothing. Such is the way of those who have cast ignorance aside from them like sleep, not esteeming it as anything, nor do they esteem its works as solid things either, but they leave them behind like a dream in the night. The knowledge of the Father they value as the dawn. This is the way each one has acted, as though asleep at the time when he was ignorant. And this is the way he has <come to knowledge>, as if he had awakened. {and} Good for the one who will return and awaken. And blessed is he who has opened the eyes of the blind.

And the Spirit ran after him, hastening from waking him up. Having extended his hand to him who lay upon the ground, he set him up on his feet, for he had not yet risen. He gave them the means of knowing the knowledge of the Father and the revelation of his Son. For, when they had seen him and had heard him, he granted them to taste him and to smell him and to touch the beloved Son.

When he had appeared instructing them about the Father, the incomprehensible one, when he had breathed into them what is in the thought, doing his will, when many had received the light, they turned to him. For the material ones were strangers and did not see his likeness and had not known him. For he came by means of fleshly form, while nothing blocked his course because incorruptibility is irresistible, since he, again, spoke new things, still speaking about what is in the heart of the Father, having brought forth the flawless word.

When light had spoken through his mouth, as well as his voice which gave birth to life, he gave them thought and understanding and mercy and salvation and the powerful spirit from the infiniteness and the sweetness of the Father. Having made punishments and tortures cease—for it was they which were leading astray from his face some who were in need of mercy, in error and in bonds— he both destroyed them with power and confounded them with knowledge. He became a way for those who were gone astray and knowledge for those who were ignorant, a discovery for those who were searching, and a support for those who were wavering, immaculateness for those who were defiled.

He is the shepherd who left behind the ninety-nine sheep which were not lost. He went searching for the one which had gone astray. He rejoiced when he found it, for ninety-nine is a number that is in the left hand which holds it. But when the one is found, the entire number passes to the right (hand). As that which lacks the one—that is, the entire right (hand)— draws what was deficient and takes it from the left-hand side and brings (it) to the right, so too the number becomes one hundred. It is the sign of the one who is in their sound; it is the Father. Even on the Sabbath, he labored for the sheep which he found fallen into the pit. He gave life to the sheep, having brought it up from the pit in order that you might know interiorly—you, the sons of interior knowledge—what is the Sabbath, on which it is not fitting for salvation to be idle, in order that you may speak from the day from above, which has no night, and from the light which does not sink because it is perfect.

Say, then, from the heart that you are the perfect day and in you dwells the light that does not fail. Speak of the truth with those who search for it and (of) knowledge to those who have committed sin in their error. Make firm the foot of those who have stumbled and stretch out your hands to those who are ill. Feed those who are hungry and give repose to those who are weary, and raise up those who wish to rise, and awaken those who sleep. For you are the understanding that is drawn forth. If strength acts thus, it becomes even stronger. Be concerned with yourselves; do not be concerned with other things which you have rejected from yourselves. Do not return to what you have vomited to eat it. Do not be moths. Do not be worms, for you have already cast it off. Do not become a (dwelling) place for the devil, for you have already destroyed him. Do not strengthen (those who are) obstacles to you who are collapsing, as though (you were) a support (for them). For the lawless one is someone to treat ill rather than the just one. For the former does his work as a lawless person; the latter as a righteous person does his work among others. So you, do the will of the Father, for you are from him.

For the Father is sweet and in his will is what is good. He has taken cognizance of the things that are yours that you might find rest in them. For by the fruits does one take cognizance of the things that are yours because the children of the Father are his fragrance, for they are from the grace of his countenance. For this reason the Father loves his fragrance and manifests it in every place, and if it mixes with matter he gives his fragrance to the light and in his repose he causes it to surpass every form (and) every sound. For it is not the ears that smell the fragrance, but (it is) the breath that has the sense of smell and attracts the fragrance to itself and is submerged in the fragrance of the Father, so that he thus shelters it and takes it to the place where it came from, from the first fragrance which is grown cold. It is something in a psychic form, being like cold water which has frozen (?), which is on earth that is not solid, of which those who see it think it is earth; afterwards it dissolves again. If a breath draws it, it gets hot. The fragrances, therefore, that are cold are from the division. For this reason faith came; it dissolved the division, and it brought the warm pleroma of love in order that the cold should not come again but there should be the unity of perfect thought. . . .

The Gospel of the Savior

The most recent Gospel to be discovered is called the Gospel of the Savior. It poses real difficulties for translator and reader alike, since so much of its text has been destroyed (i.e., there are numerous holes in the manuscript). Nonetheless, it was obviously once an intriguing account of Jesus' life—or at least of his last hours. For the surviving portion of the text recounts the final instructions of Jesus to his disciples, his prayer to God that the "cup" might be taken away from him, and then a final address—to the cross itself. Whether this Gospel originally contained an entire account of Jesus' life and death cannot be determined.[1]

There are numerous differences between the surviving passages of this Gospel and the parallel accounts in the New Testament. One of the most striking is that when Jesus asks his Father to "remove this cup from me," he does so not in the Garden of Gethsemane, but in a vision in which he has been transported to the throne room of God himself. In addition, this account records God's replies to Jesus' requests. But probably the most intriguing aspect of this hitherto lost Gospel is its ending, where Jesus (who is called "the Savior" throughout the account) speaks directly to the cross: "O cross do not be afraid! I am rich. I will fill you with my wealth. I will mount you, O cross, I will be hung upon you."

It appears that the unknown author of this Gospel made use of earlier Christian texts, including the Gospels of Matthew and, especially, John, and the book of Revelation. He evidently produced his account sometime in the second century, although the Coptic manuscript that contains it dates from the sixth or seventh century. The original language was Greek.

We do not know where the text was originally written. The surviving manuscript was discovered in Egypt and acquired for the Papyrus Collection of the Berlin Museum in 1967; but it remained unnoticed there until an American scholar, Paul Mirecki, came upon it in 1991. He and another scholar, Charles Hedrick, published the first edition of the text; an authori-

---

[1]See the comments in Ehrman, *Lost Christianities*, 50–51.

Translation by Stephen Emmel, "The Recently Published *Gospel of the Savior*," ("Unbekanntes Berliner Evangelium"): Righting the Order of Pages and Events," *Harvard Theological Review* 95 (2002) 45–72; used with permission.

tative reconstruction of its narrative with a readable translation was then made by Stephen Emmel.[2] That is the translation I reproduce here, including the places where the translator indicates that the manuscript cannot be read.

Verses 1–27: The Savior converses with his disciples (after the Last Supper)

[... 12 lines untranslatable ...] the kingdom of heaven at your right hand. 2 Blessed is he who will eat with me in the kingdom of heaven. 3 [You] are the salt [of] the earth, and [you] are the lamp that gives light to the world. 4 Do not sleep and do not slumber [until you clothe yourselves] with the garment of the kingdom, which I have bought with the blood of grapes!"

5 Andrew replied and said, "My [Lord] [... 12 ± lines untranslatable ...]."

6 [... 12 ± lines untranslatable ...]. 7 Since I have healed those of the [world], I must [also go] down to Hades on account of the others who are bound there. 8 So now what is necessary [... 23 lines untranslatable ... everything carefully]. 9 I for my part will appear to you with joy. For I know that you are able to do everything with joy. 10 For a human being [has] free will [... 9 lines untranslatable ...]. 11 So now [while] you [are] in the body, do not let matter rule over you! 12 Rise, let us go hence; for my betrayer is at hand.

13 "And you will all flee and fall away because of me. 14 You will all flee and [leave me] alone; 15 yet I am not alone, for my Father is with me. 16 I and my Father are one and the same. 17 For it is

written, 'I will strike the shepherd, and the sheep of the flock will be scattered.' 18 So I am the good shepherd. 19 I lay down my life for you. 20 You too, lay down your lives for your [friends], so that you might please my Father! 21 For there is no commandment greater than this, that I should [lay down my] life [for] humankind. 22 For [this reason] my Father loves me. 23 Because I accomplished [his] will. 24 Because [I am] divine and yet I [became human] on account of [... 4 lines untranslatable ...]."

25 [... 8 lines untranslatable ...] how soon [will you ...] or remember us, send for us, take us out of the world, and let us [come] to you? 26 [... 26 lines untranslatable ...] [...]."

27 The Savior said to us, "O my holy members, my blessed seeds, [rise] and [...] pray [... 12 ± lines untranslatable ...]."

Verses 28–36: A vision on the Mount

28 [... 12 ± lines untranslatable ...] on the mountain. 29 We became as spiritual bodies. Our eyes opened wide in every direction. The whole place was revealed before us. 30 We [saw] the heavens, and they [opened] up one after another. 31 The guardians of the gates were alarmed. 32 The angels were afraid and

[2]Charles W. Hedrick and Paul A. Mirecki, *Gospel of the Savior: A New Ancient Gospel* (Santa Rosa: Polebridge, 1999); Stephen Emmel, "The Recently Published *Gospel of the Savior* ("Unbekanntes Berliner Evangelium"): Righting the Order of Pages and Events," *Harvard Theological Review* 95 (2002) 45–72.

[fled] this [way] and that, thinking [that] they would all be destroyed. 33 We saw our Savior having penetrated all the heavens, [his] feet [placed firmly on] the [mountain with us, his head penetrating the seventh] heaven. 34 [. . . 8 lines untranslatable . . .] . . . all the heavens. 35 Then before us, the apostles, this world became as darkness. 36 We became as [those] among the [immortal] aeons, with our [eyes penetrating all] the heavens, clothed with the [power of] our apostleship, and we saw our Savior when he had reached the [seventh] heaven.

Verses 37–44: In the Father's throne room

37 [. . . 7 lines untranslatable . . .] the [heavens] were alarmed. 38 [The angels] and the archangels [bowed down] on [their faces. 39 The] cherubim [. . .] . . . [. . .]. 40 [The . . .] put down their [. . .]s. 41 The [. . .]s that [. . . the curtain (?) sang. 42 The elders, seated] on [their thrones], cast [their] crowns [down] before the Father's [throne]. 43 All [the saints brought a] robe. 44 [. . .] when [. . .] Son [. . . 4 ± lines untranslatable . . .].

Verses 45–61: The Savior prays three times to his Father

45 [. . . 4 ± lines untranslatable . . . why] are you weeping and [distressed], such that [the] entire angelic host [is alarmed]?"
46 [And] he replied [in this] manner, "[. . . 5 lines untranslatable . . .] [. . .] . . . [. . .] 47 I am [greatly distressed . . .] kill[. . .] at the hands of the [people of] Israel. 48 O my [father], if it be [possible], let this [cup] pass from me! 49 Let [me] be [. . .] at the hands of

some other [. . .] people who [. . .] if [. . .] Israel [. . . 3 ± lines untranslatable . . .]."
50 [. . . 4 ± lines untranslatable . . . so that] salvation [might come] to the entire world."
51 [Then] again the Son threw himself down at his Father's feet, [saying], 52 "[O my father . . . 5 lines untranslatable . . .] to die with joy and pour out my blood for the human race. 53 But I weep greatly on account of my beloved ones, [Abraham] and Isaac [and] Jacob, [because on the] day of judgment [they will] stand, [whereas] I will sit upon [my] throne and pass [judgment] on the world, 54 [while they] say to me, '[. . . 8 lines untranslatable . . .] the glory that was given to me [on] earth. 55 O my [father, if it be possible, let this cup] pass from me!"
56 [The Father replied] to him for [the] second time, 57 "[O my] son, you do not [. . . 28 lines untranslatable . . .]."
58 The Son [replied] for the [third] time, 59 "O [my father], if [. . .] [. . . 32 ± lines untranslatable . . .]."
60 [. . . 32 ± lines untranslatable . . .] [. . .] [. . . 29 lines untranslatable . . .] he [. . .] complete [the service until . . .] to them. 61 [. . . 27 lines untranslatable . . .]

Verses 62–72: The Savior converses with his disciples (after the vision)

62 [The Savior] said to us, "No lot surpasses your own, nor is there any glory more exalted than [your own. 63 . . . 31 lines untranslatable . . .] [. . . 31 lines untranslatable . . .] 64 O entirety [. . . 2 lines untranslatable . . .] 65 O [. . . 19 lines untranslatable . . .] cross [. . . 5 lines untranslatable . . .] three [days I will] take you[. . .] with me and and show you [the] things you desire [to]

see. **66** So [do not be alarmed] when [you] see [me]!"

67 We said to him, "Lord, in what form will you reveal yourself to us, or in what kind of body will you come? Tell us!" **68** John responded and said, "Lord, when you are ready to reveal yourself to us, do not reveal yourself to us in all your glory, but change your glory into [some other] glory so that [we might be able to bear] it, lest we see [you and] despair from [fear]!"

69 [The Savior replied], "[Rid] yourselves [of] this [fear] that [you] are afraid of, so that you might see and believe! **70** But do not touch me until I ascend to [my Father and your Father], to [my God and] your God, to my Lord and your Lord! **71** If someone [comes close] to me, he [will get burned. I] am [the] blazing [fire. Whoever is close] to [me] is close to [the fire]. Whoever is far from me is far from life. **72** So now gather [unto] me, O my holy members, [. . . 6 lines untranslatable . . .]."

Verses 73–109: **An amen responsory between the Savior and his disciples**

73 [He] said to us, "I am among you [as] a child."

74 He said, "Amen!"

75 "A little while I am among you."

76 [. . .] responded, "Amen!"

77 "[Those who] <want> [to set (?) the world] against me [are] plotting against me because I am a stranger to it. **78** So behold! Now I [am grieving] on account of the [sins] of the world. **79** [But I am rejoicing] on [your] account, because [you have . . .] well in [the world]. **80** So become acquainted with [yourselves], that you might profit me, and I will rejoice over your work!"

81 "I am the king."—"Amen!"

82 "I [am] the [son] of the king."— ["Amen!"]

83 "I [am the spring of water . . ."— "Amen!"]

84 "[I am . . .] and you have no [other]."—"Amen!"

85 "I am fighting [for] you. You too, wage war!"—"Amen!"

86 "I am being sent. I in turn want to send you."—"Amen!"

87 "[. . .], O [. . .] you [. . . I] want to [bring] you joy [for] the world. [But grieve] for [the] world instead, just as if you had not entered it!"—"Amen!"

88 "Do not weep from now on, but rejoice instead!"—"Amen!"

89 "I have overcome the world. And you, do not let the world overcome you!"—"Amen!"

90 "I have become free [from (?)] the world. You too, [become] free from [it]!"—"Amen!"

91 "[I will be] given [vinegar and gall] to drink. But [you], acquire life and [rest for yourselves]!"—"Amen!"

92 "I will be [pierced] with a spear [in my] side. **93** He who saw it, let him bear witness—and his testimony is true!"— "Amen!"

94 "[. . . 6 lines untranslatable . . .]." —"[Amen]!"

95 "Whoever has [. . .] me, I [for my part] will make him [. . .] with me."— "Amen!"

96 "Whoever does not [partake] of my body [and] my blood is a stranger to me."—"Amen!"

97 "[. . . 8 lines untranslatable . . .] you [. . .]."—"[Amen]!"

98 "[. . . 5 lines untranslatable . . .] cross."—"Amen!"

99 "I [will hasten to] you."—"Amen!"

100 "A [dispensation . . . 8 lines untranslatable . . .] cross [. . .]."— "Amen!"

101 "[For] those on the [right will] take shelter [under you, apart from] those on the [left, **102** O] cross, [. . . 5 lines untranslatable . . .], **103** O cross, [. . .]

you [...] height ... [...] for this is your desire. **104** O cross, do not be afraid! **105** I am rich. I will fill you with my wealth. **106** [I] will mount you, O cross. [I] will be [hung] upon you [...] ... [... ."]—"Amen!"]

107 "[... 6 lines untranslatable ...]. **108** [Do not] weep, O [cross], but rather [rejoice] and recognize [your] Lord as he [is coming toward] you, **109** that he is [gentle] and [lowly]!"—"Amen!"

Verses 110–119: **The Savior addresses the cross (for a second time)**

110 [The] second [... 3 lines untranslatable ...] but **111** [I am] rich. I will [fill you] with my wealth. **112** [A little while], O cross, and what is lacking will become complete, and what is stunted will become full. **113** A little while, O cross, and what has [fallen] will rise. **114** [A little while], O [cross], and the entire fullness will become complete. **115** [... 6 lines untranslatable ...] they have been waiting for you, one [laughing] and rejoicing, another weeping, [mourning], and feeling remorse. **116** [Precede] me, O cross! I [in turn] will precede you. **117** [You and] I, O [cross, we are ... **118** We are ... 10 lines untranslatable.... **119** ..., O] cross, [truly], whoever is far from [you] is far [from] [me]."

The Infancy Gospel
of Thomas

Early Christians were naturally curious to learn the details of Jesus' life. As stories circulated about the inspired teachings and miraculous deeds of Jesus' public ministry, some Christians began to speculate on what he said and did before it began. Only a couple of incidents involving Jesus prior to his baptism are found in the New Testament Gospels: the narratives of his birth and infancy in Matthew and Luke and the account, unique to Luke, of his pilgrimage to the Jerusalem Temple as a twelve-year old (Luke 2:41– 52). Other stories of Jesus as a youth, however, were soon in circulation. Behind many of these legends lay a fundamental question: if Jesus was a miracle-working Son of God as an adult, what was he like as a child?

The Infancy Gospel of Thomas, not to be confused with the Coptic Gospel of Thomas discovered near Nag Hammadi Egypt, is one of the earliest accounts of these legends. The book was allegedly written by "Thomas, the Israelite." It is not clear whether the author intended his readers to recognize him as Judas Thomas, thought by some early Christians to have been Jesus' own brother. If he did, then his accounts of Jesus as a youth, needless to say, would have been based on an impeccable authority.

The narrative begins with Jesus as a five-year old boy and relates a number of incidents, most of them miraculous, that betray a streak of the mischievous in Joseph and Mary's precocious son. Here are anecdotes of Jesus at play with his childhood companions (sometimes harming them with his divine power, sometimes healing them), in confrontation with his elders (usually bettering them), at school with his teachers (revealing their igno-rance), and in the workshop with his father (miraculously correcting his mistakes). For modern readers it is difficult to decide whether such stories were meant as serious accounts of Jesus' early life or simply as speculative and entertaining stories of the youthful Son of God.

The text provides few clues to help us fix the time of its composition.

Translation by Bart D. Ehrman, based on the Greek text of Constantin von Tischendorf, *Evangelia Apocrypha*. (Hildesheim: Georg Olms, 1987; original: Leipzig, 1867), with textual alterations made by the translator based on manuscript evidence.

Most scholars believe that such "infancy Gospels" began to circulate during the first half of the second century. The Infancy Gospel of Thomas appears to have been one of the earliest.

Tales of the Israelite Philosopher Thomas, Concerning the Childhood Activities of the Lord

1 I, Thomas the Israelite, make this report to all of you, my brothers among the Gentiles, that you may know the magnificent childhood activities of our Lord Jesus Christ—all that he did after being born in our country. The beginning is as follows:

2 When this child Jesus was five years old, he was playing by the ford of a stream; and he gathered the flowing waters into pools and made them immediately pure. These things he ordered simply by speaking a word. 2 He then made some soft mud and fashioned twelve sparrows from it. It was the Sabbath when he did this. A number of other children were also playing with him. 3 But when a certain Jew saw what Jesus had done while playing on the Sabbath, he left right away and reported to his father, Joseph, "Look, your child at the stream has taken mud and formed twelve sparrows. He has profaned the Sabbath!" 4 When Joseph came to the place and saw what had happened, he cried out to him, "Why are you doing what is forbidden on the Sabbath?" But Jesus clapped his hands and cried to the sparrows, "Be gone!" And the sparrows took flight and went off, chirping. 5 When the Jews saw this they were amazed; and they went away and reported to their leaders what they had seen Jesus do.

3 Now the son of Annas the scribe was standing there with Joseph; and he took a willow branch and scattered the water that Jesus had gathered. 2 Jesus was irritated when he saw what had happened, and he said to him: "You unrighteous, irreverent idiot! What did the pools of water do to harm you? See, now you also will be withered like a tree, and you will never bear leaves or root or fruit." 3 Immediately that child was completely withered. Jesus left and returned to Joseph's house. But the parents of the withered child carried him away, mourning his lost youth. They brought him to Joseph and began to accuse him, "What kind of child do you have who does such things?"

4 Somewhat later he was going through the village, and a child ran up and banged into his shoulder. Jesus was aggravated and said to him, "You will go no further on your way." And right away the child fell down and died. Some of those who saw what happened said, "Where was this child born? For everything he says is a deed accomplished?" 2 The parents of the dead child came to Joseph and blamed him, saying "Since you have such a child you cannot live with us in the village. Or teach him to bless and not to curse—for he is killing our children!"

5 Joseph called to the child and admonished him privately, "Why are you doing such things? These people are suffering, they hate us and are persecuting us!" But Jesus replied, "I know these

are not your words, and so I also will keep silent for your sake. But those others will bear their punishment." And immediately those who were accusing him were blinded. 2 Those who saw these things were frightened and disturbed; they began saying about him, "Everything he has said, whether good or bad, has become an amazing reality." When Joseph saw what Jesus had done, he rose up, grabbed his ear, and yanked it hard. 3 The child was irritated and said to him, "It is enough for you to seek and not find; you have not acted at all wisely. Do you not know that I am yours? Do not grieve me."

6 There was an instructor named Zachaeus standing off to the side who heard Jesus say these things to his father. And he was amazed that he was speaking such things, though just a child. 2 After a few days he approached Joseph and said to him, "You have a bright child with a good mind. Come, let me have him that he may learn to read, and through reading I will teach him everything, including how to greet all the elders and to honor them as his ancestors and fathers, and to love children his own age." 3 And he told him all the letters from Alpha to Omega, clearly and with great precision. But Jesus looked the instructor Zachaeus in the face and said to him, "Since you do not know the true nature of the Alpha, how can you teach anyone the Beta? You hypocrite! If you know it, first teach the Alpha, and then we will believe you about the Beta." Then he began to question the teacher sharply about the first letter, and he was not able to give him the answers. 4 And while many others were listening, the child said to Zachaeus, "Listen, teacher, to the arrangement of the first letter of the alphabet; observe here how it has set patterns, and middle strokes which you see collec-

tively crossing, then coming together, and proceeding upward again till they reach the top, so that it is divided into three equal parts, each of them fundamental and foundational, of equal length. Now you have the set patterns of the Alpha."

7 When the teacher Zachaeus heard the child setting forth so many allegorical interpretations like this of the first letter, he was at a complete loss about this kind of explanation and teaching, and he said to those standing there, "Woe is me! I am wretched and at complete loss; I have put myself shame, taking on this child. 2 I be you, brother Joseph, take him away not bear his stern gaze or make s a single word. This child is no world; he can even tame fire. M was born before the world ca ing. I cannot fathom what ki bore him or what kind of ished him. Woe is me, f befuddled me; I cannot soning. I have fooled my erable three times over to have a student, and to have a teacher. 3 all too well my s man, I have been may grow weak child. For at th him in the fac I have been what can I the things terns of my frie ning o Josep kno wh k

10 wood in split ope lot of blo a disturba gather, and spot. Forcin he grabbed t been struck,

8 While the Jews were giving Zacchaeus advice, the child laughed aloud and said, "Now let what is yours bear fruit, and let the blind in heart see. I have come from above to curse them and call them to the realm above, just as the one who sent me for your sake commanded." 2 When the child stopped speaking, immediately all those who had fallen under his curse were healed. No one dared to anger him from that time on, fearing that he might cripple them with a curse.

9 Some days later Jesus was playing on a flat rooftop of a house, and one of the children playing with him fell from the roof and died. When the other children saw what had happened, they ran away, so that Jesus stood there alone. 2 When the parents of the one who died arrived they accused him of throwing him down. But Jesus said, "I certainly did not throw him down." But they began to abuse him verbally. 3 Jesus leapt down from the roof and stood beside the child's corpse, and with a loud voice he cried out, "Zenon!" (for that was his name) "rise up and tell me: did I throw you down?" And right away he rose up and "Not at all Lord! You did not throw down, but you have raised me up!" they saw this they were astounded. parents of the child glorified God for that had occurred, and they worshiped Jesus.

A few days later there was a young man who was splitting secluded spot. The axe fell and the sole of his foot. He lost a and was dying. 2 There was nce and a crowd started to the child Jesus also ran to the his way through the crowd, the young man's foot that had and immediately it was

healed. And he said to the young man, "Rise now, split the wood, and remember me." When the crowd saw what had happened it worshiped the child, saying, "The Spirit of God certainly lives within this child."

11 When he was six years old, his mother gave him a water jug and sent him to draw some water to bring back home. But he was jostled by the crowd, and the water jug was shattered. 2 So Jesus unfolded the cloak he was wearing and filled it with water, and brought it back to his mother. When his mother saw the sign that had happened, she kissed him. And she kept to herself the mysterious deeds that she saw him do.

12 When it later became time for sowing, the child went out with his father to sow wheat in their field. And when his father sowed, the child Jesus also sowed a single grain of wheat. 2 When he harvested and threshed the grain, it produced a hundred large bushels. He called all the poor people of the village to the threshing floor and gave them the wheat; and Joseph took what was left of it. He was eight years old when he did this sign.

13 Now his father was a carpenter, and at that time he used to make plows and yokes. He received an order from a certain rich man to make a bed. But when the measurement for one of the beautiful crossbeams came out too short, he did not know what to do. The child Jesus said to his father Joseph, "Place the two pieces of wood on the floor and line them up from the middle to one end." 2 Joseph did just as the child said. Then Jesus stood at the other end, grabbed the shorter board, and stretched it out to make it the same length as the other. His

father Joseph saw what he had done and was amazed. He embraced the child and gave him a kiss, saying "I am blessed that God has given me this child."

14 When Joseph observed the mind of the child and saw that he was starting to mature, he again did not want him to be unable to read, and so took him out to give him over to another teacher. The teacher said to Joseph, "First I will teach him to read Greek, and then Hebrew." For the teacher knew of the child's learning and was afraid of him. Nonetheless, he wrote out the alphabet and practiced it for him for a long time; but the child gave him no response. **2** Then Jesus said to him, "If you are really a teacher and know the letters well, tell me the power of the Alpha, and I will tell you the power of the Beta." The teacher was aggravated and struck him on the head. The child was hurt and cursed him; and immediately he fainted and fell to the ground on his face. **3** The child returned to Joseph's house. Joseph was smitten with grief and ordered his mother, "Do not let him out the door; for those who anger him die."

15 Some time later there was another instructor, a close friend of Joseph, who said to him, "Bring the child to me at the school. Maybe I can use flattery to teach him to read." Joseph said to him, "If you're that courageous, brother, take him along with you." He took him with great fear and much anxiety, but the child went along gladly. **2** He entered the school with confidence and found a book lying on the reading desk. He picked it up, but instead of reading the words in it, he opened his mouth and began to speak in the Holy Spirit, teaching the Law to those who were standing there. A great crowd gathered, standing there to hear him; and they were amazed

at the great beauty of his teaching and his carefully crafted words—amazed that he could speak such things though still a babe. **3** But when Joseph heard about this he was frightened. He ran to the school, thinking that this instructor may also have proved ignorant. But the instructor said to Joseph, "You should know, brother, that I took the child as a pupil; but he is filled with great grace and wisdom. Now I ask you brother, take him home." **4** When the child heard these things, he immediately laughed at him and said, "Since you have rightly spoken and rightly borne witness, for your sake that other one who was struck down will be healed." And right away the other instructor was healed. Joseph took the child and returned home.

16 Now Joseph sent his son James to bundle some wood and bring it to the house. The child Jesus also followed him. While James was gathering the firewood, a snake bit his hand. **2** When he was stretched out on the ground dying, Jesus came up to him and breathed on the bite. The pain immediately stopped, the animal burst, and straight away James was returned to health.

17 After these things, an infant in Joseph's neighborhood became sick and died; and his mother was weeping loudly. When Jesus heard the outburst of sorrow and the disturbance, he ran up quickly and found the child dead. He touched its breast, saying "I say to you, young child, do not die but live, and be with your mother." Immediately the child opened its eyes and laughed. Jesus said to the woman, "Take him, give him milk, and remember me." **2** When the crowd standing there saw what had happened, it was amazed. The people said, "Truly this child is either God or an angel of God, for his every word is an accomplished deed." Jesus then left from there to play with the other children.

18 Some time later a house was being built and there was a great disturbance. Jesus got up and went out to the place. He saw a man lying down, dead; taking his hand he said, "I say to you, O man, rise up and do your work." Immediately he rose up and worshiped him. 2 When the crowd saw, it was amazed and said, "This child comes from heaven. For he has saved many souls from death—his entire life he is able to save them."

19 When he was twelve years old his parents made their customary trip to Jerusalem, in a caravan, for the Passover feast. After the Passover they returned home. While they were returning, the child Jesus went back up to Jerusalem. But his parents thought he was in the caravan. 2 After their first day of travel, they began looking for him among their relatives and were upset not to find him. They returned again to the city to look for him. And after the third day they found him sitting in the Temple in the midst of the teachers, both listening and asking them questions. Everyone was attending closely, amazed that though a child, he questioned the elders and teachers of the people sharply, explaining the chief points of the Law and the parables of the prophets. 3 When his mother Mary came up to him she said, "Why have you done this to us, child? See, we have been distressed, looking for you." Jesus replied to them, "Why are you looking for me? Don't you know that I must be with those who are my Father's?"[b] 4 The scribes and Pharisees said, "Are you the mother of this child?" She replied, "I am." They said to her, "You are most fortunate among women, because God has blessed the fruit of your womb. For we have never seen or heard of such glory, such virtue and wisdom. 5 Jesus got up from there and followed his mother, and he was obedient to his parents. But his mother kept to herself all these things that had happened. And Jesus grew in wisdom and stature and grace. To him be the glory forever and ever. Amen.

[b]Or: *be doing my Fathers' business;* or: *be in my Father's house*

The Proto-Gospel of James

This book is sometimes called a "Proto-Gospel" because it narrates events that took place prior to Jesus' birth (although it includes an account of the birth as well).[1] The ancient manuscripts that preserve the book have different titles, including "The Birth of Mary," "The Story of the Birth of Saint Mary, Mother of God," and "The Birth of Mary; The Revelation of James." Its author claims to be James, usually understood to be Jesus' (half-) brother known from the New Testament (e.g., Mark 6; Galatians 1). Here he is assumed to be Joseph's son by a previous marriage.

Focusing its attention on Jesus' mother, Mary, the book provides legendary accounts of (a) her miraculous birth to the wealthy Jew, Joachim, and his wife, Anna; (b) her sanctified upbringing in the Jerusalem Temple; (c) her marriage as a twelve-year old to Joseph, an old widower miraculously chosen to be her husband; (d) her supernatural conception of Jesus through the Spirit; and (e) the birth of Jesus in a cave outside of Bethlehem. Parts of the book rely heavily on the infancy narratives of Matthew and Luke, but with numerous intriguing expansions, including legendary reports of Joseph's previous marriage and grown sons, Mary's work as a seamstress for the curtain in the temple, and the supernatural events that transpired at the birth of Jesus, including a first-hand narrative told by Joseph of how time stood still when the Son of God appeared in the world (chap. 18). In one of the most striking of its narratives we are told that an originally unbelieving midwife performed a postpartum inspection of Mary to be assured of her virginity (chap. 20).

Since the book was already known to the church father Origen in the early third century, and probably to Clement of Alexandria at the end of the second, it must have been in circulation soon after 150 CE. The book was enormously popular in later centuries, and played a significant role in pictorial art of the Middle Ages.[2]

---

[1]For a fuller discussion, see Ehrman, *Lost Christianities*, 207–10. [2]See David R. Cartlidge and J. Keith Elliott, *Art and the Christian Apocrypha* (London and New York: Routledge, 2001), chap. 2.

Translation by Bart D. Ehrman, based principally on the text of Émile de Strycker, *La Forme la plus ancienne du Protévangelium de Jacques* (Brussels: Société des Bollandistes, 1961), with textual modifications made by the translator based on the manuscript evidence.

The Birth of Mary, the
Revelation of James

1 In the "Histories of the Twelve Tribes of Israel" there was a very wealthy man Joachim, who used to offer a double portion of his gifts to the Lord, saying to himself, "The portion that is a surplus will be for all the people, and the portion that is for my forgiveness will be for the Lord my God as my atonement." 2 The great day of the Lord drew near, and the sons of Israel were offering their gifts. And Reuben stood before him and said, "You are not allowed to offer your gifts first, since you have produced no offspring in Israel."

3 Joachim was very upset and went away to consult the book of the twelve tribes of the people, saying to himself, "I will examine the Book of the Twelve Tribes of Israel to see if I am the only one not to produce offspring in Israel." And he searched and found that everyone who was righteous had raised up offspring in Israel. He remembered the patriarch Abraham, that at the end of his life God had given him a son, Isaac.

4 Joachim was very upset and did not return home to his wife, but went out to the wilderness and pitched his tent there. He fasted for forty days and nights, saying to himself, "I will not come down for either food or drink until the Lord my God visits me. My prayer will be my food and drink."

2 Now his wife Anna wailed and mourned twice over, saying "I mourn for being a widow, I mourn for being childless."

2 The great day of the Lord drew near, and her servant Judith said to her, "How long will you humble your soul? See, the great day of the Lord is drawing near, and you are not allowed to lament. But take this headband that my supervisor gave me; I am not allowed to wear it, since I am your servant and it is of royal quality." 3 Anna replied, "Go away from me. I did none of these things and yet the Lord my God has severely humbled me. For all I know, some scoundrel has given this to you, and you have come to defile me with your sin." Judith said, "Why would I curse you, just because you have not listened to me? The Lord has closed your womb to keep you from bearing fruit in Israel."

4 Anna was very upset, and she wrapped herself up in her clothes of mourning; she then washed her face and put on her bridal clothes, and in mid-afternoon went down to walk in her garden. She saw a laurel tree and sat beneath it, and after resting a bit she prayed to the Master, saying, "O God of my fathers, bless me and hear my prayer, just as you blessed the womb of Sarah and gave her a son, Isaac."

3 While she was gazing at the sky she saw a nest of sparrows in the laurel tree, and she mourned to herself, "Woe is me. Who gave me birth? And what kind of womb bore me? I have been born as a curse before the sons of Israel and am despised; they have mocked me and banished me from the temple of the Lord my God. 2 Woe is me. What am I like? I am not like the birds of the sky, for even the birds of the sky are productive before you, O Lord. Woe is me. What am I like? I am not like the senseless living creatures, for even the senseless living creatures are productive before you, O Lord. Woe is me, what am I like? I am not like the wild beasts of the earth, for even the wild beasts of the earth are productive before you, O Lord. 3 Woe is me, what am I like? I am not like these waters, for even these waters are tranquil yet prance about, and their fish bless you,

O Lord. Woe is me. What am I like? I am not like this soil, for even this soil produces its fruit every season and blesses you, O Lord."

4 Then, behold, an angel of the Lord appeared and said to her, "Anna, Anna, the Lord has heard your prayer. You will conceive a child and give birth, and your offspring will be spoken of throughout the entire world." Anna replied, "As the Lord God lives, whether my child is a boy or a girl, I will offer it as a gift to the Lord my God, and it will minister to him its entire life."

2 Behold, two angels came to her, saying, "See, your husband Joachim is coming with his flocks." For an angel of the Lord had descended to him and said, "Joachim, Joachim, the Lord God has heard your prayer. Go down from here; for see, your wife Anna has conceived a child." **3** Joachim immediately went down and called his shepherds and said, "Bring me here ten lambs without spot or blemish, and they will be for the Lord God; and bring me twelve young calves, and they will be for the priests and the council leaders; and bring a hundred male goats, and they will be for all the people."

4 And behold, Joachim came with his flocks and Anna stood beside the gate and saw him coming; and running up to him she hung on his neck and said, "Now I know that the Lord God has blessed me abundantly. For see, the widow is no longer a widow and the one who is childless has conceived a child." Then Joachim rested that first day in his home.

5 On the next day he brought his gifts as an offering, saying to himself, "If the Lord is gracious to me, the leafed plate of the priest's mitre[a] will make it known to me." And Joachim offered his gifts and looked closely at the priest's

leafed mitre as he went up to the altar of the Lord; and he saw no sin in himself. Joachim then said, "Now I know that the Lord has been gracious to me and forgiven all my sins." He went down from the temple of the Lord justified and came to his house.

2 Some six months came to completion for Anna; and in the seventh month she gave birth. She asked the midwife, "What is it?" The midwife replied, "A girl." Anna said, "My soul is exalted today." And she laid the child down. And when the days came to completion, Anna washed off the blood of her impurity, gave her breast to the child, and named her Mary.

6 The child grew stronger every day. When she was six months old, her mother set her on the ground, to see if she could stand. She walked seven steps and came to her arms. She lifted her up and said, "As the Lord my God lives, you will not walk at all on this ground until I have taken you up to the temple of the Lord." Then she made a sanctuary in her bedroom and did not allow anything impure or unclean into it. And she called the undefiled daughters of the Hebrews and they entertained her.

2 When the child had her first birthday, Joachim held a great feast and invited the chief priests, priests, scribes, council leaders, and all the people of Israel. Joachim brought the child out to the priests and they blessed her, saying, "May the God of our fathers bless this child and give her a name that will be famous forever, to all generations." And all the people replied, "Let it be so! Amen." They brought her to the chief priests, and they blessed her, saying, "May the Most High

[a]Literally: *the priest's leaf*

God look upon this child and bless her with an ultimate blessing, equal to none."

3 Her mother lifted her up and took her back to the sanctuary in her bedroom, and nursed her. And Anna made a song to the Lord God, saying, "I sing a holy song to the Lord my God, for he has visited me and removed from me the reproach of my enemies. The Lord God has given me his righteous fruit, unique and abundant before him. Who will report to the sons of Reuben that Anna is now nursing a child? Listen closely, you twelve tribes of Israel: Anna is nursing a child!" And she laid her down in the sanctuary of her bedroom and went out to serve the others. When the feast ended they descended happy, giving glory to the God of Israel.

7 Months passed for the child. When she turned two, Joachim said, "Now we should take her up to the temple of the Lord, to fulfill the promise we made; otherwise the Master may send some harm our way and our gift be deemed unacceptable." Anna replied, "Let's wait until she is three; otherwise she may be homesick for her father and mother." Joseph agreed, "We will wait."

2 When the child turned three, Joachim said, "We should call the undefiled daughters of the Hebrews and have them take torches; let them set them up, blazing, that the child not turn back and her heart be taken captive away from the temple of the Lord." They did this, until they had gone up to the Lord's temple. And the priest of the Lord received her and gave her a kiss, blessing her and saying, "The Lord has made your name great for all generations. Through you will the Lord reveal his redemption to the sons of Israel at the end of time."

3 He set her on the third step of the altar, and the Lord God cast his grace down upon her. She danced on her feet, and the entire house of Israel loved her.

8 Her parents went away, amazed and praising God, the Master, that the child did not turn back. Mary was in the temple of the Lord, cared for like a dove, receiving her food from the hand of an angel.

2 But when she reached her twelfth birthday, the priests held a council and said, "See, Mary has become twelve years old in the Lord's temple. What then shall we do with her, to keep her from defiling the sanctuary of the Lord our God?" They said to the chief priest, "You have stood on the Lord's altar. Go in and pray about her, and we will do whatever the Lord God reveals to you." 3 The chief priest went in, taking the robe with twelve bells into the Holy of Holies; and he prayed about her. And behold, an angel of the Lord appeared and said to him, "Zacharias, Zacharias, go out and gather the widowers of the people, and have each of them bring a rod; she will become the wife of the one to whom the Lord God gives a sign." And the heralds went out to all the countryside of Judea and the trumpet of the Lord was blown, and everyone came running.

9 Joseph cast aside his carpenter's axe and went to their meeting. When they had gathered together they went to the chief priest, bringing their rods. And when he had taken everyone's rods he went into the temple and prayed. When he finished his prayer, he took the rods, went outside, and gave them back. And no sign appeared among them. But Joseph took the last rod, and behold! A dove came out of the rod and flew onto Joseph's head. The priest said to Joseph, "You have been called to take the Lord's virgin into your safe-keeping." 2 But

Joseph refused, saying, "I have sons and am an old man; she is but a child. I do not want to become a laughingstock to the sons of Israel." The priest replied, "Fear the Lord your God, and remember everything that he did to Dathan, Abiram, and Korah, how the earth split open and they were all devoured because of their dispute. Now, Joseph, you should be afraid of this happening to your house as well.

3 Joseph was afraid and took her into his safe-keeping. And he said to Mary, "See, I have received you from the temple of the Lord. Now I am leaving you at home, while I go out to construct my buildings; later I will come back to you. The Lord will watch over you."

10 Then the priests held a council and said, "We should make a curtain for the Lord's temple." And the priest said, "Call to me the undefiled virgins from the tribe of David." The servants went out looking for them and found seven virgins. The priest then remembered that the child Mary was from the tribe of David, and that she was undefiled before God. The servants went out and led her back and brought her into the Lord's temple. And the priest said, "Cast lots before me to see who will spin the gold, the asbestos, the fine linen, the silk, the sapphire blue, the scarlet, and the true purple." Mary drew the lot for the true purple and the scarlet, and taking them she returned home. At that time Zacharias became silent. Samuel took his place, until Zacharias spoke again. But Mary took the scarlet and began to spin it.

11 Mary took a pitcher and went out to fetch some water. And behold, she heard a voice saying, "Greetings, you who are favored. The Lord is with you. You are blessed among women." Mary looked around, right and left, to see where the voice was coming from. She then entered her house frightened and set the pitcher down. Taking up the purple she sat on her chair and began to draw it out. 2 And behold, an angel of the Lord stood before her and said, "Do not fear, Mary. For you have found favor before the Master of all, and you will conceive a child by his Word." But as she listened she was asking herself, "Am I to conceive from the living Lord God and give birth like every other woman?" 3 The angel of the Lord said to her, "Not so, Mary. For the power of God will overshadow you. Therefore the one born from you will be called holy, the Son of the Highest. And you will name him Jesus, for he will save his people from their sins." Mary replied, "Behold the slave of the Lord is before you. May it happen to me as you have said."

12 She made the purple and the scarlet, and brought them to the temple. The priest took them and blessed her, "Mary, the Lord God has made your name great; you will be blessed among all the generations of earth."

2 Full of joy, Mary went off to her relative Elizabeth. She knocked on the door; and when Elizabeth heard, she cast aside the scarlet and ran to the door. When she opened it she blessed Mary and said, "How is it that the mother of my Lord should come to me? For see, the child in me leapt up and blessed you." But Mary forgot the mysteries that the archangel Gabriel had spoken to her, and gazed at the sky and said, "Who am I, Lord, that all the women of earth will bless me?"

3 She stayed with Elizabeth for three months. Day by day her own belly grew. Mary then returned home in fear, and hid

herself from the sons of Israel. She was sixteen when these mysteries happened.

13 When she was in her sixth month, Joseph returned from his buildings. As he came into the house he saw that she was pregnant. Striking his face he cast himself to the ground on sackcloth, weeping bitterly and saying, "How can I look upon the Lord God? How can I utter a prayer for this young girl? For I received her from the temple of the Lord God as a virgin, but I did not watch over her. Who has preyed upon me? Who has done this wicked deed in my home and defiled the virgin? Has not the entire history of Adam been summed up in me? For just as Adam was singing praise to God, the serpent came and found Eve alone, and led her astray. This too has now happened to me."

2 Joseph rose up from the sackcloth, called Mary, and said to her, "You who have been cared for by God: why did you do this? Have you forgotten the Lord your God? Why have you humiliated your soul—you who were brought up in the Holy of Holies and received your food from the hand of an angel?" **3** But she wept bitterly and said, "I am pure and have not had sex with any man." Joseph replied to her, "How then have you become pregnant?" She said, "As the Lord my God lives, I do not know."

14 Joseph was very afraid and let her be, debating what to do about her: "If I hide her sin, I will be fighting the Law of the Lord; if I reveal her condition to the sons of Israel, I am afraid that the child in her is angelic, and I may be handing innocent blood over to a death sentence. What then should I do with her? I will secretly divorce her." Then night overtook him.

2 Behold, an angel of the Lord appeared to him in a dream and said, "Do not be afraid of this child. For that which is in her comes from the Holy Spirit. She will give birth to a son, and you will name him Jesus. For he will save his people from their sins." Joseph rose up from his sleep and glorified the God of Israel who had bestowed such favor on him; and he watched over her.

15 But Annas the scribe came to see Joseph and said, "Why have you not appeared before our council?" Joseph replied, "I was tired from my journey and rested on my first day back." Annas then turned and saw that Mary was pregnant. **2** He left and ran off to the priest and said to him, "Joseph, the one you have vouched for, has committed a great sin." The priest replied, "What has he done?" He said, "He has defiled the virgin he received from the Lord's temple and has stolen her wedding rights.[b] And he has not revealed this to the sons of Israel." **3** The priest asked, "Joseph, has done this?" Annas the scribe replied, "Send some servants, and you will find that the virgin is pregnant." The servants went off and found that it was just as he had said. They brought her back to the judgment hall, along with Joseph.

3 The priest said, "Mary, why have you done this? Why have you humiliated your soul and forgotten the Lord your God? You who were brought up in the Holy of Holies and received your food from the hand of an angel, and heard the hymns, and danced before him—why have you done this? But she wept bitterly and said, "As the Lord my God lives, I am pure before him and have not had sex with any man."

4 The priest then said to Joseph, "Why have you done this?" Joseph replied, "As the Lord my God lives, I am pure towards her." The priest said, "Do not bear false

[b]Or: *eloped with her*

witness, but speak the truth. You have stolen her wedding rights[c] and not revealed it to the sons of Israel; and you have not bowed your head under the mighty hand that your offspring might be blessed." Joseph kept his silence.

16 The priest said, "Hand over the virgin you received from the Lord's temple." And Joseph began to weep bitterly. The priest said, "I will have both of you drink the Lord's 'water of refutation,' and it will reveal your sins to your own eyes." **2** The priest gave it to Joseph to drink, and sent him away to the wilderness. But he came back whole. He then gave it to Mary to drink and sent her off to the wilderness. And she came back whole. All the people were amazed that no sin was revealed in them.

3 The priest said, "If the Lord God has not revealed your sins, neither do I judge you." And he released them. Joseph took Mary and returned home, rejoicing and glorifying the God of Israel.

17 An order went out from the king, Augustus, that everyone from Bethlehem of Judea was to be registered for a census. Joseph said, "I will register my sons. But what should I do about this child? How should I register her? As my wife? I would be too ashamed. As my daughter? But all the sons of Israel know that she is not my daughter. This day of the Lord will need to turn out as he wishes."

2 He saddled the donkey and seated her on it; and his son led it along, while Joseph followed behind. When they approached the third milestone, she turned to Joseph and he saw that she was gloomy. He said to himself "Maybe the child in her is causing her trouble." Then later she turned to Joseph and he saw her laughing. He said to her, "Mary, why is it that one time I see you laughing and at another time gloomy?" She replied, "Be-

cause my eyes see two peoples, one weeping and mourning and the other happy and rejoicing."

3 When they were half way there, Mary said to him, "Take me down from the donkey. The child inside me is pressing on me to come out." He took her down from the donkey and said to her, "Where can I take you to hide your shame? For this is a wilderness area."

18 He found a cave there and took her into it. Then he gave his sons to her and went out to find a Hebrew midwife in the region of Bethlehem.

2 But I, Joseph, was walking, and I was not walking. I looked up to into the air, and I saw that it was greatly disturbed. I looked up to the vault of the sky, and I saw it standing still; and the birds of the sky were at rest. I looked back to the earth and saw a bowl laid out for some workers who were reclining to eat. Their hands were in the bowl, but those who were chewing were not chewing; and those who were taking something from the bowl were not lifting it up; and those who were bringing their hands to their mouths were not bringing them to their mouths. Everyone was looking up. And I saw a flock of sheep being herded, but they were standing still. And the shepherd raised his hand to strike them, but his hand remained in the air. I looked down at the torrential stream, and I saw some goats whose mouths were over the water, but they were not drinking. Then suddenly everything returned to its normal course.

19 I saw a woman was coming down from the mountains, and she said to me, "O man, where are you going?" I replied, "I am looking for a

[c]Or: *eloped with her*

Hebrew midwife." She asked me, "Are you from Israel?" I said to her, "Yes." She asked, "Who is the one who has given birth in the cave?" I replied, "My betrothed." She said to me, "Is she not your wife?" I said to her, "Mary is the one who was brought up in the Lord's temple, and I received the lot to take her as my wife. She is not, however, my wife, but she has conceived her child by the Holy Spirit." The midwife said to him, "Can this be true?" Joseph replied to her, "Come and see." And the midwife went with him.

2 They stood in the cave, and a bright cloud overshadowed it. The midwife said, "My soul has been magnified today, for my eyes have seen a miraculous sign: salvation has been born to Israel." Right away the cloud departed from the cave, and a great light appeared within, so that their eyes could not bear it. Soon that light departed, until an infant could be seen. And it went and took hold of the breast of Mary, its mother. The midwife cried out, "This is a great day for me, for I have seen this new wonder."

3 The midwife went out of the cave and Salome met her. And she said to her, "Salome, Salome, I can describe a new wonder to you. A virgin has given birth, contrary to her natural condition." Salome replied, "As the Lord my God lives, if I do not insert my finger and examine her condition, I will not believe that the virgin has given birth."

20 The midwife went in and said to Mary, "Brace yourself, for there is no small controversy concerning you." Then Salome inserted her finger in order to examine her condition, and she cried out, "Woe to me for my sin and faithlessness. For I have put the living God to the test, and see, my hand is burning, falling away from me." 2 She kneeled before the Master and said, "O

God of my fathers, remember that I am a descendant of Abraham, Isaac, and Jacob. Do not make me an example to the sons of Israel, but deliver me over to the poor. For you know, O Master, that I have performed my services in your name and have received my wages from you."

3 And behold, an angel of the Lord appeared and said to her, "Salome, Salome, the Master of all has heard your prayer. Bring your hand to the child and lift him up; and you will find salvation and joy."

4 Salome joyfully came and lifted the child, saying, "I will worship him, for he has been born as a great king to Israel." Salome was immediately cured, and she went out of the cave justified. And behold a voice came saying, "Salome, Salome, do not report all the miraculous deeds you have seen until the child enters Jerusalem."

21 And behold, Joseph was ready to go into Judea. But there was a great disturbance in Bethlehem of Judea. For wise men came saying, "Where is the king of the Jews? For we saw his star in the east, and we have come to worship him." 2 When Herod heard, he was troubled; and he sent servants to the wise men. He then summoned the high priests and asked them in the praetorium, "What does Scripture say about where the messiah is to be born?" They replied, "In Bethlehem of Judea. For that is what is found in Scripture." He then released them and asked the wise men, "What sign did you see concerning the king who has been born?" The wise men said, "We saw a magnificent star shining among the stars and overshadowing them, so that the other stars disappeared. And thus we knew that a king had been born in Israel, and we came to worship him." Herod replied, "Go and look for him. If you find

him, let me know, that I too may come to worship him."

3 The wise men then left, and behold, the star they had seen in the east preceded them until they entered the cave, and it stood over the entrance of the cave. The wise men saw the child with its mother, Mary, and they took from their packs gifts of gold, frankincense, and myrrh. **4** When they were warned by a revelation from an angel not to enter Judea, they went home another way.

22 When Herod realized that he had been mocked by the wise men, he grew angry and sent murderers, saying to them, "Kill every infant, two years and under."

2 When Mary heard that the infants were being killed, out of fear she took her child and wrapped him in swaddling clothes and placed him in a cattle manger. **3** But when Elizabeth heard that they were looking for John, she took him and went up into the mountains, looking for a place to hide him. But there was no hiding place. Elizabeth moaned and said with a loud voice, "Mountain of God, receive a mother with her child." For Elizabeth was not able to climb the mountain. And straight away the mountain split open and received her. And a light was shining around them, for an angel of the Lord was with them, protecting them.

23 Herod was looking for John, and he sent servants to Zacharias, saying, "Where have you hidden your son?" He answered them, "I am a minister of God, constantly attending his temple. How could I know where my son is?" **2** The servants returned and reported everything to Herod. Herod became angry and said, "His son is about to rule Israel." He sent his servants to him a second time to say, "Tell me the truth:

where is your son? For you know that I can shed your blood with my hand." The servants went to report these things to him. **3** Zacharias responded, "I will be God's witness if you shed my blood. For the Master will receive my spirit, since you will be shedding innocent blood in the forecourt of the Lord's temple." And Zacharias was murdered around dawn. But the sons of Israel did not know that he was murdered.

24 The priests came out at the time of greeting, but Zacharias did not come out to meet them with his blessing, as was customary. The priests stood, waiting to greet Zacharias with a prayer and to glorify the Most High. **2** When he did not come, everyone grew afraid. One of them took courage, entered the sanctuary, and saw blood congealed beside the altar of the Lord. And he heard a voice, "Zacharias has been murdered, and his blood will not be wiped away until his avenger comes." When he heard this word he was afraid and went outside to report to the priests what he had seen and heard.

3 Taking courage they entered and saw what had happened, and the paneling around the temple cried out aloud; and they ripped their clothes from top to bottom. They did not find his body, but they found his blood turned to stone. They left in fear, and reported to all the people that Zacharias had been murdered. All the tribes of the people heard and grieved for him, mourning for three days and nights. **4** After three days the priests decided to put someone in his place, and the lot fell to Simeon. For this is the one who learned from a revelation of the Holy Spirit that he would not see death until he should see the messiah in the flesh.

25 But I James, the one who has written this account in Jerusalem, hid myself away in the wilderness when there was a disturbance at the death of Herod, until the disturbance in Jerusalem came to an end. There I glo-rified God, the Master, who gave me the gift and the wisdom to write this account.

2 Grace be with all those who fear the Lord. Amen.

The Epistle of the Apostles

The "Epistle of the Apostles" is a bit of a misnomer in that it is not really an epistle but a Gospel. The book does start out as a letter, written by the apostles to the churches around the world; but its content involves a conversation between Jesus and his eleven remaining disciples after his resurrection—Judas having already hanged himself.

This kind of Gospel, containing a post-resurrection "dialogue" of Jesus and his followers, was quite popular among Gnostic Christians, in that it allowed them to indicate that Jesus provided secret teachings to his disciples that were different from his public teachings delivered during the course of his ministry. These secret teachings, then, could become the basis for the "true" understanding of the religion that the Gnostics set forth.

But the orientation of this particular book is completely anti-gnostic. In particular, it seeks to counter the views of Simon Magus and Cerinthus, two Gnostics most despised among the proto-orthodox heresy-hunters of the second century, by insisting on the fleshly nature of Christ's body, the reality of his incarnation, death, resurrection, and future return in glory, and the importance of his followers' fleshly existence in this world and in the world to come.[1] It appears, then, that a proto-orthodox Christian has taken over a genre beloved among the Gnostics and turned it against them, to show that even after his resurrection Jesus proclaimed not a Gnostic myth but a proto-orthodox understanding of the flesh.

The "Epistle of the Apostles" was unknown through the Middle Ages down into the modern period, until a Coptic version was uncovered in Cairo near the end of the nineteenth century. Later a fuller and more accurate Ethiopic version was found.

The book was originally written in Greek, probably in the middle of the second century. The following excerpt is drawn from the Ethiopic translation.

---

[1]On the importance of Simon Magus for the early proto-orthodox heresy-hunters, see Ehrman, *Lost Christianities*, 165–67.

Translation by C. Detlef G. Muller in Wilhelm Schneemelcher, *New Testament Apocrypha*, vol. 1 (rev. ed.; Cambridge/ Louisville: Lutterworth/Westminster/John Knox, 1991) 252–64; used with permission.

1 What Jesus Christ revealed to his disciples as a letter, and how Jesus Christ revealed the letter of the council of the apostles, the disciples of Jesus Christ, to the Catholics; which was written because of the false apostles Simon and Cerinthus, that no one should follow them—for in them is deceit with which they kill people—that you may be established and not waver, not be shaken, and not turn away from the word of the Gospel that you have heard. As we have heard (it), kept (it), and have written (it) for the whole world, so we entrust (it) to you, our sons and daughters, in joy and in the name of God the Father, the ruler of the world, and in Jesus Christ. May grace increase upon you.

2 (We,) John and Thomas and Peter and Andrew and James and Philip and Bartholomew and Matthew and Nathanael and Judas Zelotes and Cephas, we have written to the churches of the East and West, towards North and South, recounting and proclaiming to you concerning our Lord Jesus Christ, as we have written; and we have heard and felt him after he had risen from the dead; and how he has revealed to us things great, astonishing, real. . . .

6 And these things our Lord and Savior revealed and showed to us, and likewise we to you, that you, reflecting upon eternal life, may be associates in the grace of the Lord and in our service and in our glory. Be firm, without wavering, in the knowledge and investigation of our Lord Jesus Christ, and he will prove gracious and will save always in all never-ending eternity.

7 Cerinthus and Simon have come to go through the world. But they are enemies of our Lord Jesus Christ, who in reality alienate those who believe in the true word and deed, namely Jesus Christ. Therefore take care and beware of them, for in them is affliction and contamination and death, the end of which will be destruction and judgment.

8 Because of that we have not hesitated with the true testimony of our Lord and Savior Jesus Christ, how he acted while we saw him, and how he constantly both explained and caused our thoughts within us.

9 He of whom we are witnesses we know as the one crucified in the days of Pontius Pilate and of the prince Archelaus, who was crucified between two thieves;[2] and was taken down from the wood of the cross together with them; and he was buried in a place which is called the place of the skull, to which three women came, Sarah, Martha, and Mary Magdalene. They carried ointment to pour out upon his body, weeping and mourning over what had happened. And they approached the tomb and found the stone where it had been rolled away from the tomb, and they opened the door and did not find his body.

10 And as they were mourning and weeping, the Lord appeared to them and said to them, "Do not weep; I am he whom you seek. But let one of you go to your brothers and say to them, 'Come, our Master has risen from the dead.' "

And Mary came to us and told us. And we said to her, "What have we to do with you, O woman? He that is dead and buried, can he then live?" And we did not believe her, that our Savior had risen from the dead.

---

[2]Matt 27–28; Mark 15–16; Luke 23–24; John 19–21.

Then she went back to our Lord and said to him, "None of them believed me concerning your resurrection." And he said to her, "Let another one of you go saying this again to them." And Sarah came and gave us the same news, and we accused her of lying. And she returned to our Lord and spoke to him as Mary had.

11 And then the Lord said to Mary and to her sisters, "Let us go to them." And he came and found us inside, veiled. And we doubted and did not believe. He came before us like a ghost and we did not believe that it was he. But it was he. And thus he said to us. "Come, and do not be afraid. I am your teacher whom you, Peter, denied three times before the cock crowed, and now do you deny again?" And we went to him, thinking and doubting whether it was he. And he said to us, "Why do you doubt and why are you not believing that I am he who spoke to you concerning my flesh, my death, and my resurrection? And that you may know that it is I, lay your hand, Peter (and your finger) in the nailprint of my hands; and you, Thomas, in my side; and also you, Andrew, see whether my foot steps on the ground and leaves a footprint. For it is written: 'But a ghost, a demon, leaves no print on the ground.' "

12 But now we felt him, that he had truly risen in the flesh. And then we fell on our faces before him, asked him for pardon, and entreated him because we had not believed him. Then our Lord and Savior said to us, "Stand up and I will reveal to you what is on earth, and what is above heaven, and your resurrection that is in the kingdom of heaven, concerning which my Father has sent me, that I may take up you and those who believe in me."

13 And what he revealed is this, as he said to us, "While I was coming from the Father of all, passing by the heavens, wherein I put on the wisdom of the Father and by his power clothed myself in his power, I was like the heavens. And passing by the angels and archangels in their form and as one of them, I passed by the orders, dominions, and princes, possessing the measure of the wisdom of the Father who sent me. And the archangels Michael and Gabriel, Raphael and Uriel followed me until the fifth firmament of heaven, while I appeared as one of them. This kind of power was given me by the Father. Then I made the archangels to become distracted with the voice and go up to the altar of the Father and serve the Father in their work until I should return to him. I did this thus in the likeness of his wisdom. For I became all in all with them, that I, fulfilling the will of the mercy of the Father and the glory of him who sent me, might return to him.

14 "Do you know that the angel Gabriel came and brought the message to Mary?" And we said to him, "Yes, O Lord." And he answered and said to us, "Do you not remember that I previously said to you that I became like an angel to the angels?" And we said to him, "Yes, O Lord." And he said to us, "At that time I appeared in the form of the archangel Gabriel to the virgin Mary and spoke with her, and her heart received (me); she believed and laughed; and I, the Word, went into her and became flesh; and I myself was servant for myself; and in the likeness of an angel, like him will I do, and after it I will go to my Father.

15 "And you therefore celebrate the remembrance of my death, which is the Passover; the one who stands beside me will be thrown into prison for my name's sake, and he will be very grieved and sorrowful, for while you celebrate the passover he who is in custody did not celebrate it with you. And I will send my power in the form of (my) angel, and the door of the prison will open, and he will come out and come to you to watch with you and to rest. And when you complete my Agape and my remembrance at the crowing of the cock, he will again be taken and thrown in prison for a testimony, until he comes out to preach, as I have commanded you." And we said to him, "O Lord, have you then not completed the drinking of the passover? Must we, then, do it again?" And he said to us, "Yes, until I come from the Father with my wounds."

16 And we said to him, "O Lord, great is this that you say and reveal to us. In what kind of power and form are you about to come?" And he said to us, "Truly I say to you, I will come as the sun which bursts forth; thus will I, shining seven times brighter than it in glory, while I am carried on the wings of the clouds in splendor with my cross going on before me, come to the earth to judge the living and the dead."

17 And we said to him, "O Lord, how many years yet?" And he said to us, "When the hundred and fiftieth year is completed, between pentecost and passover will the coming of my Father take place." And we said to him, "O Lord, now you said to us, 'I will come,' and then you said, 'he who sent me will come.' " And he said to us, 'I am wholly in the Father and the Father in me.'[3] Then we said to him, "Will you really leave us until your coming? Where will we find a teacher?" And he answered and said to us, "Do you not know that until now I am both here and there with him who

sent me?" And we said to him, "O Lord, is it possible that you should be both here and there?" And he said to us, "I am wholly in the Father and the Father in me after his image and after his likeness and after his power and after his perfection and after his light, and I am his perfect word."

18 This is, when he was crucified, had died and risen again, as he said this, and the work that was thus accomplished in the flesh, that he was crucified, and his ascension—this is the fulfilling of the number. "And the wonders and his image and everything perfect you will see in me with respect to redemption which takes place through me, and while I go to the Father and into heaven. . . ."

23 And we said again to him, "O Lord, but it is necessary, since you have commanded us to preach, prophesy, and teach, that we, having heard accurately from you, may be good preachers and may teach them, that they may believe in you. Therefore we question you."

24 He answered and said to us, "Truly I say to you, the flesh of every one will rise with his soul alive and his spirit." And we said to him, "O Lord, then can what is departed and scattered become alive? Not as if we deny it do we ask; rather we believe that what you say has happened and will happen." And he said to us, being angry, "You of little faith, how long yet do you ask me? And inquire (only) without anguish after what you wish to hear.

"Keep my commandments, and do

---

[3]John 10:38; 14:10–21.

what I tell you, without delay and without reserve and without respect of persons; serve in the strait, direct, and narrow way. And thereby will the Father in every respect rejoice concerning you."

25 And we said again to him, "O Lord, look; we have you to derision with the many questions." And he said to us, "I know that in faith and with your whole heart you question me. And I am glad because of you. Truly I say to you I am pleased, and my Father in me rejoices, that you thus inquire and ask. Your boldness makes me rejoice, and it affords yourselves life." And when he had said this to us, we were glad, for he had spoken to us in gentleness. And we said again to him, "Our Lord, in all things you have shown yourself gracious toward us and grant us life; for all we have asked you you have told us." Then he said to us, "Does the flesh or the spirit fall away?" And we said to him, "The flesh."

And he said to us, "Now what has fallen will arise, and what is ill will be sound, that my Father may be praised therein; as he has done to me, so I (will do) to you and to all who believe in me.

26 "Truly I say to you, the flesh will rise with the soul, that they may confess and be judged with the work which they have done, whether it is good or bad, in order that there may be a selection and exhibition for those who have believed and have done the commandment of my Father who sent me. Then will the righteous judgment take place; for thus my Father wills, and he said to me, 'My son, on the day of judgment you will not fear the rich and not spare the poor; rather deliver each one to eternal punishment according to his sins.' But to those who have loved me and do love me and who have done my commandment I will grant rest in life in the kingdom of my heavenly Father."

The Coptic Apocalypse of Peter

There are three surviving apocalypses allegedly written by Simon Peter, the disciple of Jesus (One other is included in this collection); the one given here was discovered at Nag Hammadi (see page 19). The book contains a series of visions given by Jesus to Peter (hence the title "apocalypse" or "revelation"), which Peter then records in the first person. In these visions, Christ issues dire warnings against the teaching of heretics who propagate falsehoods. Strikingly, the heretics here are the bishops and deacons of the proto-orthodox churches, and their false teaching is that Jesus was himself the Christ who suffered a literal death on the cross. The author deems this staunchly proto-orthodox view laughable; he labels its proponents blind.

For this author, the true significance of Jesus' death goes much deeper. Even though Jesus' flesh was killed, Christ himself was far removed from suffering; those who beheld the cross with full knowledge (gnosis) did not see the suffering Jesus but the living Christ, who was himself laughing at the entire proceeding. Jesus was merely his outward appearance, just as simple-minded Christians are nothing but the outward appearance of the living ones who have been fully enlightened by the spiritual truth of the immortal Christ.

Most scholars have dated this gnostic treatise to the third century.

And when I said these things, the Savior said, "I have told you that these (people) are blind and deaf. Now then, listen to the things that are being told to you in a mystery, and guard them. Do not tell them to the children of this age. For you will be despised in these ages, since they are ignorant of you. But you will be praised in (the age of) knowledge. For many will accept our teaching in the beginning. But they will turn away again in accordance with the will of the father of

Translation of James Brashler and Roger A. Bullard, from *Nag Hammadi Codex VII* (Nag Hammadi Studies, 30) ed. Birger Pearson (Leiden: E. J. Brill, 1996); used with permission.

their error, because they have done what he wanted. And he will make manifest in his judgment who the servants of the word are. But those who became mingled with these will become their prisoners, since they are without perception. And the guileless, good, pure one is pushed to the executioner, even into the kingdom of those who praise a restored Christ. And they praise the men of the propagation of falsehood, who will succeed you. And they will hold fast to the name of a dead man, while thinking that they will become pure. But they will become greatly defiled. And they will fall into an explicit error and into the hand of an evil, cunning man with a multifarious doctrine. And they will be ruled heretically. For some of them will blaspheme the truth and proclaim evil teaching. And they will say evil things to each other.

"And some, because they stand by virtue of the archons, will be given a name of a man and a naked woman who is multifarious and very sensual. And those who say these things will ask about dreams. And if they say that a dream came from a demon worthy of their error, then they will be given destruction instead of immortality. 'For evil cannot produce good fruit.' For each source produces what is like itself. For not every soul comes from the truth, nor from immortality. For every soul of these ages has death assigned to it, in our view. Consequently it is always a slave. It is created for its desires and their eternal destruction, for which they exist and in which they exist. They (the souls) love the material creatures which came forth with them. But the immortal souls are not like these, O Peter. But indeed, as long as the hour has not yet come, she (the immortal soul) will indeed resemble a mortal one. But she will not reveal her nature, although she alone is the immortal one and thinks about immortality. She

has faith, and desires to renounce these (material) things. 'For people neither gather figs from thorns'—or from thorn trees if they are wise—'nor grapes from brambles.' For on the one hand, a particular thing (masc.) always remains in that (condition) in which it exists. If it exists in a particular condition that is not good, that (condition) becomes its (fem.) destruction and death. On the other hand, this one (fem. = the immortal soul) abides in the Eternal One, in the one of life and immortality of life which are alike to Him.

"Therefore everything that does not abide will dissolve into that which does not exist. For deaf and blind ones join only with their own kind. But some will depart from evil words and deceptive mysteries. Others do not understand mysteries, although they speak of these things which they do not understand. Nevertheless they will boast that the mystery of the truth is theirs alone. And in haughtiness they will begin {in haughtiness} to envy the immortal soul that has become dedicated (to God). For every authority, principality, and power of the ages always wanted to remain with these (immortal souls) from the foundation of the world, in order that those who do not abide, since they have been ignorant and have not been saved, may be glorified by those who do abide. And they have not been brought to the way by them, although they have always desired that they would become the imperishable ones. For if the immortal soul receives power through an intellectual spirit, then immediately she is joined by one of those who have been misled. And others, who are numerous and who oppose the truth, who are the messengers of error, will concoct their error and their law against these pure thoughts of mine. Since they see from one (perspective), they think that good and evil are from one (source).

"They do business in my word. And they will set forth a harsh fate in which the race of the immortal souls will run in vain until my return. For they will remain among them. And I have forgiveness of their transgressions into which they fell because of the adversaries. I accepted their ransom from the slavery in which they existed (and) I gave them freedom. For they will create an imitation remnant in the name of a dead man, who is Hermas, the first-born of unrighteousness, in order that the real light might not be believed by the little ones. But those of this sort (the adversaries) are the workers who will be cast into the outer darkness, away from the children of light. For they will not enter, but neither do they permit those (to enter) who are going up to their approval and for their release. And still others of them who have sensual (natures) think that they will perfect the wisdom of the brotherhood that really exists, the spiritual friendship with those companions rooted in fellowship, those through whom the wedding of incorruptibility will be revealed.

"The kindred race of the sisterhood will appear as an imitation. These are the ones who oppress their brothers, saying to them, 'Through this our God has pity, since salvation (allegedly) comes to us through this.' They do not know the punishment of those who are delighted by what has been done to the little ones whom they sought out and imprisoned. And there will be others of those who are outside our number who name themselves 'bishop' and also 'deacons,' as if they have received their authority from God. They submit to the judgment of the leaders. Those people are dry canals."

But I said, "I am afraid because of what you have told me—that indeed little ones are, in our view, counterfeit. Indeed, there are multitudes that will mislead other multitudes of living ones, and they will be destroyed among them. And when they speak your name, they will be believed."

The Savior said, "For a period of time determined for them in proportion to their error, they will rule over the little ones. But after the completion of the error, the ageless one of immortal understanding will be renewed, and they (the little ones) will rule over those who are their rulers. The root of their error he will pull out, and he will put it to shame, and it will be exposed in all the impudence that it has assumed to itself. And such persons shall remain unchanged, O Peter. Come, therefore! Let us proceed to the completion of the will of the undefiled Father. For behold, those who will bring judgment upon themselves are coming. And they will put themselves to shame. But me they cannot touch. And you, O Peter, will stand in their midst. Do not be afraid because of your cowardice. Their minds will be closed. For the invisible one has opposed them."

When he had said those things, I saw him apparently being seized by them. And I said, "What am I seeing, O Lord? Is it you yourself whom they take? And are you holding on to me? Who is this one above the cross, who is glad and laughing? And is it another person whose feet and hands they are hammering?"

The Savior said to me, "He whom you see above the cross, glad and laughing, is the living Jesus. But he into whose hands and feet they are driving the nails is his physical part, which is the substitute. They are putting to shame that which is in his likeness. But look at him and me."

But I, when I had looked, said, "Lord, no one is looking at you. Let us flee this place." But he said to me, "I have told you, 'Leave the blind alone!' And notice how they do not know what they are saying. For the son of their glory, instead of my servant, they have put to shame."

And I saw someone about to approach us who looked like him, even him who was laughing above the cross, and he was <filled> with a pure spirit, and he (was) the Savior. And there was a great ineffable light around them and the multitude of ineffable and invisible angels blessing them. And it was I who saw him when this one who glorifies was revealed. And he said to me, "Be strong! For you are the one to whom these mysteries have been given, to know through revelation that he whom they crucified is the first-born, and the home of demons, and the clay vessel in which they dwell, belonging to Elohim, and belonging to the cross that is under the law. But he who stands near him is the living Savior, the primal part in him whom they seized. And he has been released. He stands joyfully looking at those who persecuted him. They are divided among themselves. Therefore he laughs at their lack of perception, and he knows that they are born blind. Indeed, therefore, the suffering one must remain, since the body is the substitute. But that which was released was my incorporeal body. But I am the intellectual spirit filled with radiant light. He whom you saw coming to me was our intellectual pleroma, which unites the perfect light with my pure spirit. These things, therefore, which you saw, you shall present to those of another race, who are not of this age. For there will be no grace in any one who is not immortal, but (grace will) only (be in) those who were chosen from an immortal essence that has shown that it is able to accept him who gives his abundance.

"Therefore I said, 'To every one who has, it will be given, and that one will have plenty.[1] But the one who does not have'—that is, the one of this place, being completely dead and changed by the planting of creation and begetting, who, if one of the immortal essence appears, think<s> that he (i.e. the one of immortal essence) is being seized—'it will be taken from him.' And it will be added to the one who is. You, therefore, be courageous and do not fear anything. For I will be with you so that none of your enemies will prevail over you. Peace be to you! Be strong!"

When he (the Savior) had said these things, he (Peter) came to his senses.

---

[1] Matt 25:29.

The Second Treatise of the Great Seth

In the gnostic "Second Treatise of the Great Seth," Christ himself provides a first-hand description of how he descended into the man Jesus' body, occupied it for the length of his ministry, and then died only in appearance. Like other gnostic teachers, such as Basilides, the unknown author of this book thinks that Simon of Cyrene, who bore Jesus' cross, was mistakenly crucified in his place, while Jesus looked on and laughed. Those who ascribe to a literal understanding of Christ's death are said to proclaim "a doctrine of a dead man"; in so doing they subject themselves to "fear and slavery"; they are "small and ignorant."

As in the Coptic Apocalypse of Peter, these false believers are the proto-orthodox Christians, who foolishly believe that the Jewish Scriptures are true (from Adam to the Patriarchs, Moses, and the prophets) and that the Creator of the world is almighty. In fact, the ancient Jews and their God himself are all a "laughingstock." Those who do not see the deeper truths about God and Christ from the Scriptures—i.e., those without gnosis—are "like dumb animals." They think that "they are advancing the name of Christ," especially in persecuting those who have been liberated (i.e., the Gnostics); but in fact they are completely ignorant.

The name Seth does not occur anywhere in the tractate except in the title; in the Old Testament, he is said to be the third son of Adam and Eve. Some gnostic groups maintained that he was the first to whom gnosis came, the progenitor of the Gnostics themselves. This book, which was discovered at Nag Hammadi (see page 19), probably dates from the third century.

I visited a bodily dwelling. I cast out the one who was in it previously, and I went in. And the whole multitude of the archons was disturbed. And all the physical matter of the archons along with the powers born of the earth began to tremble

Translation by Roger A. Bullard and Joseph A. Gibbons, in *Nag Hammadi Codex VII* (Nag Hammadi Studies, 30) ed. Birger Pearson (Leiden: E. J. Brill, 1996); used with permission.

when it saw the likeness of the image, since it was mixed. And I was the one who was in it, not resembling him who was in it previously. For he was a worldly man, but I, I am from above the heavens. I did not refuse them, on the one hand, and I became Christ. But on the other, I did not reveal myself to them in the love which was coming forth from me. I was revealing that I am a stranger to the regions below.

There was a great disturbance in the whole earthly region, with confusion and flight, and (in) the plan of the archons. And some were persuaded, when they saw the acts of power which were being accomplished by me. And they flee, namely all these who are descended by race from the one who fled from the throne to the Sophia of Hope—since she had previously given indication concerning us and all those who were with me— these of the race of Adonaios. Yet others fled as though (sent) from the World Ruler and those with him, and brought every punishment upon me. And there was a flight of their mind about what counsel they would take concerning me, thinking that the(ir) Greatness is (the) All, and speaking lying witness against the Man also and the whole greatness of the assembly. It was not possible for them to know who the Father of truth is, the Man of the greatness. And these took the name because of <pollution> and ig- norance—which (is) a burning and a ves- sel which they created for destruction of Adam, which they had made in order to cover up those who are equally theirs.

But they, the archons belonging to the place of Yaldabaoth, lay bare the circuit of the angels. This is what humanity was going around seeking because they did not know the Man of truth. For Adam appeared to them, the one whom they had fashioned. And a disturbance of fear occurred throughout their entire dwell-

ing, lest perhaps the surrounding angels stand against them. For on account of those who were offering (him) praise I died, though not in reality, because their archangel was vain. And then a voice of the World Ruler came to the angels "I am God and there is no other beside me."[1] But I laughed with joy when I considered his conceit. And he kept saying all the more, "Who is Man?"[2] And the entire army of his angels who had seen Adam and his dwelling were laughing at his smallness.

And in this way their thought came to be removed away from the Greatness of the heavens, who is the Man of truth, whose name they saw because he is in the smallness of a dwelling place. Since they are foolish in the senselessness of their vain thought, namely their laughter, it became defilement for them. The whole greatness of the Fatherhood of the Spirit was resting in its places, and I was with him, since I have a thought of a single emanation from the eternal ones and the unknowable ones, undefiled and immeas- urable. I placed the small Ennoia in the world, having disturbed them and fright- ened the whole multitude of the angels and their ruler. And I examined them all with burning and fire on account of my thought. And each of their activities they did on account of me. And trouble and fighting arose around the Seraphim and Cherubim, since their glory will perish, and the disturbance which is around Adonaios this side and that, and (around) their dwelling—(reaching) to the World Ruler and the one who said "Let us seize him." Others again (said), "The counsel shall not come to be." For Adonaios knows me because of Hope.

And I was in the mouths of lions. And (as for) the counsel which they planned

---

[1]Isa 45:5–6   [2]Ps 8:4.

about me against destruction of their deception and their foolishness, I did not give in to them as they had devised. And I was not afflicted at all. Those there punished me, yet I did not die in solid reality but in what appears, in order that I not be put to shame by them, because these are part of me. I cut off the shame from me and I did not become fainthearted at what happened to me at their hands. I was about to become a slave to fear, but I was struck (merely) according to their sight and thought, in order that no word might ever be found to speak about them. For my death which they think happened, (happened) to them in their error and blindness. They nailed their man up to their death. For their minds did not see me, for they were deaf and blind. But in doing these things, they render judgment against themselves.

As for me, on the one hand they saw me; they punished me. Another, their father, was the one who drank the gall and the vinegar; it was not I. They were hitting me with the reed; another was the one who lifted up the cross on his shoulder, who was Simon. Another was the one on whom they put the crown of thorns. But I was rejoicing in the height over all the riches of the archons and the offspring of their error and their conceit, and I was laughing at their ignorance. And all their powers I brought into subjection. For when I came down no one saw me. For I kept changing my forms above, transforming from appearance to appearance. And on account of this, when I was at their gates I kept taking their likeness. For I passed them by quietly, and I was viewing the places, and I did not fear nor was I ashamed, for I was undefiled. And I was speaking with them, mixing among them through those who are mine, and I tread on those who are harsh to them jealously, and the fire I extinguished.

And all these things I kept doing on account of my will in order that this which I willed in the will of the Father above I might complete. And the Son of the Greatness, who was hidden in the region below, we brought to the height, where I am with all these aeons, which no one has seen nor understood, where the wedding of the wedding robe is, the new (wedding) and not the old, nor does it perish. For the new bridal chamber is of the heavens and perfect.

I have revealed (that) there are three paths, (which are) an undefiled mystery in a spirit of this aeon, which does not perish, nor is it partial, nor is to be spoken of; rather, it is undivided, universal, and permanent. For the soul, which is from the height, will not speak about the error which is here, nor transport itself from these aeons, since it will be transported when it becomes a free person and experience nobility in the world, standing before the Father without trouble and fear, always mixed with the mind of ideal power. They will see me from every side without hatred. For while they see me, they are being seen, being mixed with them. As for me, since they did not put me to shame, they were not shamed. As for me, since they were not afraid before me, they will pass by every gate without fear, and they will be perfected in the third glory. I was the one whose cross the world did not accept, (my) apparent exaltation, my third baptism in an apparent image, when they had fled from the fire of the seven authorities. And the sun of the powers of the archons set, darkness overtook them, and the world became poor.

After they bound him with many restraints, they nailed him to the cross, and they fastened him with four nails of bronze. The veil of his temple he tore with his hands. There was a trembling that overcame the chaos of the earth, for the souls which were in the sleep below were released, and they were resurrected. They walked about boldly, having laid aside jealousy of ignorance and unlearnedness beside the dead tombs, having put on the new man, having come to know that blessed and perfect one of the eternal and incomprehensible Father and of the boundless light, which I am. When I came to my own and joined them with myself, there was no need for many words, for our thought was with their thought; on this account they understood what I was saying, for we took counsel concerning the destruction of the archons. And on this account I did the will of the Father, which I am.

When we went forth from our home, when we came down to this world and came into being in the world in bodies, we were hated and persecuted, not only (by) those who are ignorant, but by those also who think that they are advancing the name of Christ, since they are vain in ignorance. They do not know who they are, like unreasoning beasts. Those who were set free by me they persecute, since they hate them—those who, if they shut their mouth, would weep with groaning without profit because they did not know me completely. Instead, they served two masters, even a multitude. But you (pl.) will be victorious in everything, in war and battles and schism of jealousy and anger. But in the uprightness of our love we are without deceit, pure, good, having the mind of the Father in an ineffable mystery. For it (the world) was a laughingstock. It is I who bear witness that it was a laughingstock—since the archons do not know that it is an ineffable union of undefiled truth, like that which exists among the children of the light, of which they made an imitation, proclaiming the doctrine of a dead man and falsehoods to resemble the freedom and purity of the perfect assembly, uniting themselves in their doctrine to fear and slavery and

worldly concerns and discarded worship, being few (and) uninstructed.

They do not accept for themselves the nobility of the truth, hating the one for whom they exist and loving the one for whom they do not exist. For they did not know the Gnosis of the Greatness, that it is from above and (from) the fountain of truth. And it is not from slavery and jealousy and fear and love of worldly matter. For that which is not theirs and that which is theirs they use without fear and with freedom. They do not covet because they have authority and a law from themselves over the things which they would desire. But those who do not have are poor, namely, those who do not possess something and yet they desire it. And they lead astray those who through them are like those who have the truth of their freedom, so as to constrain us under a yoke and compulsion of concern and fear. This one is in slavery. And this one who is brought by compulsion of violence and threat has been guarded by God. But the noble-born one of the Fatherhood is not guarded, since he guards that which is his own by himself, without word or compulsion. He is united with his will, this one who is of the thought alone of the Fatherhood, that (the Fatherhood) may become perfect and unutterable through the living water, if it exists in wisdom among yourselves not only in word of hearing but in deed and fulfilled word.

For the perfect are worthy to be established in this way. And they are joined with me in order that they may not share in any enmity. In a wholesome friendship I accomplish everything in the Good One, for this is the joining of truth, that they should have no adversary. But everyone who causes division—and he will learn none of their wisdom because he causes division and is not a friend— he is an enemy to them all. But the one who lives in agreement and friendship of brotherly love by nature and not by decree, wholly and not in part, this one is truly the will of the Father. This one is the universal and the perfect love.

For Adam was a laughingstock, and he was created from the image of a pattern of a man by the Hebdomad, as though he had become stronger than I and my brethren. We are innocent with respect to him, since we did not sin. And Abraham was a laughing stock, and Isaac and Jacob, since they were given a name by the Hebdomad, namely "the fathers from the image," as though he had become stronger than I and my brethren. We are innocent with respect to him, since we did not sin. David was a laughingstock since his son was named the Son of Man, having been activated by the Hebdomad, as though he had become stronger than I and the friends of my race. But we are innocent with respect to him; we did not sin. Solomon was a laughingstock, since he thought that he was Christ, having become arrogant through the Hebdomad, as though he had become stronger than I and my brethren. But we are innocent with respect to him; I did not sin. The 12 prophets were laughingstocks, since they have come forth as imitations of the true prophets. They came into being from the image of the Hebdomad, as though it had become stronger than I and my brethren. But we are innocent with respect to it, since we did not sin. Moses was a laughingstock, a "faithful servant," being named "the friend"; they bore witness concerning him in iniquity, since he never knew me. Neither he nor those before him, from Adam to Moses and John the Baptist, none of them knew me nor my brethren. For a doctrine of angels is what arose through them, to keep dietary rules and bitter slavery. They never knew truth nor will they know it, for there is a great deception upon their soul, and they have no ability to find a mind of freedom ever,

in order to know him, until they come to know the Son of Man.

But concerning my Father, I am the one whom the world did not know, and on this account, it rose up against me and my brethren. But we are innocent with respect to it; we did not sin. For the Archon was a laughingstock because he said, "I am God, and there is none greater than I. I alone am the Father, the Lord, and there is no other beside me. I am a jealous God, bringing the sins of the fathers upon the children for three and four generations,"[3] as though he had become stronger than I and my brethren. But we are innocent with respect to him; for we did not sin. Though we mastered his doctrine in this way, he lives in conceit, and he does not agree with our Father. And thus through our friendship we prevailed over his doctrine, since he is arrogant in conceit and does not agree with our Father. For he was a laughingstock with (his) judgment and false prophecy.

O those who do not see! You do not see your blindness that this is who was not known. Neither did they ever know him, nor did they understand him. Concerning him they would not listen to a valid report. On this account they trained in a judgment of error, and they raised their defiled, murderous hands against him as if they were striking the air. And the senseless and the blind are senseless always, being slaves always of law and worldly fear. I am Christ, the Son of Man, the one from you (pl.) who is in you. I am despised on your account, in order that you yourselves may forget what is changeable. And do not become female, lest you give birth to their evils and kindred things: to jealousy and schism, anger and wrath, fear and a divided heart and vain coveting which is not fulfilled. But I am an ineffable mystery to you. . . .

---

[3] Isa 45:5–6; Exod 20:5.

The Secret Gospel of Mark

The Secret Gospel of Mark is a longer edition of Mark's Gospel that has been known only since 1958.[1] While cataloguing manuscripts in the library of the Greek Orthodox monastery of Mar Saba, located south-east of Jerusalem, an American scholar, Morton Smith, came upon a seventeenth-century edition of the letters of Ignatius. According to Smith's own account,[2] the final blank pages of this volume had been used by an eighteenth-century scribe to copy a portion of a letter allegedly from Clement of Alexandria, a church father who lived at the end of the second century and the beginning of the third. In this letter, Clement indicates that Mark had produced two versions of his Gospel, one for church members at large and the other for the spiritual elite who could grasp the full mysteries of the Kingdom. Clement indicates that this second expanded edition, the so-called Secret Gospel, had been entrusted to the Christians of Alexandria, his own city, but that it had come to be misused by members of the Carpocratian sect, a group of Gnostic Christians known for their illicit sexual rituals.

Clement then narrates two of the accounts found in the Secret Gospel. The contents of the stories, especially the first, show why this version of the Gospel could have seemed so dangerous to the church at large, and so interesting to the Carpocratians. Jesus raises a youth from the dead, who then loves Jesus and begs to be allowed to stay with him (the story is reminiscent of both the raising of Lazarus in John 11 and of the story of the "rich young man" of Matt 17:16–22 and Mark 10:17–31). After six days, the youth comes to Jesus in the evening, clothed with nothing but a linen garment over his naked body (cf. Mark 14:51). They spend the night together, with Jesus teaching the youth the mystery of the kingdom of God.

The highly unusual character of this story—in particular its homo-erotic overtones—have led scholars to debate virtually every aspect of the "Secret Gospel." Did Clement of Alexandria actually write this letter,

---

[1]For a full account, which focuses to some extent on the question of whether or not the Secret Gospel, and the letter of Clement that contains it, were forged, see Ehrman, *Lost Christianities*, 67–89. [2]See *The Secret Gospel: The Discovery and Interpretation of the Secret Gospel according to Mark* (New York: Harper & Row, 1973).

Translation by Bart D. Ehrman, based on the text in Morton Smith, *Clement of Alexandria and a Secret Gospel of Mark* (Cambridge, Mass: Harvard University Press, 1973).

preserved only in an eighteenth-century fragment that is no longer available for examination (Smith published photographs of the document, but the original is inaccessible)? Why is this Gospel, or even Clement's letter, never mentioned by any other ancient source? Is the letter an ancient forgery? A modern forgery? If the letter is actually by Clement, were the stories that it narrates known before the end of the second century? Do they actually come from a second edition of Mark's Gospel? Could they, instead, have originally been part of the first edition of the Gospel, only to be deleted by orthodox Christian scribes concerned with their ethical implications? Were these stories widely known by Christians already in the first century (such as the author of the Fourth Gospel?). Could they, in fact, have actually happened?

The entire letter of Clement is not translated here, but only the quotations that relate to the Secret Gospel. Clement begins the letter by providing the account summarized above, indicating that the apostle Mark produced a second version of his Gospel for the spiritually enlightened in Alexandria, which was wrongfully procured and corrupted by the Carpocratians. He then goes on to indicate two passages that were in this second version, the Secret Gospel, along with one that was not in it, that he had been queried about.

Citation 1 (following Mark 10:34)

They came to Bethany, and a woman was there whose brother had died. She came and prostrated herself before Jesus, saying to him, "Son of David, have mercy on me." But his disciples rebuked her. Jesus became angry and went off with her to the garden where the tomb was.

Immediately a loud voice was heard from the tomb. Jesus approached and rolled the stone away from the entrance to the tomb. Immediately he went in

where the young man was, stretched out his hand, and raised him by seizing his hand.

The young man looked at him intently and loved him; and he began pleading with him that he might be with him. When they came out of the tomb they went to the young man's house, for he was wealthy.

And after six days Jesus gave him a command. And when it was evening the young man came to him, wearing a linen cloth over his naked body. He stayed with him that night, for Jesus was teaching him the mystery of the Kingdom of God. When he got up from there, he returned to the other side of the Jordan."

The letter goes on to indicate a passage not found in the Secret Gospel:

Citation 2

But the phrase "naked man with naked man," and the other matters you inquired about, are not found (in the text).

Citation 3 (following Mark 10:46a)

And the sister of the young man Jesus loved was there, along with his mother and Salome. And Jesus did not receive them.

The fragment of the letter concludes with a tantalizing statement that Clement now intends to provide "a true interpretation" of these matters, "in accordance with the true philosophy." But that is exactly where the letter breaks off.

NON-CANONICAL ACTS OF THE APOSTLES

Introduction

Only one account of the activities of the apostles of Jesus came to be included in the New Testament, the book of Acts, written by the author of the Gospel of Luke. The second century, however, saw the production of numerous legendary accounts of the missionary endeavors of the apostles, who were said to have taken the gospel message far afield throughout the Roman Empire, and even outside of it. These narratives recount the apostles' heroic deeds in order to show that they were empowered by the miraculous power of the Holy Spirit to do God's will here on earth, as they heal the sick, cast out demons, and raise the dead. In addition, the accounts reveal the numerous obstacles the apostles encountered, especially in their confrontations with advocates of "pagan" religions, whose temples are occasionally destroyed by a word from an apostle, and with "heretics," who proclaim a false view of the religion. Some of the stories involve miracle-working contests between the apostolic advocates of the truth and their heretical opponents, who, naturally, come to be soundly defeated by the power of the one true God.

In addition to tales of the apostles who were known from the New Testament, there were lively accounts written about others as well—most notably a female apostle, a companion of Paul, named Thecla, whose miraculous exploits and supernatural escapes from death continue to enthrall readers today.

Throughout these accounts one finds not just a set of episodic narratives, but an ideological point, stressed time and again, relating to the need for true followers of Christ to abandon the trappings and pleasures of this world—especially the pleasures of sex—in order to participate fully in the life of the other world, the world of God. And so these tales consistently take an ascetic line, urging their readers to abandon what might be otherwise thought of as wholesome activities of daily life that bind society together (sexual love of married couples, raising of children, commitment to family life) in order to serve the God who stands over against the social conventions of this world.

Scholars have long noted that this ascetic ideology stands at tension with the "pagan" writings that are most similar to the Christian Acts and probably served as their model—ancient pagan Romances (sometimes called novels), which celebrate sexual love and the bonds of family that it creates. Numerous subplots tie the Romances together with the Christian Acts—travels and dangers on sea and land, shipwrecks, piracy, kidnappings, stories of broken marriages and frustrated love. But whereas the pagan romances affirm what today some might call "family values," the Christian Acts denounce these as worldly concerns to be overcome by the true believer. For the authors of these books, it is the true worship of God and the spread of the Christian gospel that are of ultimate importance, with society and its institutions seen as impediments to the goals of the Christians' existence, which is to be directed to life in heaven, not life on earth.

The Acts of John

Some of the most entertaining stories found among the apocryphal accounts of the apostles are in the "Acts of John," stories of the missionary adventures of the son of Zebedee, the disciple commonly regarded as Jesus' closest companion.[1] Many of the stories demonstrate the uncanny power of God at work within his great apostle, as he is able to perform remarkable miracles by healing the sick and raising the dead—evidence of the truth of his proclamation of the gospel of Christ.

The following excerpts narrate some of the apostle's most remarkable deeds, including a tale in which he raises from the dead a prominent leader in the city of Ephesus, Lycomedes, and his beautiful wife, Cleopatra (chaps. 19–25). A second resurrection account involves a gripping tale of passion gone awry, in a love triangle involving the beautiful but ascetic Christian, Drusiana, her loving husband, Andronicus, and the unbeliever Callimachus, whose unsatisfied lust becomes known to Drusiana, causing her to die of grief for being the object of temptation. In a fit of passion, however, Callimachus bribes his way into the burial vault, where he plans to fulfill his lust on Drusiana's corpse, only to be attacked by a preternatural serpent that stands as her guardian (chaps. 63–86).

Razor-sharp in its contrast between ascetic virtue and lustful vice, this intriguing Acts of John stresses both the need for purity before God and the power of the apostle, who is able to raise the dead and to right all that has gone wrong in the world (the pure Drusiana too, it should be noted, performs a resurrection in the account).

Other stories found here are somewhat more amusing—including John's encounter with a host of unwanted bed-bugs at a roadside inn (chaps. 60–61). Yet other accounts, probably from a different source, involve more mystical reflections on the nature of Christ, who is described in ways that appear docetic—that is, suggesting that he did not have a real flesh-and-blood body (see esp. chaps. 85–103).

---

[1]See further Ehrman, *Lost Christianities*, 41–44.

Translation by J. K. Elliott; *Apocryphal New Testament* (Oxford: Clarendon Press, 1993) 311–26; 328–35; used with permission.

It is difficult to know when the Acts of John was composed, but many scholars locate it to the second half of the second century.

19 When we came near the city Lycomedes, the commander-in-chief of the Ephesians, a wealthy man, met us, fell down before John and asked him for help, with these words, "Your name is John; the God whom you preach has sent you to help my wife, who has been paralyzed for seven days and lies past recovery. But glorify your God and treat her out of compassion for us. Whilst I was reflecting what to do, a man came to me and said, 'Desist, Lycomedes, from the evil thought which militates against you. Do not submit. For out of compassion for my servant Cleopatra I have sent you a man from Miletus, named John, who will comfort her and restore her to you cured.' Delay not, therefore, servant of the God who announced you to me, but hasten to the ailing woman." And John went at once from the gate with the brethren who were with him and followed Lycomedes into his house. And Cleobius said to his servants, "Go to my relative Callippus and make yourselves comfortable in his house—for I am coming there with his son—that we may find everything prepared!"

20 When Lycomedes and John had come into the house in which the woman was lying, he grasped his feet again, and said, "See, Lord, the lost beauty, see the youth, see the much talked of bloom of my unhappy wife, the admiration of all Ephesus! Woe to me, unhappy man! I was envied, humbled, the enemy's eye was fixed on me. I never wronged anyone, although I could harm many. I envisaged this situation and I was always anxious to experience no sorrow or anything like it! Of what use is my care now, Cleopatra? What good was it to me, that I was called godly to this day? I suffer more than a heathen, seeing you, Cleopatra, suffering so. The sun in his circuit shall not see me, if you are no more with me. Cleopatra, I will die before you. I will not spare my life though I am still youthful. I will justify myself before the goddess of right, whom I served in righteousness, though I might indict her for her unrighteous sentence. I will avenge myself on her by coming as a shade. I will say to her, 'You have forced me to leave the light of life, because you tore away Cleopatra. You are the cause of my death, by having prepared for me this fate. You have forced me to blaspheme Providence by destroying my joy.' "

21 And Lycomedes spoke more to Cleopatra, went to her couch, and cried bitterly. But John drew him away and said, "Abandon these tears and unbecoming words! It is not proper for you, who saw the vision, to be disbelieving. Know that your partner for life will be restored to you. Therefore join us, who have come for her sake, and pray to the God whom you saw, when he showed me to you in a vision! What is the matter, Lycomedes? Wake up and open also your soul! Cast from you heavy sleep! Call on the Lord, beseech him for your wife, and he will support her." But he fell to the ground and wept dejectedly. And John said with tears, "Woe to the treachery of the vision, woe to the new temptation prepared for me, woe to the new craft of him who devises cunnings against me!

Did the voice from heaven, which came to me by the way, intend this for me, predicting to me what should here take place? Will it deliver me up to such a great multitude of citizens, for the sake of Lycomedes? The man lies here lifeless, and I know that I shall not leave this house alive. Why do you delay, Lord? Why have you deprived us of your gracious promise? I beseech you, Lord, let him not rejoice who delights in the sorrow of others. Let him not dance who always laughs at us! But let your holy name and your compassion come quickly! Waken the bodies of the two, who are against me!"

22 While John was crying, the city of Ephesus ran to the house of Lycomedes, supposing him dead. And when John saw the great multitude, he prayed to the Lord, "Now the time of refreshing and confidence has come with you, O Christ; now is the time for us weary ones to have help from you, physician, who heal freely. Keep my entrance here free from derision! I beseech you, Jesus, help such a great multitude to come to the Lord of the universe. Behold the affliction, behold those who lie here! Even those who came here, make holy instruments for your service, after they have seen your gift. For you have said yourself, O Christ, 'Ask and it shall be given you.'[2] We therefore beseech you, O King, not for gold, not for silver, not for riches, not for possession, nor for any transient, earthly goods, but for two souls through whom you will convert those present to your way, to your knowledge, to your confidence, and to your infallible promise. For many of them shall be saved, after they have known your power through the resurrection of the departed. Give us, therefore, hope in you! I will go to Cleopatra and say, 'Arise, in the name of Jesus Christ.' "

23 And he went, touched her face, and said, "Cleopatra, he whom every ruler fears, and every creature, power, abyss, and darkness and unsmiling death and the heights of heaven and the caverns of the lower world and the resurrection of the dead and the sight of the blind and the whole power of the ruler of the world, and the pride of its prince, says, 'Rise and become not a pretext for many who will not believe, and an affliction for souls who hope and could be saved.' " And Cleopatra cried out at once, "I will rise, master, save your handmaiden!" When she had risen after the seven days, the whole city of Ephesus was stirred by the miraculous sight. . . .

38 . . . After two days the birthday of the idol's temple was celebrated. While everybody was dressed in white garments, John wore black and went to the temple. They laid hold of him and tried to kill him. But John said, "Men, you are mad to lay hold of me, the servant of the only God." And climbing on to the platform he spoke to them:

39 "Men of Ephesus, you are in danger of behaving like the sea. Every discharging river and every precipitating spring, downpours and incessant waves and torrents rushing from the rock, are permeated by the bitter salt which is in the sea. Thus to this day you are unchangeably hostile to true piety, and you perish in your old idolatry. How many miraculous deeds did you see me perform, how many cures! And still you are hardened in the heart and cannot see clearly. What now, men of Ephesus? I have ventured now to come up to this idol's temple, to convince you that you

---

[2]Matt 7:7.

are wholly without God and dead to human reasoning. Behold, here I stand. You all assert that Artemis is powerful. Pray to her, that I alone die! Or if you cannot accomplish this, I alone will call upon my God to kill you all because of your unbelief."

40 Since they already knew him and had seen the dead raised, they cried aloud, "Do not treat us so and kill us, we beseech you, John; we know indeed that you can do it." And John answered them, "If you do not wish to die, let me convince you of your idolatry. Any why? So that you may desist from your old error. Be now converted by my God or I will die at the hands of your goddess. For I will pray in your presence to my God, and ask him to have mercy upon you."

41 After these words he prayed, "God, who are God above all so-called gods, who to this day have been despised at Ephesus, you induced me to come to this place, which I never had in view. You have abrogated every form of worship through conversion to you. In your name every idol, every demon, and every unclean spirit is banished. May the deity of this place, which has deceived so many, now also give way to your name, and thus show your mercy on this place! For they walk in error."

42 And with these words of John the altar of Artemis suddenly split into many parts, and the oblations put up in the temple suddenly fell to the ground, and its glory broke, and so did more than seven of the idols. And half of the temple fell down, so that when the roof came down, the priest also was killed at one stroke. And the people of the Ephesians cried, "There is only one God, that of John, only one God who has

compassion for us; for you alone are God; now we have become converted, since we saw your miraculous deeds. Have mercy upon us, God, according to your will, and deliver us from our great error." And some of them lay on their faces and cried; others bent their knees and prayed; others rent their garments and lamented; still others tried to escape.

43 And John stretched out his hands and prayed with uplifted soul to the Lord, "Glory be to you, my Jesus, the only God of truth, who procure your servants in manifold ways!" And after these words he said to the people, "Rise up from the ground, people of Ephesus, pray to my God, and know how his invisible power was made manifest and his miraculous deeds took place before your eyes! Artemis herself should have helped. Her servant should have received help from her and not have died. Where is the power of the deity? Where are the sacrifices? Where the birthday? Where the festivals? Where the garlands? Where the great enchantment and the poison allied to it?"

44 And the people rose up from the ground and made haste to destroy the remainder of the temple, crying, "We know that the God of John is the only one, and henceforth we worship him, since we have obtained mercy from him." And as John came down, many of the people touched him, saying, "Help us, John, help us who die in vain! You see our intention; you see how the multitude following you cleaves to hope in your God. We have seen the way in which we have gone astray when we were lost. We have seen that our gods were erected in vain. We have seen their great and disgraceful derision. But give us, we beseech you, help without hindrance, when we have come to your house! Receive us, who are desperate!"

60 ... On the first day we came to a lonely inn, and when we were trying to find a bed for John we experienced a strange event. There was one bedstead with covers over which we spread our cloaks which we had brought and requested him to lie down and to rest, whilst we slept on the floor. He had hardly lain down, when he was molested by bugs. But as they became more and more troublesome, and as it was midnight already, we all heard him say to them, "I say to you, you bugs, be considerate; leave your home for this night and go to rest in a place which is far away from the servants of God!" And while we laughed and talked, John fell asleep. And we conversed quietly, and thanks to him we remained undisturbed.

61 When it was day, I rose first, and with me Verus and Andronicus. And in the door of the room which we had taken was a mass of bugs. And having called all the brethren, we went outside to have a full view of them. John was still asleep. When he woke up we showed him what we had seen. And sitting up in bed and seeing them, he said, "Since you have been wise to heed my warning, go back to your place!" When he had spoken and had risen from the bed, the bugs hastened from the door to the bed, ran up the legs into the joints and disappeared. And John said again, "This creature heard the voice of a man and kept quiet and was obedient. We, however, hear God's voice, and yet irresponsibly transgress his commandments. And how long will this go on?"

62 After this we came to Ephesus. And when the brethren who lived there had learned that John had re-

turned after this long time, they met in the house of Andronicus, where he was also staying, grasped his feet, put his hands to their faces, and kissed them because they had touched his clothes.

63 And while great love and endless joy prevailed among the brethren, one, a servant of Satan, coveted Drusiana, although he saw and knew that she was the wife of Andronicus. Very many people remonstrated with him, "It is impossible for you to obtain this woman, especially since she has separated even from her husband out of piety. Or do you alone not know that Andronicus, who was not the godly man he now is, had locked her up in a tomb, saying, 'Either I'll have you as a wife, as I had you before, or you must die?' And she preferred to die rather than to commit the repugnant act. Now, if out of piety she withheld her consent to sexual intercourse with her husband and master, but persuaded him to become like-minded, should she consent to you, who wish to commit adultery with her? Desist from your passion, which gives you no rest! Desist from your scheme, which you cannot accomplish!"

64 Though his intimate friends remonstrated with him, they could not persuade him. He was even so impudent as to send word to her. When Drusiana heard of his disgraceful passion and shameless demands, she became very despondent, and after two days she was feverish. She said, "Oh, if I only had not come back to my native city where I have become a stumbling-block to a man who believes not in the worship of God! For if he were filled with God's word, he would not fall into such a passion. Therefore, O Lord, since I have become accessory to a blow which struck an ignorant soul, deliver me from this prison and take me soon to you!" And without being understood by anyone Drusiana departed this life in the presence of John, not rejoicing but sorrowing over the physical trouble of that man.

65 And Andronicus was sad and carried a hidden sorrow in his heart, and wept bitterly, so that John could only silence him by saying to him, "Drusiana has departed this unjust life for a better hope." To this answered Andronicus, "Of this I am certain, John, and I have no doubt in the belief in my God. My hopes are grounded on the fact, that she departed this life pure."

66 After she was interred, John took Andronicus aside, and having learned of the cause he sorrowed more than Andronicus. And he kept silence, considering the threats of the enemy, and sat still a little. When the brethren were assembled to hear which words he would say concerning the departed, he began to speak:

67 "When the helmsman who crosses the ocean has landed with the ship and passengers in a quiet haven free from storms, he feels secure. The husbandman who sowed the seed-grains in the ground and cared for them with great pains is only then to enjoy a rest from his labors when he has harvested abundant corn in his barns. Whoever promises to take part in a race should rejoice only when he has obtained the prize. He whose name is entered on the list of prize-fighting should triumph only after he receives the crowns. And thus it is with all races and skills, when they do not fail at the end, but are carried out, as they were intended.

68 "So I think it is with the faith which every one of us practises,

and which can only be decided as having been the true one when it remains the same to the end of life. For there are many obstacles which cause unrest to human reasoning: cares, children, parents, glory, poverty, flattery, youth, beauty, boasting, desire for riches, anger, pride, frivolity, envy, passion, carelessness, violence, lust, slaves, money, pretence, and all the other similar obstacles which exist in life; it is the same for the helmsman who takes his course for a quiet journey and is opposed by the adverse winds and a great tempest and a mighty wave, when the heaven is serene; it is the same for the husbandman who is opposed by untimely weather and blight and creeping worms appearing from the ground; for the athletes, the near miss, and for the craftsman the obstacles to their skills.

69 "The believer must above all things consider the end and carefully examine how it will come, whether energetic and sober and without impediment, or in confusion and flattering worldly things and bound by passions. Thus one can praise the beauty of the body only when it is completely naked; and the greatness of the general when he has happily finished the whole campaign as he promised; and the excellence of the physician when he has succeeded in every cure; and so one praises a soul filled with faith and worthy of God if it has happily accomplished that which it promised, not one of which made a good beginning, and gradually descended into the errors of life and became weak, nor the numb soul which made an effort to attain higher things and was afterwards reduced to perishable, nor that which loved the temporal more than the eternal, nor that which exchanged the perishable for the lasting, nor that which honored what was not to be honored and loved works of dishonor, nor that which accepted pledges from Satan and received the serpent into its house, nor one which was reviled for God's sake and afterwards was ashamed, nor one which consented with the mouth but did not show it by the deed; but we praise one which refused to be inflamed by filthy lust, to succumb to levity, to be ensnared by thirst after money, or to be betrayed by the strength of the body and anger."

70 While John continued to preach to the brethren that they despise earthly goods for the sake of the eternal ones, the lover of Drusiana, inflamed by the influence of the polymorphous Satan to the most ardent passions, bribed the greedy steward of Andronicus with money. And he opened the tomb of Drusiana and left him to accomplish on the body that which was once denied to him. Since he had not procured her during her lifetime, he continually thought of her body after she was dead, and exclaimed, "Although when living you refused to unite with me in love, after your death I will dishonor your corpse." Being in such a frame of mind he obtained the opportunity to execute his impious plan through the accursed steward, and both went to the tomb. Having opened the door, they began to take the graveclothes from the corpse, and said, "What have you gained, unhappy Drusiana? Could you not have done this while you were alive? It need not have grieved you if you had done it willingly."

71 While they spoke and only the shift remained, there appeared something wonderful, which people that do such things deserve to experience. A serpent appeared from somewhere, bit the steward, and killed him. And the serpent did not bite the young man, but encircled his feet, hissing fearfully, and

when he fell down, the serpent sat on him.

72 On the following day John and Andronicus and the brethren went at the break of day to the tomb in which Drusiana had been for three days, so that we might break bread there. And when we were about to start, the keys were not to be found. And John said to Andronicus, "It is right that they are lost, for Drusiana is not in the tomb. Nevertheless, let us go, that you do not appear neglectful, and the doors will open of themselves, since the Lord has already given us many other things."

73 When we came to the place, the doors opened at the master's behest, and at the tomb of Drusiana we saw a beautiful youth smiling. When John saw him, he exclaimed and said, "Do you come before us here also, noble one? And why?" And he heard a voice saying to him, "For the sake of Drusiana, whom you are to raise up. I found her almost defiled on account of the dead man lying near the tomb." And when the noble one had thus spoken to John he ascended to heaven before the eyes of all. And John turned to the other side of the tomb and saw a young man, the very prominent Ephesian Callimachus—for this is what he was called—and on him a huge snake sleeping, also the steward of Andronicus, named Fortunatus, dead. On seeing both, he stood helpless and said to the brethren, "What does all this mean? Or why did the Lord not reveal to me what took place here, for he was always concerned for me?"

74 When Andronicus saw these bodies, he jumped up and went to the tomb of Drusiana. And when he saw her in her shift, he said to John, "I understand what took place, blessed servant of God. This Callimachus loved my sister. And as he could not get her, although he tried it often, he no doubt bribed this accursed steward of mine with a great sum of money with the intention— as one can now see—to accomplish his purpose through him. For this Callimachus said to many, 'If she will not yield to be me alive, rape shall be committed on her death.' This, O master, the noble one saw and did not allow her earthly remains to be violated. That is why those who engineered this are dead. And the voice which came to you 'Raise Drusiana!' foretold this. For she departed this life through sorrow. And I believe him who said that this is one of the men who was led astray. For you were asked to raise him. As for the other I know that he does not deserve salvation. But one thing I ask of you. Raise Callimachus first, and he shall confess what took place."

75 And John looked at the corpse and said to the poisonous snake, "Depart from him who is to serve Jesus Christ!" Then he rose and prayed, "God, whose name is rightly praised by us; God, who overcomes each harmful work; God, whose will is done, who always hears us, make your grace now efficacious on this youth! And if through him some dispensation is to take place, make it known to us, when he is raised!" And the young man immediately arose and kept silence for a whole hour.

76 When the man had regained his senses, John asked what his intrusion into the tomb meant. And having learned from him what Andronicus had already told him, how he passionately loved Drusiana, John asked further whether he had accomplished his wicked design to commit rape on the holy earthly remains. And he replied, "How could I

have accomplished this when this fearful beast killed Fortunatus with one bite before my eyes? And this deservedly so, for he encouraged me to such madness, after I had already desisted from the ill-timed and dreadful frenzy—but he frightened me and put me in the state in which you saw me, before I arose. But I will tell you another great miracle, which nearly slew me and almost killed me. When my soul was seized with mad passion and the incurable disease was troubling me, when I had already robbed her of the grave-clothes with which she was dressed, and went from the grave to put them down as you see, I turned back to perpetrate the abominable deed. And I saw a beautiful youth covering her with this cloak. Rays of light fell from his face upon hers, and he turned to me also and said, "Callimachus, die, that you may live." Who it was, I knew not, servant of God. Since you have come here, I know that it was an angel of God. And this I truly know, that the true God is preached by you; and I am sure of it. But I pray you, see to it that I may be delivered from this fate and dreadful crime, and bring me to your God as a man who had gone astray in scandalous, abominable, deceit. On my knees I ask for your help. I will become one of those who hope in Christ so that the voice may also prove true, which spoke here to me, 'Die to live!' And it is already fulfilled. For that unbeliever, godless, lawless man, is dead; I am raised by you as a believer, faithful and godly, that I may know the truth, which I ask of you to reveal to me."

77 And John, rejoicing, contemplated the whole spectacle of the salvation of people and said, "O Lord Jesus Christ, I do not know what your power is. I am amazed at your great mercy and endless forbearance. Oh, what greatness descended to servitude! O unspeakable freedom, which was enslaved by us! O inconceivable glory, which has come upon us! You have kept the grave from shame, and redeemed that man who contaminated himself with blood, and taught him to be chaste who meant to violate dead bodies. Father, full of mercy and compassion toward him who disregarded you, we praise, glorify, and honor you and thank you for your great goodness and long-suffering, holy Jesus, for you alone are God and none else; you against whose power all devices can do nothing now and in all eternity! Amen!"

78 After these words, John took Callimachus, kissed him, and said, "Glory be to our God, who had mercy upon you, child, and deemed me worthy to praise his power, and delivered you by a wise method from that madness and intoxication and called you to rest and renewal of life."

79 When Andronicus saw that Callimachus had been raised from the dead, he and the brethren besought John to raise Drusiana also, and said, "John, let her be raised and happily complete life's short space, which she gave up out of sorrow for Callimachus, because she thought she was a temptation to him! And when it pleases the Lord, he will take her to himself." And without delay John went to the grave, seized her hand and said, "You who alone are God, I call upon you, the immense, the unspeakable, the incomprehensible, to whom all worldly power is subject, before whom every authority bows, before whom every pride falls down and is silent, before whose voice the demons are confounded, at whose contemplation the whole creation surrenders in quiet meditation. Your name will be hallowed by us. Raise Drusiana that Callimachus be still

further strengthened in you who alone can do what is wholly impossible with man, and have given salvation and resurrection, and let Drusiana come out comforted because, in consequence of the conversion of the youth, she no more has the least impediment to long for you!"

80 Having spoken thus John said, "Drusiana, arise!" And she arose and came from the tomb. And when she saw that she wore nothing but her shirt, she was perplexed how to explain what had happened. Having learned everything from Andronicus, while John was upon his face and Callimachus with tears praised God, she also rejoiced and praised God.

81 Having dressed herself and looked around, she saw Fortunatus. And she said to John, "Father, he too shall rise, though he tried so much to become my betrayer." When Callimachus heard her speaking thus, he said, "No, I beg you, Drusiana. For the voice which I heard did not mention him, but only concerned you, and when I saw I believed. If he were good, God out of mercy would have certainly raised him through the blessed John. He knew that the man should have a bad death." And John answered him, "My son, we have not learnt to recompense evil with evil: For God had not recompensed the evil which we have done to him, but has given us repentance. And although we did not know his name, he did not forget us, but had mercy upon us. And when we reviled him, he forsook us not, but was merciful. And when we were disbelieving, he remembered not the evil. And when we persecuted his brethren, he did not requite us, but made us repent, turn away from sin, and called us to himself, as he called you also, child Callimachus, and, without remembering your former sins, made you his servant through his long-suffering mercy. If you do not wish me to raise Fortunatus, let Drusiana do it."

82 Without wavering, but in the joy of her spirit and soul, she went to the body of Fortunatus and said, "God of the ages, Jesus Christ, God of truth, you allowed me to see signs and wonders and granted me to partake of your name. You breathed into me your spirit with your polymorphous face, and showed much compassion. With your rich goodness, you protected me when my former husband, Andronicus, did violence to me, and gave me your servant Andronicus as a brother. Until now you have kept me, your maiden, pure. You raised me when I was dead through your servant John. To me, risen and freed from offence, you showed me him who was offended at me. You gave me perfect rest in you, and delivered me from the secret madness. I love you with all my heart. I beseech you, Christ, not to dismiss Drusiana's petition, who asks of you the resurrection of Fortunatus, though he tried so much to become my betrayer."

83 And she took the hand of the dead man and said, "Rise, Fortunatus, in the name of our Lord Jesus Christ!" And Fortunatus rose up. And seeing John in the tomb and Andronicus and Drusiana risen from the dead and Callimachus now a believer, he said, "O how far the power of these awful people has spread! I wish I were not raised, but remained dead, so as not to see them." And with these words he ran from the tomb.

84 And when John perceived the unchangeable soul of Fortunatus, he said, "O nature, unchanged for the better! O source of the soul, remaining in the filth! O essence of corruption, full of darkness! O death, dancing among those belonging to you! O fruitless tree, full of fire! O wood, producing coal as fruit! O forest, with trees full of unhealthy shoots, neighbor of unbelief! You showed us who you are, and you will always be convicted with your children. And the power of praising higher things is unknown to you, for you do not have it. Therefore as your issue is, so is your root and nature. Vanish away from those who hope in the Lord—from their thoughts, from their mind, from their souls, from their bodies, from their action, from their life, from their conversation, from their activity, from their deeds, from their counsel, from their resurrection to God, from their fragrance which you will share, from their fastings, from their prayers, from their holy baptism, from their eucharist, from the nourishment of their flesh, from their drink, from their dress, from their agape, from their acts of mourning, from their continence, and from their righteousness. From all these, most unholy and abominable Satan, shall Jesus Christ, our God and judge of those who are like you and your nature, remove you."

85 After these words John prayed, fetched a loaf of bread to the tomb to break it, and said, "We praise your name, who have converted us from error and unmerciful lusts. We praise you who have brought before our eyes that which we saw. We bear witness to your goodness manifested to us in various ways. We hallow your gracious name, Lord, and thank you who have convicted those who are convicted by you. We thank you, Lord Jesus Christ, that we believe in your unchangeable mercy. We thank you that you are in need of a saved human nature. We thank you that you gave this sure faith, that you alone are God, now and for ever. We, your servants, thank you, O holy One, we who are assembled with good reason and risen from the dead."

86 Having thus prayed and praised God, he made all the brethren partake of the eucharist of the Lord and then left the tomb. And when he had come into the house of Andronicus, he said to the brethren, "Dear brethren, a spirit within me has prophesied that, in consequence of the bite of the serpent, Fortunatus would die of blood-poisoning. Let someone make haste and inquire whether it is so!" And one of the young men ran and found him dead already, the poison having spread and reached his heart. And he returned to John, reporting that he had been dead three hours already. And John said, "You have your child, devil!"

Thus John rejoiced with the brethren in the Lord.

87 . . . Then those who were present inquired about the cause, and were especially perplexed because Drusiana had said, 'The Lord appeared to me in the tomb in the form of John and of a youth.' And as they were perplexed and in some ways were not yet confirmed in the faith, John said with patience:

88 "Men and brethren, you have suffered nothing that is strange or incredible in your perception of the Lord, inasmuch as we also, whom he chose for himself as apostles, were tried in many ways. I, indeed, am able neither to set forth to you nor to write the things which I saw and heard. Now I must adapt

them to your hearing; and in accordance with everyone's capabilities I will communicate to you those things whereof you are able to become hearers, that you may see the glory that surrounds him who was and is both now and forever.

"For when he had chosen Peter and Andrew, who were brothers, he came to me and to my brother James, saying, 'I have need of you, come unto me.' And my brother said, 'John, this child on the shore who called to us, what does he want?' And I said, 'What child?' He replied, 'The one who is beckoning to us.' And I answered, 'Because of our long watch that we kept at sea you are not seeing straight, brother James: but do you not see the man who stands there, fair and comely and of a cheerful countenance?' But he said to me, 'Him I do not see, brother; but let us go and we shall see what it means.' And so when we had landed the ship, we saw him helping us to beach the ship.

89 "And when we left the place, wishing to follow him again, he again appeared to me, bald-headed but with a thick and flowing beard; but to James he appeared as a youth whose beard was just starting. We were perplexed, both of us, as to the meaning of what we had seen. But when we followed him, we both became gradually more perplexed as we thought on the matter. Yet to me there appeared a still more wonderful sight; for I tried to see him as he was, and I never at any time saw his eyes closing but only open. And sometimes he appeared to me as a small man and unattractive, and then again as one reaching to heaven. Also there was in him another marvel; when I sat at table he would take me upon his breast and I held him; and sometimes his breast felt to me to be smooth and tender, and sometimes hard, like stone, so that I was perplexed in myself and said, 'What does this mean?' And when I was thinking of these things. . . .[3]

90 "At another time he took me and James and Peter to the mountain, where he used to pray, and we beheld such a light on him that it is not possible for a man who uses mortal speech to describe what it was like. Again in a similar way he led us three up to the mountain saying, 'Come with me.' And we went again and saw him at a distance praying. Now I, because he loved me, went to him quietly as though he should not see, and stood looking upon his back. And I saw that he was not dressed in garments, but was seen by us as naked and not at all like a man; his feet were whiter than snow, so that the ground there was lit up by his feet, and his head reached to heaven; so that I was afraid and cried out, and he turned and appeared as a man of small stature, and took hold of my beard and pulled it and said to me, 'John, be not unbelieving, but believing, and not inquisitive.' And I said to him, 'What have I done, Lord?' And I tell you brethren, I suffered such pain for thirty days at the place where he took hold of my beard, that I said unto him, 'Lord, if your playful tug has given me so much pain, what if you had given me a beating?' And he said to me, 'Let it be your concern from henceforth not to tempt him who is not to be tempted.'

91 "But Peter and James were angry because I spoke with the Lord and beckoned me to come to them and leave the Lord alone. And I went, and they both said to me, 'Who was speaking to the Lord when he was on top of the mountain, for we heard both of them speaking?' And I, when I considered his great grace and his unity which

has many faces, and his wisdom which without ceasing looked upon us, said, 'This you shall learn if you ask him.'

92 "Again when all of us disciples were once sleeping in a house at Gennesaret, after wrapping myself up I watched what he did, and first I heard him say, 'John, go to sleep.' And thereupon I feigned to be asleep; and I saw another like him whom I also heard saying to my Lord, 'Jesus, those whom you have chosen still do not believe in you.' And my Lord said to him, 'You are right, for they are men.'

93 "Another glory I will tell you, brethren. Sometimes when I meant to touch him, I met a material and solid body; and at other times again when I felt him, the substance was immaterial and bodiless and as if it were not existing at all. Now, if at any time he were invited by one of the Pharisees and went where he was invited, we went with him. And there was set before each one of us a loaf of bread by our host, and he also received a loaf. And he would bless his own and divide it amongst us; and from that little piece each of us was filled, and our own loaves were saved intact, so that those who had invited him were amazed. And often when I was walking with him I wished to see whether the print of his foot appeared upon the earth—for I saw him raising himself from the earth—but I never saw it. Now, these things, dear brethren, I speak to you to encourage you in your faith towards him, for we must at the present keep silent about his mighty and wonderful works, inasmuch as they are mysteries and doubtless cannot be uttered or heard.

---

[3]Gap in text.

94 "Now, before he was arrested by the lawless Jews, who received their law from a lawless serpent, he gathered us all together and said, 'Before I am delivered up to them, let us sing a hymn to the Father, and go forth to what lies before us.' So he commanded us to make a circle, holding one another's hands, and he himself stood in the middle. He said, 'Respond Amen to me.' He then began to sing a hymn, and to say:

'Glory be to you, Father!'
And we circling him said, 'Amen.'
'Glory be to you, Word! Glory be to you, Grace!' 'Amen.'
'Glory be to you, Spirit! Glory be to you, Holy One! Glory be to the glory!' 'Amen.'
'We praise you, O Father. We give thanks to you, light, in whom darkness does not abide.' 'Amen.'

95 'Now we give thanks, I say: I will be saved, and I will save.' 'Amen.'
'I will be loosed, and I will loose.' 'Amen.'
'I will be pierced, and I will pierce.' 'Amen.'
'I will be born, and I will bear.' 'Amen.'
'I will eat, and I will be eaten.' 'Amen.'
'I will hear, and I will be heard.' 'Amen.'
'I will be understood, being wholly understanding.' 'Amen.'
'I will be washed, and I will wash.' 'Amen.'

Grace is dancing.

'I will pipe, dance all of you!' 'Amen.'
'I will mourn, lament all of you!' 'Amen.'
'An Ogdoad[4] is singing with us.' 'Amen.'
'The Twelfth number is dancing above.' 'Amen.'
'The whole universe takes part in the dancing.' 'Amen.'
'He who does not dance, does not know what is being done.' 'Amen.'
'I will flee and I will stay.' 'Amen.'
'I will adorn, and I will be adorned.' 'Amen.'
'I will be united, and I will unite.' 'Amen.'
'I have no house, and I have houses.' 'Amen.'
'I have no place, and I have places.' 'Amen.'
'I have no temple, and I have temples.' 'Amen.'
'I am a lamp to you who see me.' 'Amen.'
'I am a mirror to you who perceive.' 'Amen.'
'I am a door to you who knock on me.' 'Amen.'
'I am a way to you, wayfarer.' 'Amen.'

96 " 'Now if you respond to my dancing, see yourself in me who speak; and when you have seen what I do, keep silence about my mysteries! You who dance, perceive what I do; for yours is this passion of mankind which I am to suffer! For you could not at all have comprehended what you suffer if I had not been sent to you as the Word by the Father. When you saw what I suffer, you have seen me as one suffering; and

----

[4] i.e. the eightfold power.

seeing that, you have not stood firm but were wholly moved. Moved to become wise, you have me for a support. Rest upon me! Who am I? You shall know when I go away. What I am now seen to be, that I am not. You shall see when you come. If you knew how to suffer, you would have had the power not to suffer. Learn suffering, and you shall have the power not to suffer. That which you do not know, I will teach you. I am your God, not that of the betrayer. I will that there be prepared holy souls for me. Know the word of wisdom! Say again with me:

> Glory be to you, Father; glory be
> to you, Word;
> Glory be to you, Holy Ghost!

Now concerning me, if you would know what I was: with a word I once deceived all things, and was not put to shame at all. I have leaped; but understand the whole, and having understood it say, 'Glory be to you, Father!' 'Amen.'

97 "After this dance, my beloved the Lord went out; and we were as men gone astray or dazed with sleep, and we fled all ways. Even I, when I saw him suffer, did not abide at his passion but fled to the Mount of Olives, weeping over what had taken place. And when he was hung upon the cross on Friday, at the sixth hour of the day, there came darkness over all the earth. And my Lord stood in the middle of the cave and lit it up, and said, 'John, to the multitude down below in Jerusalem I am being crucified, and pierced with lances and reeds, and gall and vinegar is given me to drink. But to you I am speaking, and pay attention to what I say. I put it into your mind to come up to this mountain, so that you might hear matters needful for a disciple to learn from his teacher, and for a man to learn from his God.'

98 "And having said this, he showed me a cross of light set up, and around the cross a great multitude which had no one form; and in the cross was one form and one likeness. And the Lord himself I beheld above the cross, not having a shape, but only a voice, and a voice not such as was familiar to us, but a sweet and kind voice and one truly divine, and it said to me, 'It is necessary that one man should hear these things from me, O John, for I have need of someone who will hear. This cross of light is sometimes called the Word by me for your sakes, sometimes Mind, sometimes Jesus, sometimes Christ, sometimes Door, sometimes Way, sometimes Bread, sometimes Seed, sometimes Resurrection, sometimes Son, sometimes Father, sometimes Spirit, sometimes Life, sometimes Truth, sometimes Faith, sometimes Grace. Thus it is called for man's sake. But in truth, as known in itself and as spoken to us, it is the marking off of all things and the uplifting and foundation of those things that are fixed but had been unstable, and the harmony of the wisdom and indeed the wisdom of the harmony. But there are on the right and on the left, powers, principalities, dominions and demons, operations, threatenings, wrath, devils, Satan and the inferior root, from which the nature of the transient things proceeded.

99 " 'This, then, is the cross which has united all things by the Word, and marked off things transient and inferior, and then compacted all into one. But this is not the cross of wood which you will see when you go down here, neither am I he who is upon the cross, whom now you do not see but only hear a voice I was reckoned to be what I am not being what I was to many others; but they will call me something else, which is vile and not worthy of me. Therefore, just as the place of rest is neither seen nor spoken of, much less shall I, the Lord of this place, be seen or spoken of.

100 " 'Now the multitude about the cross which is the lower nature is not of one form; and those whom you see in the cross, do not have one form. That is because every member of him who came down has not yet been gathered together. But when the nature of man shall be taken up, and the race which comes to me in obedience to my voice, then he who now hears me shall be united with it and shall no longer be what it now is, but shall be above them, as I am now. For as long as you do not call yourself mine, I am not that which I was. But if you hear and hearken to me, then you shall be as I am, and shall be what I was, when I have you with myself. For from this you are.[6] Therefore, ignore the many, and despise those who are outside the mystery! Know that I am wholly with the Father, and the Father with me.

101 " 'Therefore I have suffered none of the things which they will say of me: that suffering which I showed to you and to the rest in dance, I wish it to be called a mystery. For what you are, you see that I showed you; but what I am, that I alone know, and no one else. Let me, therefore, keep that which is my own, and that which is yours you must see through me. As for seeing me as I am in reality, I have told you this is impossible unless you are able to see me as my kinsman. You hear that I suffered, yet I suffered not; that I suffered not, yet I did suffer, that I was pierced, yet was I not wounded; hanged, and I was not hanged; that blood flowed from me, yet it did not flow; and, in a word, those things that they say of me I did not endure, and the things that they do not say those I suffered. Now what they are I will reveal to you for I know you will understand. Perceive in me the slaying of the Logos, the piercing of the Logos, the blood of the Logos, the wounding of the Logos, the hanging of the Logos, the passion of the Logos, the nailing of the Logos, the death of the Logos. And thus I speak, discarding manhood. Therefore, in the first place think of the Logos, then you shall perceive the Lord, and thirdly the man, and what he has suffered.'

102 "When he had spoken to me these things and others which I know not how to say as he would have me, he was taken up, without any of the multitude having seen him. And when I went down, I laughed them all to scorn, inasmuch as he had told me the things which they said about him; and I held firmly this one thing in my mind, that the Lord contrived all things symbolically and as a dispensation toward men, for their conversion and salvation.

103 "Therefore, brethren, having seen the grace of the

---

[6]Text obscure.

Lord and his affection toward us, let us worship him as those to whom he has shown mercy, not with our fingers, nor with our mouths, nor with the tongue, nor with any part of our body whatsoever, but with the disposition of our soul: let us worship him, who became man apart from this body. And let us watch because he keeps watch even now over prisons for our sakes, and in tombs, in bonds and dungeons, in shame and reproaches, by sea and land, at scourgings, condemnations, conspiracies, plots, punishments, and, in a word, he is with all of us, and suffers with us when we suffer, brethren. When he is called by any one of us he does not allow himself to shut his ears to us, but being everywhere he hearkens to all of us, and just now has hearkened to both me and Drusiana—as he is the God of those who are imprisoned—bringing help to us by his own compassion.

104 " 'You therefore must also be persuaded, beloved, that it is no man that I preach to you to worship, but God unchangeable, God invincible, God higher than all authority, and all power, and older and mightier than all the angels and creatures that are spoken of, and all ages. If then you abide in him, and are built up in him, you shall possess your soul indestructible."

105 And when he had delivered these things to the brethren, John departed with Andronicus to walk; and Drusiana also followed afar off together with all, that they might behold the acts that were done and at all times hear his word in the Lord . . .

The Acts of Paul

The "Acts of Paul" is not preserved in its entirety, but only in large fragments that are difficult to piece together. The complete book is usually thought to have included the Acts of Thecla and the pseudonymous letter of 3 Corinthians (see below). Together, the various fragments narrate legendary episodes from Paul's life, including the account, not excerpted here, of a talking lion whom Paul converts and baptizes, who then, at a later time, spares Paul when loosed upon him in the arena.

The following extract was no doubt the conclusion of the book, for it describes Paul's martyrdom. Put on trial before the evil emperor, Nero, Paul announces that even if executed, he will reappear as proof that he can never really die but will live forever. When Paul is then beheaded, we are told that milk (a symbol of life?), rather than blood, squirts from his wound, and that after his death, Paul fulfills his word by appearing to Nero and pronouncing the emperor's own imminent doom.

Most scholars identify the Acts of Paul with a book known to the church father Tertullian, who, around 200 CE, claimed that it had been forged by a presbyter of Asia Minor who, after being caught, indicated that he had done it "out of love for Paul."[1]

1 Luke, who had come from Gaul, and Titus, who had come from Dalmatia, expected Paul at Rome. When Paul saw them he rejoiced and rented a barn outside Rome where he and the brethren taught the word of truth. He became famous and many souls were added to the Lord, so that it was noised about in Rome and a great many from the house of the emperor came to him and there was much joy.

A certain Patroclus, a cupbearer of the emperor, who had come too late to the barn and could not get near to Paul on account of the throng of the people, sat on a high window, and listened as he

---

[1]See the discussion in Ehrman, *Lost Christianities,* 31–32.

Translation by J. K. Elliott, *Apocryphal New Testament* (Oxford: Clarendon Press, 1993) 385–88; used with permission.

taught the word of God. But Satan, being wicked, became jealous of the love of the brethren and Patroclus fell down from the window and died; speedily it was reported to Nero. Paul, however, having learned it by Spirit said, "Brethren, the evil one has obtained a way to tempt you; go forth and you will find a boy who has fallen down and is dying. Lift him up and bring him here." This they did. When the people saw him they were frightened. Paul said to them, "Now, brethren, show your faith. Come, let us mourn to our Lord Jesus Christ, that the boy might live and we remain unharmed." When all began to lament, the boy took breath and, having put him on an animal, they sent him away alive with all those who were of the emperor's house.

2 And Nero, having heard of Patroclus' death, became very sad, and as he came out from his bath he ordered another to be appointed for the wine. But his servants said, "Emperor, Patroclus is alive and stands at the sideboard." When the emperor heard that Patroclus was alive he was frightened and would not come in. But when he came in and saw Patroclus he cried out, "Patroclus, are you alive?" He answered, "I am alive, Caesar." But he said, "Who is he who made you alive?" And the boy, uplifted by the confidence of faith, said, "Christ Jesus, the king of the ages." The emperor asked in dismay, "Is he to be king of the ages and destroy all kingdoms?" Patroclus said to him, "Yes, he destroys all kingdoms under heaven, and he alone shall remain in all eternity, and there will be no kingdom which escapes him." And he struck his face and cried out, "Patroclus, are you also fighting for that king?" He answered, "Yes, my lord and Caesar, for he has raised me from the dead."

And Barsabas Justus the flat-footed

and Urion the Cappadocian and Festus of Galatia, the chief men of Nero, said, "And we, too, fight for him, the king of the ages." After having tortured those men whom he used to love he imprisoned them and ordered that the soldiers of the great king be sought, and he issued an edict that all Christians and soldiers of Christ that were found should be executed.

3 And among the many Paul also was brought in fetters. Those who were imprisoned with him looked at him, so that the emperor observed that he was the leader of the soldiers. And he said to him, "Man of the great king, now my prisoner, what induced you to come secretly into the Roman empire and to enlist soldiers in my territory?" But Paul, filled with the Holy Spirit, said in the presence of all, "Caesar, we enlist soldiers not only in your territory but in all lands of the earth. For thus we are commanded to exclude none who wishes to fight for my king. If it seems good to you, serve him, for neither riches nor the splendors of this life will save you; but if you become his subject and beseech him you shall be saved. For in one day he will destroy the world."

Having heard this Nero commanded all the prisoners to be burned with fire, but Paul to be beheaded according to the law of the Romans. But Paul was not silent and communicated the word to Longus the prefect and Cestus the centurion. And Nero, being instigated by the evil one, raged in Rome and had many Christians executed without trial, so that the Romans stood before the palace and cried, "It is enough, Caesar; these people are ours. You destroy the strength of the Romans." Being thus convinced, he desisted and commanded that no Christian was to be touched till his case had been investigated.

4 After the issuing of the edict Paul was brought before him, and he insisted that he should be executed. And Paul said, "Caesar, I live not merely for a short time for my king; and if you have me executed I shall do the following: I will rise again and appear to you, for I shall not be dead but alive to my king, Christ Jesus, who shall come to judge the earth."

And Longus and Cestus said to Paul, "Whence have you this king that you believe in him without changing your mind even at point of death?" And Paul answered and said, "You men, who are now ignorant and in error, change your mind and be saved from the fire which comes over the whole earth. For we fight not, as, you suppose, for a king who is from the earth but for one who is from heaven: he is the living God who comes as judge because of the lawless deeds which take place in this world. And blessed is he who will believe in him and live in eternity when he shall come with fire to purge the earth." And they besought him and said, "We entreat you, help us, and we will release you." But he answered, "I am not a deserter from Christ but a faithful soldier of the living God. If I knew that I should die I would still have done it, Longus and Cestus, but since I live to God and love myself I go to the Lord that I may come again with him in the glory of his Father." And they said to him, "How can we live after you have been beheaded?"

5 And while they were speaking Nero sent a certain Parthenius and Pheretas to see whether Paul had already been beheaded. And they found him still alive. He summoned them beside him and said, "Believe in the living God who will raise me, as well as all those who believe in him, from the dead." But they said, "We will now go to Nero but when you have died and have been raised up we will believe in your God."

But when Longus and Cestus continued to ask about salvation he said to them, "In the early dawn come quickly to my grave and you will find two men at prayer, Titus and Luke; they will give you the seal in the Lord."

And turning toward the east, Paul lifted up his hands to heaven and prayed at length; and after having conversed in Hebrew with the fathers during prayer he bent his neck, without speaking any more. When the executioner cut off his head milk splashed on the tunic of the soldier. And the soldier and all who stood near by were astonished at this sight and glorified God who had thus honored Paul. And they went away and reported everything to Caesar.

6 When he heard of it he was amazed and did not know what to say. While many philosophers and the centurion were assembled with the emperor, Paul came about the ninth hour, and in the presence of all he said, "Caesar, behold, here is Paul, the soldier of God; I am not dead but live in my God. But upon you, unhappy one, many evils and great punishment will come because you have unjustly shed the blood of the righteous not many days ago." And having spoken this Paul departed from him. When Nero had heard, he commanded that the prisoners be released, Patroclus as well as Barsabas with his friends.

7 And, as Paul had told them, Longus and Cestus, the centurion, came in fear very early to the grave of Paul. And when they drew near they found two men in prayer and Paul with them, and they became frightened when they saw the unexpected miracle, but

Titus and Luke, being afraid at the sight of Longus and Cestus, turned to run away.

But they followed and said to them, "We follow you not in order to kill you, blessed men of God, as you imagine, but in order to live, that you may do to us as Paul promised us. We have just seen him in prayer beside you." Upon hearing this Titus and Luke gave them joyfully the seal in the Lord, glorifying God and the Father of our Lord Jesus Christ to whom be glory for ever and ever. Amen.

The Acts of Thecla

The "Acts of Thecla" is a legendary account of the adventures of Thecla, a woman converted to the Christian faith through the preaching of the apostle Paul.[1] Paul himself appears on the fringes of the story, as a socially disruptive evangelist who converts women to a life of strict asceticism and sexual renunciation, much to the chagrin of their husbands and fiancés.

Thecla is portrayed here as the daughter of a woman named Theocleia and the fiancée of a prominent citizen of the city of Iconium, Thamyris. Listening to Paul preach his message of chastity, Thecla becomes enthralled and decides to become Paul's follower, renouncing her family and abandoning her fiancée. In response, Thamyris has Paul arrested. When Thecla then refuses to fulfill her social obligation of marriage, she is condemned (at her mother's own instigation) to be burned at the stake. But she is miraculously delivered from martyrdom, and joins up with Paul on his journeys.

When they arrive in Antioch, however, another series of setbacks occurs, in which Thecla is arrested for humiliating a leading aristocrat of the city while refusing his sexual advances. But once more, in a remarkable series of episodes (in which, among other things, Thecla baptizes herself in a pool of ravenous seals), God intervenes on Thecla's behalf, preserving her from death. She is eventually then reunited with her beloved apostle, Paul, who authorizes her to share fully in his ministry of teaching the word.

The Acts of Thecla was evidently in circulation near the end of the second century, along with the other narratives found in the "Acts of Paul" (see above, and below on 3 Corinthians). Thecla herself, largely based on this text and the legendary accounts that it then generated, became an enormously important saint and object of devotion, especially for women, down through the Middle Ages.[2]

---

[1]See Ehrman, *Lost Christianities*, 31–35.　[2]See Stephen J. Davies, *The Cult of Saint Thecla: A Tradition of Women's Piety in Late Antiquity* (New York: Oxford, 2001); and Cartlidge and Elliott, *Art and the Christian Apocrypha*, chap. 5.

Translation by Bart D. Ehrman, based on the Greek text in E. A. Lipsius and M. Bonnet, *Acts Apostolorum Apocrypha*; part 1 (Hildesheim: Georg Olms, 1959), with several textual alterations based on manuscript evidence.

1 As Paul was going to Iconium after his escape from Antioch, his fellow travelers were Demas and Hermogenes the bronze-smith, who were filled with hypocrisy. They kept entreating Paul earnestly, as if they loved him. But Paul was looking only at the goodness of Christ, and so did them no harm; instead, he loved them very much, giving them sweet discourses about all the Lord's sayings, involving the teaching and interpretation of the gospel, and the birth and resurrection of God's Beloved. And he was telling them word-for-word how the majestic character of Christ had been revealed to him.

2 There was a certain man named Onesiphorus who heard that Paul was coming to Iconium. He went out to meet him to give him welcome, taking along his children Simmias and Zenon and his wife Lectra. For Titus had told him what Paul looked like; for Onesiphorus had never seen him in the flesh, but only in the spirit.

3 He went out to the Royal Road that leads to Lystra and stood there waiting for him, observing those who were coming along in light of Titus's description. Then he saw Paul coming: a man short in stature, with a bald head, bowed legs, in good condition, eyebrows that met, a fairly large nose, and full of grace. At times he seemed human, at other times he looked like an angel.

4 When Paul saw Onesiphorus he smiled; and Onesiphorus said, "Greetings, servant of the Blessed God." Paul replied, "Grace be with you and your house." But Demas and Hermogenes became jealous and stirred up a great hypocrisy, so that Demas said, "Do we not also belong to the one who is Blessed? For you did not greet us like this!" Onesiphorus replied, "I did not see any fruit of righteousness in you. But if that is what you are, then come to my house as well, and be refreshed from your journey."

5 When Paul entered Onesiphorus's house there was great joy, the bending of knees in prayer, the breaking of bread, and a proclamation of the word of God concerning self-control and the resurrection, as Paul said:

"Blessed are the pure in heart, for they will see God.

Blessed are those who have kept the flesh chaste, for they will become a temple of God.

Blessed are those who are self-controlled, for God will speak to them.

Blessed are those who have renounced this world, for they will be pleasing to God.

Blessed are those who have wives as if they did not have them, for they will be the heirs of God.

Blessed are those who have the fear of God, for they will become the angels of God.

6 "Blessed are those who tremble at the sayings of God, for they will be comforted.

Blessed are those who have received the wisdom of Jesus Christ, for they will be called sons of the Highest.

Blessed are those who have kept their baptism, for they will find their rest in the Father and the Son.

Blessed are those who have a full understanding of Jesus Christ, for they will be in the light.

Blessed are those who have departed from the shell of this world because of the love of God, for they will judge angels and be blessed at the right hand of the Father.

Blessed are those who show mercy, for they will receive mercy and will not see the bitter day of judgment.

Blessed are the bodies of the virgins, for these will be pleasing to God and will not lose the reward for their chastity; for the word of the Father will be an accomplished act of salvation for them on the day of his Son, and they will receive an eternal rest."

7 While Paul was saying these things in the midst of the church in Onesiphorus's house, there was a certain virgin named Thecla, daughter of Theocleia and engaged to a man named Thamyris, who was sitting at the window of the house next door. Day and night Thecla heard what Paul said about chastity, and she did not budge from the window, but was drawn to faith with great joy. Yet when she saw many wives and virgins going in to see Paul, she also wanted to be found worthy to stand in Paul's presence to hear the word of Christ. For she had not yet seen what Paul looked like, but had only heard his word.

8 Since she would not rise up from the window, her mother sent word to Thamyris. He gladly came, as if already taking her to their wedding. Then Thamyris said to Theocleia, "Where is my Thecla?" Theocleia replied, "I have some news to tell you, Thamyra. Thecla has not gotten up from the window for three days and nights, not even to eat or drink; but she is gazing out as if watching a festival. For she has grown attached to a foreign man who is teaching various deceitful words, so that I am amazed at how the virgin's sense of modesty can be so badly disturbed.

9 "Thamyris, this man is stirring up the city of the Iconians as well as your own Thecla. For all the wives and youth are going in to see him, learning from him that, 'You must fear the one and only God and live a chaste life.' Even my daughter is bound to the window like a spider, seized by a new desire and fearful passion through his words. For she gazes at the words he speaks; and so the virgin has been captured. But you come and speak with her; for she is your fiancée."

10 So Thamyris went in, loving Thecla yet fearing that she had gone mad. He said to her, "Thecla, my future wife, why are you sitting like this? What kind of mad passion has overwhelmed you? Turn around to see your Thamyris and be ashamed." And her mother was also saying the same things, "Child, why do you sit like this looking down without answering, as if you were paralyzed?" And they were weeping bitterly: Thamyris for missing out on a wife, Thecleia for a child, and the servants for a mistress. And the household was thrown into a great confusion because of their mourning. Yet while these things were happening, Thecla did not turn aside, but continued gazing toward the words spoken by Paul.

11 Thamyris ran outside and went to the street, and began observing those who were going in to see Paul and those coming out. He saw two men having a bitter quarrel, and he said to them, "Men, tell me who you are, and who this one is who is inside with you, leading astray the youths and deceiving the virgins by telling them not to get married but to remain as they are. I promise to reward you handsomely if you tell me about him. For I am the leading citizen of the city."

12 Demas and Hermogenes said to him, "We do not know who he is. But he is depriving young men of their wives and virgins of their husbands, by saying that 'You will not be raised from the dead unless you remain chaste, abstain from polluting the flesh, and guard your chastity.' "

13 Thamyris said to them, "Men, come to my house and enjoy some refreshment with me." They went off to a lavish dinner with ample wine, a great abundance, and a splendid spread. Thamyris was plying them with drink because he loved Thecla and wanted to have her as his wife. Over dinner Thamyris said, "Men, tell me what he teaches, so I can understand it. For I am in no small agony over Thecla, because she is in love with the stranger and I am being deprived of my marriage."

14 Demas and Hermogenes said, "Make him stand trial before the governor, Castelius, for leading the crowds astray with the new teaching of the Christians. Then he will destroy him and you will have Thecla as your wife. And we will teach you that this resurrection which he claims is about to happen has already occurred in the children we have had.

15 When Thamyris heard these things from them, he was filled with jealousy and anger. Early the next morning he went off to the house of Onesiphorus with the leaders, public servants, and a large crowd carrying clubs, and he said to Paul, "You have corrupted the city of the Iconians and my own fiancée, so that she no longer desires me. Come, we are going to the governor Castelius." And the entire crowd was saying, "Take the magician away; for he has corrupted all our wives." And the crowds were persuaded.

16 When he stood before the governor's judgment seat, Thamyris called out with a loud voice, "O Proconsul, we do not know where this man comes from. But he does not allow virgins to be married. Let him tell you why he is teaching these things." But Dema and Hermogenes said to Thamyris, "Say that he is a Christian, and you will destroy him." But the governor had already decided what to do; he called Paul and asked him, "Who are you, and what are you teaching? For they are making no small accusation against you!"

17 Paul raised his voice and said, "If today I am to defend what I teach, listen to me, O Proconsul. The living God, the God of vengeance, the jealous God, the God who stands in need of nothing—this God has sent me to provide people with salvation by dragging them away from corruption and impurity and every pleasure and death, that they may no longer sin. This is also why God sent his own child, whom I proclaim, teaching that everyone must place their hope in him. For he alone has felt sympathy for this world while it was going astray, that people may no longer fall under judgment but have faith and the fear of God, along with the knowledge of holiness and the love of the truth. If, then, I am teaching what God has revealed to me, O Proconsul, how have I done anything wrong?" When the governor heard these things, he ordered Paul to be bound and taken off to prison, until he had greater leisure to listen to him more carefully.

18 But that night Thecla removed her bracelets and gave them to the gatekeeper; and when the door was opened for her, she went away to the prison. She then gave a silver mirror to the prison guard and came in to Paul. Sitting at his feet, she heard about the majestic character of God. Paul showed no sign of fear but was filled with the boldness of God. And Thecla's faith increased as she was kissing Paul's bonds.

19 But members of Thecla's own household, along with Thamyris, were looking for her, searching for her on the roads as if she were lost. Then one of the gatekeeper's fellow slaves disclosed that she had gone out at night. They examined the gatekeeper, who told them, "She has gone to the foreigner in prison." They went out just as he told them and found her, in a manner of speaking, bound together with Paul in affection. Coming out from there they roused the crowds and revealed what had happened to the governor.

20 He commanded Paul to be brought before the judgment seat. But Thecla was rolling around on the place where Paul had been teaching while sitting in the jail. The governor ordered her to be brought to the judgment seat as well. She came gladly, filled with joy. When Paul was brought forward again, the crowd began crying out more fervently, "He is a magician; away with him!" But the governor was glad to hear Paul speak of the holy deeds of Christ. When the governor had consulted his advisors, he summoned Thecla and said, "Why do you not marry Thamyris, in accordance with the law of the Iconians?" But she stood gazing at Paul. When she did not answer, her mother Theocleia cried out, "Burn the lawless one! Burn the one who will not be a bride, burn her in the midst of the theater! Then all the wives who have been taught by this one will fear!"

21 The governor was in great agony over the case. He had Paul flogged and cast out of the city; but he ordered Thecla to be burned at the stake. Immediately the governor got up and left for the theater. And the entire crowd went out, since they too had to observe the spectacle. But Thecla was like a lamb in the wilderness looking around to see its shepherd—so was she trying to catch a glimpse of Paul. Looking intently into the crowd she saw the Lord sitting there, in the appearance of Paul. And she said, "Since I am unable to endure my fate, Paul has come to watch over me." And she continued to gaze upon him. But he departed into heaven.

22 The children and virgins brought wood and hay for Thecla's burning. When she was brought into the arena naked, the governor wept, marveling at the power he saw in her. They spread out the wood, and the leaders of the people ordered her to mount the pyre. Making the shape of the cross she went up onto the wood. And they lit it. But when it roared into a great fire, the flames did not touch her. For God out of his compassion caused a great roar underground, and overhead a cloud full of water and hailstones overshadowed the place; and there was an immense cloud-burst so that many people were in danger of dying. The fire was extinguished and Thecla was saved.

23 But Paul was fasting with Onesiphorus and his wife and children in an open tomb on the path they were taking from Iconium to Daphne. After many days had passed and they were still fasting, the children said to Paul, "We are hungry." They had no money to buy bread, because Onesiphorus had left the things of the world in order to follow Paul, along with his entire household. So Paul took off his outer garment and said, "Go, child, buy plenty of bread and bring it back here." As the child was making his purchases, he saw his neighbor, Thecla. He was amazed and said to her, "Where are you going?" She replied, "I have been saved from the fire and am looking for Paul." The child said, "Come, I will take you to him. For he is mourning you, praying and fasting for six days already."

24 As she approached the tomb, Paul was kneeling and praying, "Father of Christ, do not allow the fire to touch Thecla, but be present with her, because she is yours." But she, standing behind him, cried out, "Father, maker of heaven and earth, Father of your beloved child Jesus Christ, I bless you because you have saved me from the fire, that I might see Paul." When Paul rose up he saw her and said, "O God who knows the heart, Father of our Lord Jesus Christ, I bless you because you have so quickly heard what I had to ask."

25 There was great love inside the tomb, with Paul, Onesiphorus, and everyone filled with joy. They had five loaves, vegetables, and water, and

they rejoiced in the holy deeds of Christ. Thecla said to Paul, "I will cut off my hair and follow you wherever you go." He replied, "The time is shameful and you are beautiful; another temptation may overtake you worse than the first, and you may not be able to endure but behave like a cowardly man." Thecla said, "Only give me the seal in Christ, and no temptation will touch me!" Paul replied, "Thecla, be patient and you will receive the water."

26 Paul sent Onesiphorus and his entire household back to Iconium, and took Thecla with him into Antioch. As they were entering the city, a certain leader of the Syrians named Alexander saw Thecla and was inflamed with passion for her, and began entreating Paul with money and gifts. But Paul said, "I do not know the woman you are speaking of, nor is she mine." Since Alexander was a powerful man, he began embracing her in the street. But she resisted him and was looking for Paul. Bitterly she cried out, "Do not force yourself on a stranger, do not force yourself on a slave of God. I am a leading citizen of the Iconians, and since I did not wish to marry Thamyris, I have been exiled from my city." She grabbed hold of Alexander, ripped his mantle, and pulled the crown from his head, making him an object of derision.

27 Even though Alexander loved her, he was ashamed of what had happened to him; and so he led her to the governor. When she admitted she had done these things, he condemned her to the wild beasts. But the women there were astonished and cried out before the judgment seat, "A wicked judgment! An unholy judgment!" Thecla asked the governor to be allowed to remain chaste until she had to fight the wild beasts. A certain wealthy queen named Tryphaena, whose daughter had died, took her into her care and was comforted by her.

28 For the procession of the wild beasts, they bound Thecla to a fierce lioness; and Queen Tryphaena followed her. But while Thecla was sitting on the lioness, it began licking her feet, to the amazement of the entire crowd. The charge against her was inscribed: "Sacrilegious." The women with their children were crying out again, "O God, what an unholy judgment has occurred in this city!" Tryphaena then took her home from the procession; for her daughter Falconilla had died and appeared to her in a dream, and said to her, "Mother, you should take this desolate stranger, Thecla, in my place, that she may pray for me and I be moved to the place of the righteous."

29 And so, when Tryphaena took her from the procession, she both grieved that she had to fight the wild beasts the next day and loved her deeply just as her daughter Falconilla. She said, "My second child Thecla, come, pray for my child, that she may live forever. For I saw her in a dream." And without a moment's delay, Thecla raised her voice and said, "O my God, Son of the Highest, you who are in heaven: Give her what she desires, that her daughter Falconilla may live forever." When Thecla said these things, Tryphaena began to mourn realizing that such beauty was to be cast to the wild beasts.

30 When early morning arrived, Alexander came to take her away, for he was staging the hunting games. He said, "The governor has taken his seat and the crowd is starting to cause

us problems. Hand over the one who is to fight the beasts and I will take her away." But Tryphaena put him to flight by crying out: "Our household has mourned a second time for my Falconilla; and there is no one to help us—not my child, for she has died, nor a relative, for I am a widow. O God of my child Thecla, help her!"

31 The governor then sent soldiers to bring Thecla. But Tryphaena did not leave her but led her out by the hand, saying, "I took my daughter Falconilla away to the tomb; but you, Thecla, I take away to fight the wild beasts." And Thecla wept bitterly and moaned to the Lord, saying, "O Lord God, in whom I believe, to whom I have fled for refuge, the one who saved me from the fire: Give Tryphaena her reward for showing sympathy to your servant and for keeping me chaste."

32 Then there was a disturbance, a roaring of the wild beasts and a cry of the people and of the women who were sitting together, some of them saying, "Bring in the one who has committed sacrilege," and others saying, "Let this city be destroyed for this lawless act. Destroy us all, O Proconsul. This is a bitter sight, a wicked judgment!"

33 Thecla was then taken from the hand of Tryphaena and stripped, given an undergarment to wear, and cast into the stadium. Lions and bears were cast in to attack her. And a fierce lioness ran up and lay down at her feet. The crowd of women uttered a great cry. A bear ran up to attack her; but the lioness ran up, met the bear, and ripped him apart. Then a lion owned by Alexander and trained to fight humans ran up to attack her; the lioness tangled with the lion and was destroyed along with it. The women were even more grief stricken, since the lioness that had been protecting her died.

34 Then they cast in a large number of wild beasts, while she stood, reaching out her hands and praying. When she finished her prayer she turned and saw a large vat filled with water, and said, "Now is the time for me to be cleaned!" She threw herself in, saying, "In the name of Jesus Christ, on this final day I am baptized!" When the women and the entire crowd saw what she was doing, they wailed aloud and said, "Do not throw yourself into the water!" Even the governor began to weep, because seals were about to devour such beauty. But she threw herself into the water in the name of Jesus Christ; and the seals saw a lightning bolt and floated on the water, dead. Then a cloud of fire surrounded her, so that the beasts could not attack her and no one could see her naked.

35 When yet more fearsome beasts were cast in, the women cried aloud; and some tossed leaves into the arena, others threw in nard, others cassia, and others cardamon, so that the whole place was filled with the sweet smell of perfume. All the beasts that had been cast in appeared to be overcome with sleep and did not touch her. Then Alexander told the governor, "I have some truly fearful bulls; let us bind her to them." The governor sullenly gave his consent, saying, "Do what you want." They bound her between the bulls by her feet and put red-hot irons under their genitals so that they would tear about and kill her. And they did begin to leap about, but the flame rose up around them and burned the

wooden bindings, so that she was no longer bound.

36 Tryphaena, however, passed out on the walkway beside the arena, so that her female slaves said, "The Queen Tryphaena has died." The governor stopped the festivities and the entire city was terrified. Alexander fell before the governor's feet and said, "Have mercy on me and the city, and set the prisoner free, lest the entire city be destroyed. For if Caesar hears about this, he will quickly destroy both us and the city, because his relative, the Queen Tryphaena, died on the walkway."

37 The governor called Thecla over from the midst of the wild beasts and asked, "Who are you? And what is there about you that none of the wild beasts has touched you?" She replied, "I am a slave of the living God. As to what there is about me: I have believed in God's Son, in whom he is well pleased. That is why none of the beasts has touched me. For this one alone is a boundary marker of God's salvation and a foundation of life immortal. For he is a refuge to those caught in the storm, a rest for those who are afflicted, a shelter for those who have despaired, and to put it most simply: whoever does not believe in him will not live but will die forever."

38 When the governor heard these things he ordered her clothes brought, and he said, "Put on your clothes." But she replied, "The one who clothed me when I was naked among the wild beasts will clothe me with salvation on the day of judgment." Then she took her clothes and put them on. The governor immediately sent forth an edict, saying, "I release to you Thecla, the pious slave of God." All the women cried out with a great voice and with one accord gave praise to God, "The One God! The One who saved Thecla!"—so that the entire city shook from their cry.

39 When Tryphaena was told the good news she went out and met the crowd and embraced Thecla, and said, "Now I believe that the dead are raised; now I believe that my child lives. Come inside, and I will bequeath to you all that is mine." So Thecla went in with her and rested in her house for eight days, instructing her in the word of God, so that even most of Tryphaena's female servants believed; and there was great joy in that house.

40 Thecla began to long for Paul and was trying to find him, sending around for news of him everywhere. It was reported to her that he was in Myra. She took some young men and some female servants and prepared for her journey by sewing her outer garment to make it look like a man's cloak. And so she went away to Myra and found Paul speaking the word of God; and she stood beside him. But he was astonished when he saw her and the crowd with her, wondering whether some other temptation was coming upon her. When she realized what he was thinking she said to him, "I have received my cleansing, Paul; for the one who has worked with you for the spread of the gospel has worked with me for my own cleansing."

41 Paul took her hand and led her away to the house of Hermias, and heard everything from her, so that he was greatly amazed; and those who heard were strengthened, and they prayed for Tryphaena. Thecla then rose up and told Paul, "I am going to Iconium." Paul replied, "Go and teach the word of God." And so Tryphaena sent Thecla a large amount of clothing and gold to leave for Paul's ministry to the poor.

42 And Thecla came away into Iconium. She entered Onesiphorus's house and fell on the dirt floor where Paul had sat, teaching the sayings of God. And she wept aloud, saying: "O my God and God of this house, where the light shone upon me, Christ Jesus, the Son of God, my helper in prison, my helper before governors, my helper in the fire, my helper among the wild beasts—you yourself are God. To you be the glory forever. Amen."

43 She found that Thamyris had died but that her mother was living. She called to her mother and said to her, "Theocleia, my mother, are you able to believe that the Lord in heaven lives? For if you desire riches, the Lord will give them to you through me; if you desire your child, see, here I am!" After testifying these things she went away to Seleucia and after enlightening many there with the word of God, she lay down to her glorious rest.

The Acts of Thomas

In some ways the Acts of Thomas may be the best known of the Apocryphal Acts of the Apostles, for this is the text that supports the well-known tradition that the apostle Thomas was the missionary who first brought Christianity to India. Thomas is not simply one of the apostles in this account, however. He is actually the brother of Jesus, in fact, his identical twin. (The name "Thomas" is an Aramaic word that means "twin.") Thomas and Jesus as "look alikes" serves a narrative ploy at one point in the story: when Jesus appears from heaven in a married couple's bedroom, he is mistaken for his mortal twin—creating considerable confusion, since Thomas has just been seen leaving the house (ch. 11).

The narrative recounts how Thomas is compelled to go to India, despite his reluctance: his "master" Jesus sells him as a slave to work as a carpenter for the King of India (chaps. 1–3). Both en route and while there Thomas performs miraculous deeds and proclaims a message of asceticism. For him, the gospel means renouncing this world, its wealth (see chaps. 17–24), and its pleasures—especially its sexual pleasures. Even those who are married are urged to refrain from having sexual relations, as children are a distraction on the one hand and are doomed to lives of sin on the other (see chaps. 10–16).

The cost of failing to adhere to this gospel message are extreme; in this account we find a graphic description of the torments of hell, reserved for those who did not lead lives of strict morality and renunciation, as told by a woman raised from the dead, who has seen the fates of the damned first hand (chaps. 51–58).

As with other Apocryphal Acts, it is difficult to know when the Acts of Thomas was written; most scholars have dated it to the third century and assumed that it was written in Edessa, the major city of Eastern Syria.

Translation by J. K. Elliott, *Apocryphal New Testament* (Oxford: Clarendon Press, 1993) 447–57; 468–72; used with permission.

1 At that time we apostles were all in Jerusalem—Simon called Peter, and Andrew his brother, James the son of Zebedee, and John his brother, Philip and Bartholomew, Thomas and Matthew the taxgatherer, James the son of Alphaeus and Simon the Cananaean, and Judas the son[1] of James—and we portioned out the regions of the world, in order that each one of us might go into the region that fell to him by lot, and to the nation to which the Lord had sent him. By lot India fell to Judas Thomas, also called Didymus. And he did not wish to go, saying that he was not able to travel on account of the weakness of his body. He said, "How can I, being a Hebrew, go among the Indians to proclaim the truth?" And while he was considering this and speaking, the Saviour appeared to him during the night and said to him, "Fear not, Thomas, go away to India and preach the word there, for my grace is with you." But he would not obey saying, "Wherever you wish to send me, send me, but elsewhere. For I am not going to the Indians."

2 And as he was thus speaking and considering, it happened that a merchant named Abban, who had come from India, was there, sent from King Gundaphorus, having received an order from him to buy a carpenter and bring him to him. And the Lord, having seen him walking about in the market at noon, said to him, "Do you wish to buy a carpenter?" He replied, "Yes." And the Lord said to him, "I have a slave who is a carpenter, and I wish to sell him." And having said this he showed him Thomas from a distance and agreed with him for three pounds of uncoined silver, and wrote a bill of sale saying, "I, Jesus, son of the carpenter Joseph, declare that I have sold my slave, Judas by name, to you, Abban, a merchant of Gundaphorus,

king of the Indians." When the purchase was completed the Saviour took Judas, also called Thomas, and led him to Abban, the merchant. When Abban saw him he said to him, "Is this your master?" The apostle answered and said, "Yes, he is my Lord." And he said, "I have bought you from him." And the apostle held his peace.

3 On the following morning the apostle prayed and entreated the Lord, saying, "I go wherever you wish, O Lord Jesus, your will be done."[2] And he went to the merchant Abban, carrying nothing at all with him, but only his price. For the Lord had given it to him, saying, "Let your worth also be with you along with my grace, wherever you may go." And the apostle came up with Abban, who was carrying his luggage into the boat. He too began to carry it along with him. And when they had gone on board and sat down, Abban questioned the apostle, saying, "What kind of work do you know?" And he said, "In wood, ploughs and yokes and balances and ships and boats' oars and masts and small blocks; in stone, pillars and temples and royal palaces." And Abban the merchant said to him, "We need such a workman." They began their voyage. And they had a fair wind; and they sailed cheerfully till they came to Andrapolis, a royal city.

4 And leaving the boat they went into the city. And behold, the sounds of flute-players and water-organs and trumpets echoed round them. And the apostle inquired saying, "What festival is it in this city?" And the inhabitants there answered, "The gods have brought you to keep festival in this city. For the

---

[1]Brother?   [2]Matt. 6: 10; Luke 22:42.

king has an only daughter and now he is going to give her to a husband in marriage. This festival, then, which you see to-day, is the rejoicing and public assembly for the marriage. And the king has sent forth heralds to proclaim everywhere that all are to come to the marriage, rich and poor, bond and free, strangers and citizens. But if anyone should refuse and not come to the marriage, he is answerable to the king.' And Abban, having heard this, said to the apostle, "Let us also go so that we give no offence to the king, especially as we are strangers." And he said, "Let us go." And having obtained lodgings at the inn and rested a little they went to the wedding. And the apostle, seeing them all reclining, reclined also in their midst. And they all looked at him as at a stranger, a man coming from a foreign land. And Abban the merchant, being the master, reclined in another place.

5 And whilst they were eating and drinking, the apostle tasted nothing. Those about him said to him, "Why have you come here, neither eating nor drinking?" And he answered and said to them, "For something greater than food or even drink have I come here, that I might accomplish the will of the king. For the heralds proclaim the wishes of the king, and whoever will not hear the heralds will be liable to the judgement of the king." When they had dined and drunk, and crowns and perfumes had been brought, each took perfume, and one anointed his face, another his beard, and others different parts of the body. And the apostle anointed the crown of his head, and put a little of the ointment in his nostrils, and dropped it also in his ears, and applied it also to his teeth, and carefully anointed the parts round about his heart; but the crown that was brought to him, wreathed with myrtle and other flowers, he put on his head, and he took

a branch of reed in his hand and held it. And the flute-girl, holding her flute in her hand, went round them all; and when she came to the place where the apostle was she stood over him, playing the flute over his head a long time. And that flute-girl was a Hebrew by race.

6 And as the apostle looked to the ground, one of the cupbearers stretched forth his hand and struck him. And the apostle, having raised his eyes, looked at the man who had struck him, saying, "My God will forgive you for this wrong in the world to come, but in this world he will show his wonders, and I shall soon see that hand that struck me dragged along by dogs." And having spoken he began to sing this song:

"The maiden is the daughter of the
        light,
On whom rests the majestic splen-
        dour of kings;
Delightful is the sight of her,
Resplendent with brilliant beauty
Her garments are like spring flowers
Sending forth sweet fragrance.
On the crown of her head the king
        is seated
Feeding with his own ambrosia
        those who live under him.
Truth rests upon her head,
Joy she shows forth with her feet.
Her mouth is opened, and
        becomingly.
Thirty-and-two are they who praise
        her.
Her tongue is like a door-curtain,
Drawn back for those who go in.
Made by the first creator.
Her two hands point and make se-
        cret signs predicting the
        chorus of the blessed ages,
Her fingers show the gates of the city.
Her chamber is bright,
Breathing forth scent from balsam
        and every perfume,

Sending forth a sweet smell of
    myrrh and herbs.
Within are strewn myrtle-branches
    and all manner of sweet-
    smelling flowers,
The portal is adorned with reeds.

7 She is surrounded by her grooms-
    men, seven in number,
Chosen by herself;
Her bridesmaids are seven,
Who dance before her.
Twelve in number are they who
    minister before her
And are at her bidding.
Their gaze is attentively directed at
    the bridegroom,
That they be enlightened by his
    sight,
And be for ever with him in that ev-
    erlasting joy,
And sit down at that wedding to
    which the princes assemble,
And abide at the supper, of which
    the eternal ones are deemed
    worthy,
And put on royal garments, and be
    dressed in splendid robes
That both may rejoice and exult
And praise the Father of all,
Whose majestic light they have
    received
And have been enlightened by the
    sight of their Lord,
Whose ambrosial food they received,
Of which there is no deficiency,
And drank also of his wine,
Which brings to them neither thirst
    nor desire,
And they praised and glorified with
    the living spirit
The Father of truth and the mother
    of wisdom."

8 And when he had finished this song
all who were present looked at him.
He kept silence. They also saw his form

changed, but they did not understand his
words, as he was a Hebrew and his words
were spoken in Hebrew. Only the flute-
girl understood him, being of the Hebrew
race; and leaving him she played the flute
to the others, but repeatedly looked back
and gazed at him. For she loved him as
one belonging to her race, and he was
also beautiful in appearance above all
who were there. And when the flute-girl
had finished her flute-playing, she sat
down opposite him, and looked steadily
at him. But he looked at no one at all,
neither did he pay attention to any one,
but kept his eyes only on the ground,
waiting until he could depart. And the
cupbearer that struck him came down to
the fountain to draw water. And there
happened to be a lion there which killed
him and left him lying in the place, after
tearing his limbs asunder. And dogs immediately seized his limbs, among them
a black dog, which grasped his right hand
in his mouth and brought it to the place
of the banquet.

9 When they all saw it they were
frightened and inquired who was
absent. And when it became known that
it was the hand of the cupbearer that
struck the apostle, the flute-girl broke her
flute and threw it away, and went and sat
at the feet of the apostle, saying, "This
man is either God or God's apostle. For
I heard him say in Hebrew to the cupbearer, 'I shall soon see the hand that
struck me dragged about by dogs.' This
you have now seen. For just as he said,
so also it has come to pass." Some believed her, and some not. And when the
king heard of it he came and said to the
apostle, "Rise up and go with me, and
pray for my daughter. For she is my only
child and to-day I give her away in marriage." And the apostle would not go with
him, for the Lord had not yet been revealed to him there. But the king took

him away against his will to the bridal chamber, that he might pray for them.

10 And the apostle stood and began to pray and speak thus: "My Lord and my God,[3] who accompanies his servants, guide and leader of those who believe in him, refuge and repose of the afflicted, hope of the poor and deliverer of the captives, physician of the souls laid low by disease, and saviour of every creature, who gives life to the world and strengthens the souls, you know the future and accomplish it through us; you, Lord, who reveal hidden mysteries and declare secret words; you, Lord, are the planter of the good tree and by your hand all good works are produced; you, Lord, are in all, and come through all, and exist in all your works and make yourself manifest through the working of them all; Jesus Christ, the Son of compassion and perfect Saviour; Christ, Son of the living God, the undaunted power which has overthrown the enemy; the voice, heard by the rulers, which shook all their powers; messenger, sent from on high, who went down even to Hades; who also, having opened the doors, brought out from there those who had been shut in for many ages in the treasuries of darkness, and showed them the way that leads up on high—I beseech you, Lord Jesus, offering you supplication for these young persons, that you may do to them what helps, benefits, and is profitable for them." And having laid his hands on them and said, "The Lord be with you," he left them in that place and went away.

11 The king requested the groomsmen to leave the bridal chamber. When all had left, and the doors were shut, the bridegroom raised the curtain of the bridal chamber, that he might bring the bride to himself. And he saw the Lord Jesus talking with the bride. He had the appearance of Judas Thomas, the apostle, who shortly before had blessed them and departed; and he said to him, "Did you not go out before them all? And how is it that you are here now?" And the Lord said to him, "I am not Judas Thomas, I am his brother." And the Lord sat down on the bed and ordered them to sit down on couches, and he began to speak to them.

12 "Remember, my children, what my brother said to you, and to whom he commended you; and know that if you refrain from this filthy intercourse you become temples holy and pure, being released from afflictions and troubles, known and unknown, and you will not be involved in the cares of life and of children, whose end is destruction. But if you get many children, for their sakes you become grasping and avaricious, plundering orphans and deceiving widows, and by doing this you subject yourselves to most grievous punishments. For most children become unprofitable, being possessed by demons, some openly and some secretly. For they become either lunatics or half-withered or crippled or deaf or dumb or paralytics or idiots. And though they be healthy, they will be again good-for-nothing, doing unprofitable and abominable works. For they will be detected either in adultery or in murder or in theft or in unchastity, and by all these you will be afflicted. But if you obey and preserve your souls pure to God, there will be born to you living children, untouched by these hurtful things, and you will be without care, spending an untroubled life, free from grief and care, looking forward to receive that incorruptible

---

[3]John 20: 28.

and true marriage, and you will enter as groomsmen into that bridal chamber full of immortality and light."

13 And when the young people heard this, they believed the Lord and gave themselves over to him and refrained from filthy lust, and remained thus spending the night in the place. And the Lord went away from them saying, "The grace of the Lord be with you!"[4] And when dawn came the king arrived, and having furnished the table brought it in before the bridegroom and the bride. And he found them sitting opposite each other, and he found the face of the bride uncovered, and the bridegroom was very cheerful. And the mother came in and said to the bride, "Why do you sit thus, child, and are not ashamed, but act as if you had lived for a long time with your own husband?" And her father said, "Is it because of your great love to your husband that you are unveiled?"

14 The bride answered and said, "Truly, father, I am in great love, and I pray to my Lord that the love which I have experienced this night may remain, and that I obtain that man whom I have experienced today. That I do not veil myself is because the mirror of shame has been taken away from me; I am no longer ashamed or abashed, since the work of shame and bashfulness has been removed far from me. And that I am not frightened is because alarm did not abide in me. And that I am cheerful and glad is because the day of joy has not been disturbed. And that I have set at naught this husband and these nuptials which have passed away from before my eyes is because I have been joined in a different marriage. And that I had no conjugal intercourse with a temporary husband, whose end is repentance and

bitterness of soul, is because I have been united to the true husband."

15 And when the bride was saying even more, the bridegroom answered and said, "I thank you, Lord, who have been proclaimed by the stranger and found in us; who have put corruption far from me, and have sown life in me, who have delivered me from this disease, hard to heal, hard to cure and abiding for ever, and established in me sound health; who have shown yourself to me, and have revealed to me my condition, in which I am; who have redeemed me from falling, and have led me to something better, and who have released me from things temporary, but have deemed me worthy of things immortal and everlasting; who have humbled yourself to me and my weakness, to place me beside your greatness and to unite with you; who have not kept your compassion from me, who was lost, but have shown me how to seek myself, and to know who I was and who and how I now am, that I may become again what I was; whom I did not know, but you have sought me out; of whom I did not know; but you stood by me; whom I have experienced and am not able to forget; whose love is fervent in me and of whom I cannot speak as I ought. But what I have to say about him is short and very little, and is not in proportion to his glory; but he does not find fault with me if I dare to tell him even what I know not; for it is out of love to him I say this."

16 And when the king heard these things from the bridegroom and the bride, he rent his garments and said to those standing near him, "Go out

---

[4]1 Cor. 16: 23.

quickly, and search the whole city, and seize and bring that man, the sorcerer, who has come by evil chance into this city. For I led him with my own hands into my house, and I told him to pray for my most unfortunate daughter. Whoever shall find him and bring him to me, I give him whatever he shall ask of me." They departed, therefore, and went round seeking him, and did not find him; for he had set sail. They also went into the inn where he had stayed, and found there the flute-girl weeping and in distress, because he had not taken her with him. And when they told her what had taken place with the young people, she rejoiced greatly upon hearing it, setting aside her grief, and said, "Now I also have found repose here!" And she arose and went to them, and was with them a long time, until they had instructed the king also. And many of the brethren also met there, until the rumour had spread that the apostle had gone to the cities of India, and was teaching there. And they went away and joined him.

17 When the apostle came into the cities of India with Abban the merchant, Abban went away to greet King Gundaphorus and told him about the carpenter whom he had brought with him. And the king was glad and ordered him to appear before him. When he had come in the king said to him, "What trade do you know?" The apostle said to him, "That of the carpenter and the housebuilder." The king said to him, "What work in wood do you know and what in stone?" The apostle said, "In wood, ploughs, yokes, balances, pulleys, and ships and oars and masts; in stone, monuments, temples, and royal palaces." And the king said, "Will you build me a palace?" And he answered, "Yes, I shall build it and finish it; for because of this

I have come, to build and to do carpenter's work."

18 And the king, having accepted him, took him out of the gates of the city, and on the way began to discuss with him the building of the palace, and how the foundations should be laid, till they came to the place where the work was to be carried out. And he said, "Here is where I wish the building to be!" And the apostle said, "Yes, this place is suitable for the building." For the place was wooded and there was water there. And the king said, "Begin at once!" And he answered, "I cannot commence now." The king said, "When can you?" He said, "I shall begin in November and finish in April." And the king was surprised, and said, "Every building is built in the summer, but can you build and finish a palace in the winter?" And the apostle replied "Thus it must be done; it is impossible any other way." And the king said, "If you have resolved upon this, draw a plan for me how the work is to be done, since I shall come here after some time." And the apostle took a reed, measured the place, and marked it out: the doors to be set towards the rising of the sun, to face the light; the windows toward the west, to the winds; the bakehouse he made toward the south; and the water-pipes necessary for the supply toward the north. When the king saw this, he said to the apostle, "You are truly a craftsman, and it is fitting that you should serve kings." And having left a lot of money with him, he went away.

19 And at the appointed times the king sent coined silver and the necessities for his and the workmen's living. And the apostle took everything and divided it, going about in the cities and surrounding villages, distributing to the poor and needy, and bestowing alms, and gave them relief, saying, "The king knows that he will receive royal recompense, but the poor must be refreshed, as their condition requires it." After this the king sent a messenger to the apostle, having written the following: "Let me know what you have done or what I should send to you or what you need." The apostle sent word to him saying, "The palace is built, and only the roof remains to be done." Upon hearing this the king sent him again gold and un-coined silver and wrote, "If the palace is built, let it be roofed." And the apostle said to the Lord, "I thank you, Lord, in every respect, that you died for a short time, that I may live in you for ever, and that you have sold me, to deliver many through me." And he did not cease to teach and refresh the afflicted, saying, "The Lord has dispensed this to you and he gives to each his food. For he is the support of the orphans and the nourisher of the widows, and rest and repose to all who are afflicted."

20 When the king came to the city he inquired of his friends concerning the palace which Judas, surnamed Thomas, had built for him. And they said to him, "He has neither built a palace, nor did he do anything of that which he promised to do, but he goes about in the cities and villages, and if he has anything he gives it to the poor, and teaches a new God, heals the sick, drives out demons, and performs many miracles. And we believe that he is a magician. But his acts of compassion and the cures done by him as a free gift, still more his simplicity and gentleness and fidelity, show that he is a just man, or an apostle of the new God, whom he preaches. For he continually fasts and prays and eats only bread with salt, and

his drink is water, and he wears one coat, whether in warm weather or in cold, and he takes nothing from anyone but gives to others what he has." Upon hearing this the king hit his face with his hands, shaking his head for a long time.

21 And he sent for the merchant who had brought him, and for the apostle, and said to him, "Have you built the palace?" And he said, "Yes, I have built it." The king said, "When shall we go to inspect it?" And he answered and said, "Now you cannot see it, but you shall see it when you depart this life." And the king was very angry and ordered both the merchant and Judas Thomas to be bound and cast into prison, until he should find out to whom the property of the king had been given, and so destroy him and the merchant. And the apostle went to prison rejoicing and said to the merchant, "Fear nothing, believe only in the God who is preached by me, and you shall be freed from this world, and obtain life in the world to come."

And the king considered by what death he should kill them. He decided to flog them and burn them with fire. On that very night Gad, the king's brother, fell ill; and through the grief and disappointment which the king had suffered he was grievously depressed. And having sent for the king he said to him, "Brother and king, I commend to you my house and my children. For I have been grieved on account of the insult that has befallen you, and lo, I am dying, and if you do not proceed against the life of that magician you will give my soul no rest in Hades." And the king said to his brother, "I considered the whole night by what death I should kill him, and I have decided to flog him and burn him with fire, together with the merchant who brought him."

22 While they were talking, the soul of Gad, his brother, departed, and the king mourned for Gad exceedingly, because he loved him, and ordered him to be prepared for burial in a royal and costly robe. While this was going on, angels received the soul of Gad, the king's brother, and took it up into heaven, showing him the places and mansions there, asking him, "In what place do you wish to dwell?" And when they came near the edifice of the apostle Thomas, which he had erected for the king, Gad, upon beholding it, said to the angels, "I entreat you, my lords, let me dwell in one of these lower chambers." But they said to him, "In this building you cannot dwell." And he said, "Why not?" They answered, "This palace is the one which that Christian has built for your brother." But he said, "I entreat you, my lords, allow me to go to my brother to buy this palace from him. For my brother does not know what it is like, and he will sell it to me."

23 And the angels let the soul of Gad go. And as they were putting on him the burial robe his soul came into him. And he said to those standing round him, "Call my brother to me, that I may beg of him a request." Straightway they sent the good news to their king, saying, "Your brother has become alive again!" And the king arose and with a great multitude went to his brother. And coming in he went to the bed as if stupefied, unable to speak to him. And his brother said, "I know and I am convinced, brother, that if anyone had asked of you the half of your kingdom, you would give it for my sake. Wherefore I entreat you to grant one favour, which I beg of you to do: that you sell to me that which I ask from you." And the king answered and said, "And what is it that you wish

me to sell to you?" And he said, "Assure me by an oath that you will grant it to me." And the king swore to him, "Whatever of my possession you ask, I will give you." And he said to him, "Sell me the palace which you have in heaven." And the king said, "A palace in heaven— where does this come to me from?" And he said, "It is the one that Christian built for you, the man who is now in prison, whom the merchant brought, having bought him from a certain Jesus. I mean that Hebrew slave whom you wished to punish, having suffered some deception from him, on account of whom I also was grieved and died, and now have come alive again."

24 Then the king heard and understood his words about the eternal benefits that were conferred upon him and destined for him, and said, "That palace I cannot sell you, but I pray to be permitted to enter into it and to dwell there, being deemed worthy to belong to its inhabitants. And if you really wish to buy such a palace, behold, the man is alive, and will build you a better one than that." And immediately he sent and brought the apostle out of prison, and the merchant who had been shut up along with him, saying, "I entreat you; as a man entreating the servant of God; pray for me, and ask him, whose servant you are, to pardon me and to overlook what I have done to you or intended to do, and that I may become worthy to be an inhabitant of that house for which indeed I have done nothing, but which you, labouring alone, have built for me with the help of the grace of your God, and that I may also become a servant and serve this God, whom you preach." His brother also fell down before the apostle and said, "I entreat you and supplicate before your God that I may become worthy of this service and become partaker of that which was shown to me by his angels." . . .

51 Now there was a certain young man, who had committed a nefarious deed. He came and partook of the eucharist. And his two hands withered, so that he could no longer put them to his mouth. When those present saw him, they told the apostle what had happened. And the apostle called him and said, "Tell me, my son, and be not afraid of what you have done before you came here. For the eucharist of the Lord has convicted you. For this gift, by entering many, brings healing, especially to those who come in faith and love; but you it has withered away, and what has happened has happened not without some justification." And the young man convicted by the eucharist of the Lord came up, fell at the apostle's feet, and besought him and said, "An evil deed has been done by me, whilst I thought to do something good. I loved a woman who lived in an inn outside the city, and she loved me also. And when I heard about you, believing that you proclaim the living God, I came and received the seal from you along with the others. And you said, 'Whoever shall indulge in impure intercourse, especially in adultery, shall not have life with the God whom I preach.' As I loved her very much, I entreated her and tried to persuade her to live with me in chaste and pure conduct, as you teach. And she would not. Since she would not, I took a sword and killed her. For I could not see her commit adultery with another."

52 When the apostle heard this he said, "O insane intercourse, how you lead to shamelessness! O unrestrained lust, how have you excited this man to do this! O work of the serpent, how you rage in your own!" And the apostle ordered some water to be brought in a dish. And when the water had been brought he said, "Come, waters from the living waters; everlasting, sent to us from the everlasting; rest, sent to us from the one who gives rest; power of salvation, proceeding from that power which overcomes all and subjects it to its will—come and dwell in these waters, that the gift of the Holy Spirit may be completely fulfilled in them!" And to the young man he said, "Go, wash your hands in these waters." And when he had washed them they were restored. And the apostle said to him, "Do you believe in our Lord Jesus Christ, that he can do all things?" And he said, "Though I am the least, yet I believe. But I did this in the hope of doing something good. For I entreated her, as I told you already, but she would not be persuaded by me to keep herself chaste."

53 And the apostle said to him, "Come, let us go to the inn where you committed the deed, and let us see what happened." And the young man went before the apostle on the road. When they had come to the inn they found her lying there. And when the apostle saw her he was sad, for she was a beautiful girl. And he ordered her to be brought into the middle of the inn. And putting her on a couch they carried it out and set it in the midst of the courtyard of the inn. And the apostle laid his hand on her and began to say, "Jesus, who appear to us at all times—for this is your will, that we should always seek you, and you have given us the right to ask and to receive, and have not only permitted us this, but have also taught us how to pray— who are not seen by us with the bodily eyes, but who are never hidden from those of our soul, and who are hidden in form, but manifested to us by your works; by your many deeds we have recognized you as much as we are able, and you have given us your gifts without measure saying, 'Ask, and it shall be given you; seek, and you shall find; knock, and it shall be opened unto you.'[5] We pray, therefore, being afraid of our sins. And we ask you not for riches or gold or silver or possessions or any of those things that come from earth and go into the earth again; but we beg of you and entreat that in your holy name you raise this woman lying here by your power, to your glory and to an awakening of faith in those who stand by."

54 And he said to the young man, after sealing him, "Go and take her hand and say to her, 'With iron I killed you with my hands, and with my hands I raise you because of faith in Jesus.'" And the young man went and stood by her, saying, "I have believed in you, O Christ Jesus." And looking upon Judas Thomas the apostle, he said to him, "Pray for me, that my Lord, upon whom I call, may come to my help." And laying his hand on her hand he said, "Come, Lord Jesus Christ, give her life and me the reality of your faith." And he drew her by the hand, and she sprang up and sat looking at the great multitude standing around. And she also saw the apostle standing opposite her, and leaving her couch she sprang up and fell at his feet and took hold of his garments, saying, "I pray, Lord, where is your companion who has not left me to remain in that fearful and grievous place, but has given me up to you, saying, 'Take this one, that she may be made perfect, and thereafter be brought into her own place.'?"

55 And the apostle said to her, "Tell us where you have been." And she answered, "Do you, who were with me, to whom also I was entrusted, wish to hear?" And she commenced thus:

"An ugly-looking man, entirely black, received me; and his clothing was exceedingly filthy. And he took me to a place where there were many chasms, and a great stench and most hateful vapour were given forth thence. And he made me look into each chasm, and in the first I saw blazing fire, and fiery wheels running, and souls were hung upon these wheels, dashing against each other. And there was crying and great lamentation and no Saviour was there. And that man said to me, 'These souls are akin to you, and in the days of reckoning they were delivered to punishment and destruction. And then others are brought in their stead; in like manner all these are again succeeded by others. These are they who perverted the intercourse of man and wife.' And again I looked down, and saw infants heaped upon each other, struggling and lying upon each other. And he said to me, 'These are their children, and for this they are placed here for a testimony against them.'

56 "And he brought me to another chasm, and as I looked into it I saw mud and worms spouting forth, and souls wallowing there; and I heard a great gnashing of teeth come from them. And that man said to me, 'These are the souls of women who left their husbands and committed adultery with others, and they have been brought to this torment.' And he showed me another chasm, and looking into it I saw souls hung up, some by the tongue, some by the hair, some by the hands, others by the feet, head downward, and reeking with smoke and sulphur. Concerning these the man who accompanied me said the following: 'The souls hung up by the tongue are slander-

---

[5]Matt 7:7.

ers and such as have spoken false and disgraceful words and are not ashamed. Those hung up by their hair are the shameless, who are not ashamed at all and go about with uncovered heads in the world. Those hung up by the hands are they who took that which did not belong to them and have stolen, and who never gave anything to the poor, nor helped the afflicted; but they did so because they wished to get everything, and cared neither for law nor right. And these hung up by the feet are those who lightly and eagerly walked in wicked ways and disorderly paths, not visiting the sick nor escorting those who depart this life. On this account each soul receives what it has done.'

57 "And again he led me forth and showed me a very dark cavern, exhaling a very bad stench. Many souls were peeping out thence, wishing to get some share of the air. And their keepers would not let them look out. And my companion said to me, 'This is the prison of those souls which you saw. For when they have fully received their punishment for that which each has done, others succeed them. Some are fully consumed, others are given up to other punishments.' And the keepers of the souls in the dark cavern said to the man that had charge of me, 'Give her to us, that we may bring her to the others till the time comes when she is handed over to punishment.' But he said to them, 'I will not give her to you, because I am afraid of him who delivered her to me. For I was not told to leave her here; I shall take her back with me, till I get an injunction about her.' And he took me and brought me to another place, where there were men who were cruelly tortured. He who is like you took me and gave me up to you, saying to you, 'Take her, for she is one of the sheep which have wan-

dered away.' And received by you, I now stand before you; I beg, therefore, and supplicate you that I may not come to those places of punishment which I have seen."

58 And the apostle said, "You have heard what this woman has recounted. And these are not the only punishments, but there are others worse than these. And you too, unless you turn to the God whom I preach, and abstain from your former works and from the deeds which you did in ignorance, shall find your end in these punishments. Believe, therefore, in Christ Jesus, and he will forgive you the former sins and will cleanse you from all your bodily desires that remain on the earth, and will heal you from the faults that follow after you and go along with you and are found before you. Let every one of you put off the old man and put on the new,[6] and leave your former course of conduct and behaviour. Those who steal, let them steal no more, but let them live, labouring and working.[7] The adulterers are no more to commit adultery, lest they give themselves up to everlasting punishment. For with God adultery is an evil exceedingly wicked above all other evils. Put away also covetousness and lying and drunkenness and slandering, and do not return evil for evil![8] For all these are alien and strange to the God whom I preach. But walk rather in faith and meekness and holiness and hope, in which God rejoices, that you may become his kinsmen, expecting from him those gifts which only a few receive."

59 The whole people therefore believed and presented obedient

---

[6]Cf. Col. 3: 9.   [7]Cf. Eph. 4: 28.   [8]Cf. I Pet. 3: 9.

souls to the living God and Christ Jesus, rejoicing in the blessed works of the Most High and in his holy service. And they brought money for the service of the widows. For he had them gathered together in the cities, and he sent to all of them by his deacons what was necessary, both clothing as well as food. He himself did not cease to preach and to speak to them and to show that this Jesus is the Messiah of whom the Scriptures have spoken that he should be crucified and be raised after three days from the dead. He also showed to them and explained, beginning from the prophets, what was said concerning the Messiah, that it was necessary for him to come, and that everything had to be accomplished which had been prophesied of him. And the fame of him spread over all the cities and villages, and all who had sick persons or such as were troubled by unclean spirits brought them to him; and some they laid on the road by which he was to pass, and he healed all by the power of the Lord. And those who were healed by him said with one accord and one voice, "Glory to you, Jesus, who in like manner has given healing to all through your servant and apostle Thomas! And being in good health and rejoicing, we pray that we may become members of your flock and be counted among your sheep. Receive us, therefore, O Lord, and consider not our trespasses and our former transgressions, which we did while we were in ignorance!"

The Acts of Peter

The Acts of Peter provides a number of entertaining accounts of the missionary adventures of the leader of the apostles, including several of his sermons and a number of his miracles. Much of the narrative concerns a series of contests between Peter and his nemesis, the Satanically inspired sorcerer Simon Magus, who presents himself as the true representative of God on earth. The same Simon is elsewhere portrayed as the first Gnostic and arch-heretic (see, e.g., the Epistle of the Apostles, above), although here there is less attention paid to his theology than to his claims of divine superiority.[1] These claims are completely refuted by Peter, who through the power of God is able to make dogs and newborn infants speak and to restore smoked tunas and dead people back to life.

The contests reach a climax when Simon uses his powers to fly like a bird over the temples and hills of Rome; Peter responds by calling upon God to smite him in mid-air. When Simon crashes to the ground, the crowds, convinced of Peter's superior power, rush to the scene to stone Simon and leave him for dead (chaps. 32–33).

The account ends with Peter's arrest and execution, in which, at his own request, he is crucified upside down; hanging on the cross, he explains to those nearby the symbolic reasons for his request, utters a long prayer, and then dies—only to appear to one of his followers afterwards to upbraid him for providing him with such a lavish burial (chaps. 36–40).

In many ways, the bulk of the Acts of Peter—that is, the miracle contests between Peter and Simon Magus—reflects the traditions that also lie behind the "Pseudo-Clementine" literature, including the Homilies of Clement (see below). The Acts of Peter itself appears to have been in circulation some time before the end of the second century.

---

[1]For the importance of Simon Magus as an opponent of proto-orthodox heresy-hunters, see Ehrman, *Lost Christianities*, 165–67.

Translation by J. K. Elliott, *Apocryphal New Testament* (Oxford: Clarendon Press, 1993) 401–10; 416–26; used with permission.

4 ... After a few days there was a great commotion in the congregation, for some said that they had seen things done by a man named Simon, who was at Aricia. They also added, "He claims to be the great power of God, doing nothing without God. Is he then Christ? We, however, believe in him whom Paul has preached to us. For through him we saw the dead raised and some healed from various diseases. This power seeks conflicts, we know. For it is no small disturbance that has come upon us. Perhaps he has already come to Rome. For yesterday he was invited with great acclamation to do so, being told, 'You are God in Italy, you are the savior of the Romans; hasten to Rome as quickly as possible.' And Simon addressed the people and said with a shrill voice, 'On the following day about the seventh hour you shall see me fly over the gate of the city in the same form in which I now speak to you.' Wherefore, brethren, if you agree, let us go and diligently await the end of the matter." And they all went out and came to the gate. About the seventh hour there suddenly appeared afar off a dust-cloud in the sky, looking like smoke shining with a glare of fire. And when it reached the gate it suddenly disappeared. Then he appeared standing in the midst of the people. They all worshipped him and knew that it was he whom they had seen the day before. And the brethren were exceedingly disturbed, especially as Paul was not at Rome, nor Timothy and Barnabas, whom Paul had sent to Macedonia, nor anyone who could strengthen us (*sic*) in the faith, especially the neophytes. As Simon's authority grew more and more, some of those among whom he worked in their daily conversations called Paul a sorcerer and a deceiver and all of the great multitude which had been confirmed in the faith were led astray, excepting the pres-

byter Narcissus, and two women in the hospice of the Bithynians, and four others who could not leave their house; and day and night they entreated the Lord either that Paul might return as soon as possible or that someone else might come to care for his servants, whom the devil by his wickedness had perverted.

5 While they were grieving and fasting God was already preparing Peter at Jerusalem for the future. After the twelve years had passed, according to the direction of the Lord to Peter, Christ showed to him the following vision, saying, "Peter, Simon, whom you expelled from Judaea after having exposed him as a magician, has forestalled you at Rome. And in short, all who believed in me he has perverted by the cunning and power of Satan, whose agent he proves to be. But do not delay. Go tomorrow to Caesarea, and there you will find a ship ready to sail to Italy. And within a few days I will show you my grace which is boundless." Instructed by this vision, Peter did not delay to mention it to the brethren and said, "I must go up to Rome to subdue the enemy and opponent of the Lord and of our brethren." And he went down to Caesarea and at once boarded the ship, which was ready to sail, without having obtained for himself any provisions. But the steersman, named Theon, looked at Peter and said, "What we have belongs to you. For what grace is it for us in receiving a man like ourselves in difficult circumstances, without sharing with him what we have? Let us have a safe journey." Peter thanked him for his offer. And he fasted in the ship, being dejected, and yet again comforted because God regarded him as a servant worthy of his service. A few days later the captain got up at meal time and asked Peter to eat with him, saying to him, "Whoever you are, I hardly know you. You are either a

God or a man. But as far as I can see, I think that you are a servant of God. As I was steering my ship in the middle of the night I fell asleep. It seemed to me as if a human voice from heaven said to me, "Theon, Theon!" Twice it called me by name and said to me, 'Amongst all the passengers treat Peter in the most honorable way. For, with his help, you and the rest will escape safe from an unexpected incident.' " Peter, however, thinking that God wished to show his providence to all those who were in the ship, began at once to speak to Theon of the great deeds of God, and how the Lord had chosen him among the apostles and for what cause he was sailing to Italy. Daily he spoke to him the word of God. After they had become better acquainted Peter found out that Theon was one with him in the faith and a worthy servant. When the ship was detained by the calm of the Adriatic Sea, Theon remarked on the calm to Peter and said, "If you think me worthy to be baptized with the sign of the Lord, you have the chance now." All the others in the ship were in a drunken stupor. Peter let himself down by a rope and baptized Theon in the name of the Father and of the Son and of the Holy Spirit. He came up out of the water rejoicing with great joy. Peter also had become more cheerful because God had deemed Theon worthy of his name. And it happened that in the same place where Theon was baptized, a young man, radiant in splendor, appeared and said to them, "Peace be with you." And both Peter and Theon immediately went up and entered the cabin; and Peter took bread and gave thanks to the Lord, who had deemed him worthy of his holy service, and because a young man had appeared to them saying, "Peace be with you." Peter said, "Most excellent and the only Holy One, for you appeared to us, O God Jesus Christ. In your name I have

spoken, and he was signed with your holy sign. Therefore also I give to him, in your name, your eucharist, that he may for ever be your servant, perfect and without blemish." When they were eating and rejoicing in the Lord, suddenly a moderate wind, not a violent one, arose at the prow of the ship and lasted six days and six nights till they came to Puteoli.

6 Having landed at Puteoli, Theon left the ship and went to the inn where he usually stayed, to make preparations for the reception of Peter. The innkeeper's name was Ariston, a Godfearing man, and to him he went for the sake of the Name. And when he had come to the inn and found Ariston, Theon said to him, "God, who counted you worthy to serve him, has also made known to me his grace through his holy servant Peter, who has just arrived with me from Judaea, being bidden by our Lord to go to Italy." When Ariston heard this, he fell upon Theon's neck, embraced him and asked him to bring him to the ship and show Peter to him. For Ariston said, "Since Paul has gone to Spain there was not one of the brethren who could strengthen me. Besides, a certain Jew named Simon has invaded the city. By means of his magical sayings and his wickedness he has completely perverted the entire fraternity, so that I have fled from Rome hoping for the arrival of Peter. For Paul had spoken of him, and I saw many things in a vision. Now I believe in my Lord, that he will again establish his ministry, that all deception be extinguished from his servants. For our Lord Jesus Christ is faithful, and he can renew our thoughts." When Theon heard this from the weeping Ariston, his confidence was restored, and he was even more strengthened in his faith, knowing that he believed in the living God. When they came to the ship, Peter saw them

and, filled with the Spirit, he smiled, so that Ariston fell upon his face to the feet of Peter and said, "Brother and Lord, who makes known the sacred mysteries and teaches the right way, which is in the Lord Jesus Christ, our God, through you he has shown us his coming. All whom Paul entrusted to us we have lost through the power of Satan. But now I trust in the Lord, who sent his messenger and told you to hasten to us, that he has deemed us worthy to see his great and wonderful deeds done by your hands. I therefore beg you, come quickly to the city. For I left the brethren who had stumbled, whom I saw fall into the snares of the devil, and fled here saying to them, 'Brethren, stand firm in the faith; for it is to be that within the next two months the mercy of our Lord will bring you his servant.' I saw a vision of Paul speaking to me and saying, 'Ariston, flee from the city.' Having heard this, I believed without wavering, departed from the city in the Lord, and though the flesh which I bear is weak, yet I came here, stood daily by the shore, and asked the sailors, 'Has Peter come with you?' And now that the grace of the Lord abounds, I beseech you to go up to Rome without delay, lest the teaching of the wicked man increases still more." When Ariston had spoken amidst tears Peter gave him his hand and lifted him up from the ground, and said with tears and sighs, "He who tempts the world by his angels forestalled us; but he who has the power to deliver his servants from all temptation will destroy his deceits and put them under the feet of those who believe in Christ, whom we preach." And when they entered by the gate Theon entreated Peter and said, "During the long sea voyage you never refreshed yourself on the ship, and now will you go from the ship on such a rough road? No, stay, refresh yourself and then go. From here to Rome the road is rocky, and

I fear you might hurt yourself with the shaking." But Peter answered and said to them, "But what would have happened if about my neck and that of the enemy of the Lord a millstone were hanged (as my Lord said to us, if any one should offend one of the brethren[2]), and we be drowned in the depths of the sea? Not only would it be a millstone, but what is worse, I the opponent of this persecutor of his servants would die far away from those who have believed in the Lord Jesus Christ." In no way could Theon persuade him to remain a day longer. Whereupon Theon gave everything that was in the ship to be sold at a fair price, and followed Peter to Rome, and accompanied Ariston to the house of the presbyter Narcissus.

7   Soon it became known among the scattered brethren of the city that Peter had come to Rome on account of Simon, to prove that he was a seducer and persecutor of the good. And the whole multitude came together to see the apostle of the Lord, confirming the congregation in Christ. When they gathered on the first day of the week to meet Peter he began to speak with a loud voice, "You people who are here, hoping in Christ, you who suffered a brief temptation, learn why God sent his Son into the world, or why he begot him by the virgin Mary, if it were not to dispense some mercy or means of salvation. For he meant to annul every offence and every ignorance and every activity of the devil, his instigations and powers, by means of which he once had the upper hand, before our God shone forth in the world. Since with their many and manifold weaknesses they fell to death by their ignorance, Almighty God had compassion

---

[2]Matt 18:6.

and sent his Son into the world, and I was with him. And I walked on the water and survive as a witness; I confess I was there when he was at work in the world performing signs and wonders. Dearest brethren, I denied our Lord Jesus Christ, not once, but thrice; for those who ensnared me were wicked gods, just as the prophet of the Lord said. But the Lord did not lay it to my charge; he turned to me and had mercy on the weakness of my flesh, so that I wept bitterly; and I mourned for my little faith, having been deceived by the devil, and disobeyed the word of my Lord. And now I tell you, men and brethren, who are convened in the name of Jesus Christ, Satan the deceiver sends his arrows upon you too, to make you leave the way. But do not be disloyal, brethren, nor fail in your mind, but strengthen yourselves, stand fast, and doubt not. For if Satan has subverted me, whom the Lord esteemed so highly, so that I denied the light of my hope, causing me to fall and persuading me to flee as if I believed in a man, what do you think will happen to you, who have just become converted? Do you imagine that he will not subvert you to make you enemies of the Kingdom of God and to bring you by the worst error into perdition? For every one whom he deprives of the hope in our Lord Jesus Christ is a child of perdition for all eternity. Repent, therefore, brethren whom the Lord has chosen, and be firmly established in the Almighty Lord, the Father of our Lord Jesus Christ, whom no one has ever seen nor can see except he who believes in him. Understand whence the temptation has come for you. For I came not only for the sake of convincing you with words that he whom I preach is the Christ, but by reason of miraculous deeds and powers I exhort you by faith in Jesus Christ. Let no one wait for another savior besides him who was despised and whom

the Jews reviled, this crucified Nazarene, who died and rose again on the third day."

8 The brethren repented and asked Peter to overcome Simon's claim that he was the power of God. Simon was staying at the house of the senator Marcellus whom he had won over by his magic. "Believe us, brother Peter," they said, "none among humans was so wise as this Marcellus. All the widows who hoped in Christ took their refuge in him; all the orphans were fed by him. Will you know more, brother? All the poor called Marcellus their patron; his house was called the house of the pilgrims and poor. To him the emperor said, 'I will give you no office, lest you rob the provinces to benefit the Christians.' To this Marcellus replied, 'Yet everything that is mine is yours.' Caesar said to him, 'It would be mine if you kept it for me, but now it is not mine, since you give it to whom you please, and who knows to what low people?' This, brother Peter, we know and report to you, now that the great benevolence of the man has been turned into blasphemy. For had he not been changed we certainly should not have left the holy faith in God our Lord. Now this Marcellus is enraged and repents of his good deeds and says, 'So much wealth have I spent for such a long time in the foolish belief that I spent it for the knowledge of God.' In his rage he even goes so far that when a pilgrim comes to the door of his house he beats him with a stick or has him driven off and says, 'If only I had not spent so much money on those imposters!' And he utters many more blasphemies. But if you have something of the compassion of our Lord in you and the goodness of his commandments, help this man in his error for he has shown goodness to a great many of God's servants." When Peter learned this he was very greatly moved and said, "Oh, the manifold arts and temptations of the devil! Oh, the cunnings and devices of the evil one, treasuring up to himself the great fire in the day of wrath, destruction of simple people, a ravening wolf devouring and destroying eternal life! You enticed the first man to evil lust and by your former wickedness and bodily bond bound him to you. You are the fruit of bitterness, which is entirely bitter, inducing various desires. You have forced my fellow disciple and co-apostle Judas to act wickedly and betray our Lord Jesus Christ; you must be punished. You hardened the heart of Herod and kindled Pharaoh and made him fight against Moses, the holy servant of God; you emboldened Caiaphas to deliver our Lord Jesus Christ to the cruel multitude; and now you are still firing your poisonous arrows at innocent souls. You wicked foe of all, you shall be cursed from the church of the Son of the holy, almighty God and extinguished like a firebrand thrown from the fireplace by the servants of our Lord Jesus Christ. Let your blackness turn against you and against your sons, the wicked seed; let your wickedness turn against you, also your threats, and let your temptations turn against you and your angels, you beginning of iniquity, abyss of darkness! Let the darkness which you have be with you and your vessels which you own. Depart, therefore, from those who shall believe in God; depart from the servants of Christ and from those who will serve in his army. Keep for yourself your garments of darkness; without cause you knock at strange doors which belong not to you but to Christ Jesus who keeps them. For you, ravening wolf, will carry off the sheep which do not belong to you but to Christ Jesus, who keeps them with the greatest diligence."

9 When Peter had spoken with great sorrow of soul many more believers were added to the congregation. And the brethren entreated Peter to fight with Simon and not allow him to disturb the people any longer. And without delay Peter left the meeting and went to the house of Marcellus where Simon was staying. And a great multitude followed him. When he came to the door he summoned the keeper and said to him, "Go and tell Simon, 'Peter, on whose account you left Judaea, awaits you at the door!' " The door-keeper answered and said to Peter, "I do not know, sir, if you are Peter. But I have instructions. Knowing that you arrived yesterday in the city, he said to me, 'Whether he comes in the day or at night or at whatever hour, say that I am not at home.' " But Peter said to the young man, "You were right to tell me this, although you have been forced by him not to tell me." And Peter, turning around to the people, who followed him, said, "You are about to see a great and wonderful sign." And Peter saw a big dog, tied by a big chain, and he went and loosened him. The dog, being loosed, became endowed with a human voice and said to Peter, "What will you have me do, servant of the ineffable living God?" to which Peter said, "Go inside and tell Simon in the presence of the people, 'Peter sends word to you to come outside. For on your account I have come to Rome, you wicked man and destroyer of simple souls.' " And the dog ran away at once and went into the midst of the people who were with Simon, and lifting his front legs he said with a very loud voice, "Simon, Peter, who stands at the door, bids you to come outside in public; for he says 'On your account have I come to Rome, you wicked man and destroyer of simple souls.' " When Simon heard this and saw the incredible occurrence he lost

the words with which he was deceiving the onlookers, and all were amazed.

10 When Marcellus saw this he ran outside and fell down before Peter and said, "Peter, holy servant of the holy God, I embrace your feet. I have committed many sins; do not punish my sins if you have some true faith in Christ, whom you preach. If you remember the commandments, to hate none, to do no evil to anyone, as I have learned from your fellow-apostle Paul, do not consider my sins but pray for me to the Lord, the holy Son of God, whom I angered by persecuting his servants. Pray, therefore, for me, like a good advocate of God, that I may not be given over with the sins of Simon to the everlasting fire. For by his persuasion it came about that I erected a statue to him with the following inscription: "To Simon, the young god.' If I knew, Peter, that you could be won over with money I would give you all my property. I would give it to you, to save my soul. If I had sons I would esteem them for nothing if only I could believe in the living God. I confess, however, that he seduced me only because he said that he was the power of God. Nevertheless I will tell you, dearest Peter: I was not worthy to hear you, servant of God, and I was not firmly established in the belief in God which is in Christ: for this reason I was made to stumble. I pray you, therefore, be not angry at what I am about to say. Christ our Lord, whom you preach in truth, said to your fellow-apostles in your presence, 'If you have faith like a grain of mustard-seed, you will say to this mountain: Remove yourself, and at once it shall move.'[3] But this Simon called you, Peter, an unbeliever, because you lost faith on the water. And I heard that he also said, 'Those who are with me understood me not.' If, therefore,

you, upon whom he laid his hands, whom he has also chosen, with whom he even performed miraculous deeds—if you doubted, therefore I also repent, and relying upon his testimony I resort to your intercession. Receive me, who have fallen away from our Lord and his promise. But I believe that by repenting he will have mercy on me. For the Almighty is faithful to forgive my sins." And Peter said with a loud voice, "Glory and praise be unto our Lord, Almighty God, Father of our Lord Jesus Christ. To you be praise and honor for ever and ever. Amen. Since you have now fully strengthened us and fully established us in you in the sight of all who see it, holy Lord, confirm Marcellus and give him and his house your peace today. But all who are lost or erring, you alone can restore. We worship you, O Lord, the Shepherd of the sheep which once were scattered, but now will be brought together through you. So receive Marcellus also as one of your sheep, and do not permit him to walk about any longer in error or in ignorance but receive him among the number of your sheep. Yes, Lord, receive him, since he beseeches you with sorrow and with tears."

11 Having thus spoken, and having embraced Marcellus, Peter turned to the multitude who stood beside him, when he saw one man laughing, in whom was a very bad devil. Peter said to him, "Whoever you are who have been laughing, show yourself in public." When the young man heard this he ran into the courtyard of the house, cried with a loud voice, threw himself against the wall, and said, "Peter, there is a mighty

---

[3]Matt 17:20.

contest between Simon and the dog, which you sent inside. For Simon says to the dog, 'Say I am not here.' But the dog tells him more things than you commanded. And when he has fulfilled your wish he will die at your feet." And Peter said, "Demon, whoever you are, in the name of our Lord Jesus Christ depart from this young man without hurting him. Show yourself to all present." When the young man heard this he rushed forward, took hold of a large marble statue, which stood in the courtyard of the house, and kicked it to pieces. It was a statue of Caesar. When Marcellus saw this he beat his forehead and said to Peter, "A great crime has been committed, for should Caesar hear of it through one of his spies he will greatly punish us." Peter answered, "I see that you are not the man you were a short time ago when you said you were ready to spend everything for the salvation of your soul. But if you are truly repentant and believe in Christ with all your heart, take running water into your hands and, beseeching the Lord, sprinkle it in his name on the pieces of the statue and it shall be a whole as before." Marcellus did not doubt, but believed with his whole heart, and before taking the water he lifted up his hands and said, "I believe in you, Lord Jesus Christ. For your apostle Peter has examined me whether I truly believe in your holy name. Therefore I take water in my hands and sprinkle these stones in your name that the statue become whole again as before. If it is your will, O Lord, that I live and receive no punishment from Caesar, let this statute be whole as before." And he sprinkled water on the stones, and the statue became whole. Peter, therefore, exulted that he had not hesitated to petition the Lord, and Marcellus also rejoiced in the Spirit, that the first miracle took place by his hands. He believed therefore, with all his heart in the name of Jesus Christ, the Son of my God, by whom all things impossible become possible.

12 And Simon, being inside; spoke thus to the dog, "Tell Peter that I am not in." But the dog said to him in the presence of Marcellus, "You most wicked and shameless man, worst enemy of all who live and believe in Christ Jesus. A dumb animal, which received a human voice, has been sent to you to convict you and to prove that you are a cheat and deceiver. Did it require so many hours for you to say, 'Say I am not here!' You have not been ashamed to lift up your weak and useless voice against Peter, the servant and apostle of Christ, as if you could be hidden from him who told me to speak to your face. And this is not for your sake, but on account of those whom you deceived and brought to perdition. You shall therefore be accursed, enemy and destroyer of the way of Christ's truth. He shall punish your iniquities, which you have done, with imperishable fire and you shall be in outer darkness." Having spoken these words the dog ran away. And the multitude followed so that Simon remained alone. And the dog came to Peter who was with the crowd who had come to see the face of Peter; and the dog reported what had happened with Simon. To the messenger and apostle of the true God the dog said as follows, "Peter, you shall have a hard fight with Simon, the enemy of Christ, and with his adherents, but many whom he deceived you shall convert to the faith. For this you shall receive a reward for your work from God." Having thus spoken the dog fell at the feet of Peter and expired. When the multitude with great astonishment saw the talking dog, many fell down at the feet of Peter, but others said, "Show us another miracle that we may believe in you as a servant

13 And Peter turning around saw a smoked tuna fish hanging in a window. He took it, saying to the people, "When you see this swimming in water like a fish, will you be able to believe in him whom I preach?" And all said with one voice, "Indeed we shall believe you." So he went to the pond near by, saying, "In your name, O Jesus Christ, in whom they do not yet believe, I say, 'Tuna, in the presence of all these, live and swim like a fish.' " And he cast the tuna into the pond, and it became alive and began to swim. The multitude saw the swimming fish and he made it swim not only for that hour but, lest they said that it was a deception, he made it swim longer, thereby attracting crowds from all parts and showing that the smoked tuna had again become a living fish. The success was such that many threw pieces of bread into the water, seeing that the fish was whole. Very many who had witnessed this followed Peter and believed in the Lord, and met day and night in the house of Narcissus the presbyter. And Peter spoke to them of the prophetical writings and of the things done by our Lord Jesus Christ in word and deed.

14 Marcellus was more firmly established in the faith, seeing the signs which Peter did by the grace of Jesus Christ, which was given to him. And Marcellus attacked Simon, who sat in the dining-room of his house. Cursing him, he said to him, "O you most malevolent and most pestilential of men, destroyer of my soul and of my house, who intended to lead me away from Christ, my Lord and Savior." And he laid his hand on him and ordered that he be thrown out of his house. And the servants, having obtained permission, treated him in the most shameful way; some struck him in the face, some beat him with a rod, some flung stones at him, some emptied vessels containing filth over his head. Those who, for his sake, had left their master and were imprisoned, and other servants whom he had maligned to their master, reviled him and said to him, "Now we repay to you the worthy reward, according to the will of God, who had mercy upon us and upon our master." And Simon, thus treated, left the house and went to the house in which Peter was staying. Standing at the door of the house of the presbyter Narcissus, he cried, "Behold, here am I, Simon. Come down, Peter, and I will prove that you believed in a Jewish man and the son of a carpenter."

15 When Peter heard these things he sent to him a woman with her suckling child and said to her, "Go down quickly and you shall see someone seeking me. As for you, do not speak, but keep silent and listen to what the child which you hold will say to him." And the woman went down. And her baby was seven months old. Assuming a manly voice it said to Simon, "You abomination before God and people, O destroyer of truth and most wicked seed of corruption, O unfaithful fruit of nature! After only a little while an everlasting punishment awaits you. Son of a shameless father, never taking root in good soil but in poison; unfaithful creature, destitute of all hope, when the dog accused you, you were not ashamed. I, a child, am forced by God to speak and still you do not blush. But against your will, on the coming Sabbath day, another shall lead you to the forum of Julius that you may be shown what you are. Leave by the doorway at which the saints enter. For no more shall you corrupt innocent souls whom you perverted and led away from Christ. Your whole evil nature will therefore be manifested, and your mach-inations will be spoiled. Now I say to you a last word: Jesus Christ says to you, 'Be speechless by the power of my name and leave Rome till the coming Sabbath.' "

At once he became speechless, and being constrained he left Rome till the next Sabbath and lodged in a stable. The woman returned to Peter with the baby and told Peter and the other brethren what the child had said to Simon. And they praised the Lord who had shown these things to humans.

16 When night came Peter, still awake, saw Jesus clothed with a shining garment, smiling and saying to him, "The greatest part of the brethren has already come back through me and through the signs which you have made in my name. But on the coming Sabbath you shall have a contest of faith, and many more Gentiles and Jews shall be converted in my name to me who was reviled, despised, and spat upon. For I shall show myself to you when you shall ask for signs and wonders and you shall convert many, but you will have Simon opposing you through the works of his father. But all his doings shall be manifested as sorcery and magical deception. And do not delay and you shall confirm in my name all those whom I shall send to you." When it was day he told the brethren how the Lord had appeared to him and what he had commanded him. . . .

20 When Peter had entered he saw one of the old women who was blind, and her daughter led her by the hand and conducted her into the house of Marcellus. And Peter said to her, "Come here, mother; from this day Jesus gives

you his right hand; through him we have light unapproachable which darkness cannot hide. Through me he says to you, 'Open your eyes, see and walk on your own.' " And the widow at once saw Peter put his hand upon her. When Peter came into the dining-room he saw that the gospel was being read. And rolling it up he said, "People, who believe in Christ and hope in him, you shall know how the holy scriptures of our Lord must be explained. What we have written down according to his grace, though it may seem to you as yet so little, contains what is endurable to be understood by humanity. It is necessary that we first know God's will or his goodness; for when deceit was spread and many thousands of people were plunging into perdition the Lord was moved by compassion to show himself in another form and to appear in the image of man, by whom neither the Jews nor we are worthy to be enlightened. For each of us saw him as his capacity permitted. Now, however, I will explain to you that which has been read to you. Our Lord wished to let me see his majesty on the holy mountain;[4] but when I with the sons of Zebedee saw his brightness I fell at his feet as dead, closed my eyes, and heard his voice in a manner which I cannot describe. I imagined I had been deprived of my eyesight by his splendor. I recovered a little and said to myself, 'Perhaps the Lord has brought me here to deprive me of my eyesight.' And I said, 'If such is your will, O Lord, I shall not resist.' And he took me by the hand and lifted me up. And when I arose I saw him again in a form which I could not comprehend. So the merciful God, most beloved brethren, has borne our infirmities and carried our transgressions, as the

---

[4]Mark 9:2–8.

prophet says, 'He bears our griefs; and is afflicted for us; yet we did esteem him stricken and afflicted.'[5] For he is in the Father and the Father in him; in him also is the fullness of all majesty, who has shown us all his benefits. He ate and drank on our account though he was neither hungry nor thirsty; he suffered and bore reproaches for us, he died and rose for us. He also defended and strengthened me through his greatness when I sinned; he will also comfort you, so that you may love him, this Great and Small One, this Beautiful and Ugly One, this Young Man and Old Man, appearing in time, yet utterly invisible in eternity; whom a human hand has not grasped, yet is held by his servants; whom flesh has not seen and now sees; who has not been heard, but is known now as the word which is heard; never chastised, but now chastised; who was before the world and is now perceived in time, beginning greater than all dominion, yet delivered to the princes; glorious, but lowly among us; ugly, yet foreseeing. This Jesus you have, brethren, the door, the light, the way, the bread, the water, the life, the resurrection, the refreshment, the pearl, the treasure, the seed, the abundance, the grain of mustard seed, the vine, the plough, the grace, the faith, the word: he is everything, and there is none greater than he; to him be praise in all eternity. Amen." . . .

23 The brethren and all who were in Rome came together, and on payment of a piece of gold each occupied a seat. Senators and prefects and officers also assembled. But when Peter came in he stood in the center. All cried aloud, "Show us, Peter, who your God is or which majesty it is which gave you such confidence. Be not disaffected to the Romans; they are lovers of the gods. We have had evidence from Simon, let us have yours also; show us, both of you, whom we must believe." And when they had spoken Simon also came. Dismayed, he stood by the side of Peter gazing closely at him. After a long silence Peter said, "Roman men, you shall be our true judges. I say that I believe in the living and true God, of whom I will give you proof already known to me, and to which many among you testify. You see that this man is silent because he has been refuted and because I have driven him from Judaea on account of the frauds perpetrated upon Eubola, a highly respected but simple woman, by means of his magic. Having been expelled by me from there, he has come here believing that he could remain hidden among you; and now here he stands face to face with me. Tell me, Simon, did you not fall at my feet and those of Paul, when in Jerusalem you saw the miraculous cures which took place by our hands, and say, 'I pray you, take as much money from me as you wish, that I too by laying on of hands may perform such deeds'? And when we heard this from you, we cursed you: do you think that we try to possess money? And now are you afraid? My name is Peter, because the Lord Christ had the grace to call me to be ready for every cause. For I believe in the living God, through whom I shall destroy your magic arts. Let Simon perform in your presence the wonderful things which he used to do. And will you not believe me what I just told you about him?" And Simon said, "You have the impudence to speak of Jesus the Nazarene, the son of a carpenter, himself a carpenter, whose family is from Judaea. Listen Peter. The Romans have understanding, they are no fools." And turning to the people he said, "Men

---

[5]Isa 53:4.

of Rome, is a God born? Is he crucified? Whoever has a master is no God." And when he spoke, many said, "You are right, Simon."

24 And Peter said, "Cursed be your words against Christ. You spoke in these terms whereas the prophet says of him, 'Who shall declare his generation?'[6] And another prophet says, 'And we have seen him, and he had no form not beauty.'[7] And 'In the last days a child shall be born of the Holy Spirit; his mother knows not a man and no one claims that he is his father.' And again he says, 'She has given birth and has not given birth.' And again, 'Is it a very little thing for you to go to battle? Behold, in the womb a virgin shall conceive.'[8] And another prophet says in honor of the Father, 'We neither heard her voice, nor did a midwife come.'[9] Another prophet says, 'He came not out of the womb of a woman but descended from a heavenly place,' and 'A stone cut out without hands and has broken all kingdoms,'[10] and 'The stone which the builders rejected has become the headstone of the corner,'[11] and he calls him 'the tried, precious' stone.[12] And again, the prophet says of him, 'I saw him come on a cloud like the Son of man.'[13] And what more shall I say? Men of Rome, if you knew the prophetical writings I would explain everything to you. It was necessary that through them it should be a mystery and the Kingdom of God be completed. But these things shall be revealed to you afterwards. Now I turn to you, Simon; do one of the signs whereby you deceived them before and I shall frustrate it through my Lord Jesus Christ." Simon took courage and said, "If the prefect permits."

25 The prefect wished to show his impartiality to both, so that he might not appear to be acting unjustly. And the prefect summoned one of his slaves and spoke to Simon, "Take him and kill him." To Peter he said, "And you revive him." And to the people the prefect said, "It is for you to decide which of these is accepted before God, he who kills, or he who revives." And Simon whispered something into the ear of the slave and made him speechless, and he died. But when the people began to murmur, one of the widows who had been cared for by Marcellus cried out, "Peter, servant of God, my son also is dead, the only one I had." The people made room for her, and they brought her to Peter. And she fell down at his feet and said, "I had only one son; by the labor of his hands he provided for me; he lifted me up, he carried me. Now he is dead, who will give me a hand?" Peter said to her, "In the presence of these witnesses go and bring your son, that they may be able to see and believe that he was raised up by the power of God; the other shall see it and perish." And Peter said to the young men, "We need young men such as shall believe." And at once thirty young men offered themselves to carry the widow and to fetch her dead son. When the widow had recovered, the young men lifted her up. But she cried and said, "Behold my son, the servant of Christ has sent for you," and she tore her hair and scratched her face. And the young men who had come examined the nose of the boy to see if he were really dead. When they perceived that he was dead they comforted his mother and said, "If you really believe in the God

[6]Isa 53:8. [7]Isa 53:2. [8]Isa 7:14. [9]Asc. of Isa 11:13. [10]Dan 2:34. [11]Ps 118:22; Mark 12:10. [12]Isa 28:16. [13]Dan 7:13.

of Peter, we will lift him up and bring to Peter, that he may revive him and restore him to you."

26 While the young men were saying this the prefect in the forum looked at Peter and said, "What do you say, Peter? Behold, the lad is dead; the emperor liked him, and I spared him not. I had indeed many other young men; but I trusted in you and in your Lord whom you proclaim, if indeed you are sure and truthful: therefore I allowed him to die." And Peter said, "God is neither tempted nor weighed in the balance. But he is to be worshipped with the whole heart by those whom he loves and he will hear those who are worthy. Since, however, my God and Lord Jesus Christ is now tempted among you, he is doing many signs and miracles through me to turn you from your sins. In your power, revive now through my voice, O Lord, in the presence of all, him whom Simon killed by his touch." And Peter said to the master of the lad, "Come, take hold of him by the right hand and you shall have him alive and walking with you." And the prefect Agrippa ran and came to the lad, took his hand, and restored him to life. And when the multitude saw this they cried, "There is only one God, the God of Peter."

27 Meanwhile the widow's son was brought in on a bier by the young men. The people made room, and they brought him to Peter. Peter, however, lifted up his eyes towards heaven, stretched forth his hands, and said, "Holy Father of your Son Jesus Christ who has given us power to ask and to obtain through you and to despise everything that is in this world and follow you only, who are seen by few and wish to be known by many; shine round, O Lord, enlighten, appear, revive the son of the aged widow, who is helpless without him. And I take the word of my Lord Christ and say to you, 'Young man, arise and walk with your mother as long as you can be of use to her. Afterward you shall be called to a higher ministry and serve as deacon and bishop.' " And the dead man rose immediately, and the multitude saw and were amazed, and the people cried, "You, God the Savior, you, God of Peter, invisible God and Savior." And they spoke with one another and wondered at the power of a man who with his word called upon his Lord, and they accepted what had taken place for their sanctification.

28 When the news had spread through the entire city, the mother of a senator came, and making her way through the multitude she threw herself at Peter's feet and said, "I heard many people say that you are a minister of the merciful God and that you impart his mercy to all who desire this light. Bestow, therefore, also to my son this light, since I have learned that you are not ungenerous towards any one; do not turn way from a lady, who entreats you." Peter said to her, "Do you believe in my God through whom your son shall rise?" And the mother, weeping, said with a loud voice, "I believe, Peter, I believe." The whole multitude cried out, "Give the mother her son." And Peter said, "Let him be brought here into the presence of all." And Peter, turning to the people, said, "Men of Rome, I, too, am one of you! I have human flesh and I am a sinner, but I have obtained mercy. Do not imagine that what I do, I do in my own power; I do it in the power of my Lord Jesus Christ who is the judge of the living and the dead. I believe in him, I have been sent by him, and I dare to call upon him to raise the dead. Go, therefore, woman, and have your son brought here and have him raised." And the woman made her way through the multitude, ran into the street with great joy, and believed with her heart; coming to the house she made her slaves carry him and came back to the forum. And she told the young men to cover their heads and go before the bier and carry everything that she intended to spend on the body of her son in front of the bier, so that Peter, seeing this, might have pity on the body and on her. With them all as mourners she came to the assembly, followed by a multitude of senators and ladies who came to see God's wonderful deeds. And Nicostratus (the man who had died) was very noble and respected in the senate. They brought him and placed him before Peter. And Peter asked them to be silent and said with a very loud voice, "Romans, let a righteous judgment now take place between me and Simon, and judge which of us believes in the living God, he or I. Let him revive the body which is before us, and believe in him as an angel of God. If he is not able I will call upon my God. I will restore the son alive to his mother and then you shall believe that he is a sorcerer and deceiver, this man who enjoys your hospitality." When they heard this, it seemed right to them what Peter had said. They encouraged Simon saying, "Show yourself publicly what you can do; either you convince us or you shall be convicted. Why do you stand still? Commence."

When Simon perceived that they all pushed him, he stood in silence. When the people had become quiet and were looking at him, Simon cried out and said, "Romans, when you see that the dead man is raised, will you cast Peter out of the city?" And the whole multitude said, "We shall not only cast him out but also

burn him at once." Simon came to the head of the dead man, bowed three times, and he showed the people how the dead man had lifted up his head and moved it, and opened his eyes and lightly bowed to Simon. And immediately they began to gather wood to burn Peter. But Peter, having received the power of Christ, lifted up his voice and said to those who were shouting against him, "Now I see, Romans, that I must not call you foolish and silly so long as your eyes and your ears and your senses are blinded. So long as your mind is darkened you do not perceive that you are bewitched, since you seemingly believe that a dead man rose who has not risen. I would have been content, Romans, to keep silent and to die in silence and to leave you among the illusions of this world. But the punishment of the unquenchable fire is before my eyes. If you agree, let the dead man speak, let him rise; if he is alive, let him untie the band from his chin, let him call his mother and say to you, 'Bawlers, why are you crying?' Let him beckon to you with his hand. If, therefore, you wish to see that he is dead and you are spellbound, let this man step back from the bier, this one who persuaded you to withdraw from Christ, and you shall see the dead man as you saw him when you brought him in." And the prefect Agrippa could no longer restrain himself but rose and with his own hand pushed Simon away. And the dead man looked as he had before. And the people were enraged and, converted from the magical spell of Simon, began to cry, "Hear, O Caesar, should the dead not rise let Simon be burned instead of Peter, because he has really deceived us." But Peter stretched forth his hand and said, "Romans, be patient. I do not say that Simon should be burned if the boy is restored; it is only when I tell you to do it, that you will." And the people cried, "Even if you should not wish it, Peter, we shall do it." Peter said to them, "If you continue, the boy shall not rise. We have learned not to recompense evil for evil, but we have learned to love our enemies and to pray for those who persecute us. For should even he repent, it is better. For God will not remember the evil. Let him, therefore, come to the light of Christ. But if he cannot, let him inherit the portion of his father, the devil. But do not let your hands be contaminated." Having thus spoken to the people he came to the boy, and before raising him he said to his mother, "These young men, whom you set free in honor of your son, can as free men obey their living master. For I know that the souls of some among them will be wounded when they see your risen son and serve again as slaves. But let them all be free and receive their subsistence as before— for your son shall rise again—and let them be with him." And Peter looked at her for some time awaiting the answer. And the mother of the boy said, "How can I do otherwise? Therefore I declare before the prefect that they should possess all that which I had to spend on the corpse of my son." Peter said to her, "Let the rest be divided among the widows." And Peter rejoiced in his soul and said in the spirit, "O Lord, who are merciful, Jesus Christ, manifest yourself to your servant Peter who calls upon you, as you always show mercy and goodness. In the presence of all these who have been set free, that they may be able to serve, let Nicostratus now arise." And Peter touched the side of the lad and said, "Arise." And the lad arose, took up his garment and sat and untied his chin, asked for other garments, came down from the bier, and said to Peter, "I beg you, man, let us go to our Lord Christ, whom I heard speak to you; he said to you, pointing at me, 'Bring him here, for he belongs to me.' " When Peter heard

this he was still more strengthened in the spirit by the help of the Lord and said to the people, "Romans, thus the dead are awakened, thus they speak, thus they walk when they are raised; they live for so long as it pleases God. But now I turn to you who came to see the spectacle. If you repent now from your sins and from all your human-made gods and from all uncleanness and lust, you shall receive the communion of Christ in faith so that you may obtain life for eternity."

29 From that hour on they worshipped him like a god, and the sick, whom they had at home, they brought to his feet to be cured by him. And when the prefect perceived that such a great multitude adhered to Peter he asked him to depart. And Peter bade the people come into the house of Marcellus. And the mother of the lad asked Peter to come to her house. But Peter had arranged to go to Marcellus on Sunday to see the widows, as Marcellus had promised, so that he might minister to them with his own hand. And the lad who had been raised said, "I shall not leave Peter." And his mother returned joyfully and cheerfully to her house. And on the day after the Sabbath she came into the house of Marcellus and brought two thousand pieces of gold and said to Peter, "Divide these among the virgins of Christ who minister to him." But the lad who had been raised, perceiving that he had not yet given anything to anyone, ran to his house, opened a chest, and brought four thousand pieces of gold, and said to Peter, "See, I also, who have been raised, offer the double gift and present myself from now on as a living sacrifice to God."

30 And on Sunday Peter spoke to the brethren and encouraged them in the faith of Christ. And many senators and knights and wealthy women and matrons were present, and they were strengthened in the faith. There was also present a very rich woman, named Chryse, because all her vessels were of gold—since her birth she had never used a vessel of silver or of glass, but only of gold. She said to Peter, "Peter, servant of God, in a dream the one whom you call God came and said to me, 'Chryse, bring ten thousand pieces of gold to my servant Peter; you owe them to him.' So I have brought them, fearing that some evil may come from him whom I saw and who has gone to heaven." And having said this she laid down the money and went away. And Peter seeing this praised God that the poor could now be provided for. Some of those present said to him, "Peter, is it not wrong to have accepted this money from her? All Rome knows of her fornication, and it is reported that she is not satisfied with one husband; she uses even her own slaves. Therefore have nothing to do with the Chryse's table, but let everything be sent back to her that came from her." When Peter heard this he laughed and said to the brethren, "As to her conduct, I know nothing of it; since I have received this money I received it not without reason; she brought it to me as a debtor to Christ and gives it to the servants of Christ. For he himself has provided for them."

31 And they also brought the sick to him on the Sabbath and asked him to treat them. And many paralytics and podagrous were healed, and those who had two- and four-day fevers and other diseases, and believed in the name of Jesus Christ, and very many were added every day to the grace of the Lord. When some days had passed Simon the magician promised the people that he could persuade Peter not to believe in the true God but in a fallacious one. As he performed many tricks those among the

disciples who were steadfast laughed him to scorn. In the dining halls he made some spirits appear which had the semblance of life, but in reality did not exist. And what more shall I say? Having spoken a great deal about magic[14] he seemingly cured the lame and blind for a time, and many dead persons, too, he made alive and made them move about, as well as Stratonicus.[15] In all this Peter followed him and refuted him before those who saw it. And as he was always out of favor, and was ridiculed by the Romans and lost their confidence since he promised to do something which he could not do, it came about that he said to them, "Romans, you now think that Peter has overcome me as if he were mightier than I, and you now pay more attention to him. You are mistaken. For tomorrow I shall leave you godless and impious ones and take refuge with God above, whose power I am, though enfeebled. If, therefore, you have fallen, behold I stand. I ascend to the father, and shall say to him, 'Me, your son who stands, they desired to bring low; however, I had no deal with them, but returned to myself.' "

32 And on the following day a still larger multitude gathered on the *via sacra* to see him fly. And Peter also went to the place to see the spectacle and to refute him. For when he came to Rome he astonished the people by his flying. But Peter, who rebuked him, was not yet at Rome, which he so misled and deceived that some were driven out of their senses. And standing on an elevated place, upon seeing Peter he began to speak. "Peter, now, as I am about to ascend in the

---

[14]Greek unclear. Possibly the phrase should be: "Although he had often been refuted for his magic art."
[15]Latin reads "Nicostratus."

presence of all the onlookers, I say to you, if your God is almighty, (he whom the Jews killed, and they stoned you who were chosen by him), let him show that faith in him is of God; let it be manifested by this event, whether it is worthy of God. For I ascend and will show myself to this people what kind of being I am." And, behold, he was lifted up and they saw him ascending over Rome and over its temples and hills. And the believers looked at Peter. And beholding the incredible spectacle Peter cried to the Lord Jesus Christ, "If you allow him to do what he has undertaken, all who believed in you shall be overthrown, and the signs and wonders, which you have shown to them through me, will not be believed. Make haste, O Lord, show your mercy and let him fall down and become crippled but not die; let him be disabled and break his leg in three places." And he fell down and broke his leg in three places. And they cast stones upon him, and each went to his home having faith in Peter. And one of Simon's friends, Gemellus by name, from whom Simon had received much money and who had a Greek wife, quickly ran along the street, and seeing him with his leg broken said, "Simon, if God's power is broken, shall not that God, whose power you are, be darkened?" And Gemellus ran and followed Peter and said to him, "I also wish to be one of those who believe in Christ." And Peter said, "How could I object, my brother? Come and stay with us." And Simon, being in misery, found some helpers who carried him by night on a stretcher from Rome to Aricia. There he remained and stayed with a man named Castor who on account of sorcery had been driven from Rome to Terracina. Following an operation Simon, the messenger of the devil, ended his life.

33 Now Peter remained in Rome and rejoiced with the brethren in the Lord, returning thanks day and night for the multitude who were daily added to the holy name by the grace of the Lord. And the four concubines of the prefect Agrippa also came to Peter, Agrippina, Nicaria, Euphemia, and Doris. And they heard preaching concerning chastity and all the words of the Lord, and repented and agreed among themselves to abstain from cohabitation with Agrippa, but were molested by him. When Agrippa became perplexed and distressed—for he loved them very much—he had them secretly observed where they went, and he found out that they went to Peter. When they came back he said to them, "That Christian has taught you not to consort with me. I tell you that I will destroy you and burn him alive." But they were ready to endure anything by the hand of Agrippa but would no longer allow themselves to satisfy his lust; they had become strong in the power of Jesus.

34 And a very beautiful women named Xanthippe, the wife of Albinus, a friend of the emperor, also came to Peter with the other ladies and kept away from Albinus. Being in love with Xanthippe, he became enraged and wondered why she no longer slept with him, and raging like a beast he intended to kill Peter, for he perceived that he was the cause of her leaving his bed. And many other women delighted in the preaching concerning chastity and separated from their husbands, and men too ceased to sleep with their wives, because they wished to serve God in chastity and purity. And there was a great commotion in Rome, and Albinus told Agrippa what had happened to him and said, "Either you avenge me of Peter, who has alienated my wife from me, or I shall do it myself." And Agrippa said, "I suffered the same, for he has alienated my concubines." And Albinus said to him, "Why are you waiting, Agrippa? Let us seize him and kill him as a trouble-maker, so that we may get our wives back and avenge those who cannot kill him but whose wives he has also alienated."

35 And as they made plans together, Xanthippe heard of the conspiracy which her husband had with Agrippa, and she sent word to Peter and asked him to leave Rome. And the other brethren, together with Marcellus, requested him to leave. But Peter said to them, "Shall we act like deserters, brethren?" And they said, "No; but by going you can still serve the Lord." He obeyed the brethren, and went away alone, saying, "Let none of you go with me, I will go alone in disguise." When he went out of the gate he saw the Lord come into Rome. And when he saw him he said, "Lord, where are you going?" And the Lord said to him, "I go to Rome to be crucified." And Peter said to him, "Lord, are you being crucified again?" And he said, "Yes, Peter, again I shall be crucified." And Peter came to himself; and he saw the Lord ascending to heaven. Then he returned to Rome, rejoicing and praising the Lord because he had said, "I am being crucified." This was to happen to Peter.

36 He went again to the brethren and told them of the vision which he had. And their souls were sorrowing, and they wept and said, "We entreat you, Peter, have regard for us, the young ones." And Peter said, "If it be the Lord's wish it will be, even if we would not have it so. The Lord is able to strengthen you in his faith, and he will establish you in it and increase it in you whom he has planted, so that you may

also plant others through him. I will not object so long as the Lord will keep me alive; and again if he will take me away I shall be glad and rejoice."

While Peter was speaking the brethren wept and four soldiers arrested him and brought him to Agrippa. And being enraged he ordered that he be crucified for godlessness. And the whole multitude of the brethren came together, rich and poor, widows and orphans, able-bodied and disabled alike; they wished to see Peter and rescue him. And the people cried unceasingly with one voice, "What harm has Peter done, Agrippa? What evil has he done to you? Tell the Romans." And others said, "We must be afraid lest the Lord destroy us also, should he die." And when Peter came to the place he appeased the multitude and said, "You men who are in the service of Christ, men who hope in Christ, remember the signs and wonders which you saw through me; think of the compassion of God, how he performed healings for your sakes. Wait for him, till he comes and rewards every man according to his works. And now, do not be angry with Agrippa, for he is a servant of the power of his father. And that which happens takes place as the Lord has told me that it should happen. And why do I delay and not go to the cross?"

37 And when he had come to the cross he began to say, "O name of the cross, hidden mystery; O unspeakable mercy, which is expressed in the name of the cross; O nature of man, which cannot be separated from God; O ineffable and inseparable love, which cannot be shown by impure lips; I seize you now I am standing at the end of my earthly career. I will make known what you are. I will not conceal the mystery of the cross once closed and hidden to my soul. You who hope in Christ, think

not this to be a cross which is visible; for my passion, like that of Christ, is entirely different from that which is visible. And now especially, since you who can hear can hear it from me who am in the last and parting hour of life, listen. Keep your souls from everything which you can perceive with the senses, from all that seems to be, and is not truly real. Close these your eyes, shut these your ears; withdraw from actions which are seen outwardly and you shall perceive the facts about Christ and the whole mystery of your salvation. But the hour has come for you, Peter, to deliver your body to those who are taking it. Take it, whose business it is. Of you, executioners, I ask to crucify me with head downwards, and not otherwise. And the reason I shall explain to those who listen."

38 After they had hanged him up as he wished he began to speak again, "Men, whose calling it is to hear, listen to what I, being hanged, am about to tell you now. Understand the mystery of the whole creation and the beginning of all things, how it was. For the first man, whose image I bear, in falling head downward showed a manner of birth which did not formerly exist, for it was dead, having no motion. He, having been drawn down, he who cast his origin upon the earth, established the whole of the cosmic system, suspended after the manner of his calling, whereby he showed the right as the left and the left as the right and changed all signs of nature, to behold the ugly as beautiful and the really evil as good. Concerning this the Lord says in a mystery, 'Unless you make the right as the left and the left as the right, and the top as the bottom and the front as the back, you shall not know the Kingdom.'[16] I explain this information to you, and the manner of my suspension is symbolic of that man who was first made. You, my

beloved, who now hear, and those who shall hear it, must renounce the first error and turn again. For you ought to come to the cross of Christ, who is the extended Word, the one and only, concerning whom the Spirit says, 'For what else is Christ than the Word, the sound of God?' The Word is this upright tree on which I am crucified; the sound, however, is the crossbeam, namely the nature of man; and the nail which holds the crossbeam to the upright in the middle is the conversion and repentance of man.

39 Since you have made this known and revealed these things to me, O Word of life, which is now called tree, I thank you, not with these lips which are nailed, neither with this tongue, through which comes forth truth and falsehood, nor with this word, which is produced by the skill of earthly nature, but I thank you, O King, with that voice which is heard through silence, which is not heard by all, which does not come through the organs of the body, which does not enter the ears of flesh nor is heard by corruptible substance, which is not in the world or sounds upon earth, which is also not written in books, nor belongs to one, nor to another, but with this voice, Jesus Christ, I thank you: with the silence of the voice with which the Spirit within me intercedes, who loves you, speaks with you, and sees you. You are known only to the Spirit. You are to me, father, mother, brother, friend, servant, steward. You are all, and all is in you; and you are Being, and there is nothing that is except you. To him, brethren, you also take refuge and learn that your existence is in him alone, and you shall then obtain that of which he said to

[16] Cf. Acts of Philip 140; Gospel of Thomas 22.

you, 'Eye has not seen, nor ear heard, neither has it entered into the heart of man.'[17] We now ask undefiled Jesus for that which you promised to give us; we praise you, we thank you, we confess you in glorifying you, though we are weak, because you alone are God and no other, to whom be glory now and for ever, Amen."

40 When the multitude surrounding him cried Amen, Peter, during this Amen, gave up his spirit to the Lord. When Marcellus saw that the blessed Peter had given up the ghost, without communicating with anyone, since it was not allowed, he took him down from the cross with his own hands and bathed him in milk and wine. And he ground seven pounds of mastic and also fifty pounds of myrrh and aloes and spice and anointed his body, and filled a very costly marble coffin with Attic honey and buried him in his own tomb. And Peter came to Marcellus by night and said, "Marcellus did you not hear the Lord say, 'Let the dead be buried by their own dead'?"[18] When Marcellus said, "Yes", Peter said to him, "What you spent on the dead is lost. For though alive you were like a dead man caring for the dead." When Marcellus awoke he told of the appearance of Peter to the brethren,

and he remained with those who had been strengthened by Peter in the faith of Christ, strengthening himself even more till the arrival of Paul at Rome.

41 When Nero heard that Peter had departed this life, he blamed the prefect Agrippa for having him killed without his knowledge; he had intended to punish him the more cruelly and severely because Peter had made disciples of some of his servants and alienated them from him. Therefore he was angry, and for a long time he would not speak with Agrippa. He sought how to destroy all those brethren whom Peter had instructed. And one night he saw a person striking him and saying, "Nero, you cannot now persecute or destroy the servants of Christ. Keep your hands from them." And in consequence of this vision Nero became greatly afraid and left the disciples alone from that time in which Peter had died. Thereafter the brethren continued with one accord, rejoicing and glorying in the Lord, and praised the God and Saviour of our Lord Jesus Christ with the Holy Spirit, to whom be glory for ever and ever. Amen.

---

[17]1 Cor. 2: 9; cf. Gospel of Thomas 17.   [18]Matt. 8: 22 and parallel.

NON-CANONICAL
EPISTLES AND
RELATED WRITINGS

Introduction

There are more epistles in the New Testament than any other genre: four Gospels, one book of Acts, and one apocalypse, but twenty-one epistles. It is somewhat ironic that relatively few *apocryphal* epistles exist. There are some, of course, and these still make for fascinating reading. They include a set of correspondence allegedly between the apostle Paul and the greatest philosopher of his day Seneca (the historical Seneca, of course, knew nothing of Paul) and an anti-heretical piece called "3 Corinthians" (to match the 1 and 2 Corinthians of the New Testament).

Other epistles that were not forged in the name of an apostle are included in this collection because they were revered by one group or another as bearing sacred authority. This is true even of "orthodox" productions such as the Epistle of Barnabas, which is an anonymous piece later attributed to Paul's traveling companion Barnabas, and the letter of 1 Clement, later assigned to a person thought to be a bishop of Rome. Both Barnabas and 1 Clement were considered by some orthodox Christians of later times to be canonical authorities and so were included in some manuscripts of the New Testament. Yet other non-canonical letters embody "heretical" concerns, including several that are clearly gnostic creations— which try, in fact, to convince proto-orthodox readers that a gnostic point of view is correct (e.g., Ptolemy's Letter to Flora and the Letter to Rheginus). Some of the books included here are not typical letters, but are addresses to communities providing instruction on how to conduct their communal lives (e.g., the "Didache [i.e., the "Teaching"] of the Apostles").

As is true of other writings found throughout this collection, some of these books have long been known by scholars (e.g., the Letter to the Laodiceans), whereas others—both orthodox and heretical—have been discovered just in modern times, often to much fanfare (e.g., the Didache and the Letter to Rheginus). Taken as a group, they show just how wide ranging the early Christian movement was in terms of belief, communal life, liturgical practice, and ethics.

The Third Letter to the Corinthians

The letter traditionally called 3 Corinthians is a pseudonymous reply of "Paul" to a letter from the Christians in Corinth, sent to him while he was in prison in Philippi. Both letters eventually came to be incorporated in the apocryphal Acts of Paul (see above). In some parts of the Christian church— for example, in Armenia—3 Corinthians was accepted as canonical Scripture.

The letter from the Corinthians asks for Paul's advice about the teaching of two heretics, Simon (Magus?) and Cleobius, who maintain, among other things, that (a) God was not the creator, (b) the Jewish prophets were not from God, (c) Jesus did not come in the flesh, and (d) the flesh will not be raised. All of these are clearly Gnostic ideas.[1] The pseudonymous author of 3 Corinthians replies by refuting each of them in turn. In particular, he wants to stress the proto-orthodox doctrine that the flesh was created by God and that it will be redeemed, as evident in the resurrection of Jesus himself in the flesh. The letter concludes with dire warnings of eternal torment for those who embrace the heretical teachings of Paul's opponents.

Most scholars now think that these letters were originally composed and transmitted independently of the Acts of Paul and were then at a later time incorporated in the longer narrative. If so, they may well have been in circulation already by the middle of the second century.

---

[1]For a discussion of Christian Gnosticism, see Ehrman, *Lost Christianities*, pp. 113–34.

Translation by Bart D. Ehrman, based on the Greek text in Michel Testuz, *Papyrus Bodmer X–XII; Correspondance apocryphe des Corinthiens et de l'apôtre Paul* (Cologne-Geneva: Bibliotheca Bodmeriana, 1959).

The Letter of the Corinthians to Paul

Stephanus and the Presbyters with him, Daphnus, Euboulus, Theophilus, and Zenon, to Paul, who is in the Lord. Greetings!

Two men, a certain Simon and Cleobius, have come to Corinth and upset the faith of some by their corrupt teachings, which you can evaluate for yourself. For we have never heard such teachings either from you or anyone else. But we have kept the things we received from you and our other teachers. And so, since the Lord has shown us mercy, come to us while you are in the flesh, or write back to us, that we may hear your teachings again. For we believe what was revealed to Theonoe, that the Lord has saved you from the hand of the Lawless one.

For this is what they are saying and teaching: that there is no need to consider the [Hebrew] prophets; that God is not the Almighty; that there is no resurrection of the flesh; that humans are not God's creation; that the Lord did not come (into the world) in the flesh; that he was not born from Mary; and that the world did not come from God but from angels.

For this reason, brother, make all haste to come, that the Corinthian church may continue to have no cause of stumbling and that the foolishness of these men may be made clear.

Farewell in the Lord.

The Letter of Paul to the Corinthians Concerning the Flesh

Paul, the prisoner of Jesus Christ and who is in the midst of many failures, to the brothers in Corinth. Greetings!

I am not surprised that the doctrines of the evil one have moved forward so quickly; for the Lord Christ will soon come—he who is rejected by those who have debased his sayings. For in the beginning I delivered over to you the teachings I received from the apostles who were before me, who spent their entire time with Jesus Christ: that our Lord Christ Jesus was born from Mary, from the seed of David, when the Holy Spirit was sent from heaven into her by the Father, that he might come into the world and set free all flesh through his flesh, and might raise us from the dead as fleshly beings, just as he showed himself as a model; and that humans were formed by his Father. For this reason they were sought out by him while they were perishing, that he might make them live through their adoption as God's children.

For God who is over all, the Almighty, the one who made heaven and earth, sent prophets to the Jews first of all, that they might be pulled away from their sins. For he wanted to save the house of Israel. And so he sent a portion of the Spirit of Christ into the prophets, who proclaimed the true worship of God for many years. For the unrighteous ruler who wanted to be God laid hands on them and delivered all human flesh to the bondage of pleasure.

But since God the Almighty was righteous, and did not wish to abandon his own creation, he sent down the Spirit through fire into Mary the Galilean, that the evil one might be defeated through that same perishing flesh that he used in his dealings with others. In this way he would convincingly be shown not to be God. For by his own body Christ Jesus saved all flesh, that he might show forth a temple of righteousness by his own body, by which we have been set free. Those others, therefore, are not children of righteousness but children of wrath; they try to restrain God's foreknowledge by saying that heaven and earth and all that is in them is not the work of the

Father. They have the cursed faith of the serpent. Reject such people and flee from their teaching.

There is no resurrection for those who tell you there is no resurrection of the flesh, who deny, in fact, the one who is risen. For they do not know, O men of Corinth, about the sowing of wheat or other seed, that it is cast naked on the earth and after it disintegrates in the depths it is raised by the will of God, in a body and fully clothed, so that not only is the body that is cast down raised up, but it is multiplied, erect, and blessed.

And if we are not to make a parable out of the seed, you should know that Jonah, the son of Amathias, when he refused to preach in Nineveh, was swallowed by a huge fish. After three days and nights God heard Jonah praying from the depths of Hades—and not a bit of him was corrupted, not even a hair or an eyelash. How much more will he raise you who believe in Christ Jesus, just as he himself was raised, O you of little faith!

And if a corpse was cast onto the bones of the prophet Elisha by the sons of Israel, and was then raised up in the body— what about you? When the body, bones, and spirit of Christ have been cast upon you in that last day, will you not be raised with flesh intact?

If anyone accepts some other teaching, let him not cause me trouble. For I have chains on my hands that I may gain Christ, and marks on my body that I may come to the resurrection of the dead. Anyone who remains in the rule received through the blessed prophets and the holy Gospel will receive a reward. Anyone who transgresses these things is bound for the fire, as are those atheists who have come before them—offspring of vipers, whom you should reject by the power of the Lord.

May peace be with you.

The Correspondence Between Paul and Seneca

The apostle Paul was without doubt one of the most important figures of early Christianity. Some scholars have gone so far as to label him the "second founder" of Christianity, by which they mean that his theological emphasis on the death and resurrection of Jesus for salvation from sin marked a distinct modification of Jesus' simple message of the need of repentance and forgiveness. In any event, Paul's importance in the New Testament is quite clear: thirteen of its twenty-seven books claim to be written by him, another was included in the canon because early Christians thought he wrote it (the anonymous book of Hebrews), and another is largely written *about* him (the book of Acts).

Despite his importance to the early Christian movement, Paul was not well known or influential on his world at large. It is a striking fact that he is never mentioned in any of the writings of his Jewish and Roman contemporaries. In order make up for this perceived deficit, sometime in the fourth Christian century an unknown author forged a series of fourteen letters between the apostle and the most famous philosopher of his day, Seneca. Seneca, an important statesman as well as author, had been the tutor of the young Nero; when Nero later became emperor of Rome, he appointed Seneca as a political advisor.

The pseudonymous correspondence between Seneca and Paul presupposes that historical context, as Seneca praises Paul's brilliance and indicates that he has shown Paul's letters to the emperor, who was himself impressed with his god-given ideas. Apart from a show of mutual admiration, there is little of substance in the correspondence, with the exception of letter eleven, which mentions the fire in Rome allegedly started by Nero but blamed on the Christians. The pseudonymous letters serve, then, principally to elevate the importance of Paul in the eyes of the world, as his theological insights are celebrated by a world-renowned philosopher of his day and the emperor of Rome himself.

Translation by J. K. Elliott, *Apocryphal New Testament* (Oxford: Clarendon Press, 1993) 549–53; used with permission.

1. Seneca to Paul greeting

I believe that you have been informed, Paul, of the discussion which my friend Lacilius and I held yesterday concerning the apocrypha and other matters: for some of the followers of your teachings were with me. We had retired to the gardens of Sallust, and it was our good fortune that these disciples whom I have mentioned saw us there and joined us, although they were on their way elsewhere. You may be sure that we wished that you, too, had been present, and I also want you to know this: when we had read your book, that is to say one of the many letters of admirable exhortation to an upright life which you have sent to some city or to the capital of a province, we were completely refreshed. These thoughts, I believe, were expressed not by you, but through you; though sometimes they were expressed both by you and through you; for they are so lofty and so brilliant with noble sentiments that in my opinion generations of men could hardly be enough to become established and perfected in them. I wish you good health, brother.

2. To Annaeus Seneca Paul greeting

I was extremely glad to receive your letter yesterday, and I could have answered it immediately if I had had with me the young man whom I intended to send to you. You know when and by whom and at what time and to whom a thing should be given or entrusted. Therefore I ask you not to think yourself neglected, while I pay attention to the qualities of the messenger. But you write somewhere that you are pleased with my letter, and I count myself fortunate in the approval of a man who is so great. For you, a critic, a philosopher, the teacher of so great a ruler, nay even of everyone, would not say this unless you speak the truth. I hope that you may long be in good health.

3. Seneca to Paul greeting

I have arranged some of my works and set them in order according to their proper divisions. I also intend to read them to Caesar. If only fate is kind enough to cause him to show renewed interest, perhaps you will be there also; if not, I will at some other time set a day on which we may examine this work together. I could not show him this writing without first conferring with you, if only it were possible to do so without risk, so that you may know that you are not being forgotten. Farewell, dearest Paul.

4. To Annaeus Seneca Paul greeting

Whenever I hear your letters, I think that you are present and I imagine nothing else than that you are continually with us. As soon, therefore, as you begin to come, we shall see each other face to face. I hope that you are in good health.

5. Seneca To Paul greeting

We are distressed at your exceedingly long retirement. What is the matter? What makes you stay away? If it is the displeasure of our empress because you have withdrawn from your old rite and creed and are a convert, then you will be given an opportunity of asking her to believe that you acted reasonably, not lightly. A kind farewell.

6. To Seneca and Lucilius Paul greeting

I may not speak with pen and ink concerning what you have written to me, for the one marks a thing down and defines it, while the other makes it all too clear—especially since I am certain that there are some among your number, with you and in your midst, who are able to understand me. We must show respect to everyone, the more so as they are apt to find cause for offence. If we are patient with them we shall overcome them in every way and on every side—that is, if only they are the kind of people who can be sorry for what they have done. A kind farewell.

7. Annaeus Seneca to Paul and Theophilus greeting

I admit that I enjoyed reading your letters to the Galatians, and to the Corinthians, and to the Achaeans, and may our relations be like that religious awe which you manifest in these letters. For the holy spirit that is in you and high above you expresses with lofty speech thoughts worthy of reverence. Therefore since you have such excellent matters to propose I wish that refinement of language might not be lacking to the majesty of your theme. And in order that I may not keep anything secret from you, brother, and burden my conscience, I confess that Augustus was affected by your sentiments. When your treatise on the power that is in you was read to him, this was his reply: he was amazed that one whose education had not been normal could have such ideas. I answered him that the gods are accustomed to speak through the mouths of the innocent and not through those who pride themselves on their learning. When I gave him the example of Va-

tienus, a farmer to whom appeared in the territory of Reate two men who later were found to be Castor and Pollux, he seemed thoroughly enlightened. Farewell.

8. To Seneca Paul greeting

Even though I am not unaware that our Caesar is now fond of wonders, although he may sometimes lapse, still he allows himself not to be rebuked, but to be informed. I think that it was a very serious mistake on your part to wish to bring to his notice what is against his practice and training. Inasmuch as he worships the gods of the heathen, I do not see what you had in mind wishing him to know this, unless I am to think that you are doing this from your great love for me. I beg you not to do this in the future. You must also be careful not to offend our empress while showing affection for me. Her displeasure, to be sure, cannot harm us if it lasts, nor can we be helped if it never happens. As a queen she will not be insulted; as a woman she will be angry. A kind farewell.

9. Seneca to Paul greeting

I know that it was not so much for your own sake that you were disturbed when I wrote to you that I had read my letters to Caesar as by the nature of things, which withholds the minds of men from all upright pursuits and practices,—so that I am not astonished today, particularly because I have learned this well from many clear proofs. Therefore let us begin anew, and if in the past I have been negligent in any way, you will grant pardon. I have sent you a book on elegance of expression. Farewell, dearest Paul.

10. To Seneca Paul greeting

Whenever I write to you and place my name after yours, I commit a serious fault and one incompatible with my status. For I ought, as I have often claimed, to be all things to all men and to observe towards you what the Roman law has granted for the honour of the senate—namely, to choose the last place when I have finished my letter, lest I desire to perform in an inadequate and disgraceful manner what is my own will. Farewell, most devoted of teachers. Written 27 June in the consulship of Nero III and Messala [= AD 58].

11. Seneca to Paul greeting

Greetings, my dearly beloved Paul. Do you think I am not saddened and grieved because you innocent people are repeatedly punished? Or because the whole populace believes you so implacable and so liable to guilt, thinking that every misfortune in the city is due to you? But let us endure it calmly and take advantage of whatever opportunity fortune allots to us, until invincible happiness gives us release from our troubles. Earlier ages endured the Macedonian, the son of Philip, the Cyruses, Darius, Dionysius; our own age endured Gaius Caesar; all of them were free to do whatever they pleased. The source of the frequent fires which the city of Rome suffers is plain. But if lowly people had been allowed to tell the reason, and if it were permitted to speak safely in these times of ill-fortune, everyone would now understand everything. Christians and Jews, charged with responsibility for the fire—alas!— are being put to death, as is usually the case. That ruffian, whoever he is, whose pleasure is murdering and whose refuge is lying, is destined for his time of reckoning, and just as the best is sacrificed as one life for many, so he shall be sacrificed for all and burned by fire. One hundred and thirty-two private houses and four thousand apartment-houses burned in six days; the seventh day gave respite. I hope that you are in good health, brother. Written 28 March in the consulship of Frugi and Bassus [= AD 64].

12. Seneca to Paul greeting

Greetings, my dearly beloved Paul. If such a great man as you and one who is beloved of God is to be, I do not say joined, but intimately associated in all respects with me and my name, then your Seneca will be wholly satisfied. Since, therefore, you are the peak and crest of all the most lofty mountains, do you not, then, wish me to rejoice if I am so close to you as to be considered a second self of yours? Therefore do not think that you are unworthy of having your name in first place in your letters, or else you may seem to be tempting me rather than praising me, especially since you know that you are a Roman citizen. For I wish that my position were yours, and that yours were as mine. Farewell, my dearly beloved Paul. Written 23 March in the consulship of Apronianus and Capito [= AD 59].

13. Seneca to Paul greeting

Many writings composed by you are throughout allegorical and enigmatic, and for that reason you must adorn that powerful gift of truth and talent which has been bestowed upon you not so much with embellishment of words as with a certain amount of refinement. And do not fear, as I remember I have frequently said, that many who affect such things spoil the thoughts and emasculate the force of their subject-matter. I do wish you would obey me and comply with the pure Latin style, giving a good appearance to your noble utterances, in order that the granting of this excellent gift may be worthily performed by you. A kind farewell. Written 6 July in the consulship of Lurco and Sabinus [= AD 58].

14. Paul to Seneca greeting

Things have been revealed to you in your reflections which the Godhead has granted to few. Therefore I am certain that I am sowing a rich seed in a fertile field, not a corruptible matter, but the abiding word of God, derived from him who is ever-increasing and ever-abiding. The determination which your good sense has attained must never fail—namely, to avoid the outward manifestations of the heathens and the Israelites. You must make yourself a new herald of Jesus Christ by displaying with the praises of rhetoric that blameless wisdom which you have almost achieved and which you will present to the temporal king and to the members of his household and to his trusted friends, whom you will find it difficult or nearly impossible to persuade, since many of them are not at all influenced by your presentations. Once the word of God has inspired the blessing of life within them it will create a new man, without corruption, an abiding being, hastening thence to God. Farewell, Seneca, most dear to us. Written 1 August in the consulship of Lurco and Sabinus [= AD 58].

Paul's Letter to the Laodiceans

The New Testament book of Colossians mentions a letter sent by Paul to the church of Laodicea in Asia Minor (Col 4:16).[1] No letter addressed to the Laodiceans survives from Paul's own hand, but we know that one had been placed in circulation by the second century, since the Muratorian canon (see below) warns against it as a Marcionite forgery.[2]

At a later time another letter to the Laodiceans appeared, also claiming to be from Paul; the letter became exceedingly popular: it is found in a number of Latin manuscripts of the New Testament down through the Middle Ages. This letter—which is given below—is evidently not, however, the Marcionite forgery mentioned in the Muratorian canon. For there are no clear and compelling Marcionite tendencies here. In fact, the letter shows few tendencies of any kind. It instead represents a kind of pastiche of statements drawn from Paul's canonical writings, especially Philippians: it evidences no specific occasion and addresses no clear theological or ethical issues.

It is difficult to see why a pseudonymous author would choose to forge a letter in the name of Paul without trying to achieve some kind of overarching purpose such as attacking a particular heresy (cf. 3 Corinthians) or promoting Paul's apostolic status (cf. the correspondence of Paul and Seneca). It may be that this particular letter was forged by a proto-orthodox author precisely in order to counter the *Marcionite* Letter to the Laodiceans. By compiling a number of Pauline commonplaces, the author could claim that this, rather than the heretical forgery of Marcion's followers, was actually the letter Paul had mentioned at the end of his epistle to the Colossians.

It is difficult to determine when this letter was written, but most scholars would date it to the second or third centuries.

---

[1]See further, Ehrman, *Lost Christianities*, 213–15. [2]On the life and teachings of Marcion, see Ehrman, *Lost Christianities*, 103–09.

Translation by J. K. Elliott, *Apocryphal New Testament* (Oxford: Clarendon Press, 1993) 546; used with permission.

1 Paul, an apostle not of men and not through man, but through Jesus Christ, to the brethren who are in Laodicea: 2 Grace to you and peace from God the Father and the Lord Jesus Christ.

3 I thank Christ in all my prayer that you continue in him and persevere in his works, in expectation of the promise at the day of judgement. 4 And may you not be deceived by the vain talk of some people who tell tales that they may lead you away from the truth of the gospel which is proclaimed by me. 5 And now may God grant that those who come from me for the furtherance of the truth of the gospel (. . .) may be able to serve and to do good works for the well-being of eternal life.

6 And now my bonds are manifest, which I suffer in Christ, on account of which I am glad and rejoice. 7 This to me leads to eternal salvation, which itself is brought about through your prayers and by the help of the Holy Spirit, whether it be through life or through death. 8 For my life is in Christ and to die is joy.

9 And his mercy will work in you, that you may have the same love and be of one mind. 10 Therefore, beloved, as you have heard in my presence, so hold fast and work in the fear of God, and eternal life will be yours. 11 For it is God who works in you. 12 And do without hesitation what you do. 13 And for the rest, beloved, rejoice in Christ and beware of those who are out for sordid gain. 14 May all your requests be manifest before God, and be steadfast in the mind of Christ. 15 And do what is pure, true, proper, just, and lovely. 16 And what you have heard and received, hold in your heart, and peace will be with you.

17 [3] Salute all the brethren with the holy kiss. 18 The saints salute you. 19 The grace of the Lord Jesus Christ be with your spirit. 20 And see that (this epistle) is read to the Colossians[4] and that of the Colossians to you.

---

[3] V. 17 is absent in some manuscripts.   [4] Some MSS omit "to the Colossians."

The Letter of 1 Clement

The letter of 1 Clement was an important document in the early church.[1] Some proto-orthodox Christians quoted it as canonical Scripture; it was included in several manuscripts, including the famous fifth-century Codex Alexandrinus, as one of the books of the New Testament. Eventually, though, the book fell into disuse and was lost from view until rediscovered in the seventeenth century.

The letter was sent from "the church of God that temporarily resides in Rome" to "the church of God that temporarily resides in Corinth" (1:1). Although traditionally ascribed to Clement, thought to have been the third bishop of Rome, the letter itself never names its author or mentions Clement. The purpose of the writing, in any event, is perfectly clear. There has been a division in the church in Corinth, a "vile and profane faction" (1:1) in which the elders of the church were forcibly deposed from their office and others took their place (3:2–4). For the Roman Christians, this is an altogether unacceptable arrangement: "It is shameful, loved ones, exceedingly shameful and unworthy of your conduct in Christ, that the most secure and ancient church of the Corinthians is reported to have created a faction against its presbyters, at the instigation of one or two persons" (47:6). The letter urges the congregation to do something about the situation: they are to remove the new leaders and reinstate the old.

At the core of the letter's argument against the Corinthian usurpers lies one of the earliest expressions of the notion of "apostolic succession," which came to play such a significant role in theological controversies of the second century. According to this view, the original leaders of the Christian churches had been appointed by the apostles, who were themselves chosen by Christ, who was sent from God. Anyone who deposes these leaders, therefore, is in direct rebellion against God himself (chaps. 42–44).

Much of the argument revolves around the history of the people of God as known from the Jewish Scriptures. According to 1 Clement, from the time of Cain and Abel onwards, envy and strife have always been

---

[1]For further discussion, see Ehrman, *Lost Christianities*, 141–43.

Translation by Bart D. Ehrman, in *The Apostolic Fathers*, vol. 1 (Loeb Classical Library; Cambridge, Mass.: Harvard University Press, 2003); used with permission.

promoted by sinners opposed to the righteous. The new leaders of the Corinthian congregation stand within this nefarious line: they have swindled their way into power out of jealousy and rivalry. But for this author, God opposes those who exalt themselves over the ones he has himself chosen. This is shown not only from writings of the Jewish prophets, but also from the teachings of Jesus and the writings of the apostles (e.g., chaps. 12 and 46).

The letter is generally recognized as having been written near the end of the first century, possibly around 95 CE during the reign of Domitian—before, that is, some of the books of the New Testament itself had been produced (e.g., 2 Peter).

The church of God that temporarily resides in Rome, to the church of God that temporarily resides in Corinth, to those who have been called and made holy by the will of God through our Lord Jesus Christ. May grace and peace be increased among you, from the all-powerful God, through Jesus Christ.

1 Because of the sudden and repeated misfortunes and setbacks we have experienced, we realize that we have been slow to turn our attention to the matters causing disputes among you, loved ones, involving that vile and profane faction that is alien and foreign to God's chosen people—a faction stoked by a few reckless and headstrong persons to such a pitch of madness that your venerable and renowned reputation, worthy of everyone's love, has been greatly slandered.

2 For who has ever visited you and not approved your highly virtuous and stable faith? And not been astonished by your temperate and gentle piety in Christ? And not proclaimed the magnificent character of your hospitality? And not uttered a blessing for your perfect and unwavering knowledge?

3 For you used to act impartially in all that you did, and you walked according to the ordinances of God, submitting yourselves to your leaders and rendering all due honor to those who were older[a] among you. You instructed your young people to think moderate and respectful thoughts. You directed women to accomplish all things with a blameless, respectful, and pure conscience, dutifully loving their husbands. And you taught them to run their households respectfully, living under the rule of submission, practicing discretion in every way.

2 And all of you used to be humble in mind, not arrogant in the least, being submissive rather than forcing submission, giving more gladly than receiving,[2] being satisfied with the provisions supplied by Christ. You heeded his words, carefully storing them up in your inner selves. And his sufferings were present before your eyes.

2 For this reason a deep and rich peace was given to all, along with an insatiable desire for doing good; and a full outpouring of the Holy Spirit came upon everyone.

[a]Or: *presbyters*

[2]Acts 20:35.

3 And being filled with his holy will, you used to stretch out your hands to the all-powerful God, zealous for the good, with pious confidence, begging him to be gracious if you inadvertently committed any sin.

4 Day and night you struggled on behalf of the entire brotherhood, that the total number of his chosen ones might be saved, with mortal fear and self-awareness.[b]

5 You were sincere and innocent and bore no grudges against one another.

6 Every faction and schism was loathsome to you. You used to grieve over the unlawful acts of your neighbors and considered their shortcomings your own.

7 You had no regrets when doing good; you were prepared for every good deed.[3]

8 You were adorned with a highly virtuous and honorable way of life, and you accomplished all things in reverential awe of him. The commandments and righteous demands of the Lord were inscribed upon the tablets of your heart.[4]

3 All glory and enlargement was given to you, and that which was written was fulfilled: "My loved one ate and drank and became large and grew fat and kicked out with his heels."[5]

2 From this came jealousy and envy, strife and faction, persecution and disorderliness, war and captivity.

3 And so the dishonorable rose up against the honorable, the disreputable against the reputable, the senseless against the sensible, the young against the old.[6, c]

4 For this reason, righteousness and peace are far removed,[7] since each has abandoned the reverential awe of God and become dim-sighted in faith, failing to proceed in the ordinances of his commandments and not living according to what is appropriate in Christ. Instead,

each one walks according to the desires of his evil heart, which have aroused unrighteous and impious jealousy—through which also death entered the world.[8]

4 For so it is written, "It came about that after some days, Cain brought an offering to God from the fruits of the earth; and for his part, Abel brought from the first born of the sheep and their fat.

2 And God looked favorably upon Abel and his gifts but paid no regard to Cain and his offerings.

3 And Cain was extremely upset and became downcast.

4 And God said to Cain, 'Why have you become so upset and downcast? If you brought the proper sacrifice but did not exercise proper discernment, have you not sinned?[d]

5 Be calm. He will return to you and you will rule over him.'[e]

6 And Cain said to his brother Abel, 'Let us go into the field.' And it came about that when they were in the field, Cain rose up against his brother Abel and murdered him."[9]

7 You see, brothers, jealousy and envy brought about the murder of a brother.

8 Because of jealousy our father Jacob fled from the presence of Esau, his brother.[10]

9 Jealousy caused Joseph to be perse-

[b]Or: *conscientiously;* meaning obscure [c]Or: *the presbyters.* [d]Or: *If you brought the proper sacrifice but did not divide it up properly, have you not sinned? Or, If you have rightly brought an offering but have not brought the right portion, have you not sinned? Or If you have brought, as was right, an offering but have not correctly discerned which one to bring, have you not sinned?* Meaning obscure, both in the Hebrew of Genesis and in this Greek translation. [e]Or: *It will turn to you and you will rule over it;* meaning obscure

[3]Titus 3:1. [4]Prov 7:3. [5]Deut 32:15. [6]Isa 3:5. [7]Isa 59:14. [8]Wis 2:24. [9]Gen 4:3–8. [10]Gen 27:41ff.

cuted to the point of death and to enter into slavery.[11]

10 Jealousy forced Moses to flee from the presence of Pharoah, king of Egypt, when he heard from his fellow countrymen, "Who made you an arbitrator or judge over us? Do you want to kill me, as you killed the Egyptian yesterday?"[12]

11 Because of jealousy Aaron and Miriam had to stay outside the camp.[13]

12 Jealousy brought Dathan and Abiram down into Hades while still alive because they created a faction against the servant of God, Moses.[14]

13 Because of jealousy not only did David incur envy from foreigners, but he was even persecuted by Saul, the king of Israel.[15]

5 But to stop giving ancient examples, let us come to those who became athletic contenders in quite recent times. We should consider the noble examples of our own generation.

2 Because of jealousy and envy the greatest and most upright pillars were persecuted, and they struggled in the contest even to death.

3 We should set before our eyes the good apostles.

4 There is Peter, who because of unjust jealousy bore up under hardships not just once or twice, but many times; and having thus borne his witness he went to the place of glory that he deserved.

5 Because of jealousy and strife Paul pointed the way to the prize for endurance.

6 Seven times he bore chains; he was sent into exile and stoned; he served as a herald in both the East and the West; and he received the noble reputation for his faith.

7 He taught righteousness to the whole world, and came to the limits of the West,

bearing his witness before the rulers. And so he was set free from this world and transported up to the holy place, having become the greatest example of endurance.

6 To these men who have conducted themselves in such a holy way there has been added a great multitude of the elect, who have set a superb example among us by the numerous torments and tortures they suffered because of jealousy.

2 Women were persecuted as Danaids and Dircae[f] and suffered terrifying and profane torments because of jealousy. But they confidently completed the race of faith, and though weak in body, they received a noble reward.

3 Jealousy estranged wives from their husbands and nullified what was spoken by our father Adam, "This now is bone from my bones and flesh from my flesh."[16]

4 Jealousy and strife overturned great cities and uprooted great nations.

---

[f]The author's meaning is unclear. Some scholars have suggested that he is referring to Christian women martyred under Nero, who was known for his creatively brutal excesses [see Suetonius, *Nero* 11, 12]. If so, women executed as Dircae may have been dragged to death in the arena, bound to the horns of a bull, like Dirce of Greek myth. The reference to the Danaids is more puzzling. Some scholars have seen it as an allusion to the legend that the daughters of Danaus were taken by men against their will—i.e. that the Christian women were publicly raped before being put to death. Others have thought that it refers to the punishment of Danaus's daughters in the afterlife, where they were compelled perpetually to fill leaking vessels—i.e., that the Christian women were subject to pointless and seemingly endless torments prior to their deaths. In either event, the text is so difficult that several emendations have been suggested to eliminate the reference to "Danaids and Dircae" altogether, the most popular of which changes the text to read: "persecuted as women, maidens, and slave-girls."

---

[11]Genesis 37.   [12]Exod 2:14.   [13]Numbers 12.   [14]Num 16:13.   [15]1 Samuel 18ff.   [16]Gen 2:23.

7 We are writing these things, loved ones, not only to admonish you but also to remind ourselves. For we are in the same arena and the same contest is set before us.

2 For this reason we should leave behind empty and frivolous thoughts and come to the famous and venerable rule of our tradition.

3 We should realize what is good and pleasing and acceptable before the one who made us.

4 We should gaze intently on the blood of Christ and realize how precious it is to his Father; for when it was poured out for our salvation, it brought the gracious gift of repentance to the entire world.

5 Let us review all the generations and learn that from one generation to the next the Master has provided an opportunity for repentance to those wanting to return to him.

6 Noah proclaimed repentance, and those who heeded were saved from danger.[17]

7 Jonah proclaimed an impending disaster to the Ninevites; and those who repented of their sins appeased God through their fervent pleas and received salvation, even though they had been estranged from God.[18]

8 Those who administered the gracious gift of God spoke through the Holy Spirit about repentance.

2 And the Master of all things himself spoke about repentance with an oath: "For as I live, says the Lord, I do not want the sinner to die but to repent."[19] And to this he added a good pronouncement:

3 "Repent from your lawlessness, house of Israel. Say to the children of my people, 'If your sins extend from the earth to the sky and are redder than scarlet and blacker than sackcloth, but you return to me with your whole heart and say, "Father," I will listen to you as to a holy people.' "[20]

4 And in another place he speaks as follows: "Wash and become clean; remove from yourselves the evils that are before my eyes; put an end to your evil deeds; learn to do good; pursue justice, rescue those who are treated unjustly, render a decision for the orphan and do what is right for the widow. And come, let us reason together, says the Lord. Even if your sins are like crimson, I will make them white as snow; and if they are like scarlet, I will make them white as wool. If you are willing and obey me, you will eat the good things of the earth; but if you are not willing and do not obey me, a sword will devour you. For the mouth of the Lord has spoken these things."[21]

5 Because he wanted all his loved ones to have a share in repentance, he set it in place by his all-powerful will.

9 For this reason we should obey his magnificent and glorious will and, as petitioners of his mercy and kindness, fall down before him and turn to his compassionate ways, leaving behind our pointless toil and strife and the jealousy that leads to death.

2 We should gaze intently on those who have perfectly served his magnificent glory.

3 We should consider Enoch, who was transported to another place because he was found to be righteous in his obedience; and his death was never found.[22]

---

[17]Genesis 7.   [18]Jonah 3.   [19]Cf. Ezek 33:11.   [20]Possibly drawn from Ezekiel 33.   [21]Isa 1:16–20   [22]Gen 5:24; Heb 11:5.

4 Noah, who was found to be faithful through his service, proclaimed a new beginning to the world; and through him the Master saved the living creatures that entered the ark in harmony.[23]

10 Abraham, who was called "The Friend,"[24] was found to be faithful when he became obedient to God's words.

2 In obedience he left his land, his family, and his father's house, so that by abandoning a paltry land, an insignificant family, and a small house he might inherit the promises of God. For God said to him,

3 "Depart from your land, your family, and your father's house to the land I will show you. And I will form you into a great nation and I will bless you and make your name great; and you will be blessed. And I will bless those who bless you and curse those who curse you, and all the tribes of the earth will be blessed in you."[25]

4 And again when Abraham separated from Lot, God said to him, "Lift up your eyes and look out from where you are now to the north, south, east, and west; for I will give all the land that you see to you and your offspring forever.

5 And I will make your offspring like the sand of the earth. If anyone is able to count the sand of the earth, your offspring will also be counted."[26]

6 Again it says, "God led Abraham out and said to him, 'Look up into the sky and count the stars, if you are able to number them. So will your offspring be.' And Abraham trusted God, and it was accounted to him as righteousness."[27]

7 Because of his faith and hospitality, a son was given to him in his old age; and in obedience he offered him up as a sacrifice to God on one of the mountains that he showed him.[28]

11 Because of his hospitality and piety, Lot was saved out of Sodom when all the surrounding countryside was judged by fire and brimstone.[29] The Master thus made it clear that he does not abandon those who hope in him, but hands over to punishment and torment those who turn away.

2 Lot's wife was made a sign of this: for when she left with him but then changed her mind and fell out of harmony, she was turned into a pillar of salt until this day—so that everyone may know that those who are of two minds and who doubt the power of God enter into judgment and become a visible sign for all generations.

12 Because of her faith and hospitality Rahab the prostitute was saved from danger.[30]

2 For when reconnaissance scouts had been sent into Jericho by Joshua, the son of Nun, the king of the land discovered that they had come to scout out their country and sent men to arrest them, so that once detained they could be executed.

3 And so, the hospitable Rahab brought them inside and hid them in the upper room under a pile of thatching straw.[g]

4 When the king's men arrived and said, "Those who are scouting out our land came into your house; bring them out, for so the king has ordered," she replied, "The men you are seeking did come in to see me, but they left right

---

[g]Or: *fine linen;* or: *flax.*

---

[23]Gen 6:8; Heb 11:7.   [24]Cf. Isa 41:8; Jas 2:23.
[25]Gen 12:1–3.   [26]Gen 13:14–16.   [27]Gen 15:5–6;
Rom 4:3.   [28]Gen 18:21; Genesis 22; Heb 11:17.
[29]The following account is drawn from Genesis 19.
[30]The following account is drawn from Joshua 2. Cf.
Heb 11:31; Jas 2:25.

away and are going on down the road." And she pointed them in the wrong direction.

5 And she said to the men, "I know full well that the Lord God is handing this land over to you, for fear and trembling has seized its inhabitants because of you. When you take the land, save me and my father's household."

6 They said to her, "It will be just as you have spoken to us. So, when you know that we are approaching, gather all your family under your roof and they will be saved. For whoever is found outside the house will perish."

7 And they proceeded to give her a sign[h], that she should hang a piece of scarlet from her house—making it clear that it is through the blood of the Lord that redemption will come to all who believe and hope in God.

8 You see, loved ones, not only was faith found in the woman, but prophecy as well.

13 And so we should be humble-minded, brothers, laying aside all arrogance, conceit, foolishness, and forms of anger; and we should act in accordance with what is written. For the Holy Spirit says, "The one who is wise should not boast about his wisdom, nor the one who is strong about his strength, nor the one who is wealthy about his wealth; instead, the one who boasts should boast about the Lord, seeking after him and doing what is just and right."[31] We should especially remember the words the Lord Jesus spoke when teaching about gentleness and patience.

2 For he said: "Show mercy, that you may be shown mercy; forgive, that it may be forgiven you. As you do, so it will be done to you; as you give, so it will be given to you; as you judge, so you will be judged; as you show kindness, so will

kindness be shown to you; the amount you dispense will be the amount you receive."[32]

3 Let us strengthen one another in this commandment and these demands, so that we may forge ahead, obedient to his words (which are well-suited for holiness) and humble-minded. For the holy word says,

4 "Upon whom shall I look, but upon the one who is meek and mild and who trembles at my sayings?"[33]

14 And so it is right and holy for us to obey God, brothers, rather than follow those who instigate a foul jealousy with arrogance and disorderliness.

2 For we will subject ourselves not to some ordinary harm, but to real danger, if we rashly hand ourselves over to the desires of those who rush headlong into strife and faction and so estrange us from what is good for us.

3 We should treat one another kindly, according to the compassion and sweet character of the one who made us.

4 For it is written, "Those who are kind will inhabit the land, and the innocent will be left upon it; but those who break the law will be destroyed from it."[34]

5 And again it says, "I saw one who was impious greatly exalted and raised high as the cedars of Lebanon. Then I passed by and look! He was no more. And I searched for his place, but did not find it. Protect what is innocent and focus on what is upright, because the one who lives in peace will have a posterity."[35] . . .

---

[h]Or: *in addition they told her to give a sign*

[31]Jer 9:23–24; 1 Cor 1:31; 2 Cor 10:17. [32]Matt 5:7; 6:14–15; 7:1–2, 12; Luke 6:31, 36–38. [33]Isa 66:2. [34]Prov 2:21–22; Ps 37:9, 38. [35]Ps 37:35–37.

19 The humility and obedient lowliness of so many people with such a strong reputation have improved not only us, but also the generations that came before us—indeed all those who received the sayings of God in reverential awe and truth.

2 And so, since we have shared in such numerous, great, and glorious deeds, we should forge ahead to the goal of peace that has been delivered to us from the beginning.[36] And we should gaze intently on the Father and Creator of the entire world and cling to his magnificent and superior gifts of peace and acts of kindness.

3 We should observe him with understanding and look upon his patient will with the eyes of our soul. We should realize how he feels no anger towards his entire creation.

20 The heavens, which move about under his management, are peacefully subject to him.

2 Day and night complete the racecourse laid out by him, without impeding one another in the least.

3 Sun and moon and the chorus of stars roll along the tracks that have been appointed to them, in harmony, never crossing their lines, in accordance with the arrangement he has made.

4 By his will and in the proper seasons, the fertile earth brings forth its rich abundance of nourishment for humans, beasts, and all living things that dwell on it, without dissenting or altering any of the decrees he has set forth.

5 Both the inscrutable regions of the abysses and the indescribable realms of the depths are constrained by the same commands.

6 The basin of the boundless sea, established by his workmanship to hold the waters collected, does not cross its restraining barriers, but acts just as he ordered.

7 For he said, "You shall come this far, and your waves shall crash down within you."[37]

8 The ocean, boundless to humans, and the worlds beyond it are governed by the same decrees of the Master.

9 The seasons—spring, summer, fall, and winter—succeed one another in peace.

10 The forces[i] of the winds complete their service in their own proper season, without faltering. And the eternal fountains, created for enjoyment and health, provide their life-giving breasts to humans without ceasing. The most insignificant living creatures associate with one another[j] in harmony and peace.

11 The great Creator and Master of all appointed all these things to be in peace and harmony, bringing great benefits to all things, but most especially to us, who flee to his compassion through our Lord Jesus Christ.

12 To him be the glory and the majesty forever and ever. Amen.

21 Loved ones, you should take care that his many acts of kindness do not lead to judgment against all of us. For this will happen if we fail to conduct ourselves worthily of him and do the things that are good and pleasing before him, in harmony.

2 For somewhere it says, "The Spirit of the Lord is a lamp that searches out the recesses deep within us."[38]

3 We should realize how near he is, and that none of our thoughts or the disputes we have had is hidden from him.

---

[i]Or: *stations*   [j]Or: *have sexual intercourse*

---

[36]Cf. Heb 12:1–2.   [37]Job 38:11.   [38]Prov 20:27.

4 And so it is right for us not to desert from his will.

5 It is better for us to offend foolish, senseless, and presumptuous people who boast in the arrogance of their own talk than to offend God.

6 We should revere the Lord Jesus Christ, whose blood was given for us; we should respect our leaders; we should honor the elderly;ᵏ we should discipline our youth in the reverential fear of God; we should set our wives along the straight path that leads to the good.

7 Let them display a character of purity, worthy of love; let them exhibit the innocent will of their meekness; let them manifest the gentleness of their tongues through how they speak; let them show their love not with partiality, but equally to all those who stand in reverential awe of God in a holy way.

8 Let our children partake of the discipline that is in Christ. Let them learn the strength of humility before God and the power of pure love before God. Let them learn how the reverential awe of him is beautiful and great, and how it saves all those who conduct themselves in itˡ in a holy way, with a clear understanding.

9 For he is the one who explores our understandings and desires. His breath is in us, and when he wishes, he will remove it.

22 The faith that is in Christ guarantees all these thing. For he himself calls to us through the Holy Spirit: "Come, children, and hear me; I will teach you the reverential awe of the Lord.

2 Who is the person who wants to live and yearns to see good days?

3 Stop your tongue from speaking evil and your lips from spouting deceit.

4 Move away from evil and do what is good.

5 Seek after peace and pursue it.

6 The eyes of the Lord are upon the upright, and his ears attend to their prayer. But the face of the Lord is against those who do evil and destroys any recollection of them from the face of the earth.

7 The one who is upright has called out, and the Lord has heard him and delivered him from all his afflictions."³⁹

8 "Many are the plagues of the sinner, but mercy will surround those who hope in the Lord."⁴⁰

23 The beneficent father, compassionate in every way, has pity on those who stand in awe of him; gently and kindly does he bestow his gracious gifts on those who approach him with a pure resolve.

2 And so, we should not be of two minds, nor should we entertain wild notions about his superior and glorious gifts.

3 May this Scripture be far removed from us that says: "How miserable are those who are of two minds, who doubt in their soul, who say, 'We have heard these things from the time of our parents, and look! We have grown old, and none of these things has happened to us.'

4 You fools! Compare yourselves to a tree. Take a vine: first it sheds its leaves, then a bud appears, then a leaf, then a flower, and after these an unripe grape, and then an entire bunch fully grown."⁴¹ You see that the fruit of the tree becomes ripe in just a short time.

5 In truth, his plan will come to completion quickly and suddenly, as even the Scripture testifies, when it says, "He will

ᵏOr: *the presbyters* ˡOr: *in him*

³⁹Ps 34:11–17, 19. ⁴⁰Ps 32:10. ⁴¹Source unknown. Cf. 2 Clem 11:2–3.

come quickly and not delay. And suddenly the Lord will come to his temple—he who is holy, the one you await."[42]

24 We should consider, loved ones, how the Master continuously shows us the future resurrection that is about to occur, of which he made the Lord Jesus Christ the first-fruit by raising him from the dead.[43]

2 We should look, loved ones, at the resurrection that happens time after time.

3 Day and night reveal to us a resurrection: the night sleeps and the day arises; the day departs and the night arrives.

4 We should consider the crops: how, and in what way, does the sowing occur?

5 The sower goes out and casts each of the seeds onto the soil.[44] Because they are dry and barren they decay when they fall onto the soil. But then the magnificent forethought of the Master raises them up out of their decay, and from the one seed grow more, and so bring forth the crop.

25 Let us consider the incredible sign that occurs in the eastern climes, that is, in the regions near Arabia.

2 For there is a bird called the Phoenix. This unique creature lives five hundred years. And when at last it approaches its dissolution through death, it makes a tomb for itself out of frankincense, myrrh, and other spices. Then, when the time has been fulfilled, it enters into the tomb and dies.

3 But when its flesh rots, a worm is born. And nourished by the secretions of the dead creature, it sprouts wings. Then when it becomes strong, it takes the tomb containing the bones of its predecessor and bears these from Arabia to Egypt, to the city called Heliopolis.

4 In the daytime, while all are watching, it flies onto the altar of the sun and

deposits these things, and so hastens back.

5 Then the priests examine the records of the times and discover that it has come after five hundred years have elapsed.

26 Do we then think that it is so great and marvelous that the Creator of all things will raise everyone who has served him in a holy way with the confidence of good faith, when he shows us the magnificence of his promise even through a bird?

2 For it says somewhere, "You will raise me up and I will praise you,"[45] and, "I lay down and slept, and I arose, because you are with me."[46]

3 And again, Job says, "You will raise this flesh of mine, which has endured all these things."[47] . . .

39 Those who are ignorant, unlearned, foolish, and uneducated mock and ridicule us, wishing to vaunt themselves in their own thoughts.

2 But what can a mortal accomplish? Or what power belongs to the one born of earth?

3 For it is written, "There was no form before my eyes, but I heard a puff of air and the sound of a voice.

4 What then? Can a mortal be pure before the Lord? Or can a man be blameless in what he does, when he does not trust his own servants and detects something crooked in his own messengers?[m]

5 Not even heaven is pure before him. But see! We who inhabit clay houses are ourselves made from the same clay. He smashed them like a moth, and from

---

[m]Meaning obscure

[42]Cf. Isa 13:22 (LXX); Mal 3:1.   [43]1 Cor 15:20.
[44]Mark 4:3; cf. 1 Cor 15:36ff.   [45]Ps 28:7.   [46]Ps 3:5.
[47]Job 19:26.

dawn to dusk they are no more. They perished, unable to come to their own assistance.

6 He breathed upon them and they died for want of wisdom.

7 But call out; see if anyone listens or if you observe any of the holy angels. For wrath[n] destroys the ignorant and zeal[o] kills the one who has been deceived.

8 I have seen the ignorant casting forth their roots, but their sustenance was immediately consumed.

9 May their children be far removed from safety; may they be derided before the doors of their inferiors, with no one there to deliver them. For the food prepared for them will be devoured by the upright, and they will not be delivered from those who are evil."[48]

40 Since these matters have been clarified for us in advance and we have gazed into the depths of divine knowledge, we should do everything the Master has commanded us to perform in an orderly way and at appointed times.

2 He commanded that the sacrificial offerings and liturgical rites be performed not in a random or haphazard way, but according to set times and hours.

3 In his superior plan he set forth both where and through whom he wished them to be performed, so that everything done in a holy way and according to his good pleasure might be acceptable to his will.

4 Thus, those who make their sacrificial offerings at the arranged times are acceptable and blessed. And since they follow the ordinances of the Master, they commit no sin.

5 For special liturgical rites have been assigned to the high priest, and a special place has been designated for the regular priests, and special ministries are established for the Levites. The lay person is assigned to matters enjoined on the laity.

41 Brothers, let each of us be pleasing to God by keeping to our special assignments with a good conscience, not violating the established rule of his ministry, acting in reverence.

2 The sacrifices made daily, or for vows, for sin, or for transgression, are not offered everywhere, brothers, but in Jerusalem alone; and even there a sacrifice is not made in just any place, but before the sanctuary on the altar, after the sacrificial animal has been inspected for blemishes by both the high priest and the ministers mentioned earlier.

3 Thus, those who do anything contrary to his plan bear the penalty of death.

4 You see, brothers, the more knowledge we have been deemed worthy to receive, the more we are subject to danger.

42 The apostles were given the gospel for us by the Lord Jesus Christ, and Jesus Christ was sent forth from God.

2 Thus Christ came from God and the apostles from Christ. Both things happened, then, in an orderly way according to the will of God.

3 When, therefore, the apostles received his commands and were fully convinced through the resurrection of our Lord Jesus Christ and persuaded by the word of God, they went forth proclaiming the good news that the Kingdom of God was about to come, brimming with confidence through the Holy Spirit.

4 And as they preached throughout the countryside and in the cities, they appointed the first-fruits of their ministries as bishops and deacons of those who

[n]Or: *his wrath*   [o]Or: *his zeal*

---

[48]Job 4:16–18; 15:15; 4:19–5:5.

were about to believe, testing them by the Spirit.

5 And this was no recent development. For indeed, bishops and deacons had been mentioned in writings long before. For thus the Scripture says in one place, "I will appoint their bishops in righteousness and their deacons in faith."[49]

43 And why should it be so amazing if those who were in Christ and entrusted by God with such a work appointed the leaders mentioned earlier? For even the most fortunate Moses, a faithful servant in all the house,[50] recorded in the sacred books all the directives that had been given him. And he was followed by all the other prophets, who together testified to the laws he laid down.

2 For when jealousy fell upon the tribes and created internal factions over the priesthood—concerning which of them should be adorned with that glorious name—Moses commanded the twelve tribal leaders to bring him rods, each one inscribed with the tribe's name.[51] Taking these he bound them together, sealed them with the rings of the tribal leaders, and set them in the Tent of Testimony on the table of God.

3 And he shut the Tent and sealed the keys just as he had done with the rods.

4 And he said to them, "Brothers, the tribe whose rod will blossom has been chosen by God to serve as his priests and ministers."

5 When early morning came, he called together all Israel, some six hundred thousand men, and showed the tribal leaders the seals. He opened the Tent of Testimony and brought out the rods. And the rod of Aaron was found not only to have blossomed, but even to be bearing fruit.

6 What do you think, loved ones? That Moses did not know in advance this would happen? Of course he knew. But he did this so that there might be no disorderliness in Israel, that the name of the one who is true and unique might be glorified. To him be the glory forever and ever. Amen.

44 So too our apostles knew through our Lord Jesus Christ that strife would arise over the office of the bishop.

2 For this reason, since they understood perfectly well in advance what would happen, they appointed those we have already mentioned; and afterwards they added a codicil[p] to the effect that if these should die, other approved men should succeed them in their ministry.

3 Thus we do not think it right to remove from the ministry those who were appointed by them or, afterwards, by other reputable men, with the entire church giving its approval. For they have ministered over the flock of Christ blamelessly and with humility, gently and unselfishly, receiving a good witness by all, many times over.

4 Indeed we commit no little sin if we remove from the bishop's office those who offer the gifts in a blameless and holy way.

5 How fortunate are the presbyters who passed on before, who enjoyed a fruitful and perfect departure from this life. For they have no fear that someone will remove them from the place established for them.

6 But we see that you have deposed

---

[p]The text appears here to be corrupt, and several emendations have been proposed.

---

[49]Isa 60:17 (LXX).   [50]Num 12:7; Heb 3:5.   [51]The following account is drawn from Numbers 17.

some from the ministry held blamelessly in honor among them, even though they had been conducting themselves well.

45 You should strive hard, brothers, and be zealous[q] in matters that pertain to salvation!

2 You have gazed into the holy and true Scriptures that were given through the Holy Spirit.

3 You realize that there is nothing unjust or counterfeit written in them. There you will not find the upright cast out by men who were holy.

4 The upright were persecuted, but by the lawless. They were imprisoned, but by the unholy. They were stoned by those who transgressed the law and killed by those who embraced vile and unjust envy.

5 And they bore up gloriously while suffering these things.

6 For what shall we say, brothers? Was Daniel cast into the lions' den by those who feared God?[52]

7 Or were Ananias, Azarias, and Misael shut up in the fiery furnace by those who participated in the magnificent and glorious worship of the Most High?[53] This could never be! Who then did these things? Those who were hateful and full of every evil were roused to such a pitch of anger that they tortured those who served God with holy and blameless resolve. But they did not know that the Most High is the champion and protector of those who minister to his all-virtuous name with a pure conscience. To him be the glory forever and ever. Amen.

8 But those who endured in confidence inherited glory and honor; and they were exalted and inscribed by God in their own memorial forever and ever. Amen.

46 And so, we too must cling to these examples, brothers.

2 For it is written, "Cling to those who are holy; for those who cling to them will themselves be made holy."[54]

3 And again in another place it says, "With an innocent man, you too will be innocent and with one who is chosen, you will be chosen. But with one who is corrupt, you will cause corruption."[55]

4 Therefore we should cling to those who are innocent and upright, for these are God's chosen.

5 Why are there conflicts, fits of anger, dissensions, factions, and war among you?

6 Do we not have one God, and one Christ, and one gracious Spirit that has been poured out upon us, and one calling in Christ?[56]

7 Why do we mangle and mutilate the members of Christ and create factions in our own body? Why do we come to such a pitch of madness as to forget that we are members of one another? Remember the words of our Lord Jesus,

8 for he said, "Woe to that person! It would have been good for him not to be born, rather than cause one of my chosen to stumble. Better for him to have a millstone cast about his neck and be drowned in the sea than to have corrupted one of my chosen."[57]

9 Your schism has corrupted many and cast many into despondency, many into doubt, and all of us into grief. And your faction persists even now!

47 Take up the epistle of that blessed apostle, Paul.

2 What did he write to you at first, at

---

[q]Or: *You are contentious, brothers, and envious*

[52]Dan 6:16. [53]Dan 3:19ff. [54]Source unknown. [55]Ps 18:25–26. [56]Eph 4:4–6. [57]Matt 26:24; Luke 17:2.

the beginning of his proclamation of the gospel?

3 To be sure, he sent you a letter in the Spirit[r] concerning himself and Cephas and Apollos, since you were even then engaged in partisanship.[58]

4 But that partisanship involved you in a relatively minor sin, for you were partisan towards reputable apostles and a man approved by them.

5 But now consider who has corrupted you and diminished the respect you had because of your esteemed love of others.

6 It is shameful, loved ones, exceedingly shameful and unworthy of your conduct in Christ, that the most secure and ancient church of the Corinthians is reported to have created a faction against its presbyters, at the instigation of one or two persons.

7 And this report has reached not only us but even those who stand opposed to us, so that blasphemies have been uttered against the Lord's name because of your foolishness; and you are exposing yourselves to danger.

48 And so let us dispose of this problem quickly and fall down before the Master and weep, begging him to be merciful and to be reconciled to us, and to restore us to our respected and holy conduct, seen in our love of others.

2 For this is a gate of righteousness that opens up onto life, just as it is written, "Open up for me gates of righteousness; when I enter through them I will give praises to the Lord.

3 This is the gate of the Lord, and the upright will enter through it."[59]

4 Although many gates open, this is the one that leads to righteousness—the one that is in Christ. All those who enter it are most fortunate; they make their path straight in holiness and righteousness, accomplishing all things without disorder.

5 Let a person be faithful, let him be able to speak forth knowledge, let him be wise in his discernment of words, let him be pure in deeds.

6 For the more he appears to be great, the more he should be humble, striving for the good of all, not just of himself.

49 The one who experiences love in Christ should do what Christ commanded.

2 Who can explain the bond of God's love?

3 Who is able to recount the greatness of its beauty?

4 The height to which love leads is beyond description.

5 Love binds us to God; love hides a multitude of sins;[60] love bears all things and endures all things. There is nothing vulgar in love, nothing haughty. Love has no schism, love creates no faction, love does all things in harmony. Everyone chosen by God has been perfected in love; apart from love nothing is pleasing to God.[61]

6 The Master has received us in love. Because of the love he had for us, our Lord Jesus Christ gave his blood for us, by God's will—his flesh for our flesh, his soul for our souls. . . .

53 For you know the sacred Scriptures, loved ones—and know them quite well—and you have gazed into the sayings of God. And so we write these things simply as a reminder.

2 For after Moses went up onto the mountain and spent forty days and nights in fasting and humility,[62] God said to him, "Moses, Moses, go down from here at

---

[r]Or: *with spiritual concerns*

---

[58]1 Cor 1:12. [59]Ps 118:19–20. [60]1 Pet 4:8. [61]Cf. 1 Cor 13:4–7. [62]The following account is drawn from Exod 32:7–10, 31–32 and Deut 9:12–14.

once: your people, whom you brought out of the land of Egypt, have broken the Law. They have departed quickly from the path you commanded them to take and cast metal idols for themselves."

3 And the Lord said to him, "I have spoken with you once and again: I have seen this people and know they are stiff-necked. Let me destroy them and I will blot their name out from beneath the sky; and I will make you into a great and spectacular nation, much greater than this one."

4 And Moses said, "May it never be Lord! Forgive the sin of this people—or blot me also out from the book of the living."

5 O great love! O incomparable perfection! The servant speaks boldly to the Lord, and asks for the multitude to be forgiven—or pleads for himself to be blotted out with them.

54 Who, therefore, among you is noble? Or compassionate? Or filled with love?

2 Let that one say, "If I am the cause of faction, strife, and schisms, I will depart; I will go wherever you wish and do what is commanded by the congregation. Only allow the flock of Christ to be at peace with the presbyters who have been appointed."

3 The one who does this will have made himself eminent in Christ and will be welcomed everywhere. "For the earth, and all that is in it, belongs to the Lord."[63]

4 Those who have performed their civic duty to God, without regrets, have done these things and will continue to do them.

55 But we should bring in examples from the Gentiles as well. Many kings and rulers, after receiving instruction from an oracle, have handed themselves over to death during the time

of plague, in order to deliver their fellow citizens by shedding their own blood. Many left their own cities to avoid creating more factions.

2 Among ourselves, we know many who put themselves in prison in order to ransom others; many placed themselves in slavery and fed others with the purchase price they received.

3 Many women were empowered by the gracious gift of God to perform numerous "manly" deeds.

4 The blessed Judith, when her city lay under siege, asked the elders for permission to go out to the foreigners' camp.[64]

5 And so she handed herself over to danger, going out because she loved her homeland and the people under siege. And the Lord handed Holofernes over to the hand of a female.

6 No less did Esther, a woman perfect in faith, put herself in danger to rescue the twelve tribes of Israel who were about to perish.[65] For through her fasting and humility she petitioned the all-seeing Master, the God of eternity, who saw the humbleness of her soul and rescued the people for whom she put herself in danger. . . .

59 But if some disobey the words he has spoken through us, they should realize that they entangle themselves in transgression and no little danger.

2 But we ourselves will be innocent of this sin, and we will ask with a fervent prayer and petition that the Creator of all may safeguard the number of those counted among his elect throughout the entire world, through his beloved child Jesus Christ, through whom he called us

---

[63]Ps 24:1. [64]The account is drawn from Judith 8ff. [65]The account is drawn from Esther 7; 4:16.

out of darkness into light, from ignorance into the knowledge of his glorious name.

3 Grant us, O Lord,[s] that we may hope in your name, the ultimate source of all creation. Open the eyes of our heart, that we may recognize you as the one alone who is the highest among the highest, the holy one who rests among the holy, the one who humbles the insolence of the proud, who destroys the reasonings of the nations, who exalts the humble to the heights and humiliates the exalted, the one who enriches and impoverishes, who kills and brings to life, the sole benefactor of spirits and the God of all flesh, the one who peers into the places of the abyss, who observes the works of humans and helps those in danger, the savior of those who have abandoned hope, the creator and overseer of every spirit, the one who multiplies the nations upon the earth and who from them all has chosen those who love you through Jesus Christ, your beloved child, through whom you have disciplined, sanctified, and honored us.

4 We ask you, O Master, to be our helper and defender. Save those of us who are in affliction, show mercy to those who are humble, raise those who have fallen, show yourself to those who are in need, heal those who are sick, set straight those among your people who are going astray. Feed the hungry, ransom our prisoners, raise up the weak, encourage the despondent. Let all the nations know you, that you alone are God, that Jesus Christ is your child, and that we are your people and the sheep of your pasture.

60 For you have made plain the eternal structure of the world through the works you have accomplished. You, O Lord, created the world in which we live; you are faithful from one generation to the next, upright in your judgments, spectacular in your strength and magnificence; you are wise when you create and understanding when you establish what exists; you are good in what is seen and kind to those who trust you. You who are merciful and compassionate, forgive us for our lawless acts, unjust deeds, transgressions, and faults.

2 Take into account none of the sins committed by your male slaves and female servants, but cleanse us with your truth. Set our steps straight that we may go forward with devout hearts, to do what is good and pleasing to you and to those who rule us.

3 Yes, Master, make your face shine on us in peace, for our own good, that we may be protected by your powerful hand and rescued from our every sin by your exalted arm. And rescue us from those who hate us without cause.

4 Give harmony and peace both to us and to all those who inhabit the earth, just as you gave it to our ancestors when they called upon you in a holy way, in faith and truth; and allow us to be obedient to your all-powerful and all-virtuous name, and to those who rule and lead us here on earth.

61 You have given them, O Master, the authority to rule through your magnificent and indescribable power, that we may both recognize the glory and honor you have given them

---

[s]There is an abrupt and ungrammatical shift between vv. 2 and 3 in the Greek; I have followed an emendation which restores three words to the beginning of v. 3 to indicate that the long prayer of the following chapters begins here; see 61.1

and subject ourselves to them, resisting nothing that conforms to your will. Give to them, O Lord, health, peace, harmony, and stability, so that without faltering they may administer the rule that you have given to them.

2 For you, O Master, Heavenly King forever, give humans glory, honor, and authority over the creatures of the earth. O Lord, make their plan conform with what is good and acceptable before you, that when they administer with piety the authority you have given them, in peace and meekness, they may attain your mercy.

3 You who alone can to do these things for us, and do what is more abundantly good, we praise you through the high priest and benefactor of our souls, Jesus Christ, through whom the glory and majesty be yours both now and for all generations and forever. Amen.

62 Brothers, we have written you enough about what is fitting for our worship and what is most profitable for the virtuous life, for those who want to conduct themselves in a pious and upright way.

2 For we have touched on every aspect of faith, repentance, genuine love, self-restraint, moderation, and endurance, reminding you that you must be pleasing, in a holy way, both to the all-powerful God—by acting in righteousness, truth, and patience, living in harmony, holding no grudges, living in love and peace with fervent gentleness, just as our ancestors, whom we mentioned before, were pleasing to God by being humble-minded toward the Father, who is both God and Creator—and to all people.

3 And we were all the more happy to bring these things to mind, since we knew full well that we were writing to faithful and highly respectable men, who have gazed into the sayings of God's teaching.[u]

63 Now that we have considered such great and so many examples, it is right for us to bow our necks in submission and assume a position of obedience. In this way, by putting a halt to the futile faction, we will truly reach the goal set before us, with no blame attached.

2 For you will make us joyful and happy if you become obedient to what we have written through the Holy Spirit and excise the wanton anger expressed through your jealousy, in accordance with the request we have made in this letter for your peace and harmony.

3 And we have sent faithful and temperate men who have lived blamelessly among us from youth to old age; these also will serve as witnesses between you and us.

4 We have done this that you may know that our every concern has been— and is—for you to establish the peace quickly.

64 And finally, may the God who observes all things, the Master of spirits and Lord of all flesh, who chose both the Lord Jesus Christ and us through him to be his special people—may he grant to every soul that is called by his magnificent and holy name faith, reverential awe, peace, endurance and patience, self-restraint, purity, and moderation, that they may be found pleasing to his name through our high priest and benefactor, Jesus Christ. Through whom to him be glory and greatness, power

[u]Or: *the sayings of God that bring discipline*

and honor, both now and forevermore. Amen.

65 But send back to us quickly our envoys Claudius Ephebus and Valerius Bito, along with Fortunatus, in peace and with joy, that they may inform us without delay about the peace and harmony that we have prayed and desired for you. Then we will rejoice more quickly in your stability.

2 The grace of our Lord Jesus Christ be with you and with all those everywhere who are called by God through him. Through whom be to him all glory, honor, power, greatness, and the eternal throne, forever and ever. Amen.

perishable, and to love
gs, which are good and

g the will of Christ we
e of rest; on the other
ill deliver us from eter-
if we disobey his

ipture also says in Eze-
Noah, Job, and Daniel
y will not deliver their
ptivity."[14]

ich upright men as these
eir children through acts
, with what confidence
the kingdom of God if
our baptism pure and
ho will serve as our ad-
not found doing what is
?

ny brothers, we should
the games, knowing
ion is at hand. Many set
ompetitions but not all
—only those who labor
well.

erefore compete that we
ed.

should run the straight
l competition. Many of
t and compete, that we
rown. And if all of us
e crown, we should at
o it.

ize that if someone is
while competing in an
is flogged and thrown
.

suppose? What will
who cheats in the eter-

who do not keep the
tism, he says: "Their
nor their fire be extin-
will be a spectacle for

8 And so we should repent while we are still on earth.

2 For we are clay in the hand of the artisan. As in the case of a potter: if he is making a vessel that becomes twisted or crushed in his hands, he then remolds it; but if he has already put it in the kiln, he can no longer fix it. So too with us. While we are still in the world, we should repent from our whole heart of the evil we have done in the flesh, so the Lord will save us—while there is still time for repentance.

3 For after we leave the world we will no longer be able to make confession or repent in that place.

4 So then, brothers, if we do the will of the Father and keep our flesh pure and guard the commandments of the Lord we will receive eternal life.

5 For the Lord says in the Gospel, "If you do not keep what is small, who will give you what is great? For I say to you that the one who is faithful in very little is faithful also in much."[16]

6 This then is what he means: you should keep the flesh pure and the seal of baptism stainless, so that we may receive eternal life.

9 And none of you should say that this flesh is neither judged nor raised.

2 Think about it! In what state were you saved? In what state did you regain your sight? Was it not while you were in this flesh?

3 And so we must guard the flesh like the temple of God.

4 For just as you were called in the flesh, so also you will come in the flesh.

5 Since Jesus Christ—the Lord who saved us—was first a spirit and then be-

[14]Ezek 14:14ff.   [15]Isa 66:24; cf. Mark 9:44, 46, 48.
[16]Luke 16:10–12.

The Letter of 2 Clement

In parts of early Christianity, down to at least the fifth century, the book known as 2 Clement was regarded as Scripture. It is included, along with 1 Clement, as one of the books of the New Testament in the fifth-century codex Alexandrinus.

The traditional title of the book ("The Second Letter of Clement") is a misnomer: the book was not produced by the author of 1 Clement (as is evident on stylistic grounds) and is not a letter but a sermon (see 19:1). It appears to have been delivered to an actual congregation; as such, it is the oldest freestanding homily to survive from early Christianity.[1]

The audience, and probably the author, were former pagans who had converted to Christianity (see 2:6). Based initially on an interpretation of Isaiah 54:1, the homily largely consists of exhortations backed up by sayings of Jesus, passages from the Old Testament, and writings of the apostles. One of the author's sources appears to have been a Gnostic Gospel, possibly the Gospel of Thomas (12:2). Other sources that he quotes are no longer available to us, including one that contains an intriguing interchange between Peter and Jesus (5:2–4). The author uses these sacred texts to urge his audience to repent and return to upright moral behavior in light of the coming day of judgment. In the course of his exhortation he stresses the reality of the future resurrection of the flesh and attacks those who deny it (8:1). His overarching points are that followers of Christ should recognize the enormous debt they owe to God for the salvation he has wrought. In response, they should repent of their sins, recognize that their new lives cannot be tied to this sinful world in which they temporarily reside as aliens, and commit themselves to good works and self-control in light of the judgment of God that is sure to come.

It is difficult to say when, exactly, this sermon was written, but scholars usually date it to the mid-second century, and locate its anonymous author possibly in Corinth or Alexandria.

[1]Outside, that is, of the New Testament, where several sermons can be found in the books of Acts (e.g., chaps. 2 and 13), and which includes the book of Hebrews, thought by some scholars to be an early Christian homily.

Translation by Bart D. Ehrman, in *The Apostolic Fathers*, vol. 1 (Loeb Classical Library; Cambridge, Mass.: Harvard University Press, 2003); used with permission.

1 Brothers, we must think about Jesus Christ as we think about God, as about the judge of the living and the dead.[2] And we must not give little thought to our salvation.

2 For when we think little about him, we also hope to receive but little. And we who listen as if these were little things sin, not realizing where we have been called from, by whom, and to what place, nor how many sufferings Jesus Christ endured for us.

3 What then shall we give to him in exchange? How can we produce anything comparable to what he has given us? And how many holy deeds do we owe him?

4 For he graciously bestowed light upon us. Like a father, he called us children; while we were perishing, he saved us.

5 What praise, then, shall we give him, or what can we pay in exchange for what we have received?

6 We were maimed in our understanding, worshiping stones and pieces of wood and gold and silver and copper—all of them made by humans. And our entire life was nothing other than death. Then when we were beset by darkening gloom, our vision blurred by such mist, we regained our sight through his will by setting aside the cloud that enveloped us.

7 For he showed mercy on us and through his compassion saved us. For he saw that a great error and destruction was in us, and that we had not the slightest hope of being saved, unless it came through him.

8 For he called us while we did not exist, and he wished us to come into being from non-being.

2 "Be jubilant, you who are infertile and who do not bear children! Let your voice burst forth and cry out, you who experience no pains of labor! For the one who has been deserted has more children than the one who has a husband."[3] Now when it says, "Be jubilant, you who are infertile and who do not bear children," it is referring to us. For our church was infertile before children were given to it.

2 And when it says, "Cry out, you who experience no pains of labor," it means this: we should raise our prayers up to God sincerely and not grow weary like women in labor.

3 And when it says, "For the one who has been deserted has more children than the one who has a husband," it is because our people appeared to be deserted by God, but now that we believe we have become more numerous than those who appear to have God.

4 And also another Scripture says, "I did not come to call the upright, but sinners."[4]

5 This means that he was to save[a] those who were perishing.

6 For it is a great and astonishing feat to fix in place something that is toppling over, not something that is standing.

7 Thus also Christ wished to save what was perishing. And he did save many; for he came and called us while we were on the brink of destruction.

3 He has shown us such mercy since, to begin with, we who are living do not sacrifice to dead gods or worship them; instead, through him we know the Father of truth. What then is the knowledge that is directed toward to him? Is it not refusing to deny the one through whom we have come to know him?

2 For even he himself says, "I will acknowledge before my Father the one who acknowledges me before others."[5]

---

[a]Or: that one must save

[2]Acts 10:42; 1 Pet 4:5.   [3]Isa 54:1; Gal 4:27.   [4]Matt 9:13; Mark 2:17; Luke 5:32.   [5]Matt 10:32; Luke 12:8.

3 This then is our reward, if we acknowledge the one through whom we were saved.

4 But how do we acknowledge him? By doing the things he says, not disobeying his commandments, and not honoring him only with our lips but from our whole heart and our whole understanding.[6]

5 For he also says in Isaiah, "This people honors me with their lips, but their heart is far removed from me."[7]

4 For this reason we should not merely call him Lord; for this will not save us.

2 For he says, "Not everyone who says to me, 'Lord, Lord' will be saved, but only the one who does righteousness."[8]

3 So then, brothers, we should acknowledge him by what we do, by loving one another, by not committing adultery or slandering one another or showing envy. We should be restrained, charitable, and good. We should be sympathetic with one another and not be attached to money. By doing such deeds we acknowledge him, not by doing their opposites.

4 And we must not fear people, but God.

5 For this reason, when you do these things, the Lord has said, "Even if you were cuddled up with me next to my breast but did not do what I have commanded, I would cast you away and say to you, 'Leave me! I do not know where you are from, you who do what is lawless.' "[9]

5 Therefore, brothers, having abandoned our temporary residence in this world, we should do the will of the one who called us and not fear departing from this world.

2 For the Lord said, "You will be like sheep in the midst of wolves."[10]

short-lived, a
those other th
imperishable.

7 For by d
will find a p
hand, nothing
al punishme
commandmer

8 And the
kiel, "Even
should arise,
children from

9 But if eve
cannot delive
of righteousr
can we enter
we do not k
undefiled? O
vocate, if we
holy and upr

7 So the
compe
that the com
sail for earth
receive the c
hard and con

2 We shou
all may be c

3 And so
course, the e
us should sa
may receive
cannot recei
least come c

4 We mus
caught chea
earthly conte
out of the st

5 What d
happen to th
nal competi

6 As for
seal of the
worm will r
guished; an
all to see."[15]

came flesh, and in this way called us, so also we will receive the reward in this flesh.

6 And so we should love one another, that we may all enter the Kingdom of God.

7 While we have time to be healed, let us give ourselves over to the God who brings healing, paying him what is due.

8 And what is that? Repentance from a sincere heart.

9 For he knows all things in advance and recognizes what is in our hearts.

10 And so we should give him praise, not from our mouth alone but also from our heart, that he may welcome us as children.

11 For the Lord also said, "My brothers are these who do the will of my Father."[17]

10 So my brothers, let us do the will of the Father who called us, that we may live; even more, let us pursue virtue. But we should abandon evil as a forerunner of our sins; and we should flee from impiety, lest evil overtake us.

2 For if we are eager to do good, peace will pursue us.

3 For this reason no one can find peace when they bring forward human fears and prefer the pleasure of the present to the promise that is yet to come.

4 For they do not realize the kind of torment brought by present pleasure or the kind of delight coming with the future promise.

5 It would be tolerable if they alone were doing these things; but now they persist in teaching such evil notions to innocent people, not knowing that they will bear a double penalty—both they and those who listen to them.

11 For this reason we should be enslaved to God with a pure

heart, and then we will be upright. But if we choose not to be enslaved to God, not believing in his promise, we will be miserable.

2 For the prophetic word also says, "How miserable are those of two minds, who doubt in their hearts, who say, 'We heard these things long ago, in the time of our parents, but though we have waited day after day, we have seen none of them.'

3 Fools! Compare yourselves to a tree. Take a vine: first it sheds its leaves, then a bud appears, and after these things an unripe grape, and then an entire bunch fully grown.

4 So too my people is now disorderly and afflicted; but then it will receive what is good."[18]

5 So my brothers, we should not be of two minds but should remain hopeful, that we may receive the reward.

6 For the one who has promised to reward each according to his deeds is faithful.[19]

7 If, therefore, we do what is righteous before God, we will enter into his kingdom and receive his promises, which no ear has heard nor eye seen, nor has it entered into the human heart.[20]

12 For this reason, we should await the kingdom of God with love and righteousness every hour, since we do not know the day when God will appear.

2 For when the Lord himself was asked by someone when his kingdom would come, he said, "When the two are one, and the outside like the inside, and the male with the female is neither male nor female."[21]

---

[17]Matt 12:50; Mark 3:35; Luke 8:21. [18]Source unknown. Cf. 1 Clem 23:3–4. [19]Heb 10:23. [20]1 Cor 2:9. [21]Cf. *Gosp. Thom.* 22; also quoted in Clement of Alexandria, *Stromateis* 3:13, where it is attributed to the lost *Gospel of the Egyptians.*

3 Now "the two are one" when we speak truth to one another and when one soul exists in two bodies with no posturing.[b]

4 And "the outside like the inside" means this: the "inside" refers to the soul and the "outside" to the body. Just as your body is visible, so too your soul should be clearly seen in your good deeds.

5 And the words "the male with the female is neither male nor female" mean this, that a brother who sees a sister should think nothing about her being female and she[c] should think nothing about his being male.

6 When you do these things, he says, "the kingdom of my Father will come."

13 And so brothers, now at last we should repent and be alert for the good. For we are filled with great foolishness and evil. We should wipe our former sins away from ourselves; and if we repent from deep within we will be saved. We should not be crowd-pleasers nor wish to please only ourselves, but through our righteous activity we should be pleasing as well to those outside the fold, that the name not be blasphemed because of us.

2 For the Lord says, "My name is constantly blasphemed among all the outsiders[d]."[22] And again he says, "Woe to the one who causes my name to be blasphemed."[23] How is it blasphemed? When you fail to do what I wish.

3 For when outsiders[e] hear the sayings of God from our mouths, they are astonished at their beauty and greatness. Then when they discover that our actions do not match our words, they turn from astonishment to blasphemy, saying that our faith is some kind of myth and error.

4 For, on the one hand, they hear from us that God has said, "It is no great accomplishment for you to love those who love you; it is great if you love your enemies and those who hate you."[24] And when they hear these things, they are astonished by their extraordinary goodness. But then when they see that we fail to love not only those who hate us, but even those who love us, they ridicule us and the name is blasphemed. . . .

---

[b]Or: *with no hypocrisy*   [c]Or: *he*   [d]Literally: *Gentiles, or nations*   [e]Literally: *Gentiles, or nations*

---

[22]Isa 52:5.   [23]Source unknown.   [24]Luke 6:32, 35.

The "Letter of Peter to James" and its "Reception"

The "Letter of Peter to James" is one of a number of early Christian writings pseudonymously written in the name of Jesus' disciple, Simon Peter (cf. the Gospel of Peter and the Apocalypse of Peter, both included in this collection). It does not survive as an independently transmitted letter, but only as the preface to the "Homilies of Clement" a collection of legendary stories and sermons of Clement of Rome (see below).[1] The account of its "Reception" by James, the brother of Jesus and leader of the church in Jerusalem, is also part of this preface.

The Letter of Peter urges James to pass along the accompanying sermons carefully to those who are worthy to receive them, and to no one else. The clear concern is that Peter's teachings not be corrupted by those who have a different understanding of the truth. Both the Letter and the Reception are Jewish-Christian in their orientation, as seen in their emphasis on emulating the actions of Moses, on keeping the Law, and on opposing the person Peter calls "the man who is my enemy."[2] Peter's opponent here is commonly understood to be none other than the apostle Paul (cf. Gal 2: 11–14), who taught that salvation comes to all people, Jew and Gentile, apart from following the Law of Moses, and who urged Gentiles not to be circumcised (Gal. 5:2–12). This Pauline notion stood in sharp contrast to the views of Jewish Christians like the Ebionites, as seen here, for example, in the insistence by James (the brother of Jesus himself) that only "one who has been circumcised is a believing Christian."

It is difficult to determine the date of the composition of these works, but they are probably to be situated in the early third century.

---

[1]For more information on the "Pseudo-Clementine" literature, see Ehrman, *Lost Christianities*, 182–85. [2]On Jewish Christianity, see Ehrman, *Lost Christianities*, 95–103.

Translation by Johannes Irmscher and George Strecker, in Wilhelm Schneemelcher, *New Testament Apocrypha*, vol. 2 (rev. ed.: Cambridge/ Louisville: Lutterworth/Westminister/ John Knox, 1991) 493–94; used with permission.

1 Peter to James, the lord and bishop of the holy church: Peace be with you always from the Father of all through Jesus Christ.

2 Knowing well that you, my brother, eagerly take pains about what is for the mutual benefit of us all, I earnestly beseech you not to pass on to any one of the Gentiles the books of my preachings which I (here) forward to you, nor to any one of our own tribe before probation. But if some one of them has been examined and found to be worthy, then you may hand them over to him in the same way as Moses handed over his office of a teacher to the seventy.

3 Wherefore also the fruit of his caution is to be seen up to this day. For those who belong to his people preserve everywhere the same rule in their belief in the one God and in their line of conduct, the Scriptures with their many senses being unable to incline them to assume another attitude.

4 Rather they attempt, on the basis of the rule that has been handed down to them, to harmonise the contradictions of the Scriptures, if haply some one who does not know the traditions is perplexed by the ambiguous utterances of the prophets.

5 On this account they permit no one to teach unless he first learn how the Scriptures should be used. Wherefore there obtain amongst them one God, one law, and one hope.

2 In order now that the same may also take place among us, hand over the books of my preachings in the same mysterious way to our seventy brethren that they may prepare those who are candidates for positions as teachers.

2 For if we do not proceed in this way, our word of truth will be split into many options. This I do not know as a prophet, but I have already the beginning of the evil before me.

3 For some from among the Gentiles have rejected my lawful preaching and have preferred a lawless and absurd doctrine of the man who is my enemy.

4 And indeed some have attempted, whilst I am still alive, to distort my words by interpretations of many sorts, as if I taught the dissolution of the law and, although I was of this opinion, did not express it openly. But that may God forbid!

5 For to do such a thing means to act contrary to the law of God which was made known by Moses and was confirmed by our Lord in its everlasting continuance. For he said: "The heaven and the earth will pass away, but one jot or one title shall not pass away from the law."[3]

6 This he said that everything might come to pass. But those persons who, I know not how, allege that they are at home in my thoughts wish to expound the words which they have heard of me better than I myself who spoke them. To those whom they instruct they say that this is my opinion, to which indeed I never gave a thought.

7 But if they falsely assert such a thing while I am still alive, how much more after my death will those who come later venture to do so?

3 In order now that such a thing may not happen I earnestly beseech you not to pass on the books of my preachings which I send you to any one of our own tribe or to any foreigner before probation, but if some one is examined and found

---

[3]Matt 24:35; 5:18.

to be worthy, let them then be handed over in the way

2 in which Moses handed over his office of a teacher to the seventy, in order that they may preserve the dogmas and extend farther the rule of the truth, interpreting everything in accordance with our tradition and not being dragged into error through ignorance and uncertainty in their minds to bring others into the like pit of destruction.

3 What seems to me to be necessary I have now indicated to you. And what you, my lord, deem to be right, do you carry fittingly into effect. Farewell.

The Reception of the Letter

1 Now when James had read the epistle he called the elders together, read it to them and said: "As is necessary and proper, our Peter had called our attention to the fact that we must be cautious in the matter of the truth, that we should pass on the books of his preachings that have been forwarded to us not indiscriminately, but only to a good and religious candidate for the position of a teacher, a man who as one who has been circumcised is a believing Christian, and indeed that we should not pass on all the books to him at once, so that, if he shows indiscretion in handling the first, he may not be entrusted with the others.

2 He ought therefore to be proved for not less than six years. Thereafter, according to the way of Moses, let him be brought to a river or a fountain where there is living water and the regeneration of the righteous takes place; not that he may swear, for that is not permitted, but he should be enjoined to stand by the water and to vow, as we also ourselves were made to do at the time of our re-

generation, to the end that we might sin no more.

2 And let him say: 'As witness I invoke heaven, earth, and water, in which everything is comprehended, and also in addition the all-pervading air, without which I am unable to breathe, that I shall always be obedient to him who hands over to me the books of the preachings and shall not pass on to any one in any way the books which he may give to me, that I shall neither copy them nor give a copy of them nor allow them to come into the hands of a copyist, neither shall I myself do this nor shall I do it through another, and not in any other way, through cunning or tricks, through keeping them carelessly, through depositing them with another or through underhand agreement, nor in any other manner or by means of any other artifice will I pass them on to a third party.

2 Only if I have proved someone to be worthy—proving him as I myself have been proved, or even more, in no case for less than six years—if he is a religious and good candidate for the position of a teacher, I will hand them over to him as I have received them and certainly in agreement with my bishop.

3 Otherwise, though he be either my son or a brother or a friend or any other relation, if he is unworthy, I shall keep information away from him since it does not befit him.

2 I shall allow myself neither to be frightened by persecutions nor to be deceived by gifts. And even if I should ever come to the conviction that the books of the preachings which have been handed to me do not contain the truth, then also I shall not pass them on but shall hand them back.

3 When I am on a journey, I shall carry

with me all the books that are in my possession. And if I purpose not to take them with me, I shall not leave them behind in my house, but shall consign them to the care of my bishop, who is of the same faith and of like extraction.

4 If I am sick and see death before me, I shall, if I am childless, proceed in the same way. I shall do the like if at the time of my death my son is not worthy or is not yet of age. I shall deposit the books with my bishop that if, when my son has come of age, he should prove to be worthy of the trust that he may hand them over to him as a father's legacy according to the terms of the vow.

4 And that I shall proceed in this way, I again invoke as witnesses heaven, earth, and water, in which everything is comprehended, and also in addition the all-pervading air without which I am unable to breathe: I shall be obedient to him who hands over to me the books of the preachings, I shall keep them in every respect as I have vowed and even beyond that.

2 If now I observe the agreements, then will my portion be with the saints; but if I act against my vow, then may the universe and the all-pervading ether and God, who is over all and is mightier and more exalted than any other, be hostile to me.

3 And if even I should come to believe in another god, then I swear also by him, whether he now is or is not, that I shall not proceed otherwise. In addition to all that, if I am false to my word, I shall be accursed living and dead and suffer eternal punishment.' And thereupon let him partake of bread and salt with him who hands over the books to him."

5 When James had said this, the elders were pale with fright. Accordingly, observing that they feared greatly, James said, "Hear me, brethren and fellow-servants.

2 If we pass on the books to all without discrimination and if they are falsified by audacious people and are spoiled by interpretations—as indeed you have heard that some have already done—then it will come to pass that even those who earnestly seek the truth will always be led into error.

3 On this account it is better that we keep the books and, as we have said, hand them with all caution only to those who wish to live and to save others. But if any one, after that he has made such a vow, does not adhere to it, then will he rightly suffer eternal punishment.

4 For why should he not go to ruin who has been guilty of the corruption of others?" Then were the elders pleased with James's conclusion and said, "Praised be he who has foreseen all things and destined you to be our bishop." And when they had said this, we rose up and prayed to God the Father of all, to whom be glory forever. Amen

The Homilies of Clement

The "Homilies of Clement" is an example of a pseudonymous Christian writing produced in the name of a famous person living after the apostles: Clement, thought to be the third bishop of Rome at the end of the first century (for other examples, see 1 Clement and 2 Clement, pp. 167, 185).[1] The Homilies consist of twenty legendary discourses allegedly delivered by Clement in Rome and sent to James the brother of Jesus and leader of the church in Jerusalem. In these discourses Clement narrates his family background, his search for truth, and, principally, his travels to the East, where he meets the apostle Simon Peter, whom he then accompanies, observing his words, deeds, and controversies.

As the following excerpts show, the Homilies embrace a Jewish-Christian perspective.[2] Peter is shown to be the chief apostle, bearer of Christ's power and leader of Christ's church; he claims ascendancy over his arch-rival, the magician Simon Magus, whom scholars often understand to be a thinly veiled cipher for the apostle Paul in this text, who is attacked for his view that salvation can come apart from the Jewish Law. Not so for this author, who stands within the Jewish-Christian tradition that saw the ongoing importance of the Law of Moses for salvation.[3]

The author tries to show Peter's (Jewish-Christian) understanding of the Gospel to be superior to Paul's in a number of ways. In one section in particular, Peter is said to have developed the notion that in the plan of God for humans, the lesser always precedes the greater. And so, Adam had two sons, the murderer Cain and the righteous Abel; two also sprang from Abraham, the outcast Ishmael and the chosen one Isaac; and from Isaac came the godless Esau and the godly Jacob. Bringing matters down to more recent times, there were two that appeared on the Gentile mission field, Simon (= Paul) and Peter, who was, of course, the greater of the two, "who

---

[1]For more detail, see Ehrman, *Lost Christianities*, 182–85. [2]See also the "Letter of Peter to James and its Reception"; this letter served as an introduction to the Homilies. [3]On Jewish-Christianity, see further, Ehrman, *Lost Christianities*, 95–103.

Translation by Georg Strecker, in Wilhelm Schneemelcher, *New Testament Apocrypha*, vol. 2 (rev. ed.: Cambridge/Louisville: Lutterworth/Westminister/John Knox, 1991) 504–40; used with permission.

appeared later than he did and came in upon him as light upon darkness, as knowledge upon ignorance, as healing upon sickness" (*Homilies* 2: 17).

The Homilies are closely related to another surviving work of the third century attributed to Clement, the *Recognitions;* both were evidently based on an earlier legendary account of Clement's travels that is now lost.

Book 1

18 (Peter says to Clement:) The will of God has fallen into oblivion for many sorts of reasons,

2 above all in consequence of inadequate instruction, careless upbringing, bad company, unseemly conversation and erroneous statements.

3 Thence there comes ignorance, and there come also dissoluteness, unbelief, unchastity, avarice, vanity, and innumerable vices of this kind, which have occupied the world as it were a house which, like a cloud of smoke, they have filled; they have thus made muddy the eyes of those who dwell in the house and have prevented them from looking up and recognising the Creator God from his works and inferring his will.

4 Therefore the friends of truth who are in the house must cry from the depth of their heart for help for their truth-seeking souls, that if someone is outside the smoke-filled house, he may come and open the door, so that the sunlight from outside may invade the house and that the smoke within may be dissipated.

19 Now the man who can help here, I call the true prophet; he alone can enlighten the souls of people that with their own eyes they may be able to see the way to eternal salvation.

2 That is not possible in any other way, as indeed you yourself know; only just now you said

3 that every view has its friends and opponents and counts as true or false according to the qualification of its advocate, and in consequence different opinions do not come to light as what they are, but receive the semblance of worth or worthlessness from their advocates.

4 Wherefore the world needs the godly efforts of the true prophet that he may describe things to us as they actually are and tell us what we have to believe regarding everything.

5 First of all then we must examine the prophet with all seriousness and arrive at the certainty that he is a true prophet,

6 and then we should believe him in all matters and ought not to quibble at the least small particular in his teaching, but should accept all his words as valid, as it may appear in faith, yet actually on the ground of the sound examination that we have made. . . .

Book 2

15 (Peter:) Now that he might bring people to the true knowledge of all things, God, who himself is a single person, made a clear separation by way of pairs of opposites, in that he, who from the beginning was the one and only God, made heaven and earth, day and night, life and death.

2 Among these he has gifted free-will to humans alone so that they may be just or unjust. For them he has also permuted the appearing of the pairs of opposites, in that he has set before their eyes first the small and then the great, first the world and then eternity, this world being transitory, but the one to come eternal; so also ignorance precedes knowledge.

3 In the same way he has ordered the bearers of the prophetic spirit. For since the present is womanly and like a mother gives birth to children, but the future, manly time on the other hand takes up its children in the manner of a father,

4 therefore there come first the prophets of this world (who prophesy falsely, and) those who have the knowledge of eternal things follow them because they are sons of the coming age.

5 Had the God-fearing known this secret, then they would never have been able to go wrong, and also they would even now have known that Simon, who now confounds all, is merely a helpmate of the feeble left hand (of God, i.e., the evil one).

16 As regards the disposition of the prophetic mission the case is as follows. As God, who is one person, in the beginning made first the heaven and then the earth, as it were on the right hand and on the left, he has also in the course of time established all the pairs of opposites. But with humans it is no longer so—rather does he invert the pairs.

2 For as with him the first is the stronger and the second the weaker, so with humans we find the opposite, first the weaker and then the stronger.

3 Thus directly from Adam, who was made in the image of God, there issued as the first son the unrighteous Cain and as the second the righteous Abel.

4 And in the same way from the man who amongst you is called Deucalion two symbols of the Spirit, the unclean and the clean, were sent out, the black raven and after it the white dove.

5 And also from Abraham, the progenitor of our people, there issued two sons, the older Ishmael and then Isaac, who was blessed by God.

6 Again from this same Isaac there sprang two sons, the godless Esau and the godly Jacob.

7 Likewise there came first, as firstborn into the world, the high priest (Aaron) and then the law-giver (Moses).

17 The syzygy associated with Elijah, which ought to have come, willingly held off to another time, being resolved to take its place when the occasion arises.

2 Then in the same way there came first he who was among them that are born of women and only after that did he who belongs to the sons of men appear as the second.

3 Following up this disposition it would be possible to recognise where Simon belongs, who as first and before me went to the Gentiles, and where I belong, I who came after him and followed him as the light follows darkness, knowledge ignorance, and healing sickness.

4 Thus then, as the true prophet has said, a false gospel must first come from an impostor and only then, after the destruction of the holy place, can a true gospel be sent forth for the correction of the sects that are to come.

5 And thereafter in the end Antichrist must first come again and only afterwards must Jesus, our actual Christ, appear and then, with the rising of eternal light, everything that belongs to darkness must disappear.

18 Since now, as has been said, many do not know this conformity of the syzygies with law, they do not know who this Simon, my forerunner, is. For were it known, no one would believe him. But now, as he remains unknown, confidence is wrongly placed in him.

2 Thus he who does what haters do finds love; the enemy is received as a friend; people long for him who is death as a bringer of salvation; although he is fire, he is regarded as light; although he is a cheat, he obtains a hearing as a proclaimer of truth. . . .

Book 7

1 In Tyre not a few people from the neighbourhood and numerous inhabitants of the city came to Peter and cried to him: "May God have mercy upon us through you, and may he through you bring us healing!" And Peter, having mounted a high rock that he might be seen of all, greeted them in a godly way and began as follows:

2 "God, who has made heaven and the universe, is not wanting in power to save those who desire to be saved. . . .

4 "And what is pleasing to God is this, that we pray to him and ask from him as the one who dispenses everything according to a righteous law, that we keep away from the table of devils, that we do not eat dead flesh, that we do not touch blood, that we wash ourselves clean from all defilement.

3 "Let the rest be said to you also in one word, as the God-fearing Jews heard it, while you show yourselves, many as you are, of one mind: 'What good a person wishes for himself, let him confer the same also on his neighbor!' . . ."

5 After they had thus been instructed for some days by Peter and had been healed, they were baptized. At the time of his other miraculous deeds the rest sat beside one another in the middle of the market-place in sackcloth and ashes and did penance for their former sins.

2 When the Sidonians heard this, they did likewise; and because they themselves were not able on account of their diseases to come to Peter, they sent a petition to him.

3 After he had stayed for some days in Tyre and had instructed all the inhabitants and freed them from numerous sufferings, Peter founded a church and appointed a bishop for them from the number of the elders who were accompanying him; then he set out for Sidon.

6 When Peter entered Sidon, the people brought many sick folk in beds and set them down before him.

2 And he said to them: "Do not on any account believe that I, a mortal man, myself subject to many sufferings, can do anything to heal you! But I greatly desire to tell you in what way you can be delivered. . . .

7 "For I mention to you two ways, showing you in the first place in what way people fall into misfortune and in the second place in what way under God's guidance they are delivered.

2 "The way of those who perish is broad and very easy, but it leads straight away to misfortune; the way of those who are delivered is narrow and rough, but in the end it leads to salvation those who have taken its burdens upon themselves. Before these two ways there stand belief and unbelief. . . ."

8 Such were the addresses that Peter gave in Sidon. There also within a few days many were converted and believed and were healed. So Peter founded a church there and enthroned as bishop

one of the elders who were accompanying him. He then left Sidon.

9 Immediately after the arrival of Peter in Berytus an earthquake took place; and people came to Peter saying: "Help, for we greatly fear that we shall all together perish!"

2 Then Simon dared, along with Appion, Annubion, Athenodorous and his other comrades, to turn against Peter in the presence of all the people: "Flee, people from this man;

3 "for he is a magician—you may believe me—and has himself occasioned this earthquake and has caused these diseases to frighten you, as if he himself was a god!"

4 And many other false charges of this sort did Simon and his followers bring against Peter, suggesting that he possessed superhuman power.

5 As soon as the multitude gave him a hearing, Peter with a smile and an impressive directness spoke the words: "Oh people, I admit that, God willing, I am capable of doing what these men here say and in addition am ready, if you will not hear my words, to turn your whole city upside down."

10 Now when the multitude took alarm and readily promised to carry out his commands, Peter said: "Let no one of you associate with these magicians or in any way have intercourse with them."

2 Scarcely had the people heard this summons when without delay they laid hold of cudgels and pursued these fellows till they had driven them completely out of the city. . . .

12 After he had stayed for several days with the inhabitants of Berytus, had made many conversant with the worship of the one God, and had

baptized them, Peter enthroned as bishop one of the elders who were accompanying him and then journeyed to Byblus.

3 On coming there he learned that Simon had not waited for him even for a single day, but had started at once for Tripolis. Accordingly Peter remained a few days with the people of Byblus, effected not a few healings, and gave instruction in the Holy Scriptures. He then journeyed in the track of Simon to Tripolis, being resolved to pursue him rather than to make room for him.

Book 8

1 Along with Peter there entered into Tripolis people from Tyre, Sidon, Berytus, Byblus and neighboring places, who were eager to learn, and in numbers that were not smaller, people from the city itself crowded about him desiring to get to know him. . . .

4 Astonished at this eagerness of the multitudes, Peter answered: "You see, beloved brethren, how the words of our Lord are manifestly fulfilled. For I remember how he said: 'Many will come from east and west, from north and south, and repose in the bosom of Abraham, Isaac and Jacob.'[4] Nevertheless 'many are called, but few are chosen.'[5]

2 "In their coming in response to the call so much is fulfilled.

3 "But since it rests not with them but with God who has called them and permitted them to come, on this account alone they have no reward. . . .

4 "But if after being called they do what is good, and that rests with them

---

[4]Matt 8:11.   [5]Matt 22:14.

themselves, for that they will receive their reward.

5 "For even the Hebrews who believe in Moses . . . are not saved unless they abide by what has been said to them.

2 "For their believing in Moses lies not with a decision of their own will but with God, who said to Moses. 'Behold, I come to you in a pillar of cloud that the people may hear me speaking to you and believe forever!'[6] Since then it is granted to the Hebrews and to them that are called from the Gentiles to believe the teachers of truth, while it is left to the personal decision of each individual whether he will perform good deeds, the reward rightly falls to those who do well.

4 "For neither Moses nor Jesus would have needed to come if of themselves people had been willing to perceive the way of discretion. And there is no salvation in believing in teachers and calling them lords.

6 "Therefore is Jesus concealed from the Hebrews who have received Moses as their teacher, and Moses hidden from those who believe Jesus.

2 "For since through both one and the same teaching becomes known, God accepts those who believe in one of them.

3 "But belief in a teacher has as its aim the doing of what God has ordered.

4 "That this is the case our Lord himself declares, saying: 'I confess to you, Father of heaven and earth, that you have hidden this from the wise and elder, but have revealed it to simpletons and infants.'[7] Thus has God himself hidden the teacher from some since they know beforehand what they ought to do, and has revealed him to others since they know not what they have to do.

7 "Thus the Hebrews are not condemned because they did not know Jesus . . . provided only they act according to the instructions of Moses and do not injure him whom they did not know.

2 "And again the offspring of the Gentiles are not judged, who . . . have not known Moses, provided only they act according to the words of Jesus and thus do not injure him whom they did not know.

3 "Also it profits nothing if many describe their teachers as their lords, but do not do what it befits servants to do.

4 "Therefore our Lord Jesus said to one who again and again called him Lord, but at the same time did not abide by any of his commands. 'Why call me Lord and not do what I say?'[8] For it is not speaking that can profit any one, but doing.

5 "In all circumstances goods works are needed; but if a person has been considered worthy to know both teachers as heralds of a single doctrine, then that one is counted rich in God. . . ."

---

[6]Exod 19:9.   [7]Matt 11:25; Luke 10:21.   [8]Matt 7:21; Luke 6:46.

Ptolemy's Letter to Flora

One of the most famous Christian Gnostics of the second century was Ptolemy, a renowned teacher who lived and taught in Rome. From Ptolemy's own hand comes one of the clearest expositions of Gnostic ideas, in a letter addressed to a woman named Flora, a non-Gnostic Christian whom Ptolemy is concerned to educate into the higher realms of knowledge. The letter is just the beginning of Ptolemy's instruction, but it concerns a central component of his Gnostic views, his understanding of the Bible.[1] Regrettably, his subsequent lessons have been lost.

The proper interpretation of the Bible, Ptolemy avers, depends on understanding the nature of its divine inspiration. Those who maintain that it was authored by the Perfect God and Father (e.g., the "proto-orthodox" Christians) err, because a perfect being could not inspire laws that are imperfect. Yet those who claim that it was written by God's adversary, the Devil (e.g., other groups of Gnostics?) also err, because an evil deity could not inspire laws that are just. Instead, there is a god intermediate between these two, the just but imperfect and harsh god who created the world; it was he who inspired parts of the Bible. Other parts, however, derive from Moses himself, and yet others from the elders around him. Those that are from the intermediate god can themselves be divided into three parts, those that Jesus fulfilled (e.g., the Ten Commandments), those that he abolished (e.g., "an eye for an eye"), and those that he has symbolically transformed (e.g., ceremonial laws). Ptolemy explicitly bases his views on the teachings of Paul and, especially, Jesus himself.

This letter has not been transmitted independently and was not present among the Nag Hammadi writings, but can be found only in quotations in the writings of the fourth-century heresy hunter Epiphanius (Book 33 of *The Medicine Chest*).

---

[1]See further, Ehrman, *Lost Christianities*, 129–31.

Translation by Bentley Layton, *Gnostic Scriptures: Ancient Wisdom for the New Age* (New York: Doubleday, 1987) 308–15; used with permission.

3 The law established by Moses, my dear sister Flora, has in the past been misunderstood by many people, for they were not closely acquainted with the one who established it or with its commandments. I think you will see this at once if you study their discordant opinions on this topic.

2 For some say that this law has been ordained by god the father; while others, following the opposite course, stoutly contend that it has been established by the adversary, the pernicious devil; and so the latter school attributes the craftsmanship of the world to the devil, saying that he is "the father and maker of the universe."[2]

3 <But> they are <utterly> in error, they disagree with one another, and each of the schools utterly misses the truth of the matter.

4 Now, it does not seem that the law was established by the perfect god and father: for, it must be of the same character as its giver; and yet it is imperfect and needful of being fulfilled by another and contains commandments incongruous with the nature and intentions of such a god.

5 On the other hand to attribute a law that abolishes injustice to the injustice of the adversary is the false logic of those who do not comprehend the principle of which the savior spoke. For our savior declared that a house or city divided against itself will not be able to stand.

6 And, further, the apostle states that the craftsmanship of the world is his, and that "all things were made through him, and without him was not anything made,"[3] thus anticipating these liars' flimsy wisdom. And the craftsmanship is that of a god who is just and hates evil, not a pernicious one as believed by these thoughtless people, who take no account of the craftsman's forethought and so are

blind not only in the eye of the soul but even in the eyes of the body.

7 Now, from what has been said it should be clear to you (sing.) that these (schools of thought) utterly miss the truth, though each does so in its own particular way: one (school) by not being acquainted with the god of righteousness, the other by not being acquainted with the father of the entirety, who was manifested by him alone who came and who alone knew him.

8 It remains for us, who have been deemed worthy of <acquaintance> with both, to show you (sing.) exactly what sort of law the law is, and which legislator established it. We shall offer proofs of what we say by drawing from our savior's words, by which alone it is possible to reach a certain apprehension of the reality of the matter without stumbling.

4 Now, first you must learn that, as a whole, the law contained in the Pentateuch of Moses was not established by a single author, I mean not by god alone: rather, there are certain of its commandments that were established by human beings as well. Indeed, our savior's words teach us that the Pentateuch divides into three parts.

2 For one division belongs to god himself and his legislations; while <another division> belongs to Moses—indeed, Moses ordained certain of the commandments not as god himself ordained through him, rather based upon his own thoughts about the matter; and yet a third division belongs to the elders of the people, <who> likewise in the beginning must have inserted certain of their own commandments.

---

[2]Plato *Tim* 28e.   [3]John 1:3.

3 You will now learn how all this can be demonstrated from the savior's words.

4 When the savior was talking with those who were arguing with him about divorce—and it has been ordained (in the law) that divorce is permitted—he said to them: "For your (pl.) hardness of heart Moses allowed divorce of one's wife. Now, from the beginning it was not so."[4] For god, he says, has joined together this union, and "what the lord has joined together, let no man put asunder."[5]

5 Here he shows that <the> law of god is one thing, forbidding a woman to be put asunder from her husband; while the law of Moses is another, permitting the couple to be put asunder because of hard-heartedness.

6 And so, accordingly, Moses ordains contrary to what god ordains; for <separating> is contrary to not separating.

Yet if we also scrutinize Moses' intentions with which he ordained his commandment, we find that he created the commandment not of his own inclination but of necessity because of the weakness of those to whom it was ordained.

7 For the latter were not able to put into practice god's intentions, in the matter of their not being permitted to divorce their wives. Some of them were on very bad terms with their wives, and ran the risk of being further diverted into injustice and from there into their destruction.

8 Moses, wishing to excise this unpleasant element through which they also ran the risk of being destroyed, ordained for them of his own accord a second law, the law of divorce, choosing under the circumstances the lesser of two evils, as it were,

9 so that if they were unable to keep the former (that is, god's law) they could keep at least the latter and so not be diverted into injustice and evil, through which utter destruction would follow in consequence.

10 These are Moses' intentions, with which we find him ordaining laws contrary to those of god. At any rate, even if we have for the moment used only one example in our proof, it is beyond doubt that, as we have shown, this law is of Moses himself and is distinct from god's.

11 And the savior shows also that there are some traditions of the elders interwoven in the law. He says, "For god spoke: 'Honor your father and your mother, that it may be well with you.'

12 But you have declared," the savior says, addressing the elders, " 'What you would have gained from me is given to god.' And for the sake of your tradition, O ancients, you have made void the law of god."[6]

13 And Isaiah declared this by saying, "This people honors me with their lips, but their heart is far from me; in vain do they worship me, teaching as doctrines the precepts of men."[7]

4 Thus it has been clearly shown from these passages that, as a whole, the law is divided into three parts. For we have found in it legislations belonging to Moses himself, to the elders, and to god himself. Moreover, the analysis of the law as a whole, as we have divided it here, has made clear which part of it is genuine.

5 Now, what is more, the one part that is the law of god himself divides into three subdivisions.

The first subdivision is the pure legislation not interwoven with evil, which alone is properly called law, and which the savior did not come to abolish but to fulfill. For what he fulfilled was not alien to him, <but stood in need of fulfillment>: for it did not have perfection.

---

[4]Matt 19:8. [5]Matt 19:6. [6]Matt 15:4–5. [7]Isa 29:3; Matt 15:8.

And the second subdivision is the part interwoven with the inferior and with injustice, which the savior abolished as being incongruous with his own nature.

2 Finally, the third subdivision is the symbolic and allegorical part, which is after the image of the superior, spiritual realm: the savior changed (the referent of) this part from the perceptible, visible level to the spiritual, invisible one.

3 The first, the law of god that is pure and not interwoven with the inferior, is the decalogue of Ten Commandments inscribed on two stone tablets; they divide into the prohibition of things that must be avoided and the commanding of things that must be done. Although they contain pure legislation they do not have perfection, and so they were in need of fulfillment by the savior.

4 The second, which is interwoven with injustice, is that which applies to retaliation and repayment of those who have already committed a wrong, commanding us to pluck out an eye for an eye and a tooth for a tooth and to retaliate for murder with murder.[8] This part is interwoven with injustice, for the one who is second to act unjustly still acts unjustly, differing only in the relative order in which he acts, and committing the very same act.

5 But otherwise, this commandment both was and is just, having been established as a deviation from the pure law because of the weakness of those to whom it was ordained; yet it is incongruous with the nature and goodness of the father of the entirety.

6 Now perhaps this was apt; but even more, it was a result of necessity. For when one who does not wish even a single murder to occur—by saying, "You shall not kill"—when, I say, he ordains a second law and commands the murderer to be murdered,[9] acting as judge between two murders, he who forbade even a sin-

gle murder[10] has without realizing it been cheated by necessity.

7 For this reason, then, the son who was sent from him abolished this part of the law, though he admits that it too belonged to god: this part is reckoned as belonging to the old school of thought, both where he says, "For god spoke: 'He who speaks evil of father or mother, let him surely die' "[11] and elsewhere.

8 And the third subdivision of god's law is the symbolic part, which is after the image of the superior, spiritual realm: I mean, what is ordained about offerings, circumcision, the Sabbath, fasting, Passover, the Feast of Unleavened Bread, and the like.

9 Now, once the truth had been manifested, the referent of all these ordinances was changed, inasmuch as they are images and allegories. As to their meaning in the visible realm and their physical accomplishment they were abolished; but as to their spiritual meaning they were elevated, with the words remaining the same but the subject matter being altered.

10 For the savior commanded us to offer offerings, but not dumb beasts or incense: rather, spiritual praises and glorifications and prayers of thanksgiving, and offerings in the form of sharing and good deeds.

11 And he wishes us to perform circumcision, but not circumcision of the bodily foreskin, rather of the spiritual heart;

12 and to keep the Sabbath, for he wants us to be inactive in wicked acts;

13 and to fast, though he does not wish us to perform physical fasts, rather spiritual ones, which consist of abstinence from all bad deeds.

Nevertheless, fasting as to the visible

---

[8]Lev 24:17, 20.   [9]Exod 20:13.   [10]Exod 21:12.
[11]Matt 15:4.

realm is observed by our adherents, since fasting, if practiced with reason, can contribute something to the soul, so long as it does not take place in imitation of other people or by habit or because fasting has been prescribed <for> a particular day.

14 Likewise, it is observed in memory of true fasting, so that those who are not yet able to observe true fasting might have a remembrance of it from fasting according to the visible realm.

15 Likewise, the apostle Paul makes it clear that Passover and the Feast of Unleavened Bread were images, for he says that "Christ, our paschal lamb, has been sacrificed"[12] and, he says, be without leaven, having no share in leaven—now, by "leaven" he means evil—but rather "be fresh dough."

6 And so it can be granted that the actual law of god is subdivided into three parts. The first subdivision is the part that was fulfilled by the savior: for "you shall not kill," "you shall not commit adultery," "you shall not swear falsely" are subsumed under not being angry, not looking lustfully at another, and not swearing at all.[13]

2 The second subdivision is the part that was completely abolished. For the commandment of "an eye for an eye and a tooth for a tooth,"[14] which is interwoven with injustice and itself involves an act of injustice, was abolished by the savior with injunctions to the contrary,

3 and of two contraries one must "abolish" the other: "For I say to you (pl.), Do not in any way resist one who is evil. But if any one strikes you (sing.), turn to him the other cheek also."[15]

4 And the third subdivision is the part whose referent was changed and which was altered from the physical to the spiritual—the allegorical part, which is ordained after the image of the superior realm.

5 Now, the images and allegories are indicative of other matters, and they were well and good while truth was not present. But now that truth is present, one must do the works of truth and not those of its imagery.

6 His disciples made these teachings known, and so did the apostle Paul: he makes known to us the part consisting of images, through the passage on the paschal lamb and the unleavened bread, which we have already spoken of. The part consisting of a law interwoven with injustice, he made known by speaking of "abolishing the law of commandments and ordinances";[16] and the part not interwoven with the inferior, when he says, "The law is holy, and the commandment is holy and just and good."[17]

7 Thus I think I have shown you, as well as possible in a brief treatment, both that there is human legislation which has been slipped into the law and that the law of god himself divides into three subdivisions.

2 Now it remains for us to say what sort of being this god is, who established the law. But this too I believe I have demonstrated to you (sing.) in what I have already said, providing you have followed carefully.

3 For since this division of the law (that is, god's own law) was established neither by the perfect god, as we have taught, nor surely by the devil—which it would be wrong to say—then the establisher of this division of the law is distinct from them.

4 And he is the craftsman and maker of the universe or world and of the things within it. Since he is different from the essences of the other two <and> (rather)

---

[12]Cor 5:7.   [13]Matt 5:21, 27, 33.   [14]Lev 24:20.
[15]Matt 5:39.   [16]Eph 2:15.   [17]Rom 7:12.

is in a state intermediate between them, he would rightfully be described by the term intermediateness.

5 And if the perfect god is good according to his nature—as indeed he is, for our savior showed that "one only is there who is good,"[18] namely his father whom he manifested—and if furthermore the law belonging to the nature of the adversary is both evil and wicked and is stamped in the mold of injustice, then a being that is in a state intermediate between these and is neither good, nor evil or unjust, might well be properly called just, being a judge of the justice that is his.

6 And on the one hand this god must be inferior to the perfect god and less than his righteousness precisely because he is engendered and not unengendered— for "there is one unengendered father, from whom are all things,"[19] or more exactly, from whom all things depend; and on the other hand, he must have come into being as better and more authoritative than the adversary; and must be born of an essence and nature distinct from the essences of the other two.

7 For the essence of the adversary is both corruption and darkness, for the adversary is material and divided into many parts; while the essence of the unengendered father of the entirety is both incorruptibility and self-existent light, being simple and unique. And the essence of

this intermediate produced a twofold capacity, for he is an image of the better god.

8 And now, given that the good by nature engenders and produces the things that are similar to itself and of the same essence, do not be bewildered as to how these natures—that of corruption and <that> of intermediateness—which have come to be different in essence, arose from a single first principle of the entirety, a principle that exists and is confessed and believed in by us, and which is unengendered and incorruptible and good.

9 For, god permitting, you will next learn about both the first principle and the generation of these two other gods, if you are deemed worthy of the apostolic tradition, which even we have received by succession; and along with this you will learn how to test all the propositions by means of our savior's teaching.

10 I have not failed, my sister Flora, to state these matters to you briefly. And what I have just written is a concise account, though I have treated the subject adequately. In the future these teachings will be of the greatest help to you—at least if, like good rich soil that has received fertile seeds, you bear fruit.

---

[18]Matt 19:17.   [19]1 Cor 8:6.

The Treatise on the Resurrection

The Treatise on the Resurrection was a valued document among some ancient Gnostics, but it was completely unknown in modern times until discovered among the writings of the Nag Hammadi Library (see p. 19). It is a provocative philosophical discourse addressed by an unknown Gnostic teacher to an inquirer, possibly a non-Gnostic Christian, named Rheginos.[1] Because it is in the form of a letter, the book is sometimes called "The Letter to Rheginos." In response to Rheginos's questions, it provides basic instruction about the nature of death and resurrection—both of Jesus and, more important, of humans.

The questions Rheginos had raised concerned the character of existence in the afterlife. If, as Gnostics had maintained, salvation comes *from* the body rather than *in* the body—what kind of existence will a person have after death?

The author replies by assuring Rheginos that the resurrection is by no means an illusion: it will certainly take place. But it will not involve a crass revivification of the material body—a body, the author claims, that is itself more illusory than real. After death, even though the body passes away, a person's spirit will ascend to the heavenly realm, drawn up by Jesus himself. The flesh, in other words, is completely transitory, but the spirit is eternal: just as people were not in the flesh *before* they came into the world, so too they will not be in the flesh once they leave this world.

The spiritual nature of the resurrection has clear ethical implications for this author. Those who deny their flesh in this life have begun to escape bodily existence and have started along the path to their heavenly home. And so fleshly pleasures are to be overcome for the sake of life to come.

This teaching of a spiritual resurrection stands in sharp contrast with proto-orthodox notions of the future bodily resurrection (cf. 2 Tim 2:18).

---

[1]For further discussion, see Ehrman, *Lost Christianities*, 131–32.

Translation by Malcom L. Peel, in Harold W. Attridge, *Nag Hammadi Codex 1 (The Jung Codex)* (Nag Hammadi Studies, 22) (Leiden: E. J. Brill, 1985) 148–57; used with permission.

Although it is impossible to say exactly when this intriguing treatise was written, many scholars date it to the late second century.

Some there are, my son Rheginos, who want to learn many things. They have this goal when they are occupied with questions whose answer is lacking. If they succeed with these, they usually think very highly of themselves. But I do not think that they have stood within the Word of Truth. They seek rather their own rest, which we have received through our Savior, our Lord Christ. We received it (i.e., Rest) when we came to know the truth and rested ourselves upon it. But since you ask us pleasantly what is proper concerning the resurrection, I am writing you (to say) that it is necessary. To be sure, many are lacking faith in it, but there a few who find it. So then, let us discuss the matter.

How did the Lord proclaim things while he existed in flesh and after he had revealed himself as Son of God? He lived in this place where you remain, speaking about the Law of Nature—but I call it "Death!" Now the Son of God, Rheginos, was Son of Man. He embraced them both, possessing the humanity and the divinity, so that on the one hand he might vanquish death through his being Son of God, and that on the other through the Son of Man the restoration to the Pleroma might occur; because he was originally from above, a seed of the Truth, before this structure (of the cosmos) had come into being. In this (structure) many dominions and divinities came into existence.

I know that I am presenting the solution in difficult terms, but there is nothing difficult in the Word of Truth. But since the Solution appeared so as not to leave anything hidden, but to reveal all things openly concerning existence—the destruction of evil on the one hand, the revelation of the elect on the other. This (Solution) is the emanation of Truth and Spirit, Grace is of the Truth.

The Savior swallowed up death—(of this) you are not reckoned as being ignorant—for he put aside the world which is perishing. He transformed [himself] into an imperishable Aeon and raised himself up, having swallowed the visible by the invisible, and he gave us the way of our immortality. Then, indeed, as the Apostle said, "We suffered with him, and we arose with him, and we went to heaven with him."[2] Now if we are manifest in this world wearing him, we are that one's beams, and we are embraced by him until our setting, that is to say, our death in this life. We are drawn to heaven by him, like beams by the sun, not being restrained by anything. This is the spiritual resurrection which swallows up the psychic in the same way as the fleshly.

But if there is one who does not believe, he does not have the (capacity to be) persuaded. For it is the domain of faith, my son, and not that which belongs to persuasion: the dead shall arise! There is one who believes among the philosophers who are in this world. At least he will arise. And let not the philosopher who is in this world have cause to believe that he is one who returns himself by himself—and (that) because of our faith! For we have known the Son of Man,

---

[2]cf. 1 Tim 2:10–11.

and we have believed that he rose from among the dead. This is he of whom we say, "He became the destruction of death, as he is a great one in whom they believe." <Great> are those who believe it.

The thought of those who are saved shall not perish. The mind of those who have known him shall not perish. Therefore, we are elected to salvation and redemption since we are predestined from the beginning not to fall into the foolishness of those who are without knowledge, but we shall enter into the wisdom of those who have known the Truth. Indeed, the Truth which is kept cannot be abandoned, nor has it been. "Strong is the system of the Pleroma; small is that which broke loose (and) became (the) world. But the All is what is encompassed. It has not come into being; it was existing." So, never doubt concerning the resurrection, my son Rheginos! For if you were not existing in flesh, you received flesh when you entered this world. Why will you not receive flesh when you ascend into the Aeon? That which is better than the flesh is that which is for it (the) cause of life. That which came into being on your account, is it not yours? Does not that which is yours exist with you? Yet, while you are in this world, what is it that you lack? This is what you have been making every effort to learn.

The afterbirth of the body is old age, and you exist in corruption. You have absence as a gain. For you will not give up what is better if you depart. That which is worse has diminution, but there is grace for it.

Nothing, then, redeems us from this world. But the All which we are, we are saved. We have received salvation from end to end. Let us think in this way! Let us comprehend in this way!

But there are some (who) wish to understand, in the enquiry about those things they are looking into, whether he who is saved, if he leaves his body behind, will be saved immediately. Let no one doubt concerning this. . . . indeed, the visible members which are dead shall not be saved, for (only) the living [members] which exist within them would arise.

What, then, is the resurrection? It is always the disclosure of those who have risen. For if you remember reading in the Gospel that Elijah appeared and Moses with him,[3] do not think the resurrection is an illusion. It is no illusion, but it is truth! Indeed, it is more fitting to say that the world is an illusion, rather than the resurrection which has come into being through our Lord the Savior, Jesus Christ.

But what am I telling you now? Those who are living shall die. How do they live in an illusion? The rich have become poor, and the kings have been overthrown. Everything is prone to change. The world is an illusion!—lest, indeed, I rail at things to excess!

But the resurrection does not have this aforesaid character, for it is the truth which stands firm. It is the revelation of what is, and the transformation of things, and a transition into newness. For imperishability [descends] upon the perishable; the light flows down upon the darkness, swallowing it up; and the Pleroma fills up the deficiency. These are the symbols and the images of the resurrection. He (Christ) it is who makes the good.

Therefore, do not think in part, O Rheginos, nor live in conformity with this flesh for the sake of unanimity, but flee from the divisions and the fetters, and already you have the resurrection. For if he who will die knows about himself that

---

[3]Mark 9:4.

he will die—even if he spends many years in this life, he is brought to this— why not consider yourself as risen and (already) brought to this? If you have the resurrection but continue as if you are to die—and yet that one knows that he has died—why, then, do I ignore your lack of exercise? It is fitting for each one to practice in a number of ways, and he shall be released from this Element that he may not fall into error but shall himself receive again what at first was.

These things I have received from the generosity of my Lord, Jesus Christ. [I have] taught you and your [brethren], my sons, concerning them, while I have not omitted any of the things suitable for strengthening you (pl.). But if there is one thing written which is obscure in my exposition of the Word, I shall interpret it for you (pl.) when you (pl.) ask. But now, do not be jealous of anyone who is in your number when he is able to help.

Many are looking into this which I have written to you. To these I say: peace (be) among them and grace. I greet you and those who love you (pl.) in brotherly love.

The Didache

Several proto-orthodox authors in the early church mention with approval the "Didache (literally, "The Teaching") of the Twelve Apostles"; some of them view it as standing just on the borders of the canon.[1] But the book was eventually lost from view, until a copy was discovered in 1873 in a monastery library in Constantinople. Since then the book has made a significant impact on the way scholars understand the social life and ritual practices of the early church. For this is the first "church manual" to have survived from early Christianity.

The first part of the book describes the "Two Paths of Life and Death" (see Introduction to the Epistle of Barnabas). The Path of Life (chaps. 1–4) is paved with upright behavior: the author's readers are to love one another, avoid evil desires, jealousy and anger, give alms to the poor, obey God's commandments, and generally lead morally respectable lives. Many of these instructions reflect the teachings of Jesus from Matthew's Sermon on the Mount (e.g., praying for one's enemies, turning the other cheek, and going the extra mile). As might be expected, the Path of Death (chap. 5) involves the opposite sorts of behavior: "murders, adulteries, passions, sexual immoralities, robberies," and sundry other transgressive activities.

The bulk of the rest of the book gives instructions for the ritual practices and social interactions of the Christian community (chaps. 7–15), including directions for how to perform baptisms (preferably in cold, running water), when to fast (every Wednesday and Friday), what to pray (the Lord's Prayer, three times a day), and how to celebrate the Eucharist (first giving thanks for the cup, then the bread). Near the end of these instructions the author addresses the problem of wandering "apostles," "teachers," and "prophets" of dubious moral character; evidently, some scoundrels had become itinerant Christian preachers simply for financial gain. The communities are to test the sincerity of these wandering ministers and to limit the length of their stay at the community's expense; moreover, the communities are to appoint leaders of their own to direct their affairs.

---

[1]See the Canons of Athanasius and Eusebius. For further information on the Didache, see Ehrman, *Lost Christianities*, 48–49.

Translation by Bart D. Ehrman, in *The Apostolic Fathers*, vol. 1 (Loeb Classical Library; Cambridge, Mass.: Harvard University Press, 2003); used with permission.

The book concludes with a kind of "apocalyptic discourse," an exhortation to be prepared for the imminent end of the world, to be brought by "the Lord coming on the clouds of the sky" (16:7).

The Didache's anonymous author appears to be familiar with earlier Christian traditions such as those embodied in Matthew's Gospel, but he does not evidence any familiarity with the rigid form of church hierarchy that had developed later in the second century (even though he speaks of bishops and deacons). For these reasons, scholars tend to date the book around 100 or 120 CE. It is probable, though, that the author compiled his account from several sources written at earlier times.

The teaching of the Lord through the twelve apostles to the Gentiles.[a]

1 There are two paths, one of life and one of death, and the difference between the two paths is great.

2 This then is the path of life. First, love the God who made you, and second, your neighbor as yourself.[2] And whatever you do not want to happen to you, do not do to another.[3]

3 This is the teaching relating to these matters: Bless those who curse you, pray for your enemies, and fast for those who persecute you. For why is it so great to love those who love you? Do the Gentiles[b] not do this as well? But you should love those who hate you[4]—then you will have no enemy.

4 Abstain from fleshly passions.[5] If anyone slaps your right cheek, turn the other to him as well[6]—and you will be perfect.[7] If anyone compels you to go one mile, go with him two. If anyone takes your cloak, give him your shirt as well. If anyone seizes what is yours, do not ask for it back,[8] for you will not be able to get it.

5 Give to everyone who asks, and do not ask for anything back.[9] For the Father wants everyone to be given something from the gracious gifts he himself provides. How fortunate is the one who gives according to the commandment, for he is without fault. Woe to the one who receives. For if anyone receives because he is in need, he is without fault. But the one who receives without a need will have to testify why he received what he did, and for what purpose. And he will be thrown in prison and interrogated about what he did; and he will not get out until he pays back every last cent.[10]

6 For it has also been said concerning this: "Let your gift to charity sweat in your hands until you know to whom to give it."[11]

2 And now the second commandment of the teaching.

2 Do not murder, do not commit adultery,[12] do not engage in pederasty, do not

---

[a]Or: *nations*　[b]Or: *nations*

[2]Matt 22:37–39; Mark 12:30–31; Luke 10:27; Deut 6: 5; Lev 19:18.　[3]Cf. Matt 7:12; Luke 6:31.　[4]Cf. Matt 5:44, 46–47; Luke 6:28, 32–33, 35.　[5]1 Pet 2:11.　[6]Matt 5:39.　[7]Matt 5:48.　[8]Matt 4:41, 40; Luke 6:29–30.　[9]Luke 6:30.　[10]Cf. Matt 5:26; Luke 12:59.　[11]Source unknown.　[12]The following passage elaborates Exod 20:13–17; cf. Matt 19:18; 5:33.

engage in sexual immorality. Do not steal, do not practice magic, do not use enchanted potions, do not abort a fetus or kill a child that is born.

3 Do not desire what belongs to your neighbor, do not commit perjury, do not give false testimony, do not speak insults, do not bear grudges.

4 Do not be of two minds or speak from both sides of your mouth, for speaking from both sides of your mouth is a deadly trap.

5 Your word must not be empty or false.

6 Do not be greedy, rapacious, hypocritical, spiteful, or haughty. Do not entertain a wicked plot against your neighbor.

7 Do not hate anyone—but reprove some, pray for others, and love still others more than yourself.

3 My child, flee from all evil and everything like it.

2 Do not be prone to anger, for anger leads to murder; nor be zealous, contentious, or irascible. For from all these are born acts of murder.

3 My child, do not be filled with passion, for passion leads to sexual immorality; nor be foulmouthed or lecherous. For from all these are born acts of adultery.

4 My child, do not practice divination,[c] since this leads to idolatry; nor use incantations or astrology or rites of purification, nor even wish to see or hear these things. For from all these is born idolatry.

5 My child, do not be a liar, since lying leads to robbery; nor be fond of money or vain. For from all these are born acts of robbery.

6 My child, do not be a complainer, since this leads to blasphemy; nor be insolent or evil-minded. For from all these are born blasphemies.

7 But be meek, since the meek will inherit the earth.[13]

8 Be patient, merciful, innocent, gentle, and good, trembling at the words you have heard.

9 Do not exalt yourself or become impertinent. You should not join forces with the high and mighty, but should associate with the upright and humble.

10 Welcome whatever happens to you as good, knowing that nothing occurs apart from God.

4 My child, night and day remember the one who speaks the word of God to you; honor him as the Lord. For where his lordship is discussed, there the Lord himself is.

2 Every day seek out the company of the saints, that you may find comfort in their words.

3 Do not create a schism, but bring peace to those who are at odds. Give a fair judgment; do not show favoritism when you reproach others for their unlawful acts.

4 Do not be of two minds, whether this should happen or not.

5 Do not be one who reaches out your hands to receive but draws them back from giving.

6 If you acquire something with your hands, give it as a ransom for your sins.

7 Do not doubt whether to give, nor grumble while giving. For you should recognize the good paymaster of the reward.

8 Do not shun a person in need, but share all things with your brother and do not say that anything is your own.[14] For

---

[c]i.e., through observing the flight of birds

[13]Matt 5:5; Ps 37:11. [14]Acts 4:32.

if you are partners in what is immortal, how much more in what is mortal?

9 Do not remove your hand from[d] your son or daughter, but from their youth teach them the reverential fear of God.

10 Do not give orders to your male slave or female servant—who hope in the same God—out of bitterness, lest they stop fearing the God who is over you both. For he does not come to call those of high status, but those whom the Spirit has prepared.

11 And you who are slaves must be subject to your masters as to a replica of God, with respect and referential fear.

12 Hate all hypocrisy and everything that is not pleasing to the Lord.

13 Do not abandon the commandments of the Lord, but guard what you have received, neither adding to them nor taking away.[15]

14 Confess your unlawful acts in church, and do not come to your prayer with an evil conscience. This is the path of life.

5 And the path of death is this. First of all it is evil and filled with a curse: murders, adulteries, passions, sexual immoralities, robberies, idolatries, feats of magic, sorceries, rapacious acts, false testimonies, hypocrisies, split affection, deceit, arrogance, malice, insolence, greed, obscenity, jealousy, impertinence, pride, haughtiness, irreverence.

2 It is filled with persecutors of the good, haters of the truth, lovers of the lie, who do not know the reward of righteousness, nor cling to the good nor to a fair judgment, who are alert not to do good but to do evil; from whom meekness and patience are far removed. For they love what is vain and pursue a reward, showing no mercy to the poor nor toiling for the oppressed nor knowing the one who made them; murderers of children and corruptors of what God

has fashioned, who turn their backs on the needy, oppress the afflicted, and support the wealthy. They are lawless judges of the impoverished, altogether sinful. Be delivered, children, from all such people.

6 Take care that no one lead you astray from the path of this teaching, since that one teaches you apart from God.

2 For if you can bear the entire yoke of the Lord, you will be perfect; but if you cannot, do as much as you can.

3 And concerning food, bear what you can. But especially abstain from food sacrificed to idols; for this is a ministry to dead gods.

7 But with respect to baptism, baptize as follows. Having said all these things in advance, baptize in the name of the Father and of the Son and of the Holy Spirit,[16] in running water.

2 But if you do not have running water, baptize in some other water. And if you cannot baptize in cold water, use warm.

3 But if you have neither, pour water on the head three times in the name of Father and Son and Holy Spirit.

4 But both the one baptizing and the one being baptized should fast before the baptism, along with some others if they can. But command the one being baptized to fast one or two days in advance.

8 And do not keep your fasts with the hypocrites.[17] For they fast on Monday and Thursday; but you should fast on Wednesday and Friday.

2 Nor should you pray like the hypo-

---

[d]Or: *Do not refrain from disciplining;* or *Do not shirk your responsibility toward*

---

[15]Deut 4:2; 12:32.   [16]Matt 28:19.   [17]Cf. Matt 6:16.

crites,[18] but as the Lord commanded in his gospel, you should pray as follows: "Our Father in heaven, may your name be kept holy, may your kingdom come, may your will be done on earth as in heaven. Give us today our daily bread.[e] And forgive us our debt, as we forgive our debtors. And do not bring us into temptation but deliver us from the evil one. For the power and the glory are yours forever."[19]

3 Pray like this three times a day.

9 And with respect to the thanksgiving meal,[f] you shall give thanks as follows.

2 First, with respect to the cup: "We give you thanks, our Father, for the holy vine of David, your child, which you made known to us through Jesus your child. To you be the glory forever."

3 And with respect to the fragment of bread: "We give you thanks, our Father, for the life and knowledge that you made known to us through Jesus your child. To you be the glory forever.

4 As this fragment of bread was scattered upon the mountains and was gathered to become one, so may your church be gathered together from the ends of the earth into your kingdom. For the glory and the power are yours through Jesus Christ forever."

5 But let no one eat or drink from your thanksgiving meal[g] unless they have been baptized in the name of the Lord. For also the Lord has said about this, "Do not give what is holy to the dogs."[20]

10 And when you have had enough to eat, you should give thanks as follows: "We give you thanks, holy Father, for your holy name which you have made reside in our hearts, and for the knowledge, faith, and immortality that you made known to us through Jesus your child. To you be the glory forever.

3 You, O Master Almighty, created all things for the sake of your name, and gave both food and drink to humans for their refreshment, that they might give you thanks. And you graciously provided us with spiritual food and drink, and eternal life through your child.

4 Above all we thank you because you are powerful. To you be the glory forever.

5 Remember your church, O Lord; save it from all evil, and perfect it in your love. And gather it from the four winds into your kingdom, which you prepared for it. For yours is the power and the glory forever.

6 May grace come and this world pass away. Hosanna to the God of David. If anyone is holy, let him come; if any one is not, let him repent. Maranatha![21] Amen."

7 But permit the prophets to give thanks[h] as often as they wish.[i]

11 And so, welcome anyone who comes and teaches you everything mentioned above.

2 But if the teacher should himself turn away and teach something different, undermining these things, do not listen to him. But if his teaching brings righteousness and the knowledge of the Lord, then welcome him as the Lord.

3 But act towards the apostles and prophets as the gospel decrees.

4 Let every apostle who comes to you be welcomed as the Lord.

---

[e]Or: *the bread that we need;* or: *our bread for tomorrow* [f]Literally: *eucharist* [g]Literally: *eucharist* [h]Or: *hold the eucharist* [i]Two important witnesses add a verse (with variations); *But concerning the matter of the ointment, give thanks as follows, saying, "We give you thanks, O Father, for the ointment you have made known to us through Jesus your child. To you be the glory forever, Amen."*

---

[18]Cf Matt 6:5.   [19]Matt 6:9–13.   [20]Matt 7:6.   [21]Cf. 1 Cor 16:22.

5 But he should not remain more than a day. If he must, he may stay one more. But if he stays three days, he is a false prophet.

6 When an apostle leaves he should take nothing except bread, until he arrives at his night's lodging. If he asks for money, he is a false prophet.

7 Do not test or condemn a prophet speaking in the Spirit. For every sin will be forgiven, but not this sin.[22]

8 Not everyone who speaks in the Spirit is a prophet, but only one who conducts himself like the Lord. Thus the false prophet and the prophet will both be known by their conduct.

9 No prophet who orders a meal in the Spirit eats of it; if he does, he is a false prophet.

10 Every prophet who teaches the truth but does not do what he himself teaches is a false prophet.

11 You are not to condemn any prophet who has been approved and is true, and who acts on behalf of the earthly mystery of the church, even if he does not teach others to do what he himself does, since he has his judgment with God. For even the ancient prophets behaved in this way.

12 Do not listen to anyone who says in the Spirit, "Give me money" (or something else). But if he tells you to give to others who are in need, let no one judge him.

12 Everyone who comes in the name of the Lord should be welcomed. Then, when you exercise your critical judgment, you will know him; for you understand what is true and what is false.

2 If the one who comes is simply passing through, help him as much as you can. He should not stay with you more than two or three days, if need be.

3 If he wants to remain with you, and is a tradesman, let him work and eat.

4 If he does not have a trade—use your foresight to determine how he as a Christian may live among you without being idle.[j]

5 If he does not want to behave like this, he is a Christmonger. Avoid such people.

13 Every true prophet who wants to settle down with you deserves his food.

2 So too a true teacher, like the worker, deserves his food.[23]

3 Therefore you shall take every first portion of the produce from the wine vat and the threshing floor, and the first portion of both cattle and sheep, and give it to the prophets. For they are your high priests.

4 If you do not have a prophet, then give it to the poor.

5 If you make bread, take the first portion and give it according to the commandment.

6 So too if you open a jar of wine or oil, take the first portion of it and give it to the prophets.

7 And take the first portion of your money, clothing, and everything you own, as it seems good to you, and give it according to the commandment.

14 On the Lord's own day, when you gather together, break bread and give thanks[k] after you have confessed your unlawful deeds, that your sacrifice may be pure.

2 Let no one quarreling with his neighbor join you until they are reconciled, that your sacrifice may not be defiled.[24]

3 For this is the sacrifice mentioned by

---

[j]Or: *through your understanding you should know in advance that no idle Christian is to live among you*
[k]Or: *celebrate the eucharist*

---

[22]Cf. Matt 12:31.   [23]Matt 10:10.   [24]Cf. Matt 5:23–24.

the Lord: "In every place and time, bring me a pure sacrifice. For I am a great King, says the Lord, and my name is considered marvelous among the Gentiles[l]."[25]

15 And so, elect for yourselves bishops and deacons who are worthy of the Lord, gentle men who are not fond of money, who are true and approved. For these also conduct the ministry of the prophets and teachers among you.

2 And so, do not disregard them. For these are the ones who have found honor among you, along with the prophets and teachers.

3 Do not reprimand one another in anger, but in peace, as you have learned from the gospel. Let no one speak with a person who has committed a sin against his neighbor, nor let him hear anything from you, until he repents.

4 But say your prayers, give to charity, and engage in all your activities as you have learned in the gospel of our Lord.

16 Be watchful for your life. Do not let your lamps be extinguished or your robes be loosed; but be prepared. For you do not know the hour when our Lord is coming.[26]

2 Gather together frequently, seeking what is appropriate for your souls. For the entire time of your faith will be of no use to you if you are not found perfect at the final moment.

3 For in the final days the false prophets and corruptors of the faith will be multiplied. The sheep will be turned into wolves, and love into hatred.

4 For when lawlessness increases they will hate, persecute, and betray one another.[27] Then the world-deceiver will be manifest as a son of God. He will perform signs and wonders,[28] and the earth will be delivered over into his hands. He will perform lawless deeds, unlike anything done from eternity.

5 Then all human creation will come to the fire of testing, and many will fall away and perish, but those who endure in their faith will be saved[29] by the curse itself.

6 Then the signs of truth will be manifest:[30] first a sign of a rip in the sky, then a sign of the sound of a trumpet,[31] and third a resurrection of the dead.

7 But not of all the dead. For as it has been said, "The Lord will come and all of his holy ones with him.[32]

8 Then the world will see the Lord coming on the clouds of the sky. . . ."[33] [m]

---

[l]Or: *nations*   [m]The conclusion is evidently lost

[25]Mal 1:11, 14.   [26]Cf. Matt 24:42; Luke 12:40; cf. Mark 13:35, 37.   [27]Cf. Matt 24:10–12.   [28]Cf. Mark 13:22.   [29]Cf. Matt 24:10, 13.   [30]Cf. Matt 24:30. [31]Cf. Matt 24:31; 1 Cor 15:52; 1 Thess 4:16.   [32]Zech 14:5; 1 Thess 3:13.   [33]Cf. Matt 24:30.

The Letter of Barnabas

The Letter of Barnabas was one of the most important writings for proto-orthodox Christianity.[1] Some churches regarded it as part of the New Testament canon; it is included among the books of the New Testament in the fourth-century Greek manuscript, codex Sinaiticus.

The book has traditionally been called an epistle, even though its opening contains only a greeting, with neither its author nor its recipients named (the latter features were consistently found in ancient letters). The writing appears, therefore, to be a theological treatise sent out to interested readers. The second- and third-century Christians who refer to the book attribute it to Barnabas, the companion of the apostle Paul. But this may have involved little more than guesswork on the part of Christians who were eager to have the book read and accepted as "apostolic."

The book in fact was written long after Barnabas himself would have died: it mentions, for example, the destruction of the Temple (70 CE) and refers to the possibility of its soon being rebuilt (16:3–4). This possibility was very much alive in the early decades of the second century, but evaporated when the Emperor Hadrian (117–38 CE) had a Roman shrine constructed over the Temple's ruins. Most scholars have concluded, on these grounds, that the book was written sometime during the first half of the second century, possibly around 130 CE.

The book is principally concerned with the relationship of Judaism and Christianity. Its basic thrust is that Judaism is, and always has been, a false religion. According to this author, Jews violated God's covenant from the very beginning (4:6–8); they have, as a result, never been God's people or understood their own Scriptures. For this author, the Jewish Scriptures can be understood only in light of Christ; indeed, for him, the Old Testament is a Christian, not a Jewish, book.

As a corollary, Jews who claim that their religion was given by God have been misled by an evil angel, who persuaded them to take the laws of Moses literally (9:5). In fact, claims the author, the laws of sabbath obser-

---

[1]See Ehrman, *Lost Christianities,* 145–48.

Translation by Bart D. Ehrman, in *The Apostolic Fathers,* vol. 1 (Loeb Classical Library; Cambridge, Mass.: Harvard University Press, 2003); used with permission.

vance, kosher foods, and circumcision were meant not as literal descriptions of how the Jewish people were to live, but as figurative pointers to Christ and the religion that he was to establish (chaps. 9–10, 15). A good deal of this book, therefore, tries to show how Christ and the Christian religion were foreshadowed in the Old Testament Scriptures.

The book ends on a different note, by describing the Christian doctrine of the "Two Paths": the morally upright path of "light" and the morally perverse path of "darkness" (chaps. 18–20; see Introduction to the Didache). All people must choose between these two ways, following the righteous practices of the one or the moral improprieties of the other.

1 Greetings, sons and daughters, in the name of the Lord who loved us, in peace.

2 So great and abundant are the righteous acts of God toward you that I am exceedingly overjoyed, beyond measure, by your blessed and glorious spirits. For you have received such a measure of his grace planted within you, the spiritual gift!

3 And so I share your joy all the more within myself,[a] hoping to be saved; for truly I see that, in your midst, the Spirit has been poured out upon you from the abundance of the Lord's fountain—so amazed have I been by the sight of your face, which I have so desired.

4 And so, since I have been persuaded about this and realize that I who have spoken to you know many things (since the Lord has traveled along with me in the path of righteousness), I have also felt fully compelled to love you more than my own soul. For a great faith and love dwell within you in the hope of his life.

5 I have thus come to realize that I will be rewarded for serving spirits like yours, if I care for you enough to hand over a portion of what I have received. I have hastened, then, to send you a brief letter, that you may have perfect knowledge to accompany your faith.

6 There are three firm teachings of the Lord of life: hope, which is the beginning and end of our faith; righteousness, which is the beginning and end of judgment; and love, which is a testament to our joy and gladness in upright deeds.

7 For through the prophets the Master has made known to us what has happened and what now is; and he has given us the first fruits of the taste of what is yet to be. And as we see that each and every thing has happened just as he indicated, we should make a more abundant and exalted offering in awe of him.

8 But I will show a few matters to you, not as a teacher but as one of your own; these will gladden your hearts in the present circumstances.

2 Since, then, the days are evil and the one who is at work holds sway, we should commit ourselves to seeking after the righteous acts of the Lord.

2 Reverential awe and endurance assist our faith, and patience and self-restraint do battle on our side.

3 And so while these things remain in a holy state before the Lord, wisdom, understanding, perception, and knowledge rejoice together with them.

[a]Or: *I congratulate myself all the more*

4 For through all the prophets he has shown us that he has no need of sacrifices, whole burnt offerings, or regular offerings. For he says in one place,

5 "What is the multitude of your sacrifices to me? says the Lord. I am sated with whole burnt offerings, and have no desire for the fat of lambs, the blood of bulls and goats—not even if you should come to appear before me. For who sought these things from your hands? Trample my court no longer. If you bring fine flour, it is futile; incense is loathsome to me. I cannot stand your new moons and sabbaths."[2]

6 And so he nullified these things that the new law of our Lord Jesus Christ, which is without the yoke of compulsion, should provide an offering not made by humans.

7 And again he says to them, "Did I command your fathers who came out from the land of Egypt to offer whole burnt offerings and sacrifices to me?"[3]

8 "No, this is what I commanded them: Let none of you bear a grudge against your neighbor in your heart, and do not love a false oath."[4]

9 And so, since we are not ignorant, we should perceive the good intention of our Father. For he is speaking to us, wanting us to seek how to make an offering to him without being deceived like them.

10 And so he says to us: "A sacrifice to the Lord is a crushed heart; a sweet fragrance to the Lord is a heart that glorifies the one who made it."[5] And so, brothers, we ought to learn clearly about our salvation, to keep the Evil One from hurling us away from our life after bringing error in through the backdoor.

3 And so he speaks to them again concerning these things, "Why do you fast for me, says the Lord, so that your voice is heard crying out today? This is not the fast I have chosen, says the Lord—not a person humbling his soul.

2 Not even if you bend your neck into a circle and put on sackcloth and make for yourself a bed of ashes—not even so should you call this a proper fast."[6]

3 But he says to us, "See, this is the fast I have chosen, says the Lord. Loosen every bond of injustice; unravel the strangle-hold of coercive agreements; send forth in forgiveness those who are downtrodden; tear up every unfair contract. Break your bread for the hungry, and provide clothing for anyone you see naked. Bring the homeless under your roof. And if you see anyone who has been humbled, do not despise him—neither you nor anyone from your children's household.

4 Then your light will burst forth at dawn, your garments will quickly rise up, your righteousness will go forth before you, and the glory of God will clothe you.

5 Then you will cry out and God will hear you. While you are still speaking he will say, 'See! Here I am!'—if, that is, you remove from yourself bondage, the threatening gesture, and the word of complaint, and from your heart you give your bread to the poor and show mercy to the person who has been humbled."[7]

6 The one who is patient anticipated, brothers, that the people he prepared in his beloved would believe, in a state of innocence. And so he revealed all things to us in advance, that we not be dashed against[b] their law as newcomers.[c]

4 And so by carefully investigating what is here and now, we must seek

---

[b]Or: *shipwrecked on* [c]Or: *proselytes*

---

[2]Isa 1:11–13. [3]Jer 7:22. [4]Zech 8:17. [5]Ps 51:17.
[6]Isa 58:3–5. [7]Isa 58:6–10.

for the things that can save us. We should flee, entirely, all the works of lawlessness; otherwise, they may overwhelm us. And we should hate the error of the present age, that we may be loved in the age to come.

2 We should not allow our souls to relax, thinking they can consort with sinners and the wicked; otherwise we may become like them.

3 The final stumbling block is at hand, about which it has been written, just as Enoch says, "For this reason the Master shortened the seasons and the days, that his beloved may hurry and arrive at his inheritance."

4 For also the prophet says, "Ten kingdoms will rule the earth and a small king will rise up afterwards; he will humble three of the kings at one time."[8]

5 So too Daniel speaks about the same thing: "I saw the fourth beast, wicked and strong, and worse than all the beasts of the sea, and I saw how ten horns rose up from him, and from them a small horn as an offshoot; and I saw how he humbled three of the great horns at one time."[9]

6 And so you should understand. And yet again, I am asking you this as one who is from among you and who loves each and every one of you more than my own soul: watch yourselves now and do not become like some people by piling up your sins, saying that the covenant is both theirs and ours.

7 For it is ours. But they permanently lost it, in this way, when Moses had just received it. For the Scripture says, "Moses was on the mountain fasting for forty days and forty nights, and he received the covenant from the Lord, stone tablets written with the finger of the Lord's own hand."[10]

8 But when they turned back to idols they lost it. For the Lord says this: "Moses, Moses, go down quickly, be-

cause your people, whom you led from the land of Egypt, has broken the law."[11] Moses understood and cast the two tablets from his hands. And their covenant was smashed—that the covenant of his beloved, Jesus, might be sealed in our hearts, in the hope brought by faith in him.

9 Since I want to write many things, not as a teacher, but as is fitting for one who is eager to abandon none of the things we have, I hasten to write, as your lowly scapegoat.[d] Therefore, we should pay close attention here in the final days. For the entire time of our faith will be of no use to us if we do not stand in resistance, as is fitting for the children of God, both against this present lawless age and against the stumbling blocks that are yet to come,

10 that the Black One not sneak in among us. We should flee from all that is futile and completely hate the works of the evil path. Do not sink into yourselves and live alone, as if you were already made upright; instead, gathering together for the same purpose, seek out what is profitable for the common good.

11 For the Scripture says, "Woe to those who have understanding in themselves and are knowledgeable before their own eyes."[12] We should be spiritual; we should be a perfect temple to God. As much as we can, we should concern ourselves with the reverential awe of God and struggle to guard his commandments, that we may be glad in his righteous acts.[e]

12 The Lord will judge the world, playing no favorites. Each will receive according to what he has done. If he is

---

[d]Or: *your humble servant;* literally: *offscouring*   [e]Or: *righteous demands*

---

[8]Dan 7:24.   [9]Dan 7:7–8.   [10]Exod 31:18; 34:28.
[11]Exod 32:7.   [12]Isa 5:21.

good, his righteousness will precede him; if evil, the reward for his wickedness will be before him.

13 As those who are called we must never lie down and lose consciousness of our sins, allowing the evil ruler to receive the authority against us and force us out of the Lord's kingdom.

14 And still, my brothers, consider: when you observe that Israel was abandoned even after such signs and wonders had occurred in it, we too should pay close attention, lest, as it is written, "many of us were found called, but few chosen."[13]

5 This is why the Lord allowed his flesh to be given over to corruption, that we might be made holy through the forgiveness of sins, which comes in the sprinkling of his blood.

2 For some of the things written about him concern Israel; others concern us. And so it says: "He was wounded because of our lawless acts and weakened because of our sins. By his bruising we were healed. He was led like a sheep going to slaughter; and like a lamb, silent before the one who shears it."[14]

3 Therefore we ought to give thanks to the Lord even more abundantly, because he revealed to us the things that have taken place and made us wise in the things that are now; and we are not ignorant of the things that are yet to happen.

4 And the Scripture says, "Not unjustly are the nets spread out for the birds."[15] It says this because the person who knows the path of righteousness but keeps himself in the path of darkness deserves to perish.

5 Consider this, my brothers: if the Lord allowed himself to suffer for our sake, even though he was the Lord of the entire world, the one to whom God said

at the foundation of the world, "Let us make a human according to our image and likeness,"[16] how then did he allow himself to suffer at the hands of humans? Learn this!

6 Because the prophets received his gracious gift, they prophesied looking ahead to him. He allowed himself to suffer in order to destroy death and to show that there is a resurrection of the dead. For he had to be manifest in the flesh.

7 And he allowed himself to suffer in order to redeem the promise given to the fathers and to show, while he was on earth preparing a new people for himself, that he is to execute judgment after raising the dead.

8 Moreover, while teaching Israel and doing such wonders and signs, he preached to them and loved them deeply.

9 And when he selected his own apostles who were about to preach his gospel, they were altogether lawless beyond all sin. This was to show that he did not come to call the upright but sinners. Then he revealed that he was the Son of God.

10 For if he had not come in the flesh, how would people have been able to look upon him and survive? For they cannot even look intently at the sun, gazing directly into its rays, even though it is the work of his hands and will eventually cease to exist.

11 Therefore, the Son of God came in the flesh for this reason, that he might total up all the sins of those who persecuted his prophets to death.

12 And so this is why he allowed himself to suffer. For God speaks of the blow they delivered against his flesh: "When they smite their own shepherd, then the sheep of the flock will perish."[17]

---

[13]Matt 22:14. [14]Isa 53:5, 7. [15]Prov 1:17. [16]Gen 1: 26. [17]Cf. Zech 13:7; Matt 26:31.

13 But he wished to suffer in this way, for he had to suffer on a tree. For the one who prophesied about him said, "Spare my life from the sword," and "Nail my-flesh, because an assembly[f] of evildoers has risen up against me."[18]

14 Again he says, "See! I have set my back to whips and my cheeks to blows; and I have set my face as a hard rock."[19]

6 And so, when he issued the commandment, what did he say? "Who is the one who takes me to court? Let him oppose me! Or who acquits himself before me? Let him approach the servant of the Lord!

2 Woe to you, for you will all grow old like a garment and a moth will devour you."[20] And again, since he was set in place as a strong stone used for crushing, the prophet says, "See, I will cast into Zion's foundation a precious stone that is chosen, a cornerstone, one to be valued."

3 Then what does he say? "The one who believes in him will live forever."[21] Is our hope then built on a stone? May it never be! But he says this because the Lord has set his flesh up in strength. For he says, "He set me up as a hard rock."[22]

4 And again the prophet says, "A stone that the builders rejected has become the very cornerstone." And again he says, "This is the great and marvelous day the Lord has made."[23]

5 I am writing to you in very simple terms, that you may understand. I am a lowly scapegoat[g] for your love.

6 And so what again does the prophet say? "An assembly[h] of evildoers surrounded me, they swarmed about me like bees around a honeycomb,"[24] and, "They cast lots for my clothing."[25]

7 And so, because he was about to be revealed and suffer in the flesh, his suffering was revealed in advance. For the prophet says about Israel, "Woe to their soul, because they hatched an evil plot against themselves, saying, 'Let us bind the upright one, because he is trouble for us.' "[26]

8 What does the other prophet, Moses, say to them? "See, this is what the Lord God says, 'Enter into the good land, which the Lord swore to give to Abraham, Isaac, and Jacob; and receive it as an inheritance, a land flowing with milk and honey.' "[27]

9 Learn what knowledge says. "Hope," it says, "in Jesus, who is about to be revealed to you in the flesh." For a human is earth that suffers. For Adam was formed out of the face of the earth.

10 Why then does he say, "Into the good land, a land flowing with milk and honey"? Blessed is our Lord, brothers, who placed the wisdom and knowledge of his secrets within us. For the prophet is speaking a parable of the Lord. Who will understand it, except one who is wise and learned, who loves his Lord?

11 Since, then, he renewed us through the forgiveness of our sins, he made us into a different type of person, that we might have the soul of children, as if he were indeed forming us all over again.

12 For the Scripture speaks about us when he says to his Son, "Let us make the human according to our image and likeness, and let them rule over the wild beasts of the land and the birds of the sky and the fish of the sea."[28] Once the Lord saw our beautiful form, he said "Increase and multiply and fill the earth."[29] He said these things to the Son.

---

[f]Or: *synagogue*   [g]Or: *a humble servant*; literally: *an offscouring*   [h]Or: *synagogue*

---

[18]Ps 22:20, 16.   [19]Isa 50:6–7.   [20]Isa 50:8–9.   [21]Isa 28:16.   [22]Isa 50:7.   [23]Ps 118:22, 24; cf. 1 Pet 2:7.   [24]Ps 22:16; 118:12.[25]Ps 22:18.   [26]Isa 3:9–10.   [27]Exod 33:1, 3.   [28]Gen 1:26.   [29]Gen 1: 28.

13 Again I will show you how he speaks to us. He made yet a second human form in the final days. And the Lord says, "See! I am making the final things like the first."³⁰ This is why the prophet proclaimed, "Enter into a land flowing with milk and honey, and rule over it."³¹

14 See, then, that we have been formed anew, just as he again says in another prophet, "See, says the Lord, I will remove from these people their hearts of stone" (that is to say, from those whom the Spirit of the Lord foresaw) "and cast into them hearts of flesh."³² For he was about to be revealed in the flesh and to dwell among us.

15 For the dwelling place of our heart, my brothers, is a temple holy to the Lord.

16 For again the Lord says, "And how will I appear before the Lord my God and be glorified?"³³ He answers: "I will praise you in the assembly of my brothers, and sing your praise in the midst of the assembly of saints."³⁴ And so we are the ones he has brought into the good land.

17 Why then does he speak of milk and honey? Because the child is first nourished by honey and then milk. So also, when we are nourished by faith in the promise and then by the word, we will live as masters over the earth.

18 For he already said above, "Let them increase and multiply and rule over the fish."³⁵ Who can now rule over wild beasts and fish and birds of the sky? For we ought to realize that ruling is a matter of authority, so that the one who issues commands is the master.

19 Since this is not happening now, he has told us when it will happen—when we have ourselves been perfected so as to become heirs of the Lord's covenant.

7 And so you should understand, children of gladness, that the good Lord has revealed everything to us in advance, that we may know whom to praise when we give thanks for everything.

2 And so, if the Son of God suffered, that by being beaten he might give us life (even though he is the Lord and is about to judge the living and the dead), we should believe that the Son of God could not suffer unless it was for our sakes.

3 But also when he was crucified he was given vinegar and gall to drink. Listen how the priests in the temple made a revelation about this. For the Lord gave the written commandment that "Whoever does not keep the fast must surely die,"³⁶ because he himself was about to offer the vessel of the Spirit as a sacrifice for our own sins, that the type might also be fulfilled that was set forth in Isaac, when he was offered on the altar.

4 What then does he say in the prophet? "Let them eat some of the goat offered for all sins on the day of fasting." Now pay careful attention: "And let all the priests alone eat the intestines, unwashed, with vinegar."³⁷

5 Why is this? Since you are about to give me gall mixed with vinegar to drink—when I am about to offer my flesh on behalf of the sins of my new people—you alone are to eat, while the people fast and mourn in sackcloth and ashes. He says this to show that he had to suffer at their hands.

6 Pay attention to what he commands: "Take two fine goats who are alike and offer them as a sacrifice; and let the priest take one of them as a whole burnt offering for sins."³⁸

---

³⁰Source unknown. ³¹Exod 33:3. ³²Ezek 11:19. ³³Ps 42:4. ³⁴Ps 22: 22, 25. ³⁵Gen 1:28. ³⁶Lev 23: 29. ³⁷Source unknown. Cf. Leviticus 16. ³⁸Lev 16: 7, 9.

7 But what will they do with the other? "The other," he says, "is cursed."[39] Pay attention to how the type of Jesus is revealed.

8 "And all of you shall spit on it and pierce it and wrap a piece of scarlet wool around its head, and so let it be cast into the wilderness."[40] When this happens, the one who takes the goat leads it into the wilderness and removes the wool, and places it on a blackberry bush, whose buds we are accustomed to eat when we find it in the countryside. (Thus the fruit of the blackberry bush alone is sweet.)

9 And so, what does this mean? Pay attention: "The one they take to the altar, but the other is cursed," and the one that is cursed is crowned. For then they will see him in that day wearing a long scarlet robe around his flesh, and they will say, "Is this not the one we once crucified, despising, piercing, and spitting on him? Truly this is the one who was saying at the time that he was himself the Son of God."

10 For how is he like that one? This is why "the goats are alike, fine, and equal," that when they see him coming at that time, they may be amazed at how much he is like the goat. See then the type of Jesus who was about to suffer.

11 But why do they place the wool in the midst of the thorns? This is a type of Jesus established for the church, because whoever wishes to remove the scarlet wool must suffer greatly, since the thorn is a fearful thing, and a person can retrieve the wool only by experiencing pain. And so he says: those who wish to see me and touch my kingdom must take hold of me through pain and suffering.

8 And what do you suppose is the type found in his command to Israel that men who are full of sin should offer up a heifer, and after slaughtering it burn it, and that children should then take the ashes and cast them into vessels, and then tie scarlet wool around a piece of wood (see again the type of the cross and the scarlet wool!), along with the hyssop, and that the children should thus sprinkle the people one by one, that they might be purified from their sins?

2 Understand how he speaks to you simply. The calf is Jesus; the sinful men who make the offering are those who offered him up for slaughter. Then they are no longer men and the glory of sinners is no more.

3 The children who sprinkle are those who proclaimed to us the forgiveness of sins and the purification of our hearts. To them he has given the authority to preach the gospel. There are twelve of them as a witness to the tribes, for there were twelve tribes in Israel.

4 But why are there three children who sprinkle? As a witness to Abraham, Isaac, and Jacob, because these were great before God.

5 And why is the wool placed on a piece of wood? Because the kingdom of Jesus is on the tree, and because those who hope in him will live forever.

6 But why are the wool and hyssop together? Because in his kingdom there will be evil and foul days, in which we will be saved. And because the one who is sick in the flesh is healed by the foul juice of the hyssop.

7 And thus the things that have happened in this way are clear to us, but they are obscure to them, because they have not heard the voice of the Lord.

9 For he speaks again about the ears, indicating how he has circumcised

---

[39]Cf. Lev 16:8.   [40]Cf. Lev 16:10, 20–22.

our hearts. The Lord says in the prophet, "They obeyed me because of what they heard with their ears."[41] Again he says, "Those who are far off will clearly hear; they will know what I have done."[42] And, "Circumcise your hearts,"[43] says the Lord.

2 Again he says, "Hear O Israel, for thus says the Lord your God."[44] And again the Spirit of the Lord prophesies, "Who is the one who wants to live forever? Let him clearly hear the voice of my servant."[45]

3 Again he says, "Hear, O heaven, and give ear, O earth, for the Lord has said these things as a witness."[46] And again he says, "Hear, the word of the Lord, you rulers of this people."[47] And again he says, "Hear, O children, the voice of one crying in the wilderness."[48] Thus he circumcised our hearing, that once we heard the word we might believe.

4 But even the circumcision in which they trusted has been nullified. For he has said that circumcision is not a matter of the flesh. But they violated his law, because an evil angel instructed them.

5 He says to them, "Thus says the Lord your God," (here is where I find a commandment) "Do not sow among the thorns; be circumcised to your Lord."[49] And what does he say? "Circumcise your hardened hearts and do not harden your necks."[50] Or consider again, "See, says the Lord, all the nations are uncircumcised in their foreskins, but this people is uncircumcised in their hearts."[51]

6 But you will say, "Yet surely the people have been circumcised as a seal.[i] But every Syrian and Arab and all the priests of the idols are circumcised as well. So then, do those belong to their covenant? Even the people of Egypt are circumcised!

7 Thus learn about the whole matter fully, children of love. For Abraham, the first to perform circumcision, was looking ahead in the Spirit to Jesus when he circumcised. For he received the firm teachings of the three letters.

8 For it says, "Abraham circumcised eighteen and three hundred men from his household."[52] What knowledge, then, was given to him? Notice that first he mentions the eighteen and then, after a pause, the three hundred. The number eighteen [in Greek] consists of an iota [J], 10, and an eta [E], 8. There you have Jesus.[j] And because the cross was about to have grace in the letter tau [T], he next gives the three hundred, tau. And so he shows the name Jesus by the first two letters, and the cross by the other.

9 For the one who has placed the implanted gift of his covenant in us knew these things. No one has learned a more reliable lesson from me. But I know that you are worthy.

10 And when Moses said, "Do not eat the pig, or the eagle, or the hawk, or the crow, or any fish without scales,"[53] he received three firm teachings in his understanding.

2 Moreover, he said to them in the book of Deuteronomy, "I will establish a covenant with this people in my righteous demands."[54] So, then, the commandment of God is not a matter of avoiding food; but Moses spoke in the Spirit.

3 This is why he spoke about the pig: "Do not cling," he says, "to such peo-

[i] i.e., of the covenant [j] i.e., the number eighteen in Greek is JE, taken here as an abbreviation for the name "Jesus"

[41]Ps 18:44. [42]Cf.Isa 33:13. [43]Isa 33:13; Jer 4:4. [44]Cf Jer 7:2–3; Ps 34:12–13. [45]Cf. Ps 34:12–13; Isa 50:10; Exod. 15:26. [46]Cf. Isa 1:2. [47]Cf Isa 1:10; 28:14. [48]Cf. Isa 40:3. [49]Jer 4:3–4. [50]Cf. Deut 10:16. [51]Jer 9:26. [52]Cf. Gen 14:14; 17:23. [53]Cf. Lev 11:7–15; Deut 14:8–14. [54]Cf. Deut 4:10, 13.

ple, who are like pigs." That is to say, when they live in luxury, they forget the Lord, but when they are in need, they remember the Lord. This is just like the pig: when it is eating, it does not know its master, but when hungry, it cries out— until it gets its food, and then is silent again.

4 "And do not eat the eagle, the hawk, the kite, or the crow."[55] "You must not," he says, "cling to such people or be like them, people who do not know how to procure food for themselves through toil and sweat, but by their lawless behavior seize food that belongs to others. And they are always on the watch, strolling about with ostensible innocence, but looking to see what they can plunder because of their greed." For these are the only birds that do not procure their own food, but sit by idly, waiting to see how they might devour the flesh procured by others, being pestilent in their evil.

5 "And do not," he says, "eat the lamprey-eel, the octopus, or the cuttle-fish."[56] "You must not," he says, "be like such people, who are completely impious and condemned already to death." For these fish alone are cursed and hover in the depths, not swimming like the others but dwelling in the mud beneath the depths.

6 But also "do not eat the hare."[57] For what reason? "You must not," he says, "be one who corrupts children or be like such people." For the rabbit adds an orifice every year; it has as many holes as years it has lived.

7 "Nor shall you eat the hyena."[58] "You must not," he says, "be an adulterer or a pervert nor be like such people." For what reason? Because this animal changes its nature every year, at one time it is male, the next time female.

8 And he has fully hated the weasel. "You must not," he says, "be like those who are reputed to perform a lawless deed in their mouth because of their uncleanness, nor cling to unclean women who perform the lawless deed in their mouth." For this animal conceives with its mouth.

9 And so, Moses received the three firm teachings about food and spoke in the Spirit. But they received his words according to the desires of their own flesh, as if he were actually speaking about food.

10 And David received the knowledge of the same three firm teachings and spoke in a similar way: "How fortunate is the man who does not proceed in the counsel of the impious" (like the fish who proceed in darkness in the depths) "and does not stand in the path of sinners" (like those who appear to fear God but sin like the pig) "and does not sit in the seat of the pestilent"[59] (like the birds who sit waiting for something to seize). Here you have a perfect lesson about food.

11 Again Moses said, "Eat every animal with a split hoof and that chews the cud."[60] What does he mean? He means that the one who receives food knows who has provided it and appears to be glad, having relied on him. He spoke well, looking to the commandment. What does he mean then? Cling to those who fear the Lord, to those who meditate on the special meaning of the teaching they have received in their heart, to those who discuss and keep the upright demands of the Lord, to those who know that meditation is a work that produces gladness, and to those who carefully chew over the word of the Lord. But why does he mention the split hoof? Because the one who is upright both walks in this world and

---

[55]Cf. Lev 11:13–16. [56]Source unknown. [57]Cf. Lev 11:6. [58]Source unknown. [59]Ps 1:1. [60]Cf. Lev 11:3; Deut 14:6.

waits for the holy age. Do you see how well Moses has given the Law?

12 But how could they know or understand these things? We, however, speak as those who know the commandments in an upright way, as the Lord wished. For this reason he circumcised our hearing and our hearts, that we may understand these things.

11 But we should look closely to see if the Lord was concerned to reveal anything in advance about the water and the cross. On the one hand, it is written about the water that Israel will not at all accept the baptism that brings forgiveness of sins, but will create something in its place for themselves.

2 For the prophet says, "Be astounded, O heaven, and shudder even more at this, O earth. For this people has done two wicked things: they have deserted me, the fountain of life, and dug for themselves a pit of death.

3 Is my holy mountain, Sinai, a rock that has been abandoned? For you will be like young birds who flutter about after being taken from their nest."[61]

4 Again the prophet says, "I will go before you to flatten mountains, crush gates of bronze, and smash bars of iron, and I will give you treasures that are dark, hidden, and unseen, that they may know that I am the Lord God."[62]

5 And, "You will dwell in a high cave, built of solid rock, and its water will not fail. You will see a king with glory, and your soul will meditate on the reverential fear of the Lord."[63]

6 Again in another prophet he says, "The one who does these things will be like a tree planted beside springs of water; it will produce its fruit in its season, and its leaf will not fall, and everything it does will prosper.

7 Not so with the impious, not so; but they will be like chaff driven by the wind from the face of the earth. For this reason the impious will not rise up in judgment nor sinners in the counsel of the upright; for the Lord knows the path of the upright, but the path of the impious will perish."[64]

8 Notice how he described the water and the cross in the same place. He means this: how fortunate are those who went down into the water hoping in the cross, for he indicates the reward will come "in its season." "At that time," he says, "I will pay it." Now when he says, "the leaves will not fall," he means that every word your mouth utters in faith and love will lead many to convert and hope.

9 And again another prophet says, "The land of Jacob was praised more than every other land." This means that he glorifies the vessel of his Spirit.

10 What does he say then? "And a river was flowing from the right side, and beautiful trees were rising up from it. Whoever eats from them will live forever."[65]

11 This means that we descend into the water full of sins and filth, but come up out of it bearing the fruit of reverential fear in our heart and having the hope in Jesus in our spirits.[k] And "whoever eats from these will live forever" means this: whoever, he says, hears and believes what has been said will live forever.

12 In a similar way he makes another declaration about the cross in another prophet, who says, " 'When will these things be fulfilled?' says the Lord. 'When a tree falls and rises up, and when blood flows from a tree.' "[66] Again you have a message about the

---

[k]Or: *in the Spirit*

---

[61]Jer 2:12–13; cf Isa 16:1–2. [62]Cf. Isa 45:2–3. [63]Cf. Isa 33:16–18. [64]Ps 1:3–6. [65]Cf. Ezek 47:1–12. [66]4 Ezra 4:33; 5:5.

cross and the one who was about to be crucified.

2 And he again tells Moses, when Israel was attacked by a foreign people, to remind those under assault that they were being handed over to death because of their sins. The Spirit speaks to the heart of Moses that he should make a type of the cross and of the one who was about to suffer, that they might realize, he says, that if they refused to hope in him, they would be attacked forever. And so Moses stacked weapons one on the other in the midst of the battle and standing high above all the people he began stretching out his hands; and so Israel again gained the victory. But then, when he lowered his hands, they began to be killed.[67]

3 Why was that? So that they may know that they cannot be saved unless they hope in him.

4 And again in another prophet he says, "All day long I have stretched out my hands to a disobedient people that opposes my upright path."[68]

5 Again Moses made a type of Jesus, showing that he had to suffer and that he will again make alive—this one whom they will think they have destroyed. This type came in a sign given when Israel was falling. For the Lord made every serpent bite them and they were dying (since the act of transgression came by Eve through the serpent). This was to convince them that they will be handed over to the affliction of death because of thier transgression.

6 Moreover, even though Moses himself issued this command—"You will have no molten or carved image as your god"[69]—he himself made one, that he might show forth a type of Jesus. And so Moses made a bronze serpent and displayed it prominently, and he called the people through a proclamation.

7 And when they came together they begged Moses to offer up a prayer on their behalf, that they might be healed. But Moses said to them, "When any of you is bitten, come to the serpent that is displayed on the tree and hope, in faith, that even though dead, it can restore a person to life; and you will then immediately be saved." And they did this.[70] Again you have the glory of Jesus in these things, for everything is in him and for him.

8 Again, why does Moses say to Jesus the son of Naue[l] when he gave this name to him who was a prophet, that all the people should listen to him alone? Because the Father reveals everything about his Son Jesus.

9 And so, after Moses gave Jesus the son of Naue[m] this name, he sent him as a reconnaissance scout over the land and said, "Take a small book in your hands and record what the Lord says, that in the last days the Son of God will chop down the entire house of Amalek at its roots."[71]

10 Again you see Jesus, not as son of man but as Son of God, manifest here in the flesh as a type. And so, since they are about to say that the Christ is the son of David, David himself speaks a prophecy in reverential awe, understanding the error of the sinners, "The Lord said to my Lord, 'Sit at my right side until I make your enemies a footstool for your feet.' "[72]

11 And again Isaiah says the following: "The Lord said to Christ my Lord, 'I have grasped his right hand that the nations will obey him, and I will shatter the power of kings' "[73] See how David calls him Lord; he does not call him son.

---

[l]Or: *Joshua the son of Nun; Jesus is the Greek equivalent of the Hebrew name Joshua*   [m]Or: *Joshua the son of Nun; Jesus is the Greek equivalent of the Hebrew name Joshua*

---

[67]Cf. Exod 17: 8–13.   [68]Cf. Isa 65:2.   [69]Cf. Lev 26:1; Deut 27:15.   [70]Cf. Num 21:4–8.   [71]Cf. Exod 17:14. [72]Ps 110:1.   [73]Cf. Isa 45:1.

13 Now let us see whether it is this people or the first one that receives the inheritance, and whether the covenant is for us or them.

2 Hear what the Scripture says concerning the people, "Isaac prayed for Rebecca his wife, because she was infertile. And then she conceived." Then, "Rebecca went to inquire of the Lord, and the Lord said to her, 'There are two nations in your womb and two peoples in your belly, and one people will dominate the other and the greater will serve the lesser.' "[74]

3 You ought to perceive who Isaac represents and who Rebecca, and whom he means when he shows that this people is greater than that one.

4 In another prophecy Jacob speaks more plainly to Joseph his son, when he says, "See, the Lord has not kept me from your presence. Bring your sons to me that I may bless them."[75]

5 He brought Ephraim and Manasseh, wanting him to bless Manasseh since he was the elder. So Joseph brought him to the right hand of his father Jacob. But Jacob saw in the Spirit a type of the people who was to come later. And what does it say? "Jacob crossed his hands and placed his right hand on the head of Ephraim, the second and younger, and blessed him. And Joseph said to Jacob, 'Switch your right hand onto Manasseh's head, because he is my firstborn son.' Jacob said to Joseph, 'I know, my child, I know. But the greater will serve the lesser, and it is this one who will be blessed.' "[76]

6 You see about whom he has decreed, that this people will be first, and the heir of the covenant.

7 And if this is also brought to mind through Abraham, we maintain that our knowledge is now perfect. What then does he say to Abraham, when he alone believed and was appointed for righteousness? "See, Abraham, I have made you a father of the nations who believe in God while uncircumcised."[77]

14 Yes indeed. But we should see if he has given the covenant that he swore to the fathers he would give the people. Let us pursue the question. He has given it, but they were not worthy to receive it because of their sins.

2 For the prophet says, "Moses was fasting on Mount Sinai For forty days and forty nights, that he might receive the covenant of the Lord for the people. And Moses received from the Lord the two tablets written with the finger of the Lord's hand in the Spirit."[78] When Moses received them he brought them down to give to the people.

3 And the Lord said to Moses, "Moses, Moses, go down at once, because your people, whom you brought out of the land of Egypt, has broken the Law. Moses understood that they had again made molten images for themselves, and he hurled the tablets from his hands. And the tablets of the Lord's covenant were smashed."[79]

4 So Moses received the covenant, but they were not worthy. Now learn how we have received it. Moses received it as a servant, but the Lord himself gave it to us, as a people of the inheritance, by enduring suffering for us.

5 He was made manifest so that those people might be completely filled with sins, and that we might receive the covenant through the Lord Jesus, who inherited it. He was prepared for this end, that when he became manifest he might make a covenant with us by his word, after redeeming our hearts from darkness,

[74]Cf. Gen 25:21–23. [75]Gen 48:11, 9. [76]Cf. Gen 48: 14, 19. [77]Cf. Gen 15:6; 17:4. [78]Cf. Exod. 24:18; 31: 18. [79]Cf. Exod 32:7–19.

hearts that were already paid out to death and given over to the lawlessness of deceit.

6 For it is written how the Father commanded him to prepare for himself a holy people after he redeemed us from darkness.

7 And so the prophet says, "I the Lord your God called you in righteousness; and I will grasp your hand and strengthen you. I have given you as a covenant of the people, as a light to the nations, to open the eyes of the blind, to bring out of their bondage those in shackles and out of prison those who sit in darkness."[80] And so we know the place from which we have been redeemed.

8 Again the prophet says, "See, I have set you as a light to the nations, that you may bring salvation to the end of the earth; so says the Lord God who redeems you."[81]

9 Again the prophet says, "The Spirit of the Lord is upon me, because he anointed me to preach the good news of grace to the humble; he sent me to heal those whose hearts are crushed, to proclaim a release to the captives and renewed sight to the blind, to call out the acceptable year of the Lord and the day of recompense, to comfort all those who mourn."[82]

15 Something is also written about the Sabbath in the ten commandments, which God spoke to Moses face to face on Mount Sinai: "Make the Sabbath of the Lord holy, with pure hands and a pure heart."[83]

2 In another place it says, "If my children keep the Sabbath, I will bestow my mercy on them."[84]

3 This refers to the Sabbath at the beginning of creation: "God made the works of his hands in six days, and he finished on the seventh day; and he rested on it and made it holy."[85]

4 Pay attention, children, to what it means that "he finished in six days." This means that in six thousand years the Lord will complete all things. For with him a day represents a thousand years. He himself testifies that I am right, when he says, "See, a day of the Lord will be like a thousand years."[86] And so, children, all things will be completed in six days— that is to say, in six thousand years.

5 "And he rested on the seventh day." This means that when his Son comes he will put an end to the age of the lawless one, judge the impious, and alter the sun, moon, and stars; then he will indeed rest on the seventh day.

6 Moreover, it says, "Make it holy with pure hands and a pure heart." We are very much mistaken if we think that at the present time anyone, by having a pure heart, can make holy the day that the Lord has made holy.

7 And so you see that at that time, when we are given a good rest, we will make it holy—being able to do so because we ourselves have been made upright and have received the promise, when lawlessness is no more and all things have been made new by the Lord. Then we will be able to make the day holy, after we ourselves have been made holy.

8 Moreover he says to them, "I cannot stand your new moons and Sabbaths."[87] You see what he means: It is not the Sabbaths of the present time that are acceptable to me, but the one I have made, in which I will give rest to all things and make a beginning of an eighth day, which is the beginning of another world.

9 Therefore also we celebrate the eighth day with gladness, for on it Jesus

---

[80]Isa 42:6–7.   [81]Cf. Isa 49:6–7.   [82]Isa 61:1–2.   [83]Cf. Exod 20:8; Deut 5:12.   [84]Cf. Jer 17:24–25.   [85]Gen 2: 2–3.   [86]Cf. Ps 90:4; 2 Pet 3:8.   [87]Isa 1:13.

arose from the dead, and appeared, and ascended into heaven.

16

I will also speak to you about the temple, since those wretches were misguided in hoping in the building rather than in their God who made them, as if the temple were actually the house of God.

2 For they consecrated him in the temple almost like the Gentiles do. But consider what the Lord says in order to invalidate it: "Who has measured the sky with the span of his hand or the earth with his outstretched fingers? Is it not I, says the Lord? The sky is my throne and the earth is the footstool for my feet. What sort of house will you build me, or where is the place I can rest?"[88] You knew that their hope was in vain!

3 Moreover he says again, "See, those who have destroyed this temple will themselves build it."[89]

4 This is happening. For because of their war, it was destroyed by their enemies. And now the servants of the enemies will themselves rebuild it.

5 Again it was revealed how the city, the temple, and the people of Israel were about to be handed over. For the Scripture says, "It will be in the last days that the Lord will hand over to destruction the sheep of the pasture along with their enclosure and tower."[90] And it has happened just as the Lord said.

6 But let us inquire if a temple of God still exists. It does exist, where he says that he is making and completing it. For it is written, "It will come about that when the seventh day is finished, a temple of God will be gloriously built in the name of the Lord."[91]

7 And so I conclude that a temple exists. But learn how it will be built in the name of the Lord. Before we believed in God, the dwelling place of our heart was corrupt and feeble, since it really was a temple built by hand; for it was full of idolatry and was a house of demons, because we did everything that was opposed to God.

8 "But it will be built in the name of the Lord." Now pay attention, so that the temple of the Lord may be gloriously built. And learn how: we have become new, created again from the beginning, because we have received the forgiveness of sins and have hoped in the name. Therefore God truly resides within our place of dwelling—within us.

9 How so? His word of faith, his call to us through his promise, the wisdom of his upright demands, the commandments of the teaching, he himself prophesying in us and dwelling in us who had served death, opening up to us the door of the temple, which is the mouth, and giving repentance to us—thus he brings us into his imperishable temple.

10 For the one who longs to be saved looks not merely to a person but to the one who dwells and speaks in him. For he is amazed at him since he has never heard him speak these words from his mouth nor even ever desired to hear them. This is a spiritual temple built for the Lord.

17

Insofar as I have been able to set forth these matters to you simply, I hope to have fulfilled my desire not to have omitted anything that pertains to salvation.

2 For if I should write to you about things present or things to come, you would not understand, because they are set forth in parables. And so these things will suffice.

---

[88]Cf. Isa 40:12; 66:1.   [89]Cf. Isa 49:17.   [90]Cf. 1 Enoch 89:56.   [91]Cf. Dan 9:24; 1 Enoch 91:13.

18 But let us turn to another area of knowledge and teaching. There are two paths of teaching and authority, the path of light and the path of darkness. And the difference between the two paths is great. For over the one are appointed light-bearing angels of God, but over the other angels of Satan.

2 And the one is Lord from eternity past to eternity to come; but the other is the ruler over the present age of lawlessness.

19 This then is the path of light. Anyone who wants to travel to the place that has been appointed should be diligent in his works. Such is the knowledge given to us, that we may walk in it.

2 Love the one who made you; stand in reverential awe of the one who formed you; glorify the one who ransomed you from death. Be simple in heart and rich in spirit. Do not mingle with those who walk along the path of death; hate everything that is not pleasing to God; hate all hypocrisy; do not abandon the commandments of the Lord.

3 Do not exalt yourself but be humble in every way. Do not heap glory on yourself. Do not entertain a wicked plot against your neighbor; do not make your soul impertinent.

4 Do not engage in sexual immorality, do not commit adultery, do not engage in pederasty. The word of God must not go out from you to any who are impure.[n] Do not show favoritism when you reproach someone for an unlawful act. Be meek and gentle; tremble at the words you have heard. Do not hold a grudge against your brother.

5 Do not be of two minds whether this should happen or not. Do not take the Lord's name for a futile purpose. Love your neighbor more than yourself. Do not abort a fetus or kill a child that is already born. Do not not remove your hand from your son or daughter, but from their youth teach them the reverential fear of God.

6 Do not desire your neighbor's belongings; do not be greedy. Do not join forces with the high and mighty but associate with the humble and upright. Welcome whatever happens to you as good, knowing that nothing occurs apart from God.

7 Do not be of two minds or speak from both sides of your mouth, for speaking from both sides of your mouth is a deadly trap. Be subject to your masters as to a replica[o] of God, with respect and reverential fear. Do not give orders to your male slave or female servant out of bitterness—since they hope in the same God—lest they stop fearing the God who is over you both. For he did not come to call those of high status but those whom the Spirit had prepared.

8 Share all things with your neighbor and do not say that anything is your own. For if you are partners in what is imperishable, how much more in what is perishable? Do not be garrulous, for the mouth is a deadly trap. In so far as you are able, be pure within.

9 Do not be one who reaches out your hands to receive but draws them back from giving. Love like the apple of your eye everyone who speaks the word of the Lord to you.

10 Think about the day of judgment night and day, and seek out the company of the saints every day, either laboring through the word and going out to comfort another, being concerned to save a life through the word, or working with your hands as a ransom for your sins.

11 Do not doubt whether to give, nor grumble while giving. But recognize who

---

[n]*Meaning obscure*   [o]Or: *type*

is the good paymaster of the reward. Guard the injunctions you have received, neither adding to them nor taking away. Completely hate what is evil. Give a fair judgment.

12 Do not create a schism, but make peace by bringing together those who are at odds. Confess your sins. Do not come to prayer with an evil conscience. This is the path of light.

20 But the path of the Black One is crooked and filled with a curse. For it is the path of eternal death which comes with punishment; on it are those things that destroy people's souls: idolatry, impertinence, glorification of power, hypocrisy, duplicity, adultery, murder, robbery, arrogance, transgression, deceit, malice, insolence, sorcery, magic, greed, irreverence towards God.

2 It is filled with persecutors of the good, haters of the truth, lovers of the lie; those who do not know the reward of righteousness, nor cling to the good nor to a fair judgment, who do not look out for the widow and the orphan, who are alert not to the reverential fear of God but to evil, from whom meekness and patience are far removed and remote. For they love what is vain and pursue a reward, showing no mercy to the poor nor toiling for the oppressed, who are prone to slander, not knowing the one who made them; murderers of children and corruptors of what God has fashioned, who turn their backs on the needy, oppress the afflicted, and support the wealthy. They are lawless judges of the impoverished, altogether sinful.

21 And so it is good for one who has learned all the upright demands of the Lord that have been written, to walk in them. For the one who does these things will be glorified in the kingdom of God. The one who chooses those other things will be destroyed, along with his works. This is why there is a resurrection; this is why a recompense.

2 I ask those of you who are in high positions, if you are willing to receive advice from my good counsel: keep some people among yourselves for whom you can do good, and do not fail.

3 The day is near when all things will perish, along with the wicked one. The Lord is near, as is his reward.[92]

4 Again and again I ask you, be your own good lawgivers, remain faithful advisors to yourselves, remove all hypocrisy from yourselves.

5 And may God, the one who rules the entire world, give you wisdom, understanding, perception, knowledge of his righteous demands, and patience.

6 Become those who are taught by God, enquiring into what the Lord seeks from you. And do it, that you may be found in the day of judgment.

7 And if there is any recollection of what is good, remember me by practicing these things, that my desire and vigilance may lead to a good result. I ask this of you, begging for a favor.

8 While the good vessel is still with you, do not fail in any of these things, but enquire fervently after them and fulfill every commandment. For they are worth doing.

9 Therefore I have been all the more eager to write what I could, to make you glad. Be well, children of love and peace. May the Lord of glory and of every gracious gift be with your spirit.

---

[92]Cf. Isa 40:10; Rev 22:12.

The Preaching of Peter

A popular document in early Christianity, the Preaching of Peter was widely assumed by early church fathers to have been composed by the apostle Peter himself. Most scholars today, however, think that it was written years after his death, sometime during the first part of the second century.

The book no longer survives intact but is known only through the quotations of later authors, especially Clement of Alexandria, who lived at the end of the second century and the beginning of the third. On the basis of these fragmentary remains it is impossible to judge the original length or contents of the document. Some of its major emphases, however, are reasonably clear: according to its author, Christianity is superior to both to the cults of pagans, who naively worship idols and living creatures, and to the religion of the Jews, who in their ignorance worship angels and celestial bodies rather than the true God. In particular, the book emphasizes that Christ fulfilled the predictions of the Jewish Scriptures and brought salvation to all people. Everyone who learns the truth of Christ is to repent for the forgiveness of their sins.

It is possible, given its themes, that the book was one of the first "apologies" for early Christianity, that is, a reasoned defense of the views of Christian over against the attacks of its cultured despisers among both pagans and Jews.

Clement of Alexandria
Strom. **1.29.182**

1 And in the Preaching of Peter you may find the Lord called "Law and Word."

Clement of Alexandria,
Strom. **6.5.39–41**

2 But that the most notable of the Greeks do not know God by direct knowledge but indirectly, Peter says in his Preaching, "Know then that there

Translation by J. K. Elliott, *Apocryphal New Testament* (Oxford: Clarendon Press, 1993) 21–24; used with permission.

is one God who made the beginning of all things and has power over their end," and "The invisible who sees all things, uncontainable, who contains all, who needs nothing, of whom all things stand in need and for whose sake they exist, incomprehensible, perpetual, incorruptible, increated, who made all things by the word of his power... that is, the Son." Then he goes on, "This God you must worship, not after the manner of the Greeks ... showing that we and the notable Greeks worship the same God, though not according to perfect knowledge for they had not learned the tradition of the Son." "Do not," he says, "worship"—he does not say "the God whom the Greeks worship," but "not in the manner of the Greeks": he would change the method of worship of God, not proclaim another God. What, then, is meant by "not in the manner of the Greeks"? Peter himself will explain, for he continues, "Carried away by ignorance and not knowing God as we do, according to the perfect knowledge, but shaping those things over which he gave them power for their use, wood and stones, brass and iron, gold and silver, forgetting their material and proper use, they set up things subservient to their existence and worship them; and what things God has given them for food, the fowls of the air and the creatures that swim in the sea and creep on the earth, wild beasts and four-footed cattle of the field, weasels too and mice, cats and dogs and apes; even their own food-stuffs do they sacrifice to animals that can be consumed and, offering dead things to the dead as if they were gods, they show ingratitude to God since by these practices they deny that he exists. . . ." He continues again in this fashion, "Neither worship him as the Jews do for they, who suppose that they alone know God, do not know him,

serving angels and archangels, the month and the moon: and if no moon be seen, they do not celebrate what is called the first sabbath, nor keep the new moon, nor the days of unleavened bread, nor the feast of tabernacles, nor the great day (of atonement)."

Then he adds the finale of what is required: "So then learn in a holy and righteous manner that which we deliver to you, observe, worshipping God through Christ in a new way. For we have found in the Scriptures, how the Lord said, 'Behold, I make with you a new covenant, not as the covenant with your fathers in mount Horeb.'[1] He has made a new one with us: for the ways of the Greeks and Jews are old, but we are Christians who worship him in a new way as a third generation."

Clement of Alexandra *Strom.* 6.5.43

3 Therefore Peter says that the Lord said to the apostles, "If then any of Israel will repent and believe in God through my name, his sins shall be forgiven him: and after twelve years go out into the world, lest any say, 'We did not hear'."

Clement of Alexandria *Strom.* 6.6.48

4 For example, in the Preaching of Peter the Lord says, "I chose you twelve, judging you to be disciples worthy of me, whom the Lord willed, and thinking you faithful apostles I sent you into the world to preach the gospel to people throughout the world, that they should know that there is one God; to

---

[1]Jer 31:31–32

declare by faith in me [the Christ] what shall be, so that those who have heard and believed may be saved, and that those who have not believed may hear and bear witness, not having any defence so as to say, 'We did not hear.' . . ."

And to all reasonable souls it has been said above: Whatever things any of you did in ignorance, not knowing God clearly, all his sins shall be forgiven him, if he comes to God and repents.

Clement of Alexandria
Strom. 6.15.128

5 Peter in the Preaching, speaking of the apostles, says, "But, having opened the books of the prophets which we had, we found, sometimes expressed by parables, sometimes by riddles, and sometimes directly and in so many words the name Jesus Christ, both his coming and his death and the cross and all the other torments which the Jews inflicted on him, and his resurrection and assumption into the heavens before Jerusalem was founded, all these things that had been written, what he must suffer and what shall be after him. When, therefore, we gained knowledge of these things, we believed in God through that which had been written of him."

And a little after he adds that the prophecies came by divine providence, in these terms, "For we know that God commanded them, and without the Scripture we say nothing."

John of Damascus, *Parall.* A 12

6 (Of Peter): Wretched that I am, I remembered not that God sees the mind and observes the voice of the soul. Allying myself with sin, I said to myself, "God is merciful, and will bear with me; and because I was not immediately smitten, I ceased not, but rather despised pardon, and exhausted the long-suffering of God."

(From the Teaching of Peter): Rich is the man who has mercy on many, and, imitating God, gives what he has. For God has given all things to all his creation. Understand then, you rich, that you ought to minister, for you have received more than you yourselves need. Learn that others lack the things you have in superfluity. Be ashamed to keep things that belong to others. Imitate the fairness of God, and no one will be poor.

Origen, *de Principiis* i, prol. 8

7 But if any would produce to us from that book which is called The Doctrine of Peter, the passage where the Saviour is represented as saying to the disciples, "I am not a bodiless demon," . . .

Gregory of Nazianaus,
epp. 16 and 20

8 "A soul in trouble is near to God," as Peter says somewhere—a marvellous utterance.

Pseudo-Titus

The Letter now known as "Pseudo-Titus" is later than most of the other apocrypha included in this collection. It was unknown until discovered late in the nineteenth century in a very badly translated Latin manuscript produced some time in the eighth century, probably from a Greek original.

The author claims to be Titus, the companion of Paul, to whom one of the letters of the New Testament itself is addressed. This alleged connection with the apostle provides the writer with the authority he needs to set forth his clear agenda: to promote chastity for all Christians, urging even those who are married to abstain from the pleasures of sex as detrimental to salvation. "Why," asks the pseudonymous author, "do you strive against your own salvation to find death in love?"

The author quotes numerous sources, including the books of the Old and New Testaments, in support of his views. In particular, though, he appears to be familiar with the Apocryphal Acts of the Apostles, which, as we have seen, are themselves ascetic and world-denouncing in their orientation.

It is difficult to date this strident attack against the pleasures of the flesh, but most scholars place it some time in the fifth century.

Epistle of Titus, the Disciple of Paul

Great and honorable is the divine promise which the Lord has made with his own mouth to them that are holy and pure: He will bestow upon them "what eyes have not seen nor ears heard, nor has it entered into any human heart." And from eternity to eternity there will be a race incomparable and incomprehensible.

Blessed then are those who have not polluted their flesh by craving for this world, but are dead to the world that they may live for God! To whom neither flesh nor blood has shown deadly secrets, but the Spirit has shone upon them and shown some better thing so that even in

Translation by Aurelio de Santos Otero, in Wilhelm Schneemelcher, *New Testament Apocrypha,* vol. 2 (rev. ed.; Cambridge/ Louisville: Lutterworth/Westminister/John Knox, 1991) 55–63; used with permission.

this < . . . > and instant of our <pilgrim-age on the earth> they may display an angelic appearance. As the Lord says, "Such are to be called angels."[1]

Those then who are not defiled with women[2] he calls an angelic host. Those who have not abandoned themselves to men, he calls virgins, as the apostle of Christ says: "the unmarried think day and night on godly things,"[3] i.e. to act prop-erly and to please Him alone, and not to deny by their doings what they have promised in words. Why should a virgin who is already betrothed to Christ be united with a carnal man?

It is not lawful to cling to a man and to serve him more than God. Virgin! Thou hast cast off Christ, to whom thou wert betrothed! Thou has separated thy-self from Him, thou who strivest to re-main united to another! O beauteous maidenhood, at the last thou art stuck fast in love to a male being! O (holy) ascetic state, thou disappearest (when) the saints match human offences!

O body, thou art put to the yoke of the law of God, and ever and again commit-test fornication! Thou art crucified to this world,[4] and continuest to act up to it! If the apostle Paul forbade communion to a woman caught in an adulterous relation with a strange man,[5] how much more when those concerned are saints dedi-cated to Christ! Thou art caught in the vile fellowship of this world, and yet regardest thyself as worthy of the blood of Christ or as united with his body! But this is not the case: if thou eat of the flesh of the Lord unworthily, then thou takest vainly instead of life the fire of thine everlasting punishment! O virgin: if thou strivest to please (another), then thou hast already committed a sin of volition, for the Evangelist says: "one cannot serve two masters, for he obeys the one, and despises the other."[6] O virgin! so is it also

with thee. Thou despisest God, whilst striving to please a man.

Wherefore contemplate the footprints of our ancestors! Consider the daughter of Jephthah: willing to do what had been promised by her father and vowing her own self as a sacrifice to the Lord, she first manifested her connection with God and took other virgins with her "that in the mountains throughout sixty days they might bewail her virginity."[7] O luminous secrets which disclose the future in ad-vance! Virgin is joined with virgin, and in love to her she bewails the peril of her flesh until the day of her reward comes! Rightly does he say "sixty days," since he means the sixtyfold reward of holiness which the ascetic can gain through many pains, according to the teaching of the apostle: "Let us not lose courage, he says, in the hardest labours, in affliction, in grief, in suffering abuse: we suffer per-secution, but we are not forsaken, be-cause we bear in our body the passion of Christ. Wherefore we are by no means overcome."[8] And again the same apostle left an example behind him, describing his own disasters and saying: "I have labored much, I have frequently been im-prisoned, I have suffered extremely many floggings, I have often fallen into deadly peril. Of the Jews, he says, I have five times received forty stripes save one, three times have I been beaten with rods, once have I been stoned; thrice have I suffered shipwreck, a day and a night I have spent in the depth of the sea; I have often journeyed, often been in peril of rivers in peril of robbers, in peril among

---

[1]Mark 12: 25 par.   [2]Rev 14:4.   [3]1 Cor 7:34.   [4]Cf. Gal 6:14.   [5]This happening is recorded in detail in the Actus Petri cum Simone. The name of the woman concerned is there given as Rufina.   [6]Matt 6:24. [7]Jdg. 11:38.   [8]2 Cor 4:8ff.

unbelievers in manifold ways, in peril in cities, in peril among Gentiles, in peril in the wilderness, in peril among false brethren; in trouble and labor, frequently in sorrow, in many watchings, in hunger and thirst, in many fastings, in cold and nakedness, in inward anxieties, besides the cares which do not have direct reference to my personal suffering. And in all these I have not lost courage, because Christ was and still is with me."[9]

Oh, through how much trouble does man attain to glory! Besides there is the word of the Lord, who says: "Whom I love, he says, I rebuke and chasten"[10] that the righteous man may be tested as gold in the crucible. What bodily joy can there be then in the life to come if the word of the Lord runs: "Oh! as a virgin, as a woman, so is the mystery of resurrection (which) you have shown to me, you who in the beginning of the world did institute vain feasts for yourselves and delighted in the wantonness of the Gentiles and behaved in the same way as those who take delight therein." Behold what sort of young maidens there are among you! But come and ponder over this, that there is one who tries the soul and a last day of retribution and persecution.

Where then art thou now, thou who hast passed the time of thy youth happily with a sinner, the apostle testifying moreover that "neither flesh nor blood will possess the kingdom of God?"[11]

And again the law runs: "let not a man glory in his strength, but rather let him trust in the Lord,"[12] and Jeremiah says: "Accursed is he who puts his hope in man."[13] And in the Psalms it is said: "It is better to trust in the Lord than to rely on men."[14] Why then art thou not afraid to abandon the Lord and to trust in a man who in the last judgment will not save thee but rather destroy? Consider and take note of the happening about which

the following account informs us: "A peasant had a girl who was a virgin. She was also his only daughter, and therefore he besought Peter to offer a prayer for her. After he had prayed, the apostle said to the father that the Lord would bestow upon her what was expedient for her soul. Immediately, the girl fell down dead. O reward worthy and ever pleasing to God, to escape the shamelessness of the flesh and to break the pride of the blood! But this distrustful old man, failing to recognise the worth of the heavenly grace, i.e., the divine blessing, besought Peter again that his only daughter be raised from the dead. And some days later, after she had been raised, a man who passed himself off as a believer came into the house of the old man to stay with him, and seduced the girl, and the two of them never appeared again."

For the man who dishonors his own body makes himself like the godless. And therefore the dwelling-place of the godless cannot be found out, as David says: "I sought him but he was nowhere to be found,"[15] as also in the (mentioned) case of death those two did not dare (to appear) any more. Thou oughtest then, O virgin, to fear the judgment of this law: "If," says Moses, "a betrothed virgin is caught unawares with another man, let the two of them be brought before the court of the elders and be condemned to death."[16]

These happenings have been recorded for us on whom the end of this age has come. One thing stands fast: should a virgin who is betrothed to Christ be caught unawares with another man, let them both be committed for final sen-

---

[9]2 Cor 11:23ff. [10]Rev 3:19. [11]1 Cor 15:50. [12]Jer 9:23. [13]Jer 17:5. [14]Ps 118:8. [15]Ps 37:36. [16]Deut 22:23.

tence before the court of the elders, i.e., of Abraham, Isaac and Jacob, whose charge it is to investigate the case of their children. Then will the fathers disown their own children as evildoers. And finally the malefactors will cry amidst the torment of their punishment: Hear us, O Lord God, for our father Abraham has not known us, and Isaac and Jacob have disowned us! Thus then let the children conduct themselves that (some day) they may find themselves in the bosom of father Abraham. That is to say, that they may remain praiseworthy in his remembrance and be not as the daughters of Zion whom the Holy Spirit reproaches through Isaiah: "They moved together through the streets, dancing with their heads erect. And they engaged themselves to men in the villages of Jerusalem, and heaped up iniquity to the sky, and the Lord was angry and delivered them up to king Nebuchadnezzar to slavery for seventy years."[17]

You also are disobedient and undisciplined, you who do something even worse than the first committed. In the end you also will be delivered up to the wicked king Nebuchadnezzar, as he says, i.e., to the devil who will fall upon you. And as they (the Jews), after they had spent seventy years in anguish, returned to their own places of abode, so a period of seven years is (now) appointed under Antichrist. But the pain of these seven years presents eternal anguish. And as, after their return to their homeland, they henceforth experienced much evil, so is it also now with (these): after death the soul of each one will be tormented unto the judgment day. And again, after the slaughter of the beast, the first resurrection will take place; and then will the faithless souls return to their dwellings; and according to the increase of their (earlier) evil-doings will their torment

(now) be augmented beyond the first punishment.

Therefore, beloved, we must combat the works of the flesh because of the coming retribution. In order then that ye may escape eternal torment, ye must struggle, daughters, against flesh and blood so long as a period for that continues and a few days still remain wherein ye may contend for life. Why should the man who hast renounced the flesh be held fast in its lust? Why, O virgin, thou who has renounced a man, dost thou hug this physical beauty? Why (ascetic) givest thou up to a strange woman (i.e., one belonging to Christ) the body which was not made for that? Why strivest thou against thine own salvation to find death in love? Hear the apostle who says to you: "See," he says, "that ye give not place to the flesh through the liberty of God."[18] And again: "Fulfill not the lusts of the flesh. For the flesh lusteth against the Spirit and the Spirit against the flesh. These are opposed to one another. Therefore, he says, do not what ye would. Otherwise the Spirit of God is not in you."[19] O inherently false one, to despise the commandments of the holy law and (through) a deceitful marriage to lose in secret the life everlasting! O honeyed cheat, to draw on torment in the future! O unbridled passion for glory, to offend against the devotion that has been vowed to God! O steps that lead astray from the way, that a virgin is fond of the flesh of another! O faith(less) craving, theft of fire, honor entangled in crime! O broken promise, that the mind blazes up for a stranger! O pledge of lust, beauty inclined to crime! O alluring symbol of vice that brings disdain! O seminari da

---

[17]The source of this apocryphal quotation cannot be traced.   [18]Gal. 5:13.   [19]Gal. 5:16.

membra vicinacio tenebrarum! O concealed thievery, to give an appearance of humility and chastity! O gloom of the dark deed which plunders the glory of Christ forever! O fleeting remembrance of holiness which strives after death in the name of beauty! O "silver that has been refused," which according to the saying of Isaiah "is not worthy of God!"[20] O dishonored Sabbath in which the works of the flesh come to light in the last days and times! O foot, that failest on the way to holiness and dost not arrive at a sure habitation! O ship burst open by pirates, thou that gettest away empty and miserable! O house that is undermined by burglars whilst the watchmen sleep and lose the costly treasure! O maidenly youth, thou that fallest off miserably from right conduct! O enlargement of trust in this world which turns into desolation in eternity! O consequence of unchastity which brings down upon itself the malady of melancholy! O fountain of sweet poison which springs up from the flesh as inextricable entanglement! O wretched house founded on sand! O despicable crime of (this) time, that corruptest not thine own members but those of a stranger! O fleeting enjoyment on a brink of collapse! O parcel of deceit! O unsleeping ardour for the perdition of the soul! O tower that is in building to be left unfinished! O shameful work, thou art the scorn of them that pass by! Why, O virgin, dost thou not ponder over it and estimate the heavenly charges before laying the foundation? In the beginning thou hast acted too hastily, and before the house was completed, thou hast already experienced a terrible collapse![21] In your case the saying of the law has been fulfilled, the prophecy has come to pass: Many a tract of land, it says, is built upon and soon it grows old; temples and cities are built in the land and soon they are abandoned![22]

O flames of lust! The unclean profane with their lust the temple of God and by Him are condemned to destruction! Oh, a contest is entered upon in the stadium, and when it has hardly come to grappling, the shields fall to the ground! O city captured by enemies and reduced to a wilderness!

Against this whorish behaviour the Lord turns through Ezekiel saying: "Thou hast built thee thy brothel, thou hast desecrated thy beauty and thy comeliness in every by-way, thou hast become an unclean woman, thou who hast heaped up shamelessness for thyself. Thy disgrace in the unchastity which thou hast practised with thy lovers will yet come to light. And again, As I live, saith the Lord, Sodom has not so done as thou Jerusalem and thy daughters. But the iniquity of Sodom, they sister, is fulfilled. For Samaria has not committed the half of thy sins. Thou hast multiplied iniquities beyond thy sisters in all that thou hast done. Wherefore be ashamed and take thy disgrace upon thy head."[23]

O how frequently the scourgings and beatings of God are not spared, and yet no one takes to heart the word of the Lord to be concerned about the future life! Has not Jerusalem, possessing the law, sinned more than Sodom and Gomorrah, which possessed no law? And have not the crimes of Jerusalem, whose sons and daughters have stood under the banner of faith, outweighed those of Samaria, which already from the beginning was worldly-minded?

On the unprecedented crime of this new people the apostle says: "One hears commonly of unchastity among you and

---

[20]Isa 1:22 or the Apocryphon of Isaiah.   [21]Cf. Luke 14:28ff.   [22]The source of this apocryphal quotation cannot be determined.   [23]Cf. Ezek 16:24, 25, 31, 36, 48, 49, 51, 52.

indeed of such unchastity as is never met with among the Gentiles, that one lives with his father's wife. And ye are yet puffed up, and do not rather mourn, that such an evil-doer may be removed from your midst. I am indeed absent in the body, but in the spirit am among you and already, as if I were present, I have passed sentence of on the evil-doer: to hand over that man to Satan in the name of Christ."[24]

O invention of the devil, sport for those about to perish! Oh poison instead of honey, to take a father's wife in the same way as any bride dedicated to Christ whom in thine heart thou hast craved for! O man, thou hast lent no ear to the wisdom that says to thee: the lust of the ascetic dishonors the virgin.[25] So also did the first created man fall because of a virgin: when he saw a woman giving him a smile, he fell. His senses became tied to a craving which he had never known before, assuredly he had not experienced earlier its flavour and the sweetness that proved his downfall. O man who fearest not the face of this criminal person, passing by whom many have lost their lives. The disciple of the Lord, Judas Jacobi, brings that to our remembrance when he says: "Beloved, I would bring to your remembrance, though ye know, what happened to them who were oppressed by the corruption of the flesh, as for instance the genuine persons (veraces) who did not preserve their dignity, but abandoned their heavenly abode and, enticed by lust, went to the daughters of men to dwell with them."[26]

Today also they forfeit the angelic character who crave to dwell with strange daughters, according to the word of the Lord who proclaimed by Isaiah: "Woe unto you who join house to house and add field to field that they may draw nigh one another."[27] And in Micah it is said:

"Bewail the house which you have pulled on yourselves and endure of yourselves the punishment of indignation."[28] Does the Lord mean perhaps the house or the field of this time when he warns us against pressing them together? (No) rather it is a matter here of warnings in reference to holiness, in which the separation of man and woman is ordered. So the Lord also admonishes us through Jeremiah, saying, "It is an excellent thing for a man that he bear the yoke in his youth; he will sit alone when his hope is real; he will keep quiet and have patience."[29] "To bear the yoke" is then to observe God's order. And in conclusion the Lord says: "Take my yoke upon you."[30] And further, "in his youth" means in his hope. Thus he has commanded that salvation be preserved in lonely celibacy, so that each one of you may remain as a lonely tower according to the saying of the Evangelist that house should not remain upon house, but should come down at once. Why then, O man, dost thou make haste to build you a ruin upon a strange house and thus to occasion not only your own destruction but also that of the bride of Christ who is united to you?

And also if thou art free from unchastity, already thou committest a sin in keeping up connections with women; for finally, thus says the Lord in the Gospel: "He who looks upon a woman to lust after her hath committed adultery with her already in his heart."[31] On this account a man must live for God sincerely and free from all lust. In Daniel also we read: "As these false old men, who had craved for the beauty of Susanna, were unable to practise any unchastity with her, they slandered her. Susanna was

---

[24]1 Cor 5:1ff.   [25]Ecclus 20:4?   [26]Gen 6:2 (cf. Jud. 1: 5f.)   [27]Isa 5:8.   [28]Mic 1:11 (?)   [29]Lam 3:27–28. [30]Matt 11:29.   [31]Matt 5:28.

brought before their court, and these rogues had her stand before them with her head uncovered so that they might satisfy their craving at least in looking on her beauty."[32] And thus they were unable to escape capital punishment. How much more when the last day comes! What, thinkest thou, will Christ do to those who have surrendered their own members to rape? The apostle has already shown the future in advance, saying: "Let no temptation take hold of you, he says, save what is human!"[33] O temptation to sensuality! Man is not able to control himself, and inflicts on himself the predicted fatal wounds! O exhalations of the flesh! The glowing fire hidden deep in the heart nourishes a conflagration! O ignoble fight, to strike root in a dark night! O tree of seducing fruit that shows thick foliage! O false lips, out of which honey drops and which in the end are as bitter as poison! O charming eloquence, the words of which shoot arrows into the heart! O madness of love: death fetters the young as a chain, whilst wisdom announces the future, that is, what it always orders: "Avoid, my son, every evil and everything that resembles it."[34] And further: "And every man who takes part in a foot-race abstains from all things that he may be able to obtain the crown that is prepared for him."[35]

Why takest thou, O man, a woman as a servant? Consider the conduct of (our) holy ancestors. Thus Elias, a noble man who still lives in the body, took a young man as servant, to whom also he left his mantle as a holy keepsake when he was taken up into paradise in a chariot of fire.[36] There Enoch also lives in the body, who was carried away (there) in the first age. O holy dispensation of God, who has provided for the coming age! Enoch, the righteous, from among the first people, was commissioned to commit to

writing the history of the first men, and the holy Elias (was given the task) of registering the new deeds of this later people!

All that has thus to be construed according to the condition of (our) time: each of the two springs from his own age, Enoch (as a symbol) of righteousness and Elias (as a symbol) of holiness. But we must comply with the rule of our holiness, as the apostle says: "In body and spirit genus must resemble genus and the disciple the master."[37] And the spirit of Elias rested finally on Elisha. He also begged of him that he might immediately receive from him a double blessing like the one which (later) the Lord gave to his advanced disciples, saying, "He that believes on me will also do the works that I do, and will do greater works than these."[38] But such grace is granted only to those who fulfil the commandments of the Master. What should we now say? If Elisha served in the house of Elias to comply with the rule of propriety and the boy Gehazi assisted the (prophet) Elisha as Baruch (the prophet) Jeremiah, in order to leave us an (instructive) remembrance, why does a man today take a woman as servant under a semblance of holiness? If it is a matter of a close relative, then that will do; but not if she is a strange woman. After the flood the sons of Noah looked for places for themselves where they might build cities, and they named them after their wives. Precisely so do these (men) now behave who are united (to women).

O ascetics of God who look back at women to offer them gifts, to give them

---

[32]Cf. Dan 13:32 ('Susanna' in Apocrypha).   [33]Cf. 1 Cor 10:13.   [34]Didache 3:1   [35]1 Cor 9:25.   [36]2 Kings 2:15.   [37]The source of this Paul-saying is unknown. [38]John 14:12

property, to promise them houses, to make them presents of clothes, to surrender to them their own souls and yield to their name all that belongs to them! If thou then, O man, behavest rightly and innocently, why dost thou not take thine own sister with thee? Why doest thou not give her all that belongs to thee, and thou wilt possess every thing? Further and further thou separatest thyself from her: thou hatest her, thou persecutest her. And yet they greatest safety is in her. Nay, separated from her thou attachest thyself to another. And thus dost thou think to remain wealthy in body and not be controlled by any lust, and dost say that thou possessest the heavenly hope. Hear a word that holds good for thee. Consider what the Lord in the Gospel says to Mary: "Touch me not, says he, for I am not yet ascended to my Father!"[39] O divine examples which have been written for us! And Paul, the chosen vessel (of the Lord) and the impregnable wall among the disciples, admonishes us when in the course of his mission the virgin Thecla, full of innocent faithfulness to Christ, wished to kiss his chain—mark thou what the apostle said to her: "Touch me not, he said, because of the frailty of (this) time."[40] Thou dost see then, O young man, what the present Lord and the recorded testament of the disciple have said against the flesh. For they did not order the women to withdraw for their own sakes, for the Lord cannot be tempted and just as little can Paul, his vicar, but these admonitions and commands were uttered for the sake of us who are now members of Christ.

Above all the ascetic should avoid women on that account and see to it that he does (worthily) the duty entrusted to him by God. Consider the rebuilding of Jerusalem: at the time of this laborious work every man was armed and mailclad, and with one hand he built whilst in the

other he held fast a sword, always ready to contend against the enemy. Apprehend then the mystery, how one should build the sanctuary of celibacy: in ascetic loneliness one hand must be engaged in the work that an extremely beautiful city may be built for God, whilst the other grasps the sword and is always ready for action against the wicked devil. That is then to be interpreted in this way: both hands, i.e. the spirit and the flesh, have in mutual harmony to bring the building to completion, the spirit being always on the lookout for the enemy and the flesh building on the bedrock of good conduct. Therefore it is said in the Gospel: "Let your works shine before men that they may glorify your Father in heaven."[41] Behold what a splendid structure is built in the heavenly Jerusalem. In this city one contends rightly in a lonely position, without any intercourse with the flesh, as it stands in the Gospel: "In the coming age," says the Lord, "they will neither marry nor be given in marriage, but will be as the angels in heaven."[42] Thus we must endeavour through blameless conduct to gain for ourselves everlasting honor in the future age. O man, who understandest nothing at all of the fruits of righteousness, why has the Lord made the divine phoenix and not given it a little wife, but allowed it to remain in loneliness? Manifestly only on purpose to show the standing of virginity, i.e., that young men, remote from intercourse with women, should remain holy. And its resurrection points finally to life. In this connection David says in the Psalms: "I will lay me down and sleep in peace for thou, O Lord, makest me to dwell lonesome in hope."[43] O peaceful rest given

---

[39]John 20:17. [40]The scene is described in the surviving Acts of Paul and Thecla c. 18. [41]Matt 5:16.
[42]Mark 12:25 and pars. [43]Ps 4:8. [44]Cf. Prov 6:27.

without interruption! O great security, when a man lives lonesome in the body! Thou canst not expect to bind glowing coals on thy garment, and not set the robe alight.[44] Should you do such a thing, then you will remain naked and your shame will be manifest. Add to this the word of the prophet: "All flesh is grass."[45] That a man then may not go up in flames, let him keep far from fire. Why exposest thou thine eternal salvation to loss through a trifle? Hast thou not read in the law this word that holds good for thee: The people sat down to eat and to drink; and they rose to make merry; and of them 23,000 fell there? For they had begun to have intercourse with the daughters of men, i.e. they allowed themselves to be invited by them to their unclean sacrifices, and the children of Israel dedicated themselves to Baalpeor. . . .

---

[45]Is. 40:6 [46]Exod. 32:6, 28.

NON-CANONICAL APOCALYPSES AND REVELATORY TREATISES

Introduction

There is only one "Apocalypse" (or "Revelation"—the Latin equivalent for the Greek term) in the New Testament, a vision recounted by a prophet named John concerning what would happen at the end of time when God overthrows the forces of evil in a set of cataclysmic disasters leading up to the establishment of his utopian reign over the earth. But there were other such apocalyptic visions of the end times in early Christianity, and still other kinds of visionary literature that divulged the secrets of the divine realm, the nature of reality, the revelation of how the world came into existence and of how we came to be here. One other apocalypse was widely considered canonical by orthodox Christians—the Apocalypse of Peter (one of three surviving texts that go by that name)—and another is included as Scripture in one of our oldest manuscripts of the New Testament (the *Shepherd* of Hermas). Other visionary texts were read and revered by various early Christian groups, including Jewish-Christians, Montanists, and Gnostics.

While some of these books discuss the end of the world as we know it (e.g., some of the Montanist revelations, which are still lost to us), others narrate prophetic visions of the fate of individual souls rewarded with eternal bliss in heaven or damned to never-ending torments in hell (e.g., the Apocalypse of Peter). Others provide general warnings of future catastrophes on earth for which believers needed to prepare themselves (e.g., the *Shepherd* of Hermas). And yet others show how this world came into being in the first place, along with the supernatural realm and the human race (e.g., the Secret Book of John).

As with the other non-canonical books found in this collection, there is a range of perspective found here; some of these books are completely orthodox, but were excluded from the canon because they were known not to have been written by ancient apostles (e.g., the *Shepherd*); others were suspected of being forged (Apocalypse of Peter); and yet others were widely considered in proto-orthodox circles to contain heretical teachings that were to be attacked rather than affirmed (the Secret Book of John). The communities that revered such books, of course, thought just the opposite, that they were sacred texts providing divine revelations of the true nature of the world, of how it came into being (often based on an interpretation of the book of Genesis), and how we ourselves came to inhabit it. Not until the decisions determining the shape of orthodoxy were made were these books effectively silenced, and for the most part lost, until their fortuitous discovery in modern times.

The *Shepherd* of Hermas

The *Shepherd* was a popular book among Christians of the first four centuries. Written by Hermas, brother of Pius, bishop of Rome, during the first half of the second century, the book was regarded by some churches as canonical Scripture. It was eventually excluded from the canon, however, in part because it was known not to have been written by an apostle.[1] Even so, it was still included as one of the books of the New Testament in the fourth-century codex Sinaiticus and is mentioned by other authors of the time as standing on the margins of the canon.[2]

The book takes its name from an angelic mediator who appears to Hermas in the form of a shepherd. Other angelic beings appear here as well, in particular an old woman who identifies herself as the personification of the Christian church. These various figures communicate divine revelations to Hermas and, upon request, interpret their meaning to him.

The book is divided into a series of five visions, twelve sets of commandments (or "mandates"), and ten parables (or "similitudes"). The visions and similitudes are enigmatic and symbolic; they are usually explained to Hermas as having a spiritual significance for the Christian here on earth. The mandates are somewhat easier to interpret, consisting for the most part of direct exhortations to speak the truth, give alms, do good, and avoid sexual immorality, drunkenness, gluttony, and other vices.

Indeed, the entire book is driven by an ethical concern: what can Christians do if they have fallen into sin after being baptized? A number of early Christians had insisted that those who returned to lives of sin after joining the church had lost any hope of salvation. An alternative view is advanced by Hermas, who maintains, on the basis of divine revelations, that Christians who have fallen again into sin after their baptism have a second chance (but only one second chance) to repent and return to God's good graces. Those who refuse to avail themselves of this opportunity, however, or who revert to sin again thereafter, will be forced to face the judgment of God on the day of reckoning soon to come.

---

[1]See the Muratorian Canon.   [2]See the Canons of Eusebius and Athanasius.

Translation by Bart D. Ehrman, in *The Apostolic Fathers,* vol. 2 (Loeb Classical Library; Cambridge, Mass.: Harvard University Press, 2003); used with permission.

The *Shepherd* of Hermas is the longest work to survive from the first hundred years of the Christian church. The following extracts are representative of the whole.

Vision One

(I, 1)

1 The one who raised me sold me to a certain woman named Rhoda, in Rome. After many years, I regained her acquaintance and began to love her as a sister.

2 When some time had passed, I saw her bathing in the Tiber river; and I gave her my hand to help her out of the river. When I observed her beauty I began reasoning in my heart, "I would be fortunate to have a wife of such beauty and character." This is all I had in mind, nothing else.

3 When some time had passed, I was traveling to the countryside, glorifying the creations of God and thinking how great, remarkable, and powerful they are. On the way I fell asleep and a spirit took me and carried me through a certain deserted place that was impassable, for the place was steep and split up by the courses of water. When I crossed the river I came to level ground and bowed my knees; and I began praying to the Lord and confessing my sins.

4 While I was praying the sky opened up and I saw the woman I had desired, addressing me from heaven: "Hermas, greeting!" I looked at her and said, "Lady, what are you doing here?"

5 She replied to me, "I have been taken up to accuse your sins before the Lord."

6 I said to her, "So now are you accusing me?" "No," she said, "but listen to what I have to say to you. The God who dwells in heaven and who, for the sake of his holy church, created, increased, and multiplied that which exists out of that which does not exist, is angry at you for sinning against me."

7 I answered her, "Have I sinned against you? In what way? When did I speak an inappropriate word to you? Have I not always thought of you as a goddess? Have I not always respected you as a sister? Why do you make such evil and foul accusations against me, O woman?"

8 But she laughed and said to me, "The desire for evil did rise up in your heart. Or do you not think it is evil for an evil desire to arise in the heart of an upright man? Indeed," she said, "it is a great sin. For the upright man intends to do what is right. And so, when he intends to do what is right his reputation is firmly established in heaven and he finds that the Lord looks favorably on everything he does. But those who intend in their hearts to do evil bring death and captivity on themselves—especially those who are invested in this age, who rejoice in their wealth and do not cling to the good things yet to come.

9 Those who have no hope but have already abandoned themselves and their lives will regret it. But pray to God, and he will heal your sins, along with those of your entire household and of all the saints."

(I, 2)

2 After she had spoken these words, the skies were shut; I was trembling all over and upset. I began saying

to myself, "If this sin is recorded against me, how can I be saved? Or how will I appease God for the sins I have recently committed?[a] What words can I use to ask the Lord for mercy?"

2 While I was mulling these things over in my heart and trying to reach a decision, I saw across from me a large white chair, made of wool, white as snow. And an elderly woman came, dressed in radiant clothes and holding a book in her hands. She sat down, alone, and addressed me, "Greetings, Hermas." And I said, still upset and weeping, "Greetings Lady."

3 She said to me, "Why are you sad, Hermas—you who are patient, slow to anger, and always laughing? Why are you so downcast, and not cheerful?" I replied to her, "Because of a very good woman who has been telling me that I sinned against her."

4 And she said, "May such a thing never happen to a slave of God! But probably something did rise up in your heart about her. This kind of notion brings the slaves of God into sin. For when someone longs to do what is evil, it is an evil and shocking notion, directed against a fully reverend and tested spirit—especially for Hermas, the self-controlled, who abstains from every evil desire and is full of all simplicity and great innocence.

(I, 3)

3 "Still, God is angry with you, not about this, but so that you may convert your household, which has acted lawlessly against the Lord and against you, their parents. But since you yourself are so fond of your children you do not admonish your household, and so you allow it to be terribly ruined. This is why the Lord is angry with you. But he will heal every evil your household formerly

committed. For you yourself have been brought to ruin by the affairs of daily life—because of their sins and lawless acts.

2 But the Lord's compassion has granted you and your household mercy, and it will make you strong and establish you in its glory. But you must not relax; instead, take courage and strengthen your household. For as the coppersmith hammers his work to master the material as he wants, so also the upright word spoken every day masters all evil. Do not stop exhorting your children. For I know that if they repent from their whole heart, they will be recorded with the saints in the books of the living."

3 When she finished these words, she said to me, "Do you want to hear me read?" I replied to her, "Yes, Lady, I do." She said to me, "Be a hearer and hear the glories of God." I heard great and amazing matters that I could not remember. For all the words were terrifying, more than a person can bear. But I have remembered the final words, for they were beneficial to us, and gentle:

4 "Behold, the powerful God, who with his invisible power, might, and great understanding created the world, and by his glorious plan encompassed his creation with beauty, and by his powerful word fixed the sky and founded the earth upon the waters, and by his unique wisdom and foreknowledge created his holy church, which he also blessed—behold, he transforms the skies and the mountains and the hills and the seas, and everything becomes level for his elect, that he may deliver over to them the promise he made, with great glory and joy, if they keep the ordinances of God, which they received in great faith."

[a]Or: *for the sins I am yet to commit*

(I, 4)

4 Then, when she finished reading and rose up from the chair, four young men came and took the chair and went away to the east.

2 She called me over and touched my breast and said to me, "Did my reading please you?" I said to her, "Lady, these last words are pleasing to me, but the earlier ones were difficult and hard." She said to me, "These last words are for those who are upright, but the former are for the outsiders and apostates."

3 While she was speaking with me, two other men appeared and took her by the arms and went away to the east, where the chair was. She went away cheerfully; and while she was going she said to me, "Be a man,[b] Hermas."

Vision Two

(II, 1)

5 I was traveling to the countryside at the same time as the previous year, and on the way I remembered the vision from the year before. And again a spirit took me and bore me to the same place I had been then.

2 And so, when I came to the place I bowed my knees and began praying to the Lord and glorifying his name, because he considered me worthy and showed me my former sins.

3 When I arose from prayer I saw across from me the elderly woman I had seen the year before, walking and reading a little book. And she said to me, "Can you announce these things to the ones chosen by God?" I said to her, "Lady, I cannot remember so many things. Give me the book to make a copy." "Take it," she said, "and then return it to me."

4 I took it and went away to another part of the field, where I copied the whole thing, letter by letter, for I could not distinguish between the syllables. And then, when I completed the letters of the book, it was suddenly seized from my hand; but I did not see by whom.

(II, 2)

6 Fifteen days later, after I had fasted and asked the Lord many things, the meaning of the writing was revealed to me. These are the words that were written:

2 "Your offspring, Hermas, have rejected God, blasphemed the Lord, and betrayed their parents with a great evil. And even though they have been called betrayers of their parents, they have gained nothing from their betrayal. Yet they have added still more licentious acts to their sins and piled on more evil; and so their lawless acts have gone as far as they can go.

3 But make these words known to all your children and your wife, who is about to become your sister. For she also does not restrain her tongue, but uses it to perpetrate evil. But when she hears these words she will control it and receive mercy.

4 After you have made known to them these words that the Master has commanded me to reveal to you, then all the sins they formerly committed will be forgiven them, along with those of all the saints who have sinned till this day, if they repent from their whole heart and remove double-mindedness from it.

5 For the Master swore by his own glory to his chosen ones: 'If there is any more sinning once this day has been appointed, they will not find salvation. For there is a limit to repentance for those

[b]Or: *Be courageous*

who are upright, and the days of repentance for all the saints are complete. But the outsiders[c] will be able to repent until the final day.'

6 And so, say to those who lead the church that they are to make their paths straight in righteousness, that they may fully receive the promises with great glory.

7 You who do what is righteous should stand firm and not be of two minds, that your path may lie with the holy angels. How fortunate are all you who endure the great affliction that is coming and do not deny your life.

8 For the Lord has sworn by his Son, that those who deny their Lord have lost their life—that is, those who are about to deny him in the days that are coming. But through his great compassion, mercy has been given to those who denied the Lord previously.

(II, 3)

7 "But you, Hermas, must no longer hold a grudge against your children nor leave your sister to her own devices, that they may be cleansed from their former sins. For they will be disciplined with an upright discipline, if you bear no grudge against them. A grudge produces death. But you, Hermas, have experienced great afflictions of your own because of your family's transgressions, since you paid no attention to them. You neglected them and became enmeshed in your own evil deeds.

2 But you are saved by not straying from the living God, and by your simplicity and great self-restraint. These things have saved you, if you continue; and they save all those who do them and who proceed in innocence and simplicity. Such people will overcome all evil and persist to eternal life.

3 How fortunate are all those who do righteousness. They will never perish.

4 Say to Maximus, 'See, affliction is coming. If it seems right to you, make another denial.'[d] The Lord is near to those who convert, as is written in the Book of Eldad and Modat,[e] who prophesied to the people in the wilderness."

(II, 4)

8 While I was sleeping, brothers, I received a revelation from a very beautiful young man, who said to me: "The elderly woman from whom you received the little book—who do you think she is?" "The Sibyl," I replied. "You are wrong," he said; "it is not she." "Who then is it?" I asked. "The church," he said. I said to him, "Why then is she elderly?" "Because," he said, "she was created first, before anything else. That is why she is elderly, and for her sake the world was created."

2 And afterward I saw a vision in my house. The elderly woman came and asked if I had already given the book to the presbyters. I said that I had not. "You have done well," she said. "For I have some words to add. Then, when I complete all the words, they will be made known through you to all those who are chosen.

3 And so, you will write two little books, sending one to Clement and the other to Grapte. Clement will send his to the foreign cities, for that is his commission. But Grapte will admonish the widows and orphans. And you will read yours in this city, with the presbyters who lead the church."

---

[c] Literally: *Gentiles;* or *nations*   [d] The quotation may continue to the end of the verse   [e] This was an apocryphal book written in the names of the two prophets mentioned in Num. 11:26. It no longer survives.

Vision Three

(III, 1)

9 What I saw, brothers, was this.
2 After I fasted a great deal and asked the Lord to show me the revelation that he promised to reveal through the elderly woman, that same night the elderly woman appeared and said to me, "Since you are so needy and eager to know everything, come to the field where you farm, and around eleven in the morning I will be revealed to you and show you what you must see."

3 I asked her, "Lady, in what part of the field?" "Wherever you wish," she said. I chose a beautiful spot that was secluded. But before I could speak with her to tell her the place, she said to me, "I will come there, wherever you wish."

4 And so, brothers, I went into the field and counted the hours. I arrived at the place that I had directed her to come, and I saw an ivory couch set up. On the couch was placed a linen pillow, with a piece of fine linen cloth on top.

5 When I saw these things laid out with no one there, I was astounded and seized with trembling, and my hair stood on end—terrified, because I was alone. Then when I came to myself, I remembered the glory of God and took courage. I bowed my knees and confessed my sins again to the Lord, as I had done before.

6 And she came with six young men, whom I had seen before, and she stood beside me and listened closely while I prayed and confessed my sins to the Lord. She touched me and said, "Hermas, stop asking exclusively about your sins; ask also about righteousness, that you may receive some of it in your house."

7 She raised me by the hand and led me to the couch; and she said to the young men, "Go and build."

8 After the young men left and we were alone, she said to me, "Sit here." I said to her, "Lady, let the elders sit first." "Do what I tell you," she said. "Sit."

9 But then, when I wanted to sit on the right side, she did not let me, but signaled with her hand for me to sit on the left. As I was mulling this over and becoming upset that she did not allow me to sit on the right, she said to me, "Are you upset, Hermas? The place on the right is for others, who have already pleased God and suffered on behalf of the name. Many things must happen to you before you can sit with them. But continue in your simplicity, as you are doing, and you will sit with them, as will everyone who does what they have done and endures what they have endured."

(III, 2)

10 "What have they endured?" I asked. "Listen," she said: "floggings, imprisonments, great afflictions, crucifixions, and wild beasts—for the sake of the name. For this reason, the right side of holiness belongs to them, and to anyone who suffers on account of the name. The left side is for the others. The same gifts and promises belong to both—those seated on the right and those on the left. But they alone sit on the right and have a certain glory.

2 You want to sit on the right side with them, but you have many shortcomings. But you will be cleansed of your shortcomings. And all those who are not of two minds will be cleansed from all the sins they have committed up to this day.

3 After she said these things she wanted to leave. But I fell before her feet and pled with her by the Lord to show me the vision she had promised.

4 Again she took my hand, raised me up, and seated me on the couch on the left side. She herself sat on the right. And raising up a bright rod she said to me, "Do you see a great thing?" I said to her, "Lady, I see nothing." She said to me,

"Look, do you not see a great tower being built upon the water across from you, with bright, squared stones?"

5 The tower was being built in a square by the six young men who had come with her. And thousands of other men were bringing stones, some of them from the depths of the sea and some from the land, and they were handing them over to the six young men, who were taking them and building.

6 Thus they placed all the stones drawn from the depths in the building; for they fit together and were straight at their joints with the other stones. And they were placed together so that their joints were invisible. The building of the tower seemed to have been made out of a single stone.

7 But they tossed aside some of the other stones that were brought from the dry land, while others they placed in the building. Others they broke up and cast far from the tower.

8 Many other stones were lying around the tower, and they did not use them in the building. For some of them had a rough surface, others had cracks, others were broken off, and others were white and round, and did not fit in the building.

9 I saw other stones cast far from the tower; these came onto the path, but did not remain there, but rolled from the path onto the rough terrain. Others fell into the fire and were burned. And others fell near the water, but could not be rolled into it, even though they wanted to be.

(III, 3)

11 When she had shown me these things she wanted to hurry away. I said to her, "Lady, what good is it for me to see these things if I do not know what they mean?" She answered and said to me, "You, fellow, are a crafty one, wanting to know about the tower." "Yes, Lady," I said; "I want to announce

it to the brothers that they can become more cheerful; for when they hear these things they will know the Lord in great glory."

2 She said, "Many will indeed hear; and some of those who hear will rejoice, but some will weep. But even these latter, if they hear and repent, will rejoice as well. Hear therefore the parables of the tower. For I will reveal everything to you. Then trouble me no further about the revelation. For these revelations are completed and fulfilled. But you will not stop asking about revelations, because you are shameless.

3 The tower, which you see being built, is I, the church, who has appeared to you both now and previously. And so, ask whatever you wish about the tower and I will reveal it to you, that you may rejoice with the saints."

4 I said to her, "Lady, since you have on this one occasion considered me worthy to reveal all things to me: reveal them." She said to me, "Whatever can be revealed to you, will be revealed. Only let your heart be set on God, and do not be of two minds, whatever you see."

5 I asked her, "Why, Lady, is the tower built upon water?" "I have told you already," she said, "and you keep seeking; it is by seeking, therefore, that you find the truth. As to why the tower is built upon water, listen: it is because your life was saved and will be saved through water. But the tower is founded on the word of the almighty and glorious name, and it is strengthened by the invisible power of the Master."

(III, 4)

12 I responded to her, "Lady, this is a great and amazing thing. But the six young men who are building, Lady—who are they?" "These are the holy angels of God who were created first, to whom the Lord handed over his

entire creation, so that they could increase, build up, and rule over it all. Thus, through these the building of the tower will be brought to completion."

2 "But the other—the ones bringing the stones—who are they?" "They also are holy angels of God; but these six are superior to them. And so the building of the tower will be completed, and then all of them will rejoice together around the tower and glorify God, because the building of the tower has been completed."

3 I asked her, "Lady, I want to know about the destination of the stones, and about what they mean." And she answered me, "This will be revealed to you, but not because you are more worthy than everyone else. For others are ahead of you and better than you; and these visions should have been revealed to them. But that the name of God may be glorified, the matter has been revealed to you and will be revealed, for the sake of those who are of two minds, who debate in their hearts whether these things are so or not. Tell them that all these things are true, that none of them is outside the truth, but that everything is firm and certain and established.

(III, 5)

13 "Hear now about the stones that go into the building. On the one hand, the squared and white stones that fit together at the joints are the apostles, bishops, teachers, and deacons who live reverently towards God and perform their duties as bishops, teachers, and deacons for the chosen ones of God in a holy and respectful way; some of these have fallen asleep, but others are still living. And they have always been harmonious with one another and at peace with one another, and they have listened to one another. For this reason their joints fit together in the building of the tower."

2 "But who are the ones drawn from the depths of the sea and placed into the building, who fit together at their joints with the other stones already built in it?" "These are those who have suffered on account of the name of the Lord."

3 "But I also want to know, Lady, who the other stones are, the ones brought from the dry land." She said, "Those that go into the building without being hewn are ones the Lord has approved, because they walk in the uprightness of the Lord and carry out his commandments."

4 "And who are the ones brought and placed in the building?" "These are those who are new in the faith and faithful. They are admonished by the angels to do good; for this reason, no evil has been found in them."

5 "But who are the ones who were tossed aside and cast out?" "These are those who have sinned but wish to repent. For this reason they are not cast far away from the tower, because they will be useful for the building, if they repent. And so if those who are about to repent do so, they will be strong in faith—if they repent now while the tower is still under construction. But if the building is completed, they will no longer have a place, but will be outcasts. This alone is to their advantage, that they lie next to the tower.

(III, 6)

14 "But do you want to know about the ones that are broken off and cast far from the tower? These are the children of lawlessness. For they came to faith hypocritically and no wickedness ever left them. And so they have no salvation, since, because of their wickedness, they are useless for the building. This is why they were broken off and cast far away, because of the Lord's anger, since they aggravated him.

2 But with respect to the many other stones you saw lying on the ground and not coming into the building—the ones that are rough are those who know the truth but do not remain in it nor cling to

the saints. This is why they are of no use."

3 "But who are the ones with cracks?" "These are those who hold a grudge against one another in their hearts and have no peace among themselves. Even though they seem to be peace-loving, when they leave one another's presence, their wickedness remains in their hearts. These are the cracks the stones have.

4 But the ones that are broken off are those who have believed and live, for the most part, in righteousness, but also have a certain share of lawlessness. This is why they are broken off and not whole."

5 "But who are the white stones, Lady, which are rounded and do not fit into the building?" She replied to me, "How long will you be foolish and ignorant, asking everything and understanding nothing? These are the ones who have faith, but also are wealthy in this age. But when affliction comes, because of their wealth and their business affairs, they deny their Lord."

6 And I responded to her, "And so when, Lady, will they be useful for the building?" "When the wealth that beguiles them is cut off from them," she said, "then they will be useful to God. For just as a round stone cannot be made square unless it has something cut off and discarded, so also with those who are rich in this age: if their wealth is not cut off from them, they cannot be useful to the Lord.

7 You should know this above all from your own case. When you were wealthy, you were of no use; but now you are useful and helpful in life. All of you should be useful to God. For you yourself are also being taken from the same stones.

(III, 7)

15 "But the other stones that you saw cast far from the tower and falling on the path and rolling from the path onto the rough terrain, these are the ones who have believed, but have left their true path because they are of two minds. They are lost, thinking they can find a better path; and they are miserable, walking over the rough terrain.

2 But the ones that fell into the fire and were burned are those who completely abandoned the living God; and they no longer think about repenting because of their licentious desires and the wicked deeds they have performed."

3 "But who are the other ones, which fall near the water but cannot be rolled into it?" "These are the ones who have heard the word and wanted to be baptized in the name of the Lord. But then when they recall what the life of true purity involves, they change their minds and return to pursue their evil desires."

4 And so she completed her interpretation of the tower.

5 But being completely shameless, I asked her yet another question, whether these stones that were tossed aside and not fit into the building of the tower could repent and have a place in the tower. "They can repent," she said, "but they cannot be fit into this tower.

6 They will be fit into a greatly inferior place—and then only after they have been tormented and have completed the days of their sins. That is why they will be removed from there, because they have taken part in the righteous word. And then they will be removed from the torments inflicted for the evil deeds they did. But if deep down they do not want to repent, they will not be saved, because of their hardened hearts."

(III, 8)

16 And so, when I stopped asking her about all these things, she said to me, "Do you want to see something else?" Being so eager to observe, I was excited by the prospect.

2 She looked at me and smiled, and

said to me, "Do you see seven women around the tower?" "I see them, Lady," I replied. "This tower," she said, "is supported by them according to the commandment of the Lord.

3 Hear now about the work they do. The first of them, the one clasping her hands, is called Faith. Those who are chosen by God are saved through her.

4 And the other one, the one wearing a belt and acting like a man,ᶠ is called Self-restraint. She is the daughter of Faith. Whoever follows her will be fortunate in his life, because he will abandon all his evil deeds, believing that if he abandons every evil desire, he will inherit eternal life."

5 "And the others, Lady, who are they?" "They are daughters of one another, called Simplicity, Knowledge, Innocence, Reverence, and Love. And so, when you perform all the works of their mother, you will be able to live."

6 I replied, "I wish to know, Lady, about the power that each of them has." "Listen," she said, "to the powers they have.

7 Their powers are connected and follow one another in the order of their birth. From Faith is born Self-restraint, from Self-restraint Simplicity, from Simplicity Innocence, from Innocence Reverence, from Reverence Knowledge, and from Knowledge Love. And so their deeds are pure, reverent, and godly.

8 Whoever serves as their slave and is able to adhere to their deeds will have a place to reside in the tower, along with the saints of God."

9 I began to ask her about the times, about whether the end had already come, and she cried out with a great voice, "You fool! Do you not see that the tower is still under construction? Only when its construction is finished will the end arrive. But it will be built quickly. No longer ask me anything. This reminder is enough for

you and the saints—along with the renewal of your spirits.

10 These things have not been revealed for your sake alone; for you are to show them to all the others,

11 in three days; first, however, you must think. But I enjoin you first, Hermas, with these words I am about to say; you are to speak them all in the ears of the saints, that once they have heard and done them they may be cleansed from their wicked deeds, and you along with them.

(III, 9)

17 "Listen to me, children. I raised you with great simplicity, innocence, and reverence because of the mercy of the Lord, who drizzled his righteousness upon you that you may be made upright and purified from all evil and perversity. Yet you do not wish to stop doing your wicked deeds.

2 And so, now, listen to me: be at peace with one another, take care of one another, help one another; and do not take an overabundance of God's creations for yourselves, but share with those in need.

3 For those who enjoy many kinds of food make their flesh weak and harm it; but the flesh of those without enough food is harmed by lack of proper nourishment, and their body wastes away.

4 This disparity is harmful to you who have but do not share with those in need.

5 Consider the judgment that is coming. You who have an abundance should therefore seek out the hungry before the tower is completed. For after the tower is completed you will long to do good but will have no opportunity.

6 And so, take heed, you who exult in your wealth, lest those in need complain

---

ᶠOr: *the one girded and courageous*

and their complaint rises up to the Lord, and you be shut out from the gate of the tower, along with your goods.

7 And so now I say to you who lead the church and sit in its chief seats. Do not be like the sorcerers. For the sorcerers carry their potions in boxes, but you carry your potion and poison in the heart.

8 You have grown calloused and refuse to cleanse your hearts and to join your minds together in clean hearts, so as to receive mercy from the great king.

9 And so take heed, children, lest these dissensions deprive you of your life.

10 How can you want to discipline the Lord's chosen ones, when you yourselves have no discipline? And so, discipline one another and be at peace among yourselves, that I also may stand before the Father cheerfully and so render an account to our Lord for all of you."

(III, 10)

18 Then, when she stopped speaking with me, the six young men who were building came and took her away to the tower. And four others came and took the couch and carried it off to the tower as well. I did not see their faces, because they were turned away.

2 But as she was leaving I began asking her to give me a revelation about the three forms in which she appeared to me. And she answered me, "You must ask someone else to reveal these things to you."

3 For in the first vision, brothers, the year before, she appeared to me as a very elderly woman, seated on a chair.

4 In the other vision she had a younger face, but her skin and hair were older, and she spoke to me while standing. But she was more cheerful than before.

5 And in the third vision she was very young and exceedingly beautiful in appearance; only her hair was older. But

she was completely cheerful and seated on a couch.

6 I was very sad, wanting to know about this revelation. Then I saw the elderly woman in a night vision, saying to me, "Every request requires humility. And so fast, and you will receive from the Lord what you ask."

7 So I fasted one day, and in that night a young man appeared to me and said, "Why do you constantly ask for revelations in your prayer? Take care, or you will harm your flesh by asking so much.

8 These revelations are enough for you. How can you manage to see revelations even more powerful than the ones you have already seen?"

9 I replied to him, "Lord, I am asking only about the three forms of the elderly woman, that the revelation may be complete." He answered me, "How long will you people be ignorant? You have become ignorant from being of two minds, not having your hearts set on the Lord."

10 I said to him again, "But from you, Lord, we will learn all these things more accurately."

(III, 11)

19 "Listen," he said, "concerning the forms you are inquiring after.

2 In the first vision, why did she appear to you as an elderly woman, seated on a chair? Because your spirit is elderly and already fading away, having no vigor because you are feeble and of two minds.

3 For just as elderly people who have no hope of being rejuvenated look forward to nothing but their sleep,[g] so also you, grown feeble because of your worldly affairs, have handed yourselves over to apathy, and you do not cast your

gOr: *death*

anxieties upon the Lord. Your mind has been wounded and you have grown old in your sorrows."

4 "I also want to know, Lord, why she was seated in a chair." "Because anyone who is weak sits in a chair out of weakness, to support the weakness of the body. Now you have the meaning the first vision.

(III, 12)

20 "And in the second vision you saw her standing, and she had a younger face and was more cheerful than before, even though her skin and hair looked older. Listen," he said, "to this parable as well.

2 Someone who is older and has already given up all hope because of his bodily weakness and poverty looks forward to nothing except the last day of his life. Then suddenly an inheritance is left to him. And when he hears about it he rises up and in his excitement grows strong. No longer does he recline, but he stands and his spirit becomes rejuvenated even though it has been wasting away because of his daily life from before; and he no longer sits, but becomes manly.[h] You are like this as well, when you hear what the Lord has revealed to you.

3 For he showed you compassion and rejuvenated your spirits; and you laid your feebleness to the side and strength seized you and you were empowered with faith. And when the Lord saw your renewed strength he was glad. For this reason he showed you the building of the tower, just as he will show you other things as well, if you are at peace with one another from your whole heart.

(III, 13)

21 "But in the third vision you saw her younger and beautiful and cheerful, and her form was beautiful.

2 For it is as when some good news comes to a person who is grieving: im-

mediately he forgets his former griefs and thinks about nothing but the news he has heard. And he is strengthened from that time on to do what is good, and his spirit is rejuvenated because of the exciting news he has received. So also your spirits have been rejuvenated from seeing these good things.

3 And you saw her seated on a couch because that is a strong position, since the couch has four legs and stands firmly. For the world is also held firm through the four elements.

4 And so, those who fully repent will become new and firmly established—those who have repented from their whole heart. Now you have the revelation complete. No longer ask anything about it; if anything is still needed, it will be revealed to you."

Vision Four

(IV, 1)

22 This is what I saw, brothers, twenty days after the earlier vision, as a foreshadowing of the coming affliction.

2 I was going into the country on the Via Campania. This is just over a mile off the public road; the place is easily reached.

3 While walking alone, I was asking the Lord to complete the revelations and visions he had shown me through his holy church, that he might strengthen me and give repentance to his slaves who had stumbled, so that his great and glorious name might be glorified, since he had considered me worthy to see his marvelous acts.

4 And while I was giving him glory and thanks, something like the sound of

[h]Or: *courageous*

a voice answered me, "Do not be of two minds, Hermas." I began to debate with myself, "How can I be of two minds, when I have been firmly established by the Lord and seen his glorious deeds?"

5 I passed on a bit, brothers, and suddenly saw a cloud of dust, reaching up to the sky. And I began saying to myself, "Is that a herd of cattle coming, raising the dust? But it was still about two hundred yards away from me.

6 And as the dust cloud grew larger and larger, I realized that it was something supernatural. The sun began to shine a bit and suddenly I saw an enormous wild beast, something like a sea monster, with fiery locusts spewing from its mouth. The beast was nearly a hundred feet long, and its head looked like a ceramic jar.

7 And I began to weep and ask the Lord to save me from it. Then I remembered the word I had heard: "Do not be of two minds, Hermas."

8 And so, putting on the faith of the Lord, brothers, and remembering the great things he had taught me, I courageously gave myself over to the beast. And so it came on with a roar, enough to lay waste a city.

9 But when I approached it, the enormous sea monster stretched itself out on the ground and did nothing but stick out its tongue; otherwise it did not move at all until I had passed it by.

10 And the beast had four colors on its head: black, fire- and blood-red, gold, and white.

(IV, 2)

23 After I passed by the beast and went about thirty feet ahead, a young woman suddenly met me, clothed as if coming from a bridal chamber, dressed all in white and with white sandals, veiled down to her forehead. Her veil was a headband and her hair was white.

2 From my earlier visions I knew that she was the church, and I became cheerful. She welcomed me, "Greetings, my man." And I welcomed her in return, "Greetings, Lady."

3 She said to me, "Did anything meet you?" I responded, "An enormous wild beast, Lady, able to destroy entire peoples. But by the power of the Lord and his great compassion, I escaped it."

4 "You escaped well," she said, "because you cast your anxiety upon God and opened your heart to the Lord, believing that you could not be saved except through his great and glorious name. For this reason the Lord sent his angel, named Thegri, who is in charge of the wild beasts; and he shut the beast's mouth, so that it could not harm you. You have escaped a great affliction because of your faith, and because you were not of two minds even though you saw such an enormous wild beast.

5 And so, go and explain the great acts of the Lord to his chosen ones, and tell them that this wild beast is a foreshadowing of the great affliction that is coming. If then all of you prepare and repent before the Lord from your whole heart, you will be able to escape it—if your heart becomes clean and blameless and you serve the Lord blamelessly the rest of your days. Cast your anxieties upon the Lord and he will take care of them.

6 Trust in the Lord, you who are of two minds, because he can do all things; he both diverts his anger from you and sends punishments to you who are double-minded. Woe to those who hear these words and disobey. It would be better for them not to have been born."

(IV, 3)

24 I then asked her about the four colors the beast had on its head. And she answered me, "Once again you are being overly inquisitive about these matters." "Yes Lady," I said, "explain these things to me."

2 "Listen," she said. "The black is this world, in which all of you live.

3 The fire- and blood-red shows that this world must be destroyed through blood and fire.

4 But you who escape this world are the part that is gold. For just as gold is tested through fire and thus becomes useful, so also you who dwell among them[i] are put to the test. Those who endure and are burned by them will be made pure. For just as gold casts off its dross, so also you will cast off every grief and tribulation, and be cleansed and made useful for the building of the tower.

5 But the part that is white is the age that is coming, in which the chosen ones of God will dwell. For those who have been chosen by God for eternal life will be spotless and pure.

6 And so do not stop speaking in the ears of the saints. You now have the foreshadowing of the great affliction that is coming. But if you wish, it will come to nothing. Remember the things written before."

7 When she said these things she departed; but I did not see where she went. For there was a noise, and I turned around out of fear, thinking that the beast was coming.

Vision Five

(V)

25 After I prayed in my house, sitting on my bed, an eminent looking man came to me, dressed in shepherd's clothing—wrapped with a white goat skin around his waist, with a backpack on his shoulder and a staff in his hand. He greeted me, and I greeted him in return.

2 He immediately sat next to me and said, "I have been sent from the most reverend angel to live with you for the rest of your life."

3 I thought he had come to put me to the test, and I said to him, "Who are you? For I know the one to whom I have been entrusted." He said to me, "Do you not recognize me?" "No," I replied. He said, "I am the shepherd to whom you have been entrusted."

4 While he was speaking his appearance changed, and I recognized him, since he was in fact the one to whom I had been entrusted. And I was suddenly thrown into confusion, seized with fear, and entirely broken up by grief, because I had given him such a wicked and foolish response.

5 But he said to me, "Do not be confused, but become strong in my commandments, which I am about to give you. For I was sent," he said, "to show you yet again all the things that you saw before, since these are what will chiefly benefit you. First, though, write my commandments and parables; but write the other things just as I show them to you. This is why," he said, "I am commanding you first to write the commandments and parables—that you may read them regularly and so be able to keep them."

6 And so I wrote the commandments and parables, just as he commanded me.

7 If then, after you hear them, you keep them and walk in them and accomplish them with a pure heart, you will receive from the Lord everything he promised you. But if you do not repent once you have heard them, but increase your sins still further, you will receive the opposite from the Lord. The shepherd, the angel of repentance, thus commanded me to write all these things.

---

[i] I.e., *either among the inhabitants of the world,* or *among the fire and the blood*

First Commandment

(I)

26 "First of all, believe that God is one, who created and completed all things, and made everything that exists out of that which did not, who contains all things but is himself, alone, uncontained.

2 And so believe in him and fear him, and in your fear be self-restrained. Guard these matters and you will cast all wickedness from yourselves and clothe yourselves with every righteous virtue, and you will live to God—if you guard this commandment."

Second Commandment

(II)

27 He said to me, "Hold on to simplicity and be innocent, and you will be like young children who do not know the wickedness that destroys human life.

2 First, of all, do not slander anyone. Nor listen gladly to anyone else who slanders. Otherwise, you the hearer will share the sin of the slanderer—if you believe the slander you hear. For when you believe it you also will hold something against your brother. And so you will share the sin of the one who slanders.

3 Slander is evil, a restless demon, never at peace but always living in dissension. And so, abstain from it and you will always be in good standing with all.

4 Clothe yourself with reverence, in which there is no wicked stumbling block, but everything is smooth and cheerful. Do what is good, and take what you have earned through the toils God has given you and give simply to those in need, not wavering about to whom you should give something and to whom not. Give to everyone. For God wishes everyone to be given something from his own gifts.

5 And so, those who receive something will render an account to God, about why they received something and to what end. For those who received because of hardship will not face condemnation; but those who received out of hypocrisy will pay a penalty.

6 And so the one who gives is innocent. For as he was given a ministry from the Lord to complete, he has completed it in a simple way, having no doubts about to whom he should give or not give something. This ministry that is completed in a simple way becomes glorious before God, so that the one who ministers thus, in a simple way, will live to God.

7 And so guard this commandment as I have spoken it to you, that your repentance and that of your household may be found to be in simplicity—and pure, innocent, and blameless."

Third Commandment

(III)

28 Then he spoke to me again, "Love the truth and let all truth come from your mouth, so that the spirit that God made to live in this flesh may be recognized as true by everyone; in this way the Lord who dwells in you will be glorified. For the Lord is true in his every word, and there is no lie in him.

2 And so, those who lie reject the Lord and defraud him, not handing over to him the down payment they received. For they received from him a spirit that does not lie; if they return it to him as a liar, they defile the commandment of the Lord and become defrauders."

3 When I heard these things I wept bitterly. When he saw me weeping he asked, "Why are you weeping?" "Because, Lord," I said, "I do not know if I

can be saved." "Why?" he asked. "Because, Lord" I said, "I have never in my entire life spoken a true word, but have always lived craftily with everyone, and have portrayed my lie as truth to all. And no one has ever contradicted me, but has trusted my word. How then, Lord," I asked, "can I live, having done such things?"

4 "Your thoughts are good and true," he said. "For you should have been conducting yourself as a slave of God; and a wicked conscience should not have dwelt with the spirit of truth or brought grief to the reverend and true spirit." "Never," I replied, "have I heard such words so accurately."

5 "You are hearing them now," he said. "Guard these matters so that the lies you spoke before in your daily life may themselves become trustworthy when these other words are found to be true. For even those other ones can become trustworthy. If you guard these matters and from now on speak only the truth, you will be able to give yourself life. And whoever hears this commandment and avoids lying most wickedly will live to God."

Fourth Commandment

(IV, 1)

29 "I command you," he said, "to guard your holiness, and do not allow any thought to rise up in your heart about someone else's wife, or sexual immorality, or any other similarly wicked things. Otherwise you commit a great sin. But if you always keep thinking about your own wife, you will never sin.

2 For if this notion should rise up in your heart you will sin, and if another such wicked idea should arise, you commit a sin. For this notion is a great sin for the slave of God. And anyone who

does such an evil deed brings death upon himself.

3 So be on the alert and avoid this notion. For where reverence dwells, lawlessness should not rise up in the heart of an upright man."

4 I said to him, "Lord, allow me to ask you a few questions." "Go ahead," he replied. "Lord," I said, "if someone is married to a woman who believes in the Lord, but he discovers that she is having an adulterous relationship, does the man then sin if he continues to live with her?"

5 "As long as he is ignorant of the affair," he replied, "he does not sin. But if the husband knows about her sin, and the wife does not repent, but remains in her sexual immorality, and the husband continues to live with her, he becomes guilty of her sin and a partner in her immorality."

6 "What then should the husband do, Lord" I said, "if the wife continues in her passion?" "He should divorce her," he replied, "and live alone. But if he marries someone else after the divorce, he also commits adultery."

7 "But, Lord," I said, "if after the wife is divorced she repents and wants to return to her husband, should she not be taken back?"

8 "Yes indeed," he replied. "If her husband does not take her back, he sins, and drags a great sin upon himself; for the one who sins and repents must be accepted back. But not many times. For there is but one repentance given to the slaves of God. Because of repentance, therefore, the husband ought not to marry. The same applies to both wife and husband.

9 Not only is it adultery," he continued, "if a person defiles his flesh; but also, whoever behaves like the outsiders commits adultery. And so, if anyone continues doing such deeds and does not repent, you should avoid him and not allow him

to live in your midst. Otherwise you also share in his sin.

10 This is why you have been ordered to remain by yourselves, whether a husband or wife; for repentance is possible in such cases.

11 And so," he said, "I am not giving an occasion for matters to turn out this way; I am saying that the sinner should sin no more. But with respect to his former sin, there is one who can provide healing. For he has the authority over all things."

(IV, 2)

30 I asked him again, "Since the Lord has considered me worthy to have you live with me always, bear with me for a few more words, since I understand nothing and my heart has been hardened because of my former actions. Give me insight, for I am extremely senseless and comprehend nothing at all."

2 He answered me, "I am in charge of repentance," he said, "and I give understanding to all those who repent. Or do you not realize," he said, "that repentance is itself a form of understanding? Repentance," he said, "is indeed a great understanding. For the one who sins understands that he has done something evil before the Lord, and what he has done rises up in his heart; then he repents and no longer does what is evil, but lavishly does what is good; and he humbles and torments himself, because he has sinned. So you see that repentance is a great understanding."

3 I replied, "This is why, Lord, I am carefully inquiring about everything from you—chiefly because I am a sinner, and I need to know what sorts of things I must do to live; for my sins are many and various."

4 "You will live," he said, "if you guard my commandments and proceed in them. And whoever guards these command-

ments, once he has heard them, will live to God."

(IV, 3)

31 "I still have some things to ask, Lord," I said. "Go ahead," he replied. "I have heard from some teachers, Lord," I said, "that there is no repentance apart from the one that came when we descended into the water and received forgiveness for the sins we formerly committed."

2 He said to me, "You have heard well, for that is so. For the one who has received forgiveness of sins must sin no more, but live in holiness.

3 And since you are carefully inquiring about all things, I will show this to you as well—not, however, to give an occasion for those who are about to believe in the Lord or who have already come to believe. For those who now believe or who are about to believe have no further repentance for their sins, but have received forgiveness for the sins they previously committed.

4 And so the Lord has given those who were called before these days an opportunity to repent. For the Lord knows the heart, and knowing all things in advance he recognized the weakness of humans and the intricate plots of the devil—that he will do some harm to the slaves of God and will reek havoc among them.

5 And so, since the Lord is full of compassion, he had mercy on his creation and provided this opportunity to repent; and the authority for this repentance was given to me.

6 But this also I say to you," he said: "whoever is tempted by the devil and sins after that great and reverend calling has one repentance. But if he should sin and repent repeatedly it is of no benefit to him. For he will find it difficult to live."

7 I said to him, "I have been made alive by hearing these things from you so accurately. For I know that if I no longer increase my sins, I will be saved." "You will be saved," he replied, "as will everyone else who does these things."

(IV, 4)

32 I asked him again, "Lord, since you have borne with me once, reveal this to me as well." "Speak," he said. "Lord," I said, "if a wife or, again, a husband, should die and the survivor marry, does the one who marries commit a sin?"

2 "That one does not sin," he said, "but anyone who remains alone has provided a superior honor for himself and a great glory to the Lord. But if such a one does marry, it is not a sin.

3 And so, maintain your purity and reverence, and you will live to God. From now on, from this day in which you have been entrusted to me, guard all these things that I say and am about to say to you, and I will reside in your house.

4 For your former transgressions will be forgiven if you guard my commandments. And everyone will be forgiven, if they guard these my commandments and proceed in this purity."

Fifth Commandment

(V, 1)

33 "Be patient," he said, "and understanding, and you will rule over every evil work and do all that is righteous.

2 For if you are patient, the holy spirit that dwells in you will be pure and will not be overshadowed by another, evil spirit; but dwelling in a broad place it will rejoice and be glad with the vessel it inhabits, and it will serve God with great cheerfulness, flourishing in itself.

3 But if any irascibility should enter in, immediately the holy spirit, which is sen-

sitive, feels cramped; and not having a pure place it seeks to leave. For it is suffocated by the evil spirit, not having a place to serve the Lord as it wishes, being polluted by the irascibility. For the Lord dwells in patience, but the devil in irascibility.

4 And so, when both spirits dwell in the same place, it is unprofitable and evil for that person in whom they dwell.

5 For if you take a very small portion of wormwood and pour it into a jar of honey, is not all the honey spoiled? A great deal of honey is ruined by the least bit of wormwood. It destroys the sweetness of the honey, which is no longer pleasing to the master, because it has become bitter and lost its value. But if the wormwood is not put into the honey, the honey is found to be sweet and is valuable to the master.

6 You see that patience is sweeter than honey and is valuable to the Lord, and he dwells in it. But irascibility is bitter and useless. And so, if irascibility is mixed with patience, the patience is defiled and its prayer is of no use to God."

7 "I wish to know, Lord," I said, "the inner workings of irascibility, that I may guard against it." "Yes indeed," he replied, "if you and your household do not guard against it, you destroy your entire hope. But guard against it, for I am with you. And all those who repent from their whole heart will abstain from it; for I will be with them and protect them. For all have been made upright by the most reverend angel."

(V, 2)

34 "Hear, now," he said, "the inner workings of irascibility, how it is evil and brings ruin on the slaves of God by the way it works, and misleads them away from righteousness. It does not mislead those who are full of faith, nor is it able to work against them, because the power of God is with them. But it misleads those who are empty and of two minds.

2 For when it sees such people at rest it inserts itself into their hearts, and with no warning the woman or man becomes embittered on account of some business deals, or because of food or something trivial, or because of a friend or something received or given, or because of other such foolish matters. For all these things are foolish, empty, senseless, and unprofitable for the slaves of God.

3 But patience is great and mighty; it has a forceful power that flourishes in a spacious arena; it is cheerful, glad, and free of anxiety, glorifying the Lord at all times, having no bitterness in itself but remaining always meek and mild. This patience, therefore, dwells with all those who hold on to faith intact.

4 But irascibility is first of all foolish, fickle, and senseless. And then, from senselessness comes bitterness, from bitterness anger, from anger wrath, and from wrath rage. Then this rage, which is compounded of such evil things, becomes a great and incurable sin.

5 For when these spirits dwell in one and the same vessel with the holy spirit, the vessel no longer has sufficient space but is stuffed to the brim.

6 And so the sensitive spirit, which is not accustomed to dwelling with an evil spirit nor with harshness, leaves the person and seeks to live with meekness and mildness.

7 Then when it leaves the one it had inhabited, the person becomes devoid of the upright spirit and at last, being filled with evil spirits, vacillates in everything he does, being dragged back and forth by the evil spirits, entirely blinded from any good understanding. This then is what happens to everyone who is irascible.

8 And so, avoid irascibility, which is the most wicked spirit. Clothe yourself with patience and stand against irascibility and bitterness, and you will be found with the reverence that is loved by the Lord. Take care that you never neglect this commandment. For if you master it, you will be able to guard the other commandments, which I am about to give you. And so, be strong and empowered in them, and may everyone who wishes to proceed in them be so empowered." . . .

The Parables That He Spoke With Me

(I)

50 He said to me, "You know that you slaves of God are living in a foreign land. For your own city is a long way from this one. If, then," he said, "you know your own city, where you are about to live, why are you preparing fields, expensive furnishings, buildings, and pointless rooms for yourselves here?

2 Anyone who prepares these things in this city, therefore, cannot return to his own city.

3 You foolish, double-minded, and miserable person! Do you not understand that all these things belong to another and are under someone else's control? For the ruler of this city will say, 'I do not want you living in my city; leave it, because you are not living by my laws.'

4 And so, you who have fields and houses and many other possessions—when he casts you out, what will you do with your field and house and whatever else you have prepared for yourself? For the ruler of this country rightly says to you, 'Either live by my laws or leave my country.'

5 And so what will you do, you who have a law from your own city? Will you completely renounce your own law for the sake of your fields and whatever else you own, and follow the law of the city

you are in now? Take care, because renouncing your law may be contrary to your own interests. For if you want to return to your own city, you will not be welcomed, because you have renounced its law; and you will be shut out of it.

6 And so take care. Since you are dwelling in a foreign land, fix nothing up for yourself except what is absolutely necessary; and be ready, so that when the master of this city wants to banish you for not adhering to his law, you can leave his city and go to your own, and live according to your own law gladly, suffering no mistreatment.

7 Take care, then, you who are enslaved to the Lord and have him in your heart. Do the works of God, remembering his commandments and the promises he made; and trust in him, because he will do these things, if his commandments are guarded.

8 Instead of fields, then, purchase souls that have been afflicted, insofar as you can, and take care of widows and orphans and do not neglect them; spend your wealth and all your furnishings for such fields and houses as you have received from God.

9 For this is why the Master made you rich, that you may carry out these ministries for him. It is much better to purchase the fields, goods, and houses you will find in your own city when you return to it.

10 This kind of extravagance is good and makes one glad; it has no grief or fear, but joy instead. And so, do not participate in the extravagance sought by outsiders; for it is of no profit for you who are slaves of God.

11 But participate in your own extravagance in which you can rejoice. And do not counterfeit or touch what belongs to another, or desire it. For it is evil to desire someone else's goods. But do your own work, and you will be saved."

Another Parable

(II)

51 While I was walking in the field and considering an elm tree and a vine, reflecting on them and their fruits, the shepherd appeared to me and said, "Why are you asking yourself about the elm tree and the vine?" "I am thinking, Lord," I replied, "that they are extremely well suited for one another."

2 "These two trees," he replied, "symbolize the slaves of God." "I would like to know," I said, "what these two trees you are speaking about symbolize." "You see," he said, "the elm and the vine?" "I see them, Lord," I replied.

3 "This vine," he said, "bears fruit; but the elm is a tree that does not. Yet if this vine did not grow up onto the elm, it could not bear much fruit, since it would be lying on the ground, and the fruit it bore would be rotten, since it would not be clinging to the elm. And so, when the vine attaches to the elm, it bears fruit both of itself and because of the elm.

4 And so you see that the elm also gives much fruit—no less than the vine, but rather more." "How does it bear more, Lord" I asked. "Because," he said, "it is by clinging to the elm that the vine gives an abundance of good fruit; but when it is lying on the ground it bears just a little rotten fruit. And so this parable applies to the slaves of God, the poor and the rich."

5 "How so, Lord?" I asked. "Explain it to me." "Listen," he said. "The rich person has money, but is poor towards the Lord, since he is distracted by his wealth. The prayer and confession he makes to the Lord are very small—weak, small, and of no real effect. And so, when the rich person depends upon the one who is poor and supplies him with what he needs, he believes that by helping the one who is poor he will find his recom-

pense before God. For the poor person is rich in his petition and confession, and his petition has a great effect before God. And so the rich person supplies everything to the one who is poor, without hesitation.

6 And then the poor person, having his needs supplied by the one who is rich, prays to God and thanks him for the one who has given him what he needs. And that one becomes even more eager to help out the poor person, so that he may lack nothing in his life. For he knows that the petition of the poor person is acceptable and rich before the Lord.

7 And so both accomplish their work. The poor person works at his prayer in which he is rich and which he received from the Lord; and he gives it back to the Lord who supplied it to him in the first place. So too the rich person does not hesitate to supply his wealth to the poor person, since he received it from the Lord. And this is a great and acceptable thing to do before God, because the rich person has gained understanding by his wealth and has worked for the poor person out of the gifts provided by the Lord, and he has accomplished his ministry well.

8 And so, people may think that the elm tree bears no fruit; but they neither know nor understand that when a drought comes, the elm nourishes the vine by holding water; and the vine, since it has an undiminished supply of water, produces fruit for two, both for itself and for the elm. Thus also those who are poor who pray to the Lord on behalf of the rich bring their own wealth to completion; and again those who are rich and supply the poor with what they need bring their souls to completion.

9 Both then share in an upright work. And so the one who does these things will not be abandoned by God, but will be recorded in the books of the living.

10 Happy are those who have possessions and understand that their riches have come from the Lord; for the one who understands this will also be able to perform a good ministry."

Third Parable

(III)

52 He showed me many trees that did not have leaves but appeared to me to be withered. And they were all alike. He said to me, "Do you see these trees?" "I see them, Lord," I replied. "They are like one another and withered." He replied, "These trees you see are the people who dwell in this age."

2 "Why, then, Lord," I asked, "do they seem withered and like one another?" "Because," he said, neither the upright nor the sinners stand out clearly in this age, but they are like one another. For this age is a winter for those who are upright: they do not stand out clearly while dwelling with the sinners.

3 For just as the trees that shed their leaves in the winter all look alike, with the withered indistinguishable from the living, so too in this age it is not clear who the upright are and who the sinners, but they all appear alike."

Another Parable

(IV)

53 He showed me again a number of trees, some of them budding, others withered. And he said to me, "Do you see these trees?" "I see them, Lord," I replied. "Some of them are budding and others withered."

2 "These trees that are budding," he said, "are the upright who are about to dwell in the age that is coming. For the coming age is a summer for the upright,

but a winter for sinners. And so, when the mercy of the Lord shines forth, those who serve as slaves to God will stand out clearly, and everyone will be able to recognize them.

3 For just as the fruits of each individual tree appear in the summer and their species are recognized, so too the fruits of the upright will appear, and they will all be known in that age because they will be blossoming.

4 But the outsiders and sinners—who are the withered trees you saw—will be found withered and fruitless in that age, and they will be burned like withered trees and shown for what they are, because they did what was evil in their lifetimes. The sinners will be burned for sinning and not repenting. But the outsiders will be burned for not knowing the one who created them.

5 You, therefore, bear fruit in yourself, that your fruit may appear in that summer. But avoid many business activities and you will not sin at all. For those involved with numerous business dealings are also involved in numerous sins, since they are distracted by their affairs and do not serve as the Lord's slaves.

6 How then," he continued, "can someone like this receive anything he asks from the Lord, if he does not serve as the Lord's slave? For his slaves will receive what they request, but those who are not his slaves will receive nothing.

7 But if someone should engage in just one kind of business,[j] he will also be able to serve as the Lord's slave. For his thoughts will in no way be corrupted away from the Lord, but he will be enslaved to him, keeping his thoughts pure.

8 So then, if you do these things you will be able to bear fruit in the age that is coming. And whoever else does these things will bear fruit."

Another Parable, Five

(V, 1)

54 While I was fasting and sitting on a certain mountain, thanking the Lord for everything he had done for me, I saw the shepherd sitting next to me. And he said to me: "Why have you come here so early?" "Because, Lord," I said, "I have a duty to perform."[k]

2 "What is the duty?"[l] he asked. "I am fasting, Lord," I replied. "But what is this fast you people are keeping?" he asked. "I am fasting according to my custom, Lord," I said.

3 "You people do not know how to fast for God," he said, "and this worthless fast you are keeping for him is not a fast." "Why do you say this, Lord," I asked. "I say this," he said, "because what you think you are keeping is not a fast. But I will teach you a fast that is acceptable and complete to the Lord." "Yes, Lord," I said, "you will make me blessed if you show me the fast acceptable to God." "Listen," he said.

4 "God does not want this kind of vain fast. For when you fast like this to God you do nothing at all righteous. But fast to God as follows:

5 Do no evil in your life, but serve as the Lord's slave with a pure heart, keeping his commandments and proceeding in his injunctions; and let no evil desire rise up in your heart. Trust in God, because if you do these things and fear him and are self-restrained from every evil deed, you will live to God. If you do these things, you will accomplish a fast that is great and acceptable to the Lord.

[j]Or: *one business transaction* [k]Literally: *I have a station* [l]Or: *What is a station?*

(V, 2)

55 "Listen to this parable I am about to tell you; for it relates to fasting.

2 There was a person who owned a field and many slaves, and he planted a vineyard in part of the field. And he chose a certain slave who was most trustworthy and pleasing to him; and when he was about to go on a journey, he called him in and said to him, 'Take this vineyard that I have planted and build a fence around it before I return, and do nothing else to the vineyard. Do what I have commanded and I will set you free.' And the master of the slave went away on his journey.

3 When he had gone, his slave took the vineyard and built a fence around it. And when he finished the fence he saw that the vineyard was full of weeds.

4 And so he reasoned to himself, 'I have finished what the lord commanded; so now I will dig in this vineyard. Once it is dug it will be more attractive, and without the weeds it will give more fruit, since it will not be choked by the weeds.' So he dug the vineyard and removed all the weeds that were in it. And that vineyard became more attractive and flourishing, since there were no weeds that could choke it.

5 After some time the master of both field and slave returned and came into the vineyard. When he saw that the vineyard was attractively fenced and even more that it was dug, with all the weeds removed, and that the vines were flourishing, he was extremely pleased with what the slave had done.

6 So he called his beloved son, who was to be his heir, and his friends, who served as his advisors, and he told them everything he had commanded his slave and everything he found accomplished. And they congratulated the slave for the good testimony that the master had given him.

7 He said to them, 'I promised to free this slave if he did what I commanded him. And he did what I commanded and an additional good work in my vineyard besides. He has pleased me greatly. In exchange for the work he has done I want to make him a fellow heir with my son; for when he thought of the good deed, he did not leave it alone, but he accomplished it.'

8 The master's son approved of the idea that the slave should become his fellow heir.

9 After some days the master of the house gave a dinner and sent a number of foods to the slave from his table. When the slave received the food his master sent, he took what he needed and distributed the rest to his fellow slaves.

10 His fellow slaves took the food gladly, and began also to pray for him, that he might find even greater favor with the master, since he had treated them so well.

11 The master heard everything that happened and was again extremely pleased at what the slave had done. And so he once more assembled his friends and his son, and he reported to them what the slave had done with the foods he had received. And they approved even more heartily his plan to make the slave his son's fellow heir."

(V, 3)

56 I said to him, "Lord, I do not know what these parables mean and cannot understand them, unless you explain them to me."

2 "I will explain everything to you," he said, "and show you the meaning of everything I tell you. Guard what the Lord commands and you will be acceptable to him and enrolled among those who keep his commandments.

3 But if you do anything good beyond

what God commands, you will be glorified even more and even more highly honored before God than you were bound to be. If, then, you do what God commands and perform any of these services in addition, you will be filled with joy—if you keep them according to my commandment."

4 I said to him, "Lord, I will guard whatever you command me. For I know you are with me." "I will be with you," he said, "because you are so eager to do good; and I will be with everyone who is just as eager.

5 This fast that consists of keeping the Lord's commandments," he said, "is very good. And so guard the fast.

6 First of all, be on your guard against every evil word and desire, and cleanse your heart from all the vain affairs of this age. If you guard these things, this fast will be complete.

7 And act as follows: when you have completed the things that have already been written, taste nothing but bread and water on the day you fast. Then estimate the cost of the food you would have eaten on that day and give that amount to a widow or orphan or someone in need. Be humble in this way, that the one who receives something because of your humility may fill his own soul and pray to the Lord for you.

8 If then you complete your fast like this, as I have commanded you, your sacrifice will be acceptable before God and the fast will be recorded. The service done in this way will be good and cheerful and pleasing to the Lord.

9 Thus you should keep these things, as should your children and your entire household. When you do so, you will be blessed. Everyone who hears these things and keeps them will be blessed, and they will receive whatever they ask from the Lord."

(V, 4)

57 I begged him fervently to explain to me the parable of the field, the master, the vineyard, the slave who built a fence around the vineyard, the fence posts, the weeds that were removed from the vineyard, the son, and the friends who were advisors. For I understood that all these things were a parable.

2 He answered me, "You are extremely brazen in your requests. You should ask nothing at all, for if anything needs to be explained to you, it will be." I said to him, "Lord, there is no point in showing me something that you do not explain, when I do not know what it is. And if you tell me parables without explaining them to me, there is no point in my hearing them from you."

3 Again he said to me, "Whoever is a slave of God and has the Lord in his heart asks him for understanding and receives it. And he interprets every parable; and the words of the Lord spoken in parables are made known to him. But all those who are weak and lazy in prayer hesitate to ask anything from the Lord.

4 The Lord has great compassion and gives without hesitation to everyone who asks of him. But you have been empowered by the glorious angel and have received from him this petition; since you are not lazy, why do you not ask for understanding from the Lord and receive it directly from him?"

5 I said to him, "Lord, since I have you with me I need to ask and inquire of you. For you are the one showing everything to me and speaking with me. If I had seen or heard these things without you, I would ask the Lord to clarify them for me."

(V, 5)

58 "I told you just now," he said, "that you are crafty and brazen,

asking for the interpretations of the parables. But since you are so persistent, I will interpret for you the parable of the field and everything that follows it, that you may make these things known to all. Listen, now," he said, "and understand these things.

2 The field is this world. And the lord of the field is the one who created all things and completed them and empowered them. The son is the Holy Spirit and the slave is the Son of God. The vines are this people, which he has planted.

3 The fence-posts are the Lord's holy angels who surround his people. The weeds that were removed from the vineyard are the lawless deeds of the slaves of God. The foods that he sent to him from his dinner are the commandments he has given his people through his Son. The friends and advisors are the holy angels who were created first. And the absence of the master is the time that remains until his coming."

4 I said to him, "Lord, all these things are great, marvelous, and glorious. How could I have understood them? No one else could have understood them either, even if he were extremely insightful. Yet, Lord," I said, "explain to me what I am about to ask you."

5 "Say what you wish," he said. "Why, Lord," I asked, "is the Son of God represented as a slave in the parable?"

(V, 6)

59 "Listen," he said; "the Son of God is not represented as a slave, but as one who has great authority and lordship." "I don't see how, Lord," I replied.

2 "Because," he said, "God planted the vineyard—that is, he created the people and handed them over to his Son. And the Son appointed the angels over them, to protect each one. And he cleansed their

sins through great labor, bearing up under his many labors. For a vine cannot be dug around without labor or toil.

3 And so, when he had cleansed the sins of the people he showed them the paths of life, giving them the law, which he received from his Father.

4 You see, then," he said, "that he is the Lord of the people, having received all authority from his Father. But listen to what it means that the Lord took his Son, along with the glorious angels, as a counselor about the slave's inheritance.

5 God made the Holy Spirit dwell in the flesh that he desired,[m] even though it pre-existed and created all things. This flesh, then, in which the Holy Spirit dwelled, served well as the Spirit's slave, for it conducted itself in reverence and purity, not defiling the Spirit at all.

6 Since it lived in a good and pure way, cooperating with the Spirit and working with it in everything it did, behaving in a strong and manly way, God chose it to be a partner with the Holy Spirit. For the conduct of this flesh was pleasing, because it was not defiled on earth while bearing the Holy Spirit.

7 Thus he took his Son and the glorious angels as counselors, so that this flesh, which served blamelessly as the Spirit's slave, might have a place of residence and not appear to have lost the reward for serving as a slave. For all flesh in which the Holy Spirit has dwelled— and which has been found undefiled and spotless—will receive a reward.

8 Now you have the interpretation of this parable."

(V, 7)

60 "I am very glad to have heard this interpretation, Lord," I

---

[m]Meaning obscure

said. "And now listen," he replied: "Guard this flesh of yours to keep it clean and undefiled, so that the spirit dwelling in it may bear a good testimony to it, and your flesh may be made upright.

2 Take care that the thought never occur to you that this flesh of yours is corrupt, and never misuse it in a defiling way. If you defile your flesh, you defile the Holy Spirit as well. And if you defile your flesh, you will not live."

3 "But Lord," I said, "if anyone was ignorant earlier—before having heard these words—and defiled his flesh, how will he be saved?" "God alone," he replied, "can bring healing to those who were ignorant earlier. For all authority is his.

4 But guard these things for now, and the Lord who has great compassion will provide healing for these things, if here at the end you defile neither your flesh nor your spirit. For these two go together, and one cannot be defiled without the other. Keep both of them pure, therefore, and you will live to God."

Parable Six

(VI, 1)

61 While I was sitting in my house and giving glory to the Lord for all the things I had seen, and reflecting that his commandments are good, powerful, cheerful, glorious, and able to save a person's soul, I was telling myself, "I will be fortunate if I proceed in these commandments; for whoever proceeds in them is fortunate."

2 While I was telling myself these things, I suddenly saw him sitting next to me and saying, "Why are you of two minds about the commandments I have given you? They are good. Do not be at all of two minds, but clothe yourself with

the faith of the Lord and proceed in them. For I will empower you to do them.

3 These commandments are profitable to those who are about to repent. For if they do not proceed in them, their repentance is in vain.

4 And so, you who repent should cast aside the evil affairs of this age, which wear you down. For when you are clothed with every righteous virtue, you will be able to keep these commandments and no longer increase your sins. And so, by not increasing them, you will greatly cut off your former sins. Proceed therefore in my commandments, and you will live to God. For I have spoken these things to all of you."

5 After he spoke these things to me, he said, "Let us go into the country, and I will show you the shepherds of the sheep." "Yes, Lord," I said, "let us go." We came to a certain plain and he showed me a young shepherd, wearing a bright yellow suit of clothes.

6 He was tending a large flock of sheep. These sheep were luxuriously fed and extremely frisky and cheerful, leaping about here and there; and the shepherd also was cheerful with his flock. The shepherd's appearance was very cheerful, and he was running about among the sheep.

(VI, 2)

62 He said to me, "Do you see this shepherd?" "I see him, Lord," I replied. "This," he said, "is the angel of luxury and deceit. He, then, is the one who wears down the souls of the vacuous slaves of God and turns them away from the truth, deceiving them with evil desires that destroy them.

2 For they forget the commandments of the living God and proceed in vain deceits and luxuries and are destroyed by this angel—some to death and others to ruin."

3 I said to him, "Lord, I do not know what you mean that some are destroyed to death and others to ruin." "Listen," he said. "All the sheep you saw that were extremely cheerful and leaping about are the ones who have finally fallen away from God and have delivered themselves over to the desires of this age. Among these there is no repentance that leads to life, because they have also committed blasphemy against the name of the Lord. Death therefore belongs to them.

4 But the ones you saw that were not leaping about but were grazing in one place, these are the ones who have delivered themselves over to luxuries and deceits, without committing blasphemy against the Lord. They have been ruined by falling from the truth. For these there is a hope of repentance, and it can make them live. And so, those who have experienced this kind of ruin have some hope of new life, but death brings eternal destruction."

5 Then we went a little way ahead, and he showed me a large shepherd with a wild kind of appearance, clothed in the skin of a white goat, with a bag on his shoulder, a very hard and knotty staff, and a great whip. He had an extremely bitter look about him. I was afraid of him, he had such a look.

6 This shepherd was taking the sheep from the young shepherd—those that were frisky and luxuriously fed, but not leaping—and driving them into an area that was steep and filled with thorns and thistles. And the sheep could not extricate themselves from the thorns and thistles but became entangled in them.

7 And so they had to graze while being entangled among the thorns and thistles; and they were being miserably beaten by the shepherd. He was forcing them to move here and there, giving them no rest at all, so that those sheep were not at all tranquil.

(VI, 3)

63 When I saw them flogged like this and made so miserable, I started to grieve for them, because they were tormented in this way and had no respite.

2 I said to the shepherd who was speaking with me, "Lord," I said, "who is this merciless and bitter shepherd, who is showing no compassion at all for these sheep?" "This," he replied, "is the angel of punishment. He is one of the upright angels, but he has been appointed to mete out punishment.

3 And so he takes those who have strayed from God and proceeded in the desires of this age, and he punishes them with the various terrifying punishments that each of them deserves."

4 "I want to know, Lord," I said, "what sorts of punishments there are." "Listen," he said, "to the various torments and punishments. For the torments come in the present life. Some people are punished with financial losses, others with deprivations, various diseases, or every kind of disruption, or by being abused by miscreants and many other kinds of suffering.

5 For many people undertake numerous projects but go back and forth in their minds, and nothing at all goes well for them. And they say that they do not prosper in what they do, but it never occurs to them that they have done what is evil; instead, they blame the Lord.

6 And so, when they have suffered every affliction, they are handed over to me for good discipline, and they are made strong in the faith of the Lord, and they serve as the Lord's slaves the remaining days of their lives, with pure hearts. When they repent, they think about the evil deeds they have done, and then they give glory to God, because he is an upright judge and each one has rightly suffered everything in light of what he has done. For the rest of their lives they will serve as the Lord's slave with pure hearts, and they will prosper in their every deed, receiving everything they ask from the Lord. Then they glorify the Lord, because they have been delivered over to me, and they no longer suffer any evil."

(VI, 4)

64 I said to him, "Lord, explain something else to me." "What do you want to know?" he asked. "Are those who live in luxury and deceit," I asked, "tormented for the same amount of time they lived in luxury and deceit?" He replied to me, "They are tormented the same amount of time."

2 "Then they are tormented very little, Lord," I said. "For those who have lived in luxury like this and forgotten God should be tormented seven times as long."

3 He said to me, "You are a fool and do not understand the force of the torment." "If I had understood it, Lord," I replied, "I would not have asked you to explain it to me." "Listen," he said, "and I will tell you the force of both things.

4 The time of luxury and deceit is a single hour. But an hour's worth of torment has the force of thirty days. And so, if someone lives in luxury and deceit for a single day, and is then tormented for a single day, that day of torment has the force of an entire year. Thus, a person is tormented for the same number of years as the days he has lived in luxury.ⁿ You see," he said, "that the time of luxury and deceit is very brief, but that of punishment and torment is long."

(VI, 5)

65 I said, "Lord, since I have not completely understood about the times of deceit and luxury and torment, explain them to me more clearly."

2 He answered me, "You are persistently foolish and do not wish to cleanse your heart and serve God. Take care," he said, "lest the time be fulfilled and you be found foolish. Listen, now," he said, "to what you want to know, so that you may understand these things.

3 The one who lives in luxury and deceit for a single day, doing whatever he wants, is clothed with great foolishness and does not understand what he is doing. The next day he forgets what he did the day before. For luxury and deceit have no memories, because the person is clothed in foolishness. But when punishment and torment cling to a person for a single day, he is punished and tormented for a year, because punishment and torment have great memories,

4 And so, when he is tormented and punished over the course of the entire year, then he remembers his luxury and deceit and he knows that he is suffering because of these evil deeds. All those who live in luxury and deceit are tormented in this way, because even though they are alive they have handed themselves over to death."

5 "What sorts of luxuries, Lord," I asked, "are harmful?" He replied, "Everything that brings a person pleasure is a luxury," he said. "For even the foul-tempered person who acts as he desires enjoys a luxury. So too does the adulterer, the drunkard, the slanderer, the liar, the greedy, the defrauder, and anyone who does anything similar, as he desires, in his own diseased way. Such a person, then, enjoys a luxury in what he does.

6 All these luxuries are harmful to the slaves of God. Those who are punished and tormented, therefore, suffer because of these deceitful practices.

7 But there are also luxuries that save people. For many people who do what is good enjoy luxury by being borne along

---

ⁿNote: the calculations are based on a twelve-hour day

by their own pleasure. And so this kind of luxury can be profitable for the slaves of God, and provides life to such a person. But the harmful luxuries that I mentioned before provide torments and punishments. If people remain in them without repenting, they provide death for themselves."

Parable Seven

(VII)

66 After a few days I saw him in the same plain where I had seen the shepherds, and he said to me, "What are you looking for?" "I have come here, Lord," I said, "to ask you to order the punishing angel to leave my house, because he is afflicting me terribly." "You need to be afflicted," he replied, "because this is what the glorious angel commanded for you. For he wants you to be put to the test." "What evil thing have I done, Lord, to be handed over to this angel?" I asked.

2 "Listen," he said, "your sins are many, but not enough for you to be handed over to this angel. But your household has committed great sins and lawless acts, and the glorious angel is embittered by their deeds. This is why he commanded you to be afflicted for a time, to lead them to repent and cleanse themselves from all worldly desires. When they repent and are cleansed, then the punishing angel will leave."

3 I said to him, "Lord, even if they are acting in ways that embitter the glorious angel—what have I done?" "It cannot be otherwise," he said. "They cannot be afflicted unless you are as well, since you are the head of the household. For if you are afflicted, of necessity they are too; but if you are flourishing, they can experience no affliction."

4 "But look, Lord," I said, "they have in fact repented from their whole heart." "I myself know they have repented from their whole heart," he replied. "But do you think," he said, "that the sins of those who repent are forgiven on the spot? Not at all! But the one who repents must torment his own soul and become mightily humble in his every deed and be afflicted with many and various afflictions. And if he should endure the afflictions that come upon him, the one who created and empowered all things will be fully compassionate and bring him some healing.

5 This will certainly happen if he sees that the heart of the one who repents is pure from every evil deed. And it is to your advantage, and to your household's, to be afflicted now. But why am I telling you so much? You must be afflicted, just as that angel of the Lord commanded, the one who delivered you over to me. Give the Lord thanks for this—for he considered you worthy to have the affliction explained in advance, that by knowing about it in advance you could endure it strongly."

6 I said to him, "Lord, be with me and I will be able to endure every affliction." "I will be with you," he said. "And I will also ask the punishing angel to afflict you less severely. You will be afflicted for a brief time, and you will again be restored to your place. But continue by being humble, serving the Lord with a pure heart, you, your children, and your household, and proceed in my commandments, which I have given you, and your repentance will be able to be strong and pure.

7 And if you guard these matters, along with your household, every affliction will leave you. And affliction will leave everyone who proceeds in these my commandments." . . .

The Apocalypse of Peter

Three different apocalypses surviving from ancient Christianity claim to have been written by Peter. The one presented here was discovered in 1887 in the tomb of a Christian monk, along with the Gospel of Peter; it was subsequently found in a fuller Ethiopic translation.[1] This apocalypse was well-known in early Christianity; some churches counted it among the New Testament Scriptures.[2] Eventually, though, it came to be excluded from the canon, in part because Christians realized that it was pseudonymous. Even then, however, the book continued to exercise a significant influence on Christian thought. This is the first Christian writing to describe a journey through hell and heaven, an account that inspired a large number of successors, including, ultimately, Dante's *Divine Comedy*.

The book begins with Peter and the other disciples on the Mount of Olives listening to Jesus deliver his "apocalyptic discourse" (see Mark 13). Peter asks about the coming judgment. Jesus responds by describing the terrifying events that will occur when the world is destroyed by fire at the last judgment. He then details the eternal torments that await those destined for hell and the perpetual blessings of those bound for heaven.

There is some ambiguity over whether Jesus actually takes Peter on a journey through these two abodes of the dead or simply describes them in such vivid detail that it feels as if Peter is seeing them. There is no ambiguity, however, concerning the respective fates of those destined for one place or the other. In an unsettling way, the horrific punishments of the damned are made to fit their crimes (chaps. 7–12). Those who have followed Christ and kept the commandments of God, however, will be brought into the eternal kingdom, where they will enjoy the blissful life of heaven forever. The book ends with Peter describing first-hand what he saw on the Mount of Transfiguration, possibly in order to validate the legitimacy of the rest of his vision (cf. 2 Pet 1:17–18). The ultimate goal of this first-hand description of hellish and heavenly realities is reasonably clear: the way to escape eternal torment is to avoid sin.

---

[1]For a full discussion, see Ehrman, *Lost Christianities,* 24–27. [2]See the Muratorian Canon and the Canon of Eusebius.

Translation by J. K. Elliott, *Apocryphal New Testament* (Oxford: Clarendon Press, 1993) 600–609; used with permission.

The following translation follows the more complete and, probably, more accurate Ethiopic version of the text.

1 The Second Coming of Christ and Resurrection of the Dead which Christ revealed through Peter to those who died for their sins, because they did not keep the commandment of God, their creator.

And he (Peter) pondered thereon, that he might perceive the mystery of the Son of God, the merciful and lover of mercy.

And when the Lord was seated upon the Mount of Olives, his disciples came to him.

And we besought and entreated him severally and implored him, saying to him, "Declare to us what are the signs of your coming and of the end of the world, that we may perceive and mark the time of your coming and instruct those who come after us, to whom we preach the word of your gospel, and whom we install in your church, that they, when they hear it, may take heed to themselves and mark the time of your coming."

And our Lord answered us saying, "Take heed that no one deceive you and that you be not doubters and serve other gods. Many shall come in my name saying, 'I am the Christ.' Believe them not, neither draw near to them. For the coming of the Son of God shall not be plain; but as the lightning that shines from the east to the west, so will I come upon the clouds of heaven with a great host in my majesty; with my cross going before my face will I come in my majesty; shining seven times brighter than the sun will I come in my majesty with all my saints, my angels. And my Father shall set a crown upon my head, that I may judge the quick and the dead and recompense every one according to his works."

2 "And you learn a parable from the fig-tree: as soon as its shoots have come forth and the twigs grown, the end of the world shall come."

And I, Peter, answered and said to him, "Interpret the fig-tree to me: how can we understand it? For throughout all its days the fig-tree sends forth shoots and every year it brings forth its fruit for its master. What then does the parable of the fig-tree mean? We do not know."

And the Master answered and said to me, "Do you not understand that the fig-tree is the house of Israel? It is like a man who planted a fig-tree in his garden and it brought forth no fruit. And he sought the fruit many years, and when he did not find it he said to the keeper of his garden, 'Uproot this fig-tree so that it does not make our ground unfruitful.' And the gardener said to his master, 'Let us rid it of weeds and dig the ground round about it and water it. If then it does not bear fruit, we will straightway uproot it from the garden and plant another in place of it.' Have you not understood that the fig-tree is the house of Israel? Verily I say to you, when its twigs have sprouted forth in the last days, then shall false Christs come and awake expectation, saying, 'I am the Christ who has now come into the world.' And when they perceive the wickedness of their deeds they shall turn away and deny him whom our fathers praised, the first Christ whom they crucified and therein sinned a great sin. But this deceiver is not the Christ. And when they reject him, he shall slay them with the sword, and there shall be many martyrs. Then shall the twigs of the fig-tree, that is, the house of Israel, shoot forth: many shall become martyrs at his hand. Enoch and Elijah shall be sent to teach them that this is the deceiver who must come into the world and do signs and wonders in order to deceive. And therefore those who die by his hand shall be martyrs, and shall be reckoned among the good and righteous martyrs who have pleased God in their life."

3 And he showed me in his right hand the souls of all people. And on the palm of his right hand the image of that which shall be accomplished at the last day; and how the righteous and the sinners shall be separated, and how those who are upright in heart will fare, and how the evil-doers shall be rooted out to all eternity. We beheld how the sinners wept in great affliction and sorrow, until all who saw it with their eyes wept, whether righteous or angels, and he himself also.

And I asked him and said to him, "Lord, allow me to speak your word concerning the sinners, 'It were better for them if they had not been created.' " And the Saviour answered and said to me, "Peter, why do you say that not to have been created were better for them? You resist God. You would not have more compassion than he for his image: for he has created them and brought them forth out of not-being. Now because you have seen the lamentation which shall come upon the sinners in the last days, therefore your heart is troubled; but I will show you their works, whereby they have sinned against the Most High."

4 "Behold now what shall come upon them in the last days, when the day of God and the day of the decision of the judgment of God comes. From the east to the west shall all the children of men be gathered together before my Father who lives for ever. And he shall

command hell to open its bars of adamant and give up all that is therein.

"And the wild beasts and the fowls shall he command to restore all the flesh that they have devoured, because he wills that people should appear; for nothing perishes before God and nothing is impossible with him, because all things are his.

"For all things come to pass on the day of decision, on the day of judgment, at the word of God: and as all things were done when he created the world and commanded all that is therein and it was done, even so shall it be in the last days; for all things are possible with God. And therefore he said in the scripture, 'Son of man, prophesy upon the several bones and say to the bones: bone unto bone in joints, sinew, nerves, flesh, and skin and hair thereon.'[3]

"And soul and spirit shall the great Uriel give them at the commandment of God; for God has set him over the resurrection of the dead at the day of judgment.

"Behold and consider the corns of wheat that are sown in the earth. As something dry and without soul do men sow them in the earth: and they live again and bear fruit, and the earth restores them as a pledge entrusted to it.

"And this which dies, that is sown as seed in the earth, and shall become alive and be restored to life, is man.

"How much more shall God raise up on the day of decision those who believe in him and are chosen of him, for whose sake he made the world? And all things shall the earth restore on the day of decision, for it also shall be judged with them, and the heaven with it."

---

[3]Ezek 37:4–6

5 "And this shall come at the day of judgment upon those who have fallen away from faith in God and have committed sin. Cataracts of fire shall be let loose; and darkness and obscurity shall come up and clothe and veil the whole world; and the waters shall be changed and turned into coals of fire, and all that is in them shall burn, and the sea shall become fire. Under the heaven there shall be a sharp fire that cannot be quenched, and it flows to fulfil the judgment of wrath. And the stars shall be melted by flames of fire, as if they had not been created, and the firmaments of the heaven shall pass away for lack of water and shall be as though they had not been. And the lightnings of heaven shall be no more, and by their enchantment they shall affright the world. The spirits of the dead bodies shall be like them and shall become fire at the commandment of God.

"And as soon as the whole creation dissolves, the people who are in the east shall flee to the west, [and those who are in the west] to the east; those in the south shall flee to the north, and those who are in the north to the south. And in all places shall the wrath of a fearful fire overtake them; and an unquenchable flame driving them shall bring them to the judgment of wrath, to the stream of unquenchable fire which flows, flaming with fire, and when the waves thereof part themselves one from another, burning, there shall be a great gnashing of teeth among the children of men.

6 "Then shall they all behold me coming upon an eternal cloud of brightness; and the angels of God who are with me shall sit upon the throne of my glory at the right hand of my heavenly Father; and he shall set a crown upon my head. And when the nations behold it, they shall weep, every nation for itself.

"Then shall he command them to enter into the river of fire while the works of every one of them shall stand before them. [Rewards shall be given] to everyone according to his deeds. As for the elect who have done good, they shall come to me and not see death by the devouring fire. But the unrighteous, the sinners, and the hypocrites shall stand in the depths of darkness that shall not pass away, and their chastisement is the fire, and angels bring forward their sins and prepare for them a place wherein they shall be punished for ever, every one according to his transgression.

"Uriel the angel of God shall bring forth the souls of those sinners who perished in the flood, and of all who dwelt in all idols, in every molten image, in every object of love, and in pictures, and of those who dwelt on all hills and in stones and by the wayside, whom people called gods: they shall be burned with them in everlasting fire; and after all of them with their dwelling-places are destroyed, they shall be punished eternally."

7 "Then shall men and women come to the place prepared for them. By their tongues where-with they have blasphemed the way of righteousness shall they be hanged up. There is spread under them unquenchable fire so that they do not escape it.

"Behold another place: there is a pit, great and full. In it are those who have denied righteousness: and angels of punishment chastise them and there they kindle upon them the fire of their torment.

"And again behold two women: they hang them up by their neck and by their hair; they shall cast them into the pit. These are those who plaited their hair, not to make themselves beautiful but to turn them to fornication, that they might ensnare the souls of men to perdition. And the men who lay with them in fornication shall be hung by their loins in that place of fire; and they shall say one to another, 'We did not know that we should come to everlasting punishment.'

"And the murderers and those who have made common cause with them shall they cast into the fire, in a place full of venomous beasts, and they shall be tormented without rest, feeling their pains; and their worms shall be as many in number as a dark cloud. And the angel Ezrael shall bring forth the souls of those who have been slain, and they shall behold the torment of those who slew them and say one to another, 'Righteousness and justice is the judgment of God. For we heard, but we believed not, that we should come into this place of eternal judgment."

8 "And near this flame there is a pit, great and very deep, and into it flows from above all manner of torment, foulness, and excrement. And women are swallowed up therein up to their necks and tormented with great pain. These are they who have caused their children to be born untimely and have corrupted the work of God who created them. Opposite them shall be another place where children sit alive and cry to God. And flashes of lightning go forth from those children and pierce the eyes of those who for fornication's sake have caused their destruction.

"Other men and women shall stand above them, naked; and their children stand opposite them in a place of delight, and sigh and cry to God because of their parents saying, 'These are they who despised and cursed and transgressed your commandments and delivered us to death: they have cursed the angel that formed us and have hanged us up and begrudged us the light which you have given to all creatures. And the milk of their mothers flowing from their breasts shall congeal and from it shall come beasts devouring flesh, which shall come

forth and turn and torment them for ever with their husbands because they forsook the commandments of God and slew their children. As for their children, they shall be delivered to the angel Temlakos. And those who slew them shall be tormented eternally, for God wills it so."

9 "Ezrael the angel of wrath shall bring men and women, with half of their bodies burning, and cast them into a place of darkness, the hell of men; and a spirit of wrath shall chastise them with all manner of torment, and a worm that never sleeps shall devour their entrails; and these are the persecutors and betrayers of my righteous ones.

"And beside those who are there, shall be other men and women, gnawing their tongues; and they shall torment them with red-hot irons and burn their eyes. These are they who slander and doubt my righteousness.

'Other men and women whose works were done in deceitfulness shall have their lips cut off; and fire enters into their mouth and their entrails. These are they who caused the martyrs to die by their lying.

'And beside them, in a place near at hand, upon the stone shall be a pillar of fire, and the pillar is sharper than swords. And there shall be men and women clad in rags and filthy garments, and they shall be cast thereon to suffer the judgment of an unceasing torment; these are the ones who trusted in their riches and despised the widows and the women with fatherless children . . . before God."

10 "And into another place nearby, full of filth, they cast men and women up to the knees. These are they who lent money and took usury.

"And other men and women cast themselves down from a high place and return again and run, and devils drive them. These are the worshippers of idols, and they drive them up to the top of the height and they cast themselves down. And this they do continually and are tormented for ever. These are they who have cut their flesh as apostles of a man: and the women with them . . . and these are the men who defiled themselves together as women.

"And beside them . . . and beneath them shall the angel Ezrael prepare a place of much fire: and all the idols of gold and silver, all idols, the work of human hands, and the semblances of images of cats and lions, of creeping things and wild beasts, and the men and women that have prepared the images thereof, shall be in chains of fire and shall be chastised because of their error before the idols, and this is their judgment for ever.

"And beside them shall be other men and women, burning in the fire of the judgment, and their torment is everlasting. These are they who have forsaken the commandment of God and followed the (persuasions?) of devils."

11 "And there shall be another place, very high . . . The men and women whose feet slip shall go rolling down into a place where is fear. And again while the fire that is prepared flows, they mount up and fall down again and continue to roll down. Thus shall they be tormented for ever. These are they who honored not their father and mother and of their own accord withheld themselves from them. Therefore shall they be chastised eternally.

"Furthermore the angel Ezrael shall bring children and maidens, to show them those who are tormented. They shall be chastised with pains, with hanging up(?) and with a multitude of wounds which flesh-devouring birds shall inflict upon them. These are they who trust in their sins and do not obey their parents and do not follow the instruction of their fathers and do not honor those more aged than they.

"Beside them shall be girls clad in darkness for a garment, and they shall be seriously punished and their flesh shall be torn in pieces. These are they who did not preserve their virginity until they were given in marriage and with these torments shall they be punished and shall feel them.

"And again, other men and women, gnawing their tongues without ceasing, and being tormented with everlasting fire. These are the servants who were not obedient to their masters; and this then is their judgment for ever."

12 "And near by this place of torment shall be men and women who are dumb and blind and whose raiment is white. They shall crowd one upon another, and fall upon coals of unquenchable fire. These are they who give alms and say, 'We are righteous before God,' whereas they have not sought after righteousness.

"Ezrael the angel of God shall bring them forth out of this fire and establish a judgment of decision(?). This then is their judgment. A river of fire shall flow, and all those judged shall be drawn down into the middle of the river. And Uriel shall set them there.

"And there are wheels of fire, and men and women hung thereon by the force of the whirling. And those in the pit shall burn; now these are the sorcerers and sorceresses. Those wheels shall be in all decision by fire without number."

13 "Thereafter shall the angels bring my elect and righteous who are perfect in all uprightness and bear them in their hands and clothe them with the raiment of the life that is above. They shall see their desire on those who hated them, when he punishes them and the torment of every one shall be for ever according to his works.

"And all those in torment shall say with

one voice, 'Have mercy upon us, for now we know the judgment of God, which he declared to us before-time and we did not believe.' And the angel Tatirokos shall come and chastise them with even greater torment, and say to them, 'Now do you repent, when it is no longer the time for repentance, and nothing of life remains.' And they shall say, 'Righteous is the judgment of God, for we have heard and perceived that his judgment is good, for we are recompensed according to our deeds.' "

14 "Then will I give to my elect and righteous the baptism and the salvation for which they have besought me, in the field of Akrosja (Acherusia) which is called Aneslasleja (Elysium). They shall adorn with flowers the portion of the righteous, and I shall go . . . I shall rejoice with them. I will cause the peoples to enter into my everlasting kingdom, and show them eternal good things to which I have made them set their hope, I and my Father in heaven.

"I have spoke this to you, Peter, and declared it to you. Go forth therefore and go to the city of the west and enter into the vineyard which I shall tell you of, in order that by the sufferings of the Son who is without sin the deeds of corruption may be sanctified. As for you, you are chosen according to the promise which I have given you. Spread my gospel throughout all the world in peace. Verily people shall rejoice; my words shall be the source of hope and of life, and suddenly shall the world be ravished."

15 And my Lord Jesus Christ, our King, said to me, "Let us go to the holy mountain." And his disciples went with him, praying.

And behold there were two men there, and we could not look upon their faces,

for a light came from them, shining more than the sun and their raiment also was shining and cannot be described and nothing is sufficient to be compared to them in this world. And the sweetness of them . . . that no mouth is able to utter the beauty of their appearance, for their aspect was astonishing and wonderful. And the other, great, I say, shines in his aspect above crystal. Like the flower of roses is the appearance of the color of his aspect and of his body . . . his head. And upon his shoulders . . . and on their foreheads was a crown of nard woven from fair flowers. As the rainbow in the water, so was their hair. And such was the comeliness of their countenance, adorned with all manner of ornament.

16 And when we suddenly saw them, we marvelled. And I drew near to God, Jesus Christ, and said to him, "O my Lord, who are these?" And he said to me, "They are Moses and Elijah." And I said to him, "Where then are Abraham and Isaac and Jacob and the rest of the righteous fathers?" And he showed us a great garden, open, full of fair trees and blessed fruits and of the odor of perfumes. The fragrance was pleasant and reached us. And of that tree . . . I saw many fruits. And my Lord and God Jesus Christ said to me, "Have you seen the companies of the fathers?"

"As is their rest, such also is the honor and the glory of those who are persecuted for my righteousness' sake." And I rejoiced and believed and understood that which is written in the book of my Lord Jesus Christ. And I said to him, "O my Lord, do you wish that I make here three tabernacles, one for you, and one for Moses, and one for Elijah?"[4] And he said to me in wrath, "Satan makes war against

---

[4]Matt 17:4; Mark 9:5; Luke 9:33

you, and has veiled your understanding; and the good things of this world prevail against you. Your eyes therefore must be opened and your ears unstopped that you may see a tabernacle, not made with human hands, which my heavenly Father has made for me and for the elect." And we beheld it and were full of gladness.

17 And behold, suddenly there came a voice from heaven, saying, "This is my beloved Son in whom I am well pleased:[5] [he has kept] my commandments." And then came a great and exceedingly white cloud over our heads and bore away our Lord and Moses and Elijah. And I trembled and was afraid; and we looked up, and the heaven opened and we beheld men in the flesh and they came and greeted our Lord and Moses and Elijah and went to another heaven. And the word of the scripture was fulfilled: "This is the generation that seeks him and seeks the face of the God of Jacob."[6] And great fear and commotion took place in heaven, and the angels pressed one upon another that the word of the scripture might be fulfilled which says, "Open the gates, you princes."[7]

Thereafter was the heaven shut, that had been open.

And we prayed and went down from the mountain, glorifying God, who has written the names of the righteous in heaven in the book of life.

---

[5]Matt 17:5   [6]Ps 24:6   [7]Ps 24:7, 9

The Apocalypse of Paul

In a well-known passage from 2 Corinthians 12, Paul claims that he had once been caught up into heaven to behold a vision of things that could not be uttered. A later Christian nonetheless decided to give utterance to these things, and the present apocalypse is the result. The book describes Paul's ascent into heaven to receive a revelation concerning the fate of individual souls after death. He observes souls that leave their bodies to appear before God, who knows every detail about their lives and metes out rewards or punishments accordingly. The vision continues with a narrative description of Paradise and a graphic portrayal of the torments of the damned. These parallel in many ways those found in the Apocalypse of Peter (p. 280), which the pseudonymous author—claiming to be Paul—appears to have used as a source.

In its present form, the Apocalypse of Paul dates from the end of the fourth century, but it contains materials that were composed earlier, as they are alluded to by the proto-orthodox church father Origen in the early third century. The book became quite popular in Western Christianity, and was responsible for propagating many of the wide-spread notions of heaven and hell that have come down even till today.

The excerpts here are often thought to be among the older portions of the book.

In the consulship of Theodosius Augustus the Younger and Cynegius, a certain nobleman was then living in Tarsus, in the house which was that of Saint Paul; an angel appeared in the night and revealed it to him, saying that he should open the foundations of the house and should publish what he found, but he thought that these things were dreams.

2 But the angel coming for the third time beat him and forced him to open the foundation. And digging he found a marble box, inscribed on the

Translation by J. K. Elliott, *Apocryphal New Testament* (Oxford: Clarendon Press, 1993) 620; 624–27; 629; 631; 633–35; used with permission.

sides; there was the revelation of Saint Paul, and his shoes in which he walked teaching the word of God. But he feared to open that box and brought it to the judge; when he had received it, the judge, because it was sealed with lead, sent it to the emperor Theodosius, fearing lest it might be something else; when the emperor had received it he opened it, and found the revelation of Saint Paul, a copy of which he sent to Jerusalem, and retained the original himself.

3 While I was in the body in which I was snatched up to the third heaven, . . .

14 And I said to the angel, "I wish to see the souls of the just and of sinners, and to see in what manner they go out of the body." And the angel answered and said to me, "Look again upon the earth." And I looked and saw all the world, and people were as naught and growing weak; and I looked carefully and saw a certain man about to die, and the angel said to me, "This one whom you see is a just man." And I looked again and saw all his works, whatever he had done for the sake of God's name, and all his desires, both what he remembered, and what he did not remember; they all stood in his sight in the hour of need; and I saw the just man advance and find refreshment and confidence, and before he went out of the world the holy and the impious angels both attended; and I saw them all, but the impious found no place of habitation in him, but the holy angels took possession of his soul, guiding it till it went out of the body; and they roused the soul saying, "Soul, know the body you leave, for it is necessary that you should return to the same body on the day of the resurrection, that you may receive the things promised to all the just." Receiving therefore the soul from

the body, they immediately kissed as if it were familiar to them, saying to it, "Be of good courage, for you have done the will of God while placed on earth." And there came to meet it the angel who watched it every day, and said to it, "Be of good courage, soul; I rejoice in you, because you have done the will of God on earth; for I related to God all your works just as they were." Similarly also the spirit proceeded to meet it and said, "Soul, fear not, nor be disturbed, until you come to a place which you have never known, but I will be a helper to you: for I found in you a place of refreshment in the time when I dwelt in you, while I was on earth." And his spirit strengthened it, and his angel received it, and led it into heaven; and an angel said, "Where are you running to, O soul, and do you dare to enter heaven? Wait and let us see if there is anything of ours in you; and behold we find nothing in you. I see also your divine helper and angel, and the spirit is rejoicing along with you, because you have done the will of God on earth." And they led it along till it should worship in the sight of God. And when it had ceased, immediately Michael and all the army of angels, with one voice, adored the footstool of his feet and his doors, saying at the same time to the soul, "This is your God of all things, who made you in his own image and likeness." Moreover, the angel ran on ahead and pointed him out, saying, "God, remember his labors; for this is the soul, whose works I related to you, acting according to your judgment." And the spirit said likewise, "I am the spirit of vivification inspiring it; for I had refreshment in it, in the time when I dwelt in it, acting according to your judgment." And there came the voice of God and said, "In as much as this man did not grieve me, neither will I grieve him; as he had pity, I also will have pity. Let it therefore be handed over to Michael, the angel of the Covenant, and let him lead it into the Paradise of joy, that it may become coheir with all the saints." And after these things I heard the voices of a thousand thousand angels and archangels and cherubim and twenty-four elders, saying hymns and glorifying the Lord and crying, "You are just, O Lord, and just are your judgments, and there is no respect of persons with you, but you reward every one according to your judgment." And the angel answered and said to me, "Have you believed and known that whatever each one of you has done he sees in the hour of need?" And I said, "Yes, sir."

15 And he said to me, "Look again down on the earth, and watch the soul of an impious man going out of the body, which grieved the Lord day and night, saying, "I know nothing else in this world, I eat and drink, and enjoy what is in the world; for who is there who has descended into hell and, ascending, has declared to us that there is judgment there!' " And again I looked carefully, and saw all the scorn of the sinner, and all that he did, and they stood together before him in the hour of need; and it was done to him in that hour, when he was led out of his body at the judgment, and he said, "It were better for me if I had not been born." And after these things, there came at the same time the holy angels and the evil angels, and the soul of the sinner saw both and the holy angels did not find a place in it. Moreover the evil angels cursed it; and when they had drawn it out of the body the angels admonished it a third time, saying, "O wretched soul, look upon your flesh from which you have come out; for it is necessary that you should return to your flesh in the day of resurrection, that you may receive what is the due for your sins and your impieties."

16 And when they had led it forth the guardian angel preceded it, and said to it, "O wretched soul, I am the angel belonging to you, relating daily to the Lord your evil works, whatever you did by night or day; and if it were in my power, not for one day would I minister to you, but none of these things was I able to do: the judge is full of pity and just, and he himself commanded us that we should not cease to minister to the soul till you should repent, but you have lost the time of repentance. I have become a stranger to you and you to me. Let us go on then to the just judge; I will not dismiss you before I know from today I am to be a stranger to you." And the spirit afflicted it, and the angel troubled it. When they had arrived at the powers, when it started to enter heaven, a burden was imposed upon it, above all other burden: error and oblivion and murmuring met it, and the spirit of fornication, and the rest of the powers, and said to it, "Where are you going, wretched soul, and do you dare to rush into heaven? Hold, that we may see if we have our qualities in you, since we do not see that you have a holy helper." And after that I heard voices in the height of heaven saying, "Present that wretched soul to God, so it may know that it is God whom it despised." When, therefore, it had entered heaven all the angels saw it; a thousand thousand exclaimed with one voice, all saying, "Woe to you, wretched soul, for the sake of your works which you did on earth; what answer are you about to give to God when you have approached to adore him?" The angel who was with it answered and said, "Weep with me, my beloved, for I have not found rest in this soul." And the angels answered him and said, "Let such a soul be taken away from our midst, for from the time it entered the stink of it crosses to us angels." And after these things it was presented, that it might worship in the sight of God, and an angel of God showed it God who made it after his own image and likeness. Moreover its angel ran before it saying, "Lord God Almighty, I am the angel of this soul, whose works I presented to you day and night, not acting in accordance with your judgment. And the spirit likewise said, "I am the spirit who dwelt in it from the time it was made; in itself I know it, and it has not followed my will; judge it, Lord, according to your judgment." And there came the voice of God to it and said, "Where is your fruit which you have made worthy of the goods which you have received? Have I put a distance of one day between you and the just person? Did I not make the sun to arise upon you as upon the just?" But the soul was silent, having nothing to answer, and again there came a voice saying, "Just is the judgment of God, and there is no respect of persons with God, for whoever shall have done mercy, on him shall have mercy, and whoever shall not have been merciful, neither shall God pity him. Let it therefore be handed over to the angel Tartaruchus, who is set over the punishments, and let him cast it into outer darkness, where there is weeping and gnashing of teeth, and let it be there till the great day of judgment." And after these things I heard the voice of angels and archangels saying, "You are just, Lord, and your judgment is just."

17 And again I saw and, behold, a soul which was led forward by two angels, weeping and saying, "Have pity on me, just God, God the judge, for today it is seven days since I went out of my body, and I was handed over to these two angels, and they brought me to those places which I had never seen." And God, the just judge, said to it, "What have you done? For you never showed mercy, therefore you were handed over to such angels as have no mercy, and because you did no right, so neither did they act compassionately with you in your hour of need. Confess your sins which you committed when placed in the world." And it answered and said, "Lord, I did not sin." And the Lord, the just Lord, was angered in fury when it said, "I did not sin," because it lied; and God said, "Do you think you are still in the world where any one of you, sinning, may conceal and hide his sin from his neighbor? Here nothing whatever shall be hidden, for when the souls come to worship in sight of the throne both the good works and the sins of each one are made manifest." And hearing these things the soul was silent, having no answer. And I heard the Lord God, the just judge, again saying, "Come, angel of this soul, and stand in the midst." And the angel of the sinful soul came, having in his hands a document, and said, "These, Lord, in my hands, are all the sins of this soul from its youth till today, from the tenth year of its birth; and if you command, Lord, I will also relate its acts from the beginning of its fifteenth year." And the Lord God, the just judge, said, "I say to you, angel, I do not expect of you an account of it since it began to be fifteen years old, but state its sins for five years before it died and before it came hither." And again God, the just judge, said, "For by myself I swear, and by my holy angels, and by my virtue, that if it had repented five years before it died, on account of a conversion one year old, oblivion would now be thrown over all the evils which it sinned before, and it would have indulgence and remission of sins; now indeed it shall perish." And the angel of the sinful soul answered and said, "Lord, command that angel to exhibit those souls."

18 And in that same hour the souls were exhibited in the midst, and the soul of the sinner knew them; and the Lord said to the soul of the sinner, "I say to you, soul, confess your work which you wrought in these souls whom you see, when they were in the world." And it answered and said, "Lord, it is not yet a full year since I slew this one and poured his blood upon the ground, and with another I committed fornication; not only this, but I also greatly harmed her in taking away her goods." And the Lord God, the just judge, said, "Did you not know that if someone does violence to another and the person who sustains the violence dies first, he is kept in this place until the one who was committed the offence dies, and then both stand in the presence of the judge, and now each receives according to his deed?" And I heard a voice of one saying, "Let that soul be delivered into the hands of Tartarus, and led down into hell; he shall lead it into the lower prison, and it shall be put in torments and left there till the great day of judgment." And again I heard a thousand thousand angels saying hymns to the Lord, and crying, "You are just, O Lord, and just are your judgments."

19 The angel answered and said to me, "Have you perceived all these things?" And I said, "Yes, sir." And he said to me, "Follow me again, and I will take you, and show you the places of the just." And I followed the angel, and he raised me to the third heaven and placed me at the entry of the door; and looking, I saw that the door was of gold, and two columns of gold above it full of golden letters, and the angel turned again to me and said, "Blessed are you if you enter through these doors, for it is not permitted for any to enter except those who have goodness and purity of body in all things." . . .

22 And I looked around upon that land, and I saw a river flowing with milk and honey, and there were trees planted by the bank of that river, full of fruit; moreover, each single tree bore twelve fruits in the year, having various and diverse fruits; and I saw the created things which are in that place and all the work of God, and I saw there palms of twenty cubits, but others of ten cubits; and that land was seven times brighter than silver. And there were trees full of fruits from the roots to the highest branches, of ten thousand fruits of palms upon ten thousand fruits. The grapevines had ten thousand plants. Moreover in the single vines there were ten thousand thousand bunches and in each of these a thousand single grapes; moreover these single trees bore a thousand fruits. And I said to the angel, "Why does each tree bear a thousand fruits?" The angel answered and said to me, "Because the Lord God gives an abounding profusion of gifts to the worthy and because they of their own will afflicted themselves when they were placed in the world doing all things on account of his holy name." And again I said to the angel, "Sir, are these the only promises which the Most Holy God makes?" And he answered and said to me, "No! There are seven times greater than these. But I say to you that when the just go out of the body they shall see the promises and the good things which God has prepared for them. Till then, they shall sigh and lament, saying, "Have we uttered any word from our mouth to grieve our neighbor even on one day?" I asked and said again, "Are these alone the promises of God?" And the angel answered and said to me, "These whom you now see are the souls of the married and those who kept the chastity of their nuptials, controlling themselves. But to the virgins and those who hunger and thirst after righteousness and those who afflicted themselves for the sake of the name of God, God will give seven times greater than these, which I shall now show you." . . .

26 Again he led me where there is a river of milk, and I saw in that place all the infants whom Herod slew because of the name of Christ, and they greeted me, and the angel said to me, "All who keep their chastity and purity, when they have come out of the body, after they adore the Lord God are delivered to Michael and are led to the infants, and they greet them, saying that they are our brothers and friends and members; among them they shall inherit the promises of God."

27 Again he took me up and brought me to the north of the city and led me where there was a river of wine, and there I saw Abraham and Isaac and Jacob, Lot and Job and other saints, and they greeted me; and I asked and said, "What is this place, my lord?" The angel answered and said to me, "All who have given hospitality to strangers when they go out of the world first adore the Lord God, and are delivered to Michael and by this route are led into the city, and all the just greet them as son and brother, and say to them, 'Because you have observed humanity and helped pilgrims, come, have an inheritance in the city of the Lord our God: every righteous person shall receive good things of God in the city, according to his own action.' "

28 And again he carried me near the river of oil on the east of the city. And I saw there men rejoicing and singing psalms, and I said, "Who are those, my lord?" And the angel said to

me, "These are they who devoted themselves to God with their whole heart and had no pride in themselves. For all those who rejoice in the Lord God and sing psalms to the Lord with their whole heart are here led into this city. . . ."

31 When he had ceased speaking to me, he led me outside the city through the midst of the trees and far from the places of the land of the good, and put me across the river of milk and honey; and after that he led me over the ocean which supports the foundations of heaven.

The angel answered and said to me, "Do you understand why you go hence?" And I said, "Yes, sir." And he said to me, "Come and follow me, and I will show you the souls of the godless and sinners, that you may know what manner of place it is." And I went with the angel, and he carried me towards the setting of the sun, and I saw the beginning of heaven founded on a great river of water, and I asked, "What is this river of water?" And he said to me, "This is the ocean which surrounds all the earth." And when I was at the outer limit of the ocean I looked, and there was no light in that place, but darkness and sorrow and sadness; and I sighed.

And I saw there a river boiling with fire, and in it a multitude of men and women immersed up to the knees, and other men up to the navel, others even up to the lips, others up to the hair. And I asked the angel and said, "Sir, who are those in the fiery river?" And the angel answered and said to me, "They are neither hot nor cold, because they were found neither in the number of the just nor in the number of the godless. For those spent the time of their life on earth passing some days in prayer, but others in sins and fornications, until their death."

And I asked him and said, "Who are these, sir, immersed up to their knees in fire?" He answered and said to me, "These are they who when they have gone out of church occupy themselves with idle disputes. Those who are immersed up to the navel are those who, when they have taken the body and blood of Christ, go and fornicate and do not cease from their sins till they die. Those who are immersed up to the lips are those who slander each other when they assemble in the church of God; those up to the eyebrows are those who nod to each other and plot spite against their neighbor."

32 And I saw to the north a place of various and diverse punishments full of men and women, and a river of fire ran down into it. I observed and I saw very deep pits and in them several souls together, and the depth of that place was about there thousand cubits, and I saw them groaning and weeping and saying, "Have pity on us, O Lord!", and no one had pity on them. And I asked the angel and said, "Who are these, sir?" And the angel answered and said to me, "These are they who did not hope in the Lord, that they would be able to have him as their helper." And I asked and said, "Sir, if these souls remain for thirty or forty generations thus one upon another, I believe the pits would not hold them unless they were dug deeper." And he said to me, "The Abyss has no measure, for beneath it there stretches down below that which is below it; and so it is that if perchance anyone should take a stone and throw it into a very deep well after many hours it would reach the bottom, such is the abyss. For when the souls are thrown in there, they hardly reach the bottom in fifty years."

33 When I heard this, I wept and groaned over the human race.

The angel answered and said to me, "Why do you weep? Are you more merciful than God? For though God is good, he knows that there are punishments, and he patiently bears with the human race, allowing each one to do his own will in the time in which he dwells on the earth."

34 I observed the fiery river and saw there a man being tortured by Tartaruchian angels having in their hands an iron instrument with three hooks with which they pierced the bowels of that old man; and I asked the angel and said, "Sir, who is that old man on whom such torments are imposed?" And the angel answered and said to me, "He whom you see was a presbyter who did not perform his ministry well: when he had been eating and drinking and committing fornication he offered the host to the Lord at his holy altar."

35 And I saw not far away another old man led on by evil angels running with speed, and they pushed him into the fire up to his knees, and they struck him with stones and wounded his face like a storm and did not allow him to say, "Have pity on me!" And I asked the angel, and he said to me, "He whom you see was a bishop and did not perform his episcopate well, who indeed accepted the great name but did not enter into the witness of him who gave him the name all his life, seeing that he did not give judgment and did not pity widows and orphans, but now he receives retribution according to his iniquity and his works."

36 And I saw another man in the fiery river up to his knees. His hands were stretched out and bloody, and worms proceeded from his mouth and nostrils, and he was groaning and weeping, and crying he said, "Have pity on me! For I am hurt more than the rest who are in this punishment." And I asked, "Sir, who is this?" And he said to me, "This man whom you see was a deacon who devoured the oblations and committed fornication and did not do right in the sight of God; for this cause he unceasingly pays this penalty."

And I looked closely and saw alongside of him another man, whom they delivered up with haste and cast into the fiery river, and he was in it up to the knees; and the angel who was set over the punishments came with a great fiery razor, and with it he cut the lips of that man and the tongue likewise. And sighing, I lamented and asked, "Who is that, sir?" And he said to me, "He whom you see was a reader and read to the people, but he himself did not keep the precepts of God; now he also pays the proper penalty."

37 And I saw another multitude of pits in the same place, and in the midst of it a river full with a multitude of men and women, and worms consumed them. But I lamented, and sighing asked the angel and said, "Sir, who are these?" And he said to me, "These are those who exacted interest on interest and trusted in their riches and did not hope in God that he was their helper."

And after that I looked and saw another place, very narrow, and it was like a wall, and fire round about it. And I saw inside men and women gnawing their tongues, and I asked, "Sir, who are these?" And he said to me, "These are they who in church disparage the Word of God, not attending to it, but as it were making naught of God and his angels; for that reason they now likewise pay the proper penalty."

38 And I observed and saw another pool in the pit and its appearance was like blood, and I asked and said, "Sir, what is this place?" And he said to me, "Into that pit stream all the punishments." And I saw men and women immersed up to the lips, and I asked, "Sir, who are these?" And he said to me, "These are the magicians who prepared for men and women evil magic arts and did not cease till they died."

And again I saw men and women with very black faces in a pit of fire, and I sighed and lamented and asked, "Sir, who are these?" And he said to me, "These are fornicators and adulterers who committed adultery, having wives of their own; likewise also the women committed adultery, having husbands of their own; therefore they unceasingly suffer penalties."

39 And I saw there girls in black raiment, and four terrifying angels having in their hands burning chains, and they put them on the necks of the girls and led them into darkness; and I, again weeping, asked the angel, "Who are these, sir?" And he said to me. "These are they who, when they were virgins, defiled their virginity unknown to their parents; for which cause they unceasingly pay the proper penalties."

And again I observed there men and women with hands cut and their feet placed naked in a place of ice and snow, and worms devoured them. Seeing them I lamented and asked, "Sir, who are these?" And he said to me, "These are they who harmed orphans and widows and the poor, and did not hope in the Lord, for which cause they unceasingly pay the proper penalties."

And I observed and saw others hanging over a channel of water, and their tongues were very dry, and many fruits were placed in their sight, and they were not permitted to take of them, and I asked, "Sir, who are these?" And he said to me, "These are they who broke their fast before the appointed hour; for this cause they unceasingly pay these penalties."

And I saw other men and women hanging by their eyebrows and their hair, and a fiery river drew them, and I said, "Who are these, sir?" And he said to me, "These are they who join themselves not to their own husbands and wives but to whores, and therefore they unceasingly pay the proper penalties."

And I saw other men and women covered with dust, and their countenance was like blood, and they were in a pit of pitch and sulphur running in a fiery river, and I asked, "Sir, who are these?" And he said to me, "These are they who committed the iniquity of Sodom and Gomorrah, the male with the male, for which reason they unceasingly pay the penalties." . . .

The Secret Book of John

The Secret Book (sometimes called "Apocryphon") of John was one of the most remarkable discoveries of the Nag Hammadi Library (see p. 19), where it was found in multiple versions that differ from one another in some ways.[1] Cast as a post-resurrection discussion of Jesus with his disciple, John the son of Zebedee, the book contains one of the clearest expositions of the Gnostic myth of creation and redemption, an exposition designed, ultimately, to explain the existence of evil in the world and the path of escape for those who recognize their plight.[2]

In intricate detail the account discusses the propagation of the divine realm from the one invisible, imperishable, incomprehensible God prior to creation, and the tragic mistake of the aeon Sophia, who produced an offspring apart from her divine consort. The result was the monster Creator God, whom Sophia named Yaltabaoth; this, in fact, is none other than the God of the Bible, who is portrayed here as a malformed and imperfect divine being, who out of ignorance proclaims "I am God, and there is no other God beside me" (Isa 45:5–6).

Yaltabaoth is ultimately responsible for the creation of the world and humans; but he is tricked into breathing the breath of life into the human he has made, thus imparting the power of his mother, Sophia, to them, making them animate, with an element of the divine within. As with other forms of the Gnostic myth, a good deal of the Secret Book of John represents a creative exposition of the stories of creation found in Genesis 1–4. The tale continues with the appearance of Christ from above to provide the divine souls entrapped within mortal bodies the knowledge necessary for escape.

Since this particular version of the Gnostic myth was known, in a slightly different form, to the late second-century church father Irenaeus, most scholars date the Secret Book of John sometime prior to 180 CE.

---

[1]See further Ehrman, *Lost Christianities*, 123–25.   [2]For a fuller explanation of Christian Gnosticism, see Ehrman, *Lost Christianities*, 122–25.

Translation by Frederik Wisse, in James Robinson, *Nag Hammadi Library in English*, 3rd ed. (Leiden: E. J. Brill, 1988) 105–13; 116; 117–120; 123; used with permission.

The teaching [of the savior], and [the revelation] of the mysteries, [and the] things hidden in silence, [even these things which] he taught John, [his] disciple.

[And] it happened one [day], when John, [the brother] of James—who are the sons of Zebedee—had come up to the temple, that a Pharisee named Arimanius approached him and said to him, "Where is your master [whom] you followed?" And he [said] to him, "He has gone to the [place] from which he came." The Pharisee [said to him, "With deception did this Nazarene] deceive you (pl.), and he filled [your ears with lies], and closed [your hearts (and) turned you] from the traditions [of your fathers."]

[When] I, [John], heard these things [I turned] away from the temple [to a desert place]. And I grieved [greatly in my heart saying]. "How [then was] the savior [appointed], and why was he sent [in to the world] by [his Father, and who is his] Father who [sent him, and of what sort] is [that] aeon [to which we shall go?] For what did he [mean when he said to us], 'This aeon to [which you will go is of the] type of the [imperishable] aeon,' [but he did not teach] us concerning [the latter of what sort it is."]

Straightway, [while I was contemplating these things,] behold, the [heavens opened and] the whole creation [which is] below heaven shone, and [the world] was shaken. [I was afraid, and behold I] saw in the light [a youth who stood] by me. While I looked [at him he became] like an old man. And he [changed his] likeness (again) becoming like a servant. There was [not a plurality] before me, but there was a [likeness] with multiple forms in the light, and the [likenesses] appeared through each other, [and] the [likeness] had three forms.

He said to me, "John, John, why do you doubt, or why [are you] afraid? You

are not unfamiliar with this image, are you?—that is, do not [be] timid!—I am one who is [with you (pl.)] always. I [am that Father], I am the Mother, I am the Son. I am the undefiled and incorruptible one. Now [I have come to teach you] what is [and what was] and what will come to [pass], that [you may know the] things which are not revealed [and those which are revealed, and to teach you] concerning the [unwavering race of] the perfect [Man]. Now, [therefore, lift up] your [face, that] you may [receive] the things that I [shall teach you] today, [and] may [tell them to your] fellow spirits who [are from] the [unwavering] race of the perfect Man."

[And I asked] to [know it, and he said] to me, "The Monad [is a] monarchy with nothing above it. [It is he who exists] as [God] and Father of everything, [the invisible] One who is above [everything, who exists as] incorruption, which is [in the] pure light into which no [eye] can look.

"He [is the] invisible [Spirit] of whom it is not right [to think] of him as a god, or something similar. For he is more than a god, since there is nothing above him, for no one lords it over him. [For he does] not [exist] in something inferior [to him, since everything] exists in him. [For it is he who establishes] himself. [He is eternal] since he does [not] need [anything]. For [he] is total perfection. [He] did not [lack anything] that he might be completed by [it; rather] he is always completely perfect in [light]. He is [illimitable] since there is no one [prior to him] to set limits to him. He is unsearchable [since there] exists no one prior to him to [examine him. He is] immeasurable since there [was] no one [prior to him to measure] him. [He is invisible since no] one saw [him. He is eternal] since he [exists] eternally. He is [ineffable since] no one was able to comprehend him to speak [about him]. He is unnameable since [there is no one prior to him] to give [him] a name.

"He is [immeasurable light] which is pure, holy, [(and) immaculate]. He is ineffable [being perfect in] incorruptibility. (He is) [not] in perfection, nor in blessedness, nor in divinity, but he is far superior. He is not corporeal [nor] is he incorporeal. He is neither large [nor] is he small. [There is no] way to say, 'What is his quantity?' or, 'What [is his quality?'], for no one can [know him]. He is not someone among (other) [beings, rather he is] far superior. [Not] that [he is (simply) superior], but his essence does not [partake] in the aeons nor in time. For he who partakes in [an aeon] was prepared beforehand. Time [was not] apportioned to him, [since] he does not receive anything from another, [for it would be received] on loan. For he who precedes someone does not [lack] that he may receive from [him]. For [rather] it is the latter that looks expectantly at him in his light.

"For the [perfection] is majestic. He is pure, immeasurable [mind]. He is an aeon-giving aeon. He is [life]-giving life. He is a blessedness-giving blessed one. He is knowledge-giving knowledge. [He is] goodness-giving goodness. [He is] mercy and redemption-[giving mercy]. He is grace-giving grace, [not] because he possesses it, but because he gives [the] immeasurable, incomprehensible [light].

"[How am I to speak] with you about him? His [aeon] is indestructible, at rest and existing in [silence, reposing] (and) being prior [to everything. For he] is the head of [all] the aeons, [and] it is he who gives them strength in his goodness. For [we know] not [the ineffable things, and we] do not understand what [is immeasurable], except for him who came forth [from] him, namely (from) [the] Father. For it is he who [told] it to us [alone].

For it is he who looks at him[self] in his light which surrounds [him], namely the spring [of the] water of life. And it is he who gives to [all] the [aeons] and in every way, (and) who [gazes upon] his image which he sees in the spring of the [Spirit]. It is he who puts his desire in his [water]-light [which is in the] spring of the [pure light]-water [which] surrounds him.

"And [his thought performed] a deed and she came forth, [namely] she who had [appeared] before him in [the shine of] his light. This is the first [power which was] before all of them (and) [which came] forth from his mind. She [is the forethought of the All]—her light [shines like his] light—the [perfect] power which is [the] image of the invisible, virginal Spirit who is perfect. [The first power], the glory of Barbelo, the perfect glory in the aeons, the glory of the revelation, she glorified the virginal Spirit and it was she who praised him, because thanks to him she had come forth. This is the first thought, his image; she became the womb of everything, for it is she who is prior to them all, the Mother-Father, the first man, the holy Spirit, the thrice-male, the thrice-powerful, the thrice-named androgynous one, and the eternal aeon among the invisible ones, and the first to come forth.

"<She> requested from the invisible, virginal Spirit—that is Barbelo—to give her foreknowledge. And the Spirit consented. And when he had [consented], the foreknowledge came forth, and it stood by the forethought; it originates from the thought of the invisible, virginal Spirit. It glorified him [and] his perfect power, Barbelo, for it was for her sake that it had come into being.

"And she requested again to grant her [indestructibility], and he consented. When he had [consented], indestructibility [came] forth, and it stood by the thought and the foreknowledge. It glorified the invisible One and Barbelo, the one for whose sake they had come into being.

"And Barbelo requested to grant her eternal life. And the invisible Spirit consented. And when he had consented, eternal life came forth, and [they attended] and glorified the invisible [Spirit] and Barbelo, the one for whose sake they had come into being.

"And she requested again to grant her truth. And the invisible Spirit consented. And [when he had] consented truth came forth, and they attended and glorified the invisible, excellent Spirit and his Barbelo, the one for whose sake they had come into being.

"This is the pentad of the aeons of the Father, which is the first man, the image of the invisible Spirit; it is the forethought, which is Barbelo, and the thought, and the foreknowledge, and the indestructibility, and the eternal life, and the truth. This is the androgynous pentad of the aeons, which is the decad of the aeons, which is the Father.

"And he looked at Barbelo with the pure light which surrounds the invisible Spirit and (with) his spark, and she conceived from him. He begot a spark of light with a light resembling blessedness. But it does not equal his greatness. This was an only-begotten child of the Mother-Father which had come forth; it is the only offspring, the only-begotten one of the Father, the pure Light.

"And the invisible, virginal Spirit rejoiced over the light which came forth, that which was brought forth first by the first power of his forethought which is Barbelo. And he anointed it with his goodness until it became perfect, not lacking in any goodness, because he had anointed it with the goodness of the invisible Spirit. And it attended him as he poured upon it. And immediately when it had received from the Spirit, it glorified the holy Spirit and the perfect forethought for whose sake it had come forth.

"And it requested to give it a fellow worker, which is the mind, and he consented [gladly]. And when the invisible Spirit had consented, the mind came forth, and it attended Christ glorifying him and Barbelo. And all these came into being in silence.

"And the mind wanted to perform a deed through the word of the invisible Spirit. And his will became a deed and it appeared with the mind; and the light glorified it. And the word followed the will. For because of the word, Christ the divine Autogenes created everything. And the eternal life <and> his will and the mind and the foreknowledge attended and glorified the invisible Spirit and Barbelo, for whose sake they had come into being.

"And the holy Spirit completed the divine Autogenes, his son, together with Barbelo, that he may attend the mighty and invisible, virginal Spirit as the divine Autogenes, the Christ whom he had honored with a mighty voice. He came forth through the forethought. And the invisible, virginal Spirit placed the divine Autogenes of truth over everything. And he subjected to him every authority, and the truth which is in him, that he may know the All which had been called with a name exalted above every name. For that name will be mentioned to those who are worthy of it.

"For from the light, which is the Christ, and the indestructibility, through the gift of the Spirit the four lights (appeared) from the divine Autogenes. He expected that they might attend him. And the three (are) will, thought, and life. And the four powers (are) understanding, grace, perception, and prudence. And grace belongs to the lightaeon Armozel, which is the first angel. And there are three other aeons with this aeon: grace, truth, and form. And the second light (is) Oriel, who has been placed over the second aeon. And there are three other aeons with him: conception, perception, and memory. And the third light is Daveithai, who has been placed over the third aeon. And there are three other aeons with him: understanding, love, and idea. And the fourth aeon was placed over the fourth light Eleleth. And there are three other aeons with him: perfection, peace, and wisdom. These are the four lights which attend the divine Autogenes, (and) these are the twelve aeons which attend the son of the mighty one, the Autogenes, the Christ, through the will and the gift of the invisible Spirit. And the twelve aeons belong to the son of the Autogenes. And all things were established by the will of the holy Spirit through the Autogenes.

"And from the foreknowledge of the perfect mind, through the revelation of the will of the invisible Spirit and the will of the Autogenes, <the> perfect Man (appeared), the first revelation, and the truth. It is he whom the virginal Spirit called Pigera-Adamas, and he placed him over the first aeon with the mighty one, the Autogenes, the Christ, by the first light Armozel; and with him are his powers. And the invisible one gave him a spiritual, invincible power. And he spoke and glorified and praised the invisible Spirit, saying, 'It is for your sake that everything has come into being and everything will return to you. I shall praise and glorify you and the Autogenes and the aeons, the three: the Father, the Mother, and the Son, the perfect power.'

"And he placed his son Seth over the second aeon in the presence of the second light Oriel. And in the third aeon the seed of Seth was placed over the third light Daveithai. And the souls of the saints were placed (there). And in the fourth aeon the souls were placed of those who do not know the Pleroma and who did not repent at once, but who persisted for a while and repented afterwards; they are by the fourth light Eleleth. These are creatures which glorify the invisible Spirit.

"And the Sophia of the Epinoia, being an aeon, conceived a thought from herself and the conception of the invisible Spirit and foreknowledge. She wanted to bring forth a likeness out of herself without the consent of the Spirit—he had not approved—and without her consort, and without his consideration. And though the person of her maleness had not approved, and she had not found her agreement, and she had thought without the consent of the Spirit and the knowledge of her agreement, (yet) she brought forth. And because of the invincible power which is in her, her thought did not remain idle and something came out of her which was imperfect and different from her appearance, because she had created it without her consort. And it was dissimilar to the likeness of its mother for it has another form.

"And when she saw (the consequences of) her desire, it changed into a form of a lion-faced serpent. And its eyes were like lightening fires which flash. She cast it away from her, outside that place, that no one of the immortal ones might see it, for she had created it in ignorance. And she surrounded it with a luminous cloud, and she placed a throne in the middle of the cloud that no one might see it except the holy Spirit who is called the mother of the living. And she called his name Yaltabaoth.

"This is the first archon who took a great power from his mother. And he removed himself from her and moved away from the places in which he was born. He became strong and created for himself other aeons with a flame of luminous fire which (still) exists now. And he joined with his arrogance which is in him and begot authorities for himself. The name of the first one is Athoth, whom the generations call [the reaper]. The second one is Harmas, who [is the eye] of envy. The third one is Kalila-Oumbri. The fourth one is Yabel. The fifth one is Adonaiou, who is called Sabaoth. The sixth one is Cain, whom the generations of men call the sun. The seventh is Abel. The eighth is Abrisene. The ninth is Yobel. The tenth is Armoupieel. The eleventh is Melceir-Ardonein. The twelth is Belias, it is he who is over the depth of Hades. And he placed seven kings—each corresponding to the firmaments of heaven—over the seven heavens, and five over the depth of the abyss, that they may reign. And he shared his fire with them, but he did not send forth from the power of the light which he had taken from his mother, for he is ignorant darkness.

"And when the light had mixed with the darkness, it caused the darkness to shine. And when the darkness had mixed with the light, it darkened the light and it became neither light nor dark, but it became dim.

"Now the archon who is weak has three names. The first name is Yaltabaoth, the second is Saklas, and the third is Samael. And he is impious in his arrogance which is in him. For he said, 'I am God and there is no other God beside me,'[3] for he is ignorant of his strength, the place from which he had come.

"And the archons created seven powers for themselves, and the powers created for themselves six angels for each one until they became 365 angels. And there are the bodies belonging with the names: the first is Athoth, he has a sheep's face; the second is Eloaiou, he has a donkey's face; the third is Astaphaios, he has a [hyena's] face; the fourth is Yao, he has a [serpent's] face with seven heads; the fifth is Sabaoth, he has a dragon's face;

the sixth is Adonin, he had a monkey's face; the seventh is Sabbede, he has a shining fire-face. This is the sevenness of the week.

"But Yaltabaoth had a multitude of faces more than all of them so that he could put a face before all of them, according to his desire, when he is in the midst of seraphs. He shared his fire with them; therefore he became lord over them. Because of the power of the glory he possessed of his mother's light, he called himself God. And he did not obey the place from which he came. And he united the seven powers in his thought with the authorities which were with him. And when he spoke it happened. And he named each power beginning with the highest: the first is goodness with the first (authority), Athoth; the second is foreknowledge with the second one, Eloaio; and the third is Astraphaio; the fourth is lordship with the fourth one, Yao; the fifth is kingdom with the fifth one, Sabaoth; the sixth is envy with the sixth one, Adonein; the seventh is understanding with the seventh one, Sabbateon. And these have a firmament corresponding to each aeon-heaven. They were given names according to the glory which belongs to heaven for the [destruction of the] powers. And in the names which were given to [them by] their Originator there was power. But the names which were given them according to the glory which belongs to heaven mean for them destruction and powerlessness. Thus they have two names.

"And having created [   ] everything he organized according to the model of the first aeons which had come into being, so that he might create them like the indestructible ones. Not because he had

_____

[3]Isa 45:5–6; cf. Exod 20:2–3.

seen the indestructible ones, but the power in him, which he had taken from his mother, produced in him the likeness of the cosmos. And when he saw the creation which surrounds him and the multitude of the angels around him which had come forth from him, he said to them, 'I am a jealous God and there is no other God beside me.'[4] But by announcing this he indicated to the angels who attended him that there exists another God. For if there were no other one, of whom would he be jealous?

"Then the mother began to move to and fro. She became aware of the deficiency when the brightness of her light diminished. And she became dark because her consort had not agreed with her."

And I said, "Lord, what does it mean that she moved to and fro?" But he smiled and said, "Do not think it is, as Moses said, 'above the waters.'[5] No, but when she had seen the wickedness which had happened, and the theft which her son had committed, she repented. And she was overcome by forgetfulness in the darkness of ignorance and she began to be ashamed. And she did not dare to return, but she was moving about. And the moving is the going to and fro.

"And the arrogant one took a power from his mother. For he was ignorant, thinking that there existed no other except his mother alone. And when he saw the multitude of the angels which he had created, then he exalted himself above them.

"And when the mother recognized that the garment of darkness was imperfect, then she knew that her consort had not agreed with her. She repented with much weeping. And the whole pleroma heard the prayer of her repentance and they praised on her behalf the invisible, virginal Spirit. And he consented; and when the invisible Spirit had consented, the holy Spirit poured over her from their whole pleroma. For it was not her consort who came to her, but he came to her through the pleroma in order that he might correct her deficiency. And she was taken up not to her own aeon but above her son, that she might be in the ninth until she has corrected her deficiency.

"And a voice came forth from the exalted aeon-heaven: 'The Man exists and the son of Man.' And the chief archon, Yaltabaoth, heard (it) and thought that the voice had come from his mother. And he did not know from where it came. And he taught them, the holy and perfect Mother-Father, the complete foreknowledge, the image of the invisible one who is the Father of the all (and) through whom everything came into being, the first Man. For he revealed his likeness in a human form.

"And the whole aeon of the chief archon trembled, and the foundations of the abyss shook. And of the waters which are above matter, the underside was illuminated by the appearance of his image which had been revealed. And when all the authorities and the chief archon looked, they saw the whole region of the underside which was illuminated. And through the light they saw the form of the image in the water. And he said to the authorities which attend him, 'Come, let us create a man according to the image of God and according to our likeness that his image may become a light for us.'[6] And they created by means of their respective powers in correspondence with the characteristics which were given. And each authority supplied a characteristic in the form of the image which he had seen in its natural (form). He created

---

[4]Exod 20:5; Isa 45:5–6, 12.   [5]Gen 1:2.   [6]Gen 1:26.

a being according to the likeness of the first, perfect Man. And they said, 'Let us call him Adam, that his name may become a power of light for us.' . . . And all the angels and demons worked until they had constructed the natural body. And their product was completely inactive and motionless for a long time.

"And when the mother wanted to retrieve the power which she had given to the chief archon, she petitioned the Mother-Father of the All who is most merciful. He sent, by means of the holy decree, the five lights down upon the place of the angels of the chief archon. They advised him that they should bring forth the power of the mother. And they said to Yaltabaoth, 'Blow into his face something of your spirit and his body will arise.' And he blew into his face the spirit which is the power of his mother; he did not know (this), for he exists in ignorance. And the power of the mother went out of Yaltabaoth into the natural body which they had fashioned after the image of the one who exists from the beginning. The body moved and gained strength, and it was luminous.

"And in that moment the rest of the powers became jealous, because he had come into being through all of them and they had given their power to the man, and his intelligence was greater than that of those who had made him, and greater than that of the chief archon. And when they recognized that he was luminous, and that he could think better than they, and that he was free from wickedness, they took him and threw him into the lowest region of all matter.

"But the blessed One, the Mother-Father, the beneficent and merciful One, had mercy on the power of the mother which had been brought forth out of the chief archon, for they (the archons) might gain power over the natural and perceptible body. And he sent, through his beneficent Spirit and his great mercy, a

helper to Adam, luminous Epinoia which comes out of him, who is called Life. And she assists the whole creature, by toiling with him and by restoring him to his fullness and by teaching him about the descent of his seed (and) by teaching him about the way of ascent, (which is) the way he came down. And the luminous Epinoia was hidden in Adam, in order that the archons might not know her, but that the Epinoia might be a correction of the deficiency of the mother. . . . And the archons took him and placed him in paradise. And they said to him, 'Eat, that is at leisure,' for their luxury is bitter and their beauty is depraved. And their luxury is deception and their trees are godlessness and their fruit is deadly poison and their promise is death. And the tree of their life they had placed in the midst of paradise.

"And I shall teach you (pl.) what is the mystery of their life, which is the plan which they made together, which is the likeness of their spirit. The root of this (tree) is bitter and its branches are death, its shadow is hate and deception is in its leaves, and its blossom is the ointment of evil, and its fruit is death and desire is its seed, and it sprouts in darkness. The dwelling place of those who taste from it is Hades and the darkness is their place of rest.

"But what they call the tree of knowledge of good and evil, which is the Epinoia of the light, they stayed in front of it in order that he (Adam) might not look up to his fullness and recognize the nakedness of his shamefulness. But it was I who brought about that they ate."

And I said to the savior, "Lord, was it not the serpent that taught Adam to eat?" The savior smiled and said, "The serpent taught them to eat from wickedness of begetting, lust, (and) destruction, that he (Adam) might be useful to him. And he (Adam) knew that he was disobedient to him (the chief archon) due to light of the

Epinoia which is in him, which made him more correct in his thinking than the chief archon. And (the latter) wanted to bring about the power which he himself had given him. And he brought a forgetfulness over Adam. . . .

"Then the Epinoia of the light hid herself in him (Adam). And the chief archon wanted to bring her out of his rib. But the Epinoia of the light cannot be grasped. Although darkness pursued her, it did not catch her. And he brought a part of his power out of him. And he made another creature in the form of a woman according to the likeness of the Epinoia which had appeared to him. And he brought the part which he had taken from the power of the man into the female creature, and not as Moses said, 'his rib-bone.'[7]

"And he (Adam) saw the woman beside him. And in that moment the luminous Epinoia appeared, and she lifted the veil which lay over his mind. And he became sober from the drunkenness of darkness. And he recognized his counterimage, and he said, 'This is indeed bone of my bones and flesh of my flesh.'[8] Therefore the man will leave his father and his mother and he will cleave to his wife and they will both be one flesh. For they will send him his consort, and he will leave his father and his mother.

"And our sister Sophia (is) she who came down in innocence in order to rectify her deficiency. Therefore she was called Life, which is the mother of the living, by the foreknowledge of the sovereignty of heaven and [ ] to him [ ]. And through her they have tasted the perfect Knowledge. I appeared in the form of an eagle on the tree of knowledge, which is the Epinoia from the foreknowledge of the pure light, that I might teach them and awaken them out of the depth of sleep. For they were both in a fallen state and they recognized their nakedness. The

Epinoia appeared to them as a light (and) she awakened their thinking.

"And when Yaldabaoth noticed that they withdrew from him, he cursed his earth. He found the woman as she was preparing herself for her husband. He was lord over her though he did not know the mystery which had come to pass through the holy decree. And they were afraid to blame him. And he showed his angels his ignorance which is in him. And he cast them out of paradise and he clothed them in gloomy darkness. And the chief archon saw the virgin who stood by Adam, and that the luminous Epinoia of life had appeared in her. And Yaldabaoth was full of ignorance. And when the foreknowledge of the All noticed (it), she sent some and they snatched life out of Eve. . . .

"And the two archons he set over principalities so that they might rule over the tomb. And when Adam recognized the likeness of his own foreknowledge, he begot the likeness of the son of man. He called him Seth according to the way of the race in the aeons. Likewise the mother also sent down her spirit which is in her likeness and a copy of those who are in the pleroma, for she will prepare a dwelling place for the aeons which will come down. And he made them drink water of forgetfulness, from the chief archon, in order that they might not know from where they came. Thus the seed remained for a while assisting (him) in order that, when the Spirit comes forth from the holy aeons, he may raise up and heal him from the deficiency, that the whole pleroma may (again) become holy and faultless."

And I said to the savior, "Lord, will all the souls then be brought safely into the

---

[7]Gen 2:21–22.   [8]Gen 2:23.

pure light?" He answered and said to me, "Great things have arisen in your mind, for it is difficult to explain them to others except to those who are from the immovable race. Those on whom the Spirit of life will descend and (with whom) he will be with the power, they will be saved and become perfect and be worthy of the greatness and be purified in that place from all wickedness and the involvements in evil. Then they have no other care than the incorruption alone, to which they direct their attention from here on, without anger or envy or jealousy or desire and greed of anything. They are not affected by anything except the state of being in the flesh alone; which they bear while looking expectantly for the time when they will be met by the receivers (of the body). Such then are worthy of the imperishable, eternal life and the calling. For they endure everything and bear up under everything, that they may finish the good fight and inherit eternal life."

I said to him, "Lord, the souls of those who did not do these works, (but) on whom the power and Spirit descended, will they be rejected?" He answered and said to me, "If the Spirit descended upon them, they will in any case be saved and they will change (for the better). For the power will descend on every one, for without it no one can stand. And after they are born, then, when the Spirit of life increases and the power comes and strengthens that soul, no one can lead it astray with works of evil. But those on whom the counterfeit spirit descends are drawn by him and they go astray."

And I said, "Lord, where will the souls of these go when they have come out of their flesh?" And he smiled and said to me, "The soul, in which the power will become stronger than the counterfeit spirit, is strong and it flees from evil and, through the intervention of the incorrupt-

ible one, it is saved and it is taken up to the rest of the aeons."

And I said, "Lord, those, however, who have not known to whom they belong, where will their souls be?" And he said to me, "In those the despicable spirit has gained strength when they went astray. And he burdens the soul and draws it to the works of evil, and he casts it down into forgetfulness. And after it comes out of (the body), it is handed over to the authorities, who came into being through the archon, and they bind it with chains and cast it into prison and consort with it until it is liberated from the forgetfulness and acquires knowledge. And if thus it becomes perfect, it is saved." . . .

And I said, "Lord, these also who did not know but have turned away, where will their souls go?" Then he said to me, "To that place where the angels of poverty go they will be taken, the place where there is no repentance. And they will be kept for the day on which those who have blasphemed the spirit will be tortured, and they will be punished with eternal punishment. . . . And behold, now I shall go up to the perfect aeon. I have completed everything for you in your hearing. And I have said everything to you that you might write them down and give them secretly to your fellow spirits, for this is the mystery of the immovable race."

And the savior presented these things to him that he might write them down and keep them secure. And he said to him, "Cursed be everyone who will exchange these things for a gift or for food or for drink or for clothing or for any other such thing." And these things were presented to him in a mystery, and immediately he disappeared from him. And he went to his fellow disciples and related to them what the savior had told him.

On the Origin of the World

This tractate, which was discovered for the first time as part of the Nag Hammadi Library (see p. 9), is not provided with a title in its manuscript. Modern scholars have called it "On the Origin of the World" simply as a summation of its contents. The unknown author appears to be writing for outsiders, and is concerned to provide in involved and intricate detail a Gnostic view of how the world came into being. Many important aspects of Gnostic mythology are covered here: the existence of the divine pleroma before all things, the emergence of Yaldabaoth the creator God, his generation of other divine beings, the creation of the material world, and the formation of the human race. As with other Gnostic myths, "On the Origin of the World" is largely based on an imaginative exposition of the opening chapters of Genesis, in which a number of the gaps of the narrative (including the events that transpired before Gen 1:1) are filled in.

In many ways the mythological exposition here is similar to what can be found in other important treatises of the Nag Hammadi Library; but as a comparison with the Secret Book of John shows, there are key differences as well. Gnostic Christians did not have a single myth at the root of their religion, but a number of different ways of explaining the existence of the world and the place of humans within it.

Scholars debate the dating of the work; possibly it was written near the end of the third century. The following excerpt gives approximately two-thirds of the treatise, from its beginning through the creation of Adam.

Seeing that everybody, gods of the world and humankind, says that nothing existed prior to chaos, I in distinction to them shall demonstrate that they are all mistaken, because they are not acquainted with the origin of chaos, nor with its root. Here is the demonstration. How well it suits all people, on the subject of chaos, to say that it is a kind of darkness! But in fact it comes from a shadow, which

Translation by Hans-Gebhard Bethge, Bentley Layton, Societas Coptica Hierosolymitana in James Robinson, *Nag Hammadi Library in English,* 3rd ed. (Leiden: E. J. Brill, 1988) 172–81; used with permission.

has been called by the name darkness. And the shadow comes from a product that has existed since the beginning. It is, moreover, clear that it (viz., the product) existed before chaos came into being, and that the latter is posterior to the first product.

Let us therefore concern ourselves with the facts of the matter; and furthermore, with the first product, from which chaos was projected. And in this way the truth will be clearly demonstrated.

After the natural structure of the immortal beings had completely developed out of the infinite, a likeness then emanated from Pistis (Faith); it is called Sophia (Wisdom). It exercised volition and became a product resembling the primeval light. And immediately her will manifested itself as a likeness of heaven, having an unimaginable magnitude; it was between the immortal beings and those things that came into being after them, like . . . : she (Sophia) functioned as a veil dividing mankind from the things above.

Now the eternal realm (aeon) of truth has no shadow outside it, for the limitless light is everywhere within it. But its exterior is shadow, which has been called by the name darkness. From it there appeared a force, presiding over the darkness. And the forces that came into being subsequent to them called the shadow "the limitless chaos." From it, every [kind] of divinity sprouted up . . . together with the entire place, [so that] also, [shadow] is posterior to the first product. It was <in> the abyss that [it] (shadow) appeared, deriving from the aforementioned Pistis.

Then shadow perceived that there was something mightier than it, and felt envy; and when it had become pregnant of its own accord, suddenly it engendered jealousy. Since that day, the principle of jealousy amongst all the eternal realms and

their worlds has been apparent. Now as for that jealousy, it was found to be an abortion without any spirit in it. Like a shadow it came into existence in a vast watery substance. Then the bile that had come into being out of the shadow was thrown into a part of chaos. Since that day, a watery substance has been apparent. And what sank within it flowed away, being visible in chaos: as with a woman giving birth to a child—all her superfluities flow out; just so, matter came into being out of shadow and was projected apart. And it (viz., matter) did not depart from chaos; rather, matter was in chaos, being in a part of it.

And when these things had come to pass, then Pistis came and appeared over the matter of chaos, which had been expelled like an aborted fetus—since there was no spirit in it. For all of it (viz., chaos) was limitless darkness and bottomless water. Now when Pistis saw what had resulted from her defect, she became disturbed. And the disturbance appeared, as a fearful product; it rushed [to] her in the chaos. She turned to it and [blew] into its face in the abyss, which is below all the heavens.

And when Pistis Sophia desired to cause the thing that had no spirit to be formed into a likeness and to rule over matter and over all her forces, there appeared for the first time a ruler, out of the waters, lionlike in appearance, androgynous, having great authority within him and ignorant of whence he had come into being. Now when Pistis Sophia saw him moving about in the depth of the waters she said to him, "Child, pass through to here," whose equivalent is "yalda baōth."

Since that day there appeared the principle of verbal expression, which reached the gods and the angels and mankind. And what came into being as a result of verbal expression, the gods and the angels and mankind finished. Now as for the ruler Yaltabaoth, he is ignorant of the force of Pistis: he did not see her face, rather he saw in the water the likeness that spoke with him. And because of that voice, he called himself Yaldabaoth. But Ariael is what the perfect call him, for he was like a lion. Now when he had come to have authority over matter, Pistis Sophia withdrew up to her light.

When the ruler saw his magnitude—and it was only himself that he saw: he saw nothing else, except for water and darkness—then he supposed that it was he alone who existed. His [. . .] was completed by verbal expression: it appeared as a spirit moving to and fro upon the waters. And when that spirit appeared, the ruler set apart the watery substance. And what was dry was divided into another place. And from matter he made for himself an abode, and he called it heaven. And from matter, the ruler made a footstool, and he called it earth.

Next, the ruler had a thought—consistent with his nature—and by means of verbal expression he created an androgyne. He opened his mouth and cooed to him. When his eyes had been opened, he looked at his father, and he said to him, "Eee!" Then his father called him Eee-a-o (Yao). Next he created the second son. He cooed to him. And he opened his eyes and said to his father, "Eh!" His father called him Eloai. Next he created the third son. He cooed to him. And he opened his eyes and said to his father, "Asss!" His father called him Astaphaios. These are the three sons of their father.

Seven appeared in chaos, androgynous. They have their masculine names and their feminine names. The feminine name is Pronoia (Forethought) Sambathas, which is "week." And his son is called Yao: his feminine name is Lordship.

Sabaoth: his feminine name is Deity.

Adonaios: his feminine name is Kingship.

Eloaios: his feminine name is Jealousy.

Oraios: his feminine name is Wealth.

And Astaphaios: his feminine name is Sophia (Wisdom).

These are the [seven] forces of the seven heavens of [chaos]. And they were born androgynous, consistent with the immortal pattern that existed before them, according to the wish of Pistis: so that the likeness of what had existed since the beginning might reign to the end.

You (sg.) will find the effect of these names and the force of the male entities in the *Archangelic (Book) of the Prophet Moses,* and the names of the female entities in the first *Book (biblos) of Noraia.*

Now the prime parent Yaldabaoth, since he possessed great authorities, created heavens for each of his offspring through verbal expression—created them beautiful, as dwelling places—and in each heaven he created great glories, seven times excellent. Thrones and mansions and temples, and also chariots and virgin spirits up to an invisible one and their glories, each one has these in his heaven; mighty armies of gods and lords and angels and archangels—countless myriads—so that they might serve.

The account of these matters you (sg.) will find in a precise manner in the first *Account of Oraia.*

And they were completed from this heaven to as far up as the sixth heaven, namely that of Sophia. The heaven and his earth were destroyed by the troublemaker that was below them all. And the six heavens shook violently; for the forces of chaos knew who it was that had destroyed the heaven that was below them. And when Pistis knew about the breakage resulting from the disturbance, she sent forth her breath and bound him and cast him down into Tartaros. Since that day, the heaven, along with its earth, has consolidated itself through Sophia the daughter of Yaldabaoth, she who is below them all.

Now when the heavens had consolidated themselves along with their forces and all their administration, the prime parent became insolent. And he was honored by all the army of angels. And all the gods and their angels gave blessing and honor to him. And for his part he was delighted and continually boasted, saying to them, "I have no need of anyone." He said, "It is I who am God, and there is no other one that exists apart from me."[1] And when he said this, he sinned against all the immortal beings who give answer. And they laid it to his charge.

Then when Pistis saw the impiety of the chief ruler she was filled with anger. She was invisible. She said, "You are mistaken, Samael," that is, "blind god." "There is an immortal man of light who has been in existence before you and who will appear among your modelled forms; he will trample you to scorn just as potter's clay is pounded. And you will descend to your mother, the abyss, along with those that belong to you. For at the consummation of your (pl.) works the entire defect that has become visible out of the truth will be abolished, and it will cease to be and will be like what has never been." Saying this, Pistis revealed her likeness of her greatness in the waters. And so doing she withdrew up to her light.

Now when Sabaoth the son of Yaldabaoth heard the voice of Pistis, he sang praises to her, and [he] condemned the father . . . at the word of Pistis; and he praised her because she had instructed them about the immortal man and his light. Then Pistis Sophia stretched out her finger and poured upon him some light from her light, to be a condemnation of

his father. Then when Sabaoth was illumined, he received great authority against all the forces of chaos. Since that day he has been called "Lord of the Forces."

He hated his father, the darkness, and his mother, the abyss, and loathed his sister, the thought of the prime parent, which moved to and fro upon the waters. And because of his light all the authorities of chaos were jealous of him. And when they had become disturbed, they made a great war in the seven heavens. Then when Pistis Sophia had seen the war, she dispatched seven archangels to Sabaoth from her light. They snatched him up to the seventh heaven. They stood before him as attendants. Furthermore she sent him three more archangels and established the kingdom for him over everyone so that he might dwell above the twelve gods of chaos.

Now when Sabaoth had taken up the place of repose in return for his repentance, Pistis also gave him her daughter Zoe (Life) together with great authority so that she might instruct him about all things that exist in the eighth heaven. And as he had authority, he made himself first of all a mansion. It is huge, magnificent, seven times as great as all those that exist in the seven heavens.

And before his mansion he created a throne, which was huge and was upon a four-faced chariot called "Cherubin." Now the Cherubin has eight shapes per each of the four corners, lion forms and calf forms and human forms and eagle forms, so that all the forms amount to sixty-four forms—and (he created) seven archangels that stand before it; he is the eighth, and has authority. All the forms amount to seventy-two. Furthermore,

---

[1]Isa 45:5–6, 12.

from this chariot the seventy-two gods took shape; they took shape so that they might rule over the seventy-two languages of the peoples. And by that throne he created other, serpent-like angels, called "Saraphin," which praise him at all times.

Thereafter he created a congregation (*ekklesia*) of angels, thousands and myriads, numberless, which resembled the congregation in the eighth heaven; and a firstborn called Israel—which is, "the man that sees God"; and another being, called Jesus Christ, who resembles the savior above in the eighth heaven and who sits at his right upon a revered throne, and at his left, there sits the virgin of the holy spirit, upon a throne and glorifying him. And the seven virgins stand before her, . . . possessing thirty harps, and psalteries and trumpets, glorifying him. And all the armies of the angels glorify him, and they bless him. Now where he sits is upon a throne of light <with a> great cloud that covers him. And there was no one with him in the cloud except Sophia <the daughter of> Pistis, instructing him about all the things that exist in the eighth heaven, so that the likenesses of those things might be created, in order that his reign might endure until the consummation of the heavens of chaos and their forces.

Now Pistis Sophia set him apart from the darkness and summoned him to her right, and the prime parent she put at her left. Since that day, right has been called justice, and left called wickedness. Now because of this they all received a realm (*kosmos*) in the congregation of justice and wickedness, . . . stand . . . upon a creature . . . all.

Thus when the prime parent of chaos saw his son Sabaoth and the glory that he was in, and perceived that he was greatest of all the authorities of chaos, he envied him. And having become wrathful

he engendered Death out of his death: and he (viz., Death) was established over the sixth heaven, <for> Sabaoth had been snatched up from there. And thus the number of the six authorities of chaos was achieved. Then Death, being androgynous, mingled with his (own) nature and begot seven androgynous offspring. These are the names of the male ones: Jealousy, Wrath, Tears, Sighing, Suffering, Lamentation, Bitter Weeping. And these are the names of the female ones: Wrath, Pain, Lust, Sighing, Curse, Bitterness, Quarrelsomeness. They had intercourse with one another, and each one begot seven, so that they amount to forty-nine androgynous demons.

Their names and their effects you will find in the *Book of Solomon*.

And in the presence of these, Zoe, who was with Sabaoth, created seven good androgynous forces. These are the names of the male ones; the Unenvious, the Blessed, the Joyful, the True, the Unbegrudging, the Beloved, the Trustworthy. Also, as regards the female ones, these are their names: Peace, Gladness, Rejoicing, Blessedness, Truth, Love, Faith (Pistis). And from these there are many good and innocent spirits.

Their influences and their effects you will find in the *Configurations of the Fate of Heaven That Is Beneath the Twelve.*

And having seen the likeness of Pistis in the waters, the prime parent grieved very much, especially when he heard her voice, like the first voice that had called to him out of the waters. And when he knew that it was she who had given a name to him, he sighed. He was ashamed on account of his transgression. And when he had come to know in truth that an immortal man of light had been existing before him, he was greatly disturbed; for he had previously said to all the gods and their angels, "It is I who am god. No other one exists apart from me."[2] For he had been afraid they might know that another had been in existence before him, and might condemn him. But he, being devoid of understanding, scoffed at the condemnation and acted recklessly. He said, "If anything has existed before me, let it appear, so that we may see its light."

And immediately, behold! Light came out of the eighth heaven above and passed through all of the heavens of the earth. When the prime parent saw that the light was beautiful as it radiated, he was amazed. And he was greatly ashamed. As that light appeared, a human likeness appeared within it, very wonderful. And no one saw it except for the prime parent and Pronoia, who was with him. Yet its light appeared to all the forces of the heavens. Because of this they were all troubled by it.

Then when Pronoia saw that emissary, she became enamored of him. But he hated her because she was on the darkness. But she desired to embrace him, and she was not able to. When she was unable to assuage her love, she poured out her light upon the earth. Since that day, that emissary has been called "Adam of Light," whose rendering is "the luminous man of blood," and the earth spread over him, holy Adaman, whose rendering is "the Holy Land of Adamantine." Since that day, all the authorities have honored the blood of the virgin. And the earth was purified on account of the blood of the virgin. But most of all, the water was purified through the likeness of Pistis Sophia, who had appeared to the prime parent in the waters. Justly, then, it has been said: "through the waters." The holy water, since it vivifies the all, purifies it.

Out of that first blood Eros appeared, being androgynous. His masculinity is Himireris (i.e., Himeros), being fire from the light. His femininity that is with him— a soul of blood—is from the stuff of Pronoia. He is very lovely in his beauty, having a charm beyond all the creatures of chaos. Then all the gods and their angels, when they beheld Eros, became enamored of him. And appearing in all of them he set them afire: just as from a single lamp many lamps are lit, and one and the same light is there, but the lamp is not diminished. And in this way Eros became dispersed in all the created beings of chaos, and was not diminished. Just as from the midpoint of light and darkness Eros appeared and at the midpoint of the angels and mankind the sexual union of Eros was consummated so out of the earth the primal pleasure blossomed. The woman followed earth. And marriage followed woman. Birth followed marriage. Dissolution followed birth.

After that Eros, the grapevine sprouted up out of that blood, which had been shed over the earth. Because of this, those who drink of it conceive the desire of sexual union. After the grapevine, a fig tree and a pomegranate tree sprouted up from the earth, together with the rest of the trees, all species, having within them their seed from the seed of the authorities and their angels.

Then Justice created Paradise, being beautiful and being outside the orbit of the moon and the orbit of the sun in the Land of Wantonness, in the East in the midst of the stones. And desire is in the midst of the beautiful, appetizing trees. And the tree of eternal life is as it appeared by God's will, to the north of Paradise, so that it might make eternal the souls of the pure, who shall come forth from the modelled forms of poverty at the consummation of the age. Now the color of the tree of life is like the sun.

---

[2]Isa 45:5–6, 12.

And its branches are beautiful. Its leaves are like those of the cypress. Its fruit is like a bunch of grapes when it is white. Its height goes as far as heaven. And next to it (is) the tree of acquaintance (*gnosis*), having the strength of God. Its glory is like the moon when fully radiant. And its branches are beautiful. Its leaves are like fig leaves. Its fruit is like a good appetizing date. And this tree is to the north of Paradise, so that it might arouse the souls from the torpor of the demons, in order that they might approach the tree of life and eat of its fruit and so condemn the authorities and their angels.

The effect of this tree is described in the *Sacred Book,* to wit: "It is you who are the tree of acquaintance, which is in Paradise, from which the first man ate and which opened his mind; and he loved his female counterpart and condemned the other, alien likenesses and loathed them."

Now after it, the olive tree sprouted up, which was to purify the kings and the high priests of righteousness, who were to appear in the last days, since the olive tree appeared out of the light of the first Adam for the sake of the unguent that they were to receive.

And the first soul (*psyche*) loved Eros, who was with her, and poured her blood upon him and upon the earth. And out of that blood the rose first sprouted up, out of the earth, out of the thorn bush, to be a source of joy for the light that was to appear in the bush. Moreover after this the beautiful, good-smelling flowers sprouted up from the earth, different kinds, from every single virgin of the daughters of Pronoia. And they, when they had become enamored of Eros, poured out their blood upon him and upon the earth. After these, every plant sprouted up from the earth, different kinds, containing the seed of the authorities and their angels. After these, the authorities created out of the waters all species of beast, and the reptiles and birds—different kinds—containing the seed of the authorities and their angels.

But before all these, when he had appeared on the first day, he remained upon the earth, something like two days, and left the lower Pronoia in heaven, and ascended towards his light. And immediately darkness covered all the universe. Now when she wished, the Sophia who was in the lower heaven received authority from Pistis, and fashioned great luminous bodies and all the stars. And she put them in the sky to shine upon the earth and to render temporal signs and seasons and years and months and days and nights and moments and so forth. And in this way the entire region upon the sky was adorned.

Now when Adam of Light conceived the wish to enter his light—i.e., the eighth heaven—he was unable to do so because of the poverty that had mingled with his light. Then he created for himself a vast eternal realm. And within that eternal realm he created six eternal realms and their adornments, six in number, that were seven times better than the heavens of chaos and their adornments. Now all these eternal realms and their adornments exist within the infinity that is between the eighth heaven and the chaos below it, being counted with the universe that belongs to poverty.

If you (sg.) want to know the arrangement of these, you will find it written in the *Seventh Universe of the Prophet Hieralias.*

And before Adam of Light had withdrawn in the chaos, the authorities saw him and laughed at the prime parent because he had lied when he said, "It is I who am God. No one exists before me."[3]

---

[3]Isa 45:5–6, 12

When they came to him, they said, "Is this not the god who ruined our work?" He answered and said, "Yes. If you do not want him to be able to ruin our work, come let us create a human being out of earth, according to the image of our body and according to the likeness of this being (viz., Adam of Light), to serve us; so that when he (viz., Adam of Light) sees his likeness he might become enamored of it. No longer will he ruin our work; rather, we shall make those who are born out of the light our servants for all the duration of this eternal realm. Now all of this came to pass according to the forethought of Pistis, in order that a human being should appear after his likeness, and should condemn them because of their modelled form. And their modelled form became an enclosure of the light.

Then the authorities received the acquaintance (*gnosis*) necessary to create man. Sophia Zoe—she who is with Sabaoth—had anticipated them. And she laughed at their decision. For they are blind: against their own interests they ignorantly created him. And they do not realize what they are about to do. The reason she anticipated them and made her own human being first, was in order that he might instruct their modelled form how to despise them and thus to escape from them.

Now the production of the instructor came about as follows. When Sophia let fall a droplet of light, it flowed onto the water, and immediately a human being appeared, being androgynous. That droplet she molded first as a female body. Afterwards, using the body she molded it in the likeness of the mother which had appeared. And he finished it in twelve months. An androgynous human being was produced, whom the Greeks call Hermaphrodites; and whose mother the Hebrews call Eve of Life (Eve of Zoe),

namely, the female instructor of life. Her offspring is the creature that is lord. Afterwards, the authorities called it "Beast," so that it might lead astray their modelled creatures. The interpretation of "the beast" is "the instructor." For it was found to be the wisest of all beings.

Now, Eve is the first virgin, the one who without a husband bore her first offspring. It is she who served as her own midwife.

For this reason she is held to have said:
"It is I who am the part of my
    mother;
And it is I who am the mother;
It is I who am the wife;
It is I who am the virgin;
It is I who am pregnant;
It is I who am the midwife;
It is I who am the one that
    comforts pains of travail;
It is my husband who bore me;
And it is I who am his mother,
And it is he who is my father and
    my lord.
It is he who is my force;
What he desires, he says with
    reason.
I am in the process of becoming.
Yet I have borne a man as lord."

Now these through the will < ... >. The souls that were going to enter the modelled forms of the authorities were manifested to Sabaoth and his Christ. And regarding these the holy voice said, "Multiply and improve! Be lord over all creatures." And it is they who were taken captive, according to their destinies, by the prime parent. And thus they were shut into the prisons of the modelled forms. . . . And at that time, the prime parent then rendered an opinion concerning man to those who were with him. Then each of them cast his sperm into the midst of the navel of the earth. Since that day, the seven rulers have fashioned man with his body resembling their body, but his likeness resembling the man that had appeared to them. His modelling took place by parts, one at a time. And their leader fashioned the brain and the nervous system. After- wards he appeared as prior to him. He became a soul-endowed man. And he was called Adam, that is, "father," ac- cording to the name of the one that ex- isted before him.

The First Thought in Three Forms

Discovered at Nag Hammadi (see p. 19), the "First Thought in Three Forms" (sometimes called the "Trimorphic Protennoia") contains a series of three mystical discourses on the world, humans, and salvation through knowledge, placed on the lips of a female aeon (= divine being). Comparable in many ways to the Secret Book of John, the discourses contain several of the key elements of the Gnostic myth. Particularly emphasized are the revelations of divine knowledge from on high, culminating in the incarnation of the Word (cf. John 1:1–18).

The "First Thought" (= Protennoia), is the first emanation from the one true inscrutable God. She begins her discourse by revealing her own mysterious greatness, which is so great that it cannot even be spoken of. She then describes the three descents that she made from the heavenly realm in order to bring humans the heavenly knowledge that can illuminate their souls, delivering them from darkness into light. Each of these descents is associated with one of her three forms, since she is the Thought of the Father (or Voice), the Mother (or Sound), and the Son (or Word, i.e., the Logos). It is her final descent in the appearance of human flesh that brings the ultimate illumination to those who dwell in ignorance and darkness, leading to their ascent into the world of Light.

It is difficult to date this work, but many scholars think it was written around 200 CE.

[I] am [Protennoia, the] Thought that [dwells] in [the Light. I] am the movement that dwells in the [All, she in whom the] All takes its stand, [the first]-born among those who [came to be, she who exists] before the All. [She (Protennoia) is called] by three names, although she dwells alone, [since she is perfect]. I

Translation by John D. Turner, in James Robinson, *Nag Hammadi Library in English*, 3rd ed. (Leiden: E. J. Brill, 1988) 13–22; used with permission.

am invisible within the Thought of the Invisible One. I am revealed in the immeasurable, ineffable (things). I am incomprehensible, dwelling in the incomprehensible, I move in every creature.

I am the life of my Epinoia that dwells within every Power and every eternal movement and (in) invisible Lights and within the Archons and Angels and Demons and every soul dwelling in [Tartaros] and (in) every material soul. I dwell in those who came to be. I move in everyone and I delve into them all. I walk uprightly, and those who sleep I [awaken]. And I am the sight of those who dwell in sleep.

I am the Invisible One within the All. It is I who counsel those who are hidden, since I know the All that exists in it. I am numberless beyond everyone. I am immeasurable, ineffable, yet whenever I [wish, I shall] reveal myself of my own accord. I [am the head of] the All. I exist before the [All, and] I am the All, since I [exist in] everyone.

I am a Voice [speaking softly]. I exist [from the first. I dwell] within the Silence [that surrounds every one] of them. And [it is] the [hidden Voice] that [dwells within] me, [within the] incomprehensible, immeasurable [Thought, within the] immeasurable Silence.

I [descended to the] midst of the underworld and I shone [down upon the] darkness. It is I who poured forth the [water]. It is I who am hidden within [radiant] waters. I am the one who gradually put forth the All by my Thought. It is I who am laden with the Voice. It is through me that Gnosis comes forth. [I] dwell in the ineffable and unknowable ones. I am perception and knowledge, uttering a Voice by means of thought. [I] am the real Voice. I cry out in everyone, and they recognize it (the voice], since a seed indwells [them]. I am the Thought

of the Father and through me proceeded [the] Voice, that is, the knowledge of the everlasting things. I exist as Thought for the [All]—being joined to the unknowable and incomprehensible Thought—I revealed myself—yes, I—among all those who recognize me. For it is I who am joined with everyone by virtue of the hidden Thought and an exalted <Voice>, even a Voice from the invisible Thought. And it is immeasurable, since it dwells in the Immeasurable One. It is a mystery; it is [unrestrainable] by [the Incomprehensible One]. It is invisible [to all those who are] visible in the All. [It is a Light] dwelling in Light.

It is we [also who] alone [have separated] [from the] visible [world] since we [are saved by the] hidden [wisdom by means of the] ineffable, immeasurable [Voice]. And he who is hidden within us pays the tributes of his fruit to the Water of Life.

Then the Son who is perfect in every respect—that is, the Word who originated through that Voice; who proceeded from the height; who has within him the Name; who is a Light—he (the Son) revealed the everlasting things and all the unknowns were known. And those things difficult to interpret and secret, he revealed, and as for those who dwell in Silence with the First Thought, he preached to them. And he revealed himself to those who dwell in darkness, and he showed himself to those who dwell in the abyss, and to those who dwell in the hidden treasuries he told ineffable mysteries, and he taught unrepeatable doctrines to all those who became Sons of the Light.

Now the Voice that originated from my Thought exists as three permanences: the Father, the Mother, the Son. Existing perceptibly as Speech, it (Voice) has within it a Word endowed with every <glory>, and it has three masculinities, three powers, and three names. They exist in the manner of Three □ □ □—which are quadrangles—secretly within a silence of the Ineffable One.

[It is he] alone who came to be, that [is, the Christ. And] as for me I anointed him as the glory [of the] Invisible [Spirit] with [goodness]. Now [the Three] I established [alone in] eternal [glory] over [the Aeons in the] Living [Water], that [is, the glory that surrounds him] who first came forth to the Light of those exalted Aeons, and it is in glorious Light that he firmly perseveres. And [he] stood in his own Light that surrounds him, that is, the Eye of the Light that gloriously shines on me. He perpetuated the Father of all <the> Aeons, who am I, the Thought of the Father, Protennoia, that is, Barbelo, the [perfect] Glory and the [immeasurable] Invisible One who is hidden. I am the Image of the Invisible Spirit and it is through me that the All took shape, and (I am) the Mother (as well as) the Light which she appointed as Virgin, she who is called Meirothea, the incomprehensible Womb, the unrestrainable and immeasurable Voice.

Then the Perfect Son revealed himself to his Aeons who originated through him, and he revealed them and glorified them and gave them thrones and stood in the glory with which he glorified himself. They blessed the Perfect Son, the Christ, the only-begotten God. And they gave glory, saying, "He is! He is! The Son of God! The Son of God! It is he who is! The Aeon of Aeons beholding the Aeons which he begot! For you have begotten by your own desire! Therefore [we] glorify you: ma mō ō ō ō eia ei on ei! The [Aeon] of [Aeons! The] Aeon which he gave!"

Then, moreover, the [God who was begotten] gave them (the Aeons) a power of [life, on which they might rely] and

[he] established [them. The] first Aeon, he established [over the first]: Armedon, Nousa[nios, Armozel; the] second he established [over the second Aeon]: Phaionios, Ainios, Oroiael; the third over the third Aeon: Mellephaneus, Loios, Daveithai; the fourth over the fourth: Mousanios, Amethes, Eleleth. Now those Aeons were begotten by the God who was begotten—the Christ—and these Aeons received as well as gave glory. They were the first to appear, exalted in their thought, and each Aeon gave myriads of glories within great untraceable lights and they all together blessed the Perfect Son, the God who was begotten.

Then there came forth a word from the great Light Eleleth and said, "I am King! Who belongs to Chaos and who belongs to the underworld?" And at that instant his Light appeared radiant, endowed with the Epinoia. The Powers of the Powers did not entreat him and likewise immediately there appeared the great Demon who rules over the lowest part of the underworld and Chaos. He has neither form nor perfection, but on the contrary possesses the form of the glory of those begotten in the darkness. Now he is called "Saklas," that is, "Samael," "Yaltabaoth," he who had taken power; who had snatched it away from the innocent one (Sophia); who had earlier overpowered her who is the Light's Epinoia (Sophia) who had descended, her from whom he (Yaltabaoth) had come forth originally.

Now when the Epinoia of the [Light] realized that [he (Yaltabaoth)] had begged him (the Light), for another [order, even though he was lower] than she, she said, "Grant [me another order so that] you may become for me [a dwelling place lest I dwell] in disorder [forever." And the order of the] entire house of glory [was agreed] upon her word. A blessing was brought for her and the higher order released it to her.

And the great Demon began to produce aeons in the likeness of the real Aeons, except that he produced them out of his own power.

Then I too revealed by Voice secretly, saying, "Cease! Desist, (you) who tread on matter; for behold I am coming down to the world of mortals for the sake of my portion that was in that place from the time when the innocent Sophia was conquered, she who descended, so that I might thwart their aim which the one revealed by her appoints." And all were disturbed, each one who dwells in the house of the ignorant light, and the abyss trembled. And the Archigenetor of ignorance reigned over Chaos and the underworld and produced a man in my likeness. But he neither knew that that one would become for him a sentence of dissolution nor does he recognize the power in him.

But now I have come down and reached down to Chaos. And I was [with] my own who were in that place. [I am hidden] within them, empowering [them and] giving them shape. And [from the first day] until the day [when I will grant mighty power] to those who [are mine, I will reveal myself to] those who have [heard my mysteries], that is, the [Sons] of [the] Light.

I am their Father and I shall tell you a mystery, ineffable and indivulgeable by [any] mouth: Every bond I loosed from you, and the chains of the Demons of the underworld, I broke, these things which are bound on my members, restraining them. And the high walls of darkness I overthrew, and the secure gates of those pitiless ones I broke, and I smashed their bars. And the evil Force and the one who beats you, and the one who hinders you, and the Tyrant, and the Adversary, and the one who is King, and the present Enemy, indeed all these I explained to those who are mine, who are the Sons of the light, in order that they might nullify them all and be saved from all those bonds and enter into the place where they were at first.

I am the first one who descended on account of my portion which remains, that is, the Spirit that (now) dwells in the soul, (but) which originated from the Water of Life and out of the immersion of the mysteries, and I spoke, I together with the Archons and Authorities. For I had gone down below their language and I spoke my mysteries to my own—a hidden mystery—and the bonds and eternal oblivion were nullified. And I bore fruit in them, that is, the Thought of the unchanging Aeon, and my house, and their [Father]. And I went down [to those who were mine] from the first and I [reached them and broke] the first strands that [enslaved them. Then] everyone [of those] within me shone, and I prepared [a pattern] for those ineffable Lights that are within me. Amen.

I am the Voice that appeared through my Thought, for I am "He who is syzygetic," since I am called "the Thought of the Invisible One." Since I am called "the unchanging Speech," I am called "She who is syzygetic."

I am a single one (fem.) since I am undefiled. I am the Mother [of] the Voice, speaking in many ways, completing the All. It is in me that knowledge dwells, the knowledge of <things> everlasting. It is I [who] speak within every creature and I was known by the All. It is I who lift up the Speech of the Voice to the ears of those who have known me, that is, the Sons of the Light.

Now I have come the second time in the likeness of a female and have spoken with them. And I shall tell them of the coming end of the Aeon and teach them of the beginning of the Aeon to come, the one without change, the one in which our appearance will be changed. We shall be purified within those Aeons from which I revealed myself in the Thought of the likeness of my masculinity. I settled among those who are worthy in the Thought of my changeless Aeon.

For I shall tell you a mystery [of] this particular Aeon and tell you about the forces that are in it. The birth beckons: [hour] begets hour, [day begets day]. The months made known the [month. Time] has [gone round] succeeding [time]. This particular Aeon was completed in [this] fashion, and it was estimated, and it (was) short, for it was a finger that released a finger and a joint that was separated from a joint. Then when the great Authorities knew that the time of fulfillment had appeared—just as in the pangs of the parturient it (the time) had drawn near, so also had the destruction approached—all together the elements trembled, and the foundations of the underworld and the ceilings of Chaos shook and a great fire shone within their midst, and the rocks and the earth were shaken like a reed shaken by the wind. And the lots of Fate and those who apportion the domiciles were greatly disturbed over a great thunder. And the thrones of the Powers were disturbed since they were overturned, and their King was afraid. And those who pursue Fate paid their allotment of visits to the path, and they said to the Powers, "What is this disturbance and this shaking that has come upon us through a Voice <belonging> to the exalted Speech? And our entire habitation has been shaken, and the entire circuit of our path of ascent has met with destruction, and the path upon which we go, which takes us up to the Archigenetor of our birth, has ceased to be established for us." Then the Powers answered, saying, "We

too are at a loss about it since we did not know what was responsible for it. But arise, let us go up to the Archigenetor and ask him." And the Powers all gathered and went up to the Archigenetor. [They said to] him, "Where is your boasting in which [you boast]? Did we not [hear you say], 'I am God [and I am] your Father and it is I who [begot] you and there is no [other] beside me'? Now behold, there has appeared [a] Voice belonging to that invisible Speech of [the Aeon] (and) which we know not. And we ourselves did not recognize to whom we belong, for that Voice which we listened to is foreign to us, and we do not recognize it; we did not know whence it was. It came and put fear in our midst and weakening in the members of our arms. So now let us weep and mourn most bitterly! As for the future, let us make our entire flight before we are imprisoned perforce and taken down to the bosom of the underworld. For already the slackening of our bondage has approached, and the times are cut short and the days have shortened and our time has been fulfilled, and the weeping of our destruction has approached us so that we may be taken to the place we recognize. For as for our tree from which we grew, a fruit of ignorance is what it has; and also its leaves, it is death that dwells in them, and darkness dwells under the shadow of its boughs. And it was in deceit and lust that we harvested it, this (tree) through which ignorant Chaos became for us a dwelling place. For behold, even he, the Archigenetor of our birth, about whom we boast, even he did not know this Speech."

So now, O Sons of the Thought, listen to me, to the Speech of the Mother of your mercy, for you have become worthy of the mystery hidden from (the beginning of) the Aeons, so that [you might receive] it. And the consummation of this [particular] Aeon [and] of the evil life [has approached and there dawns the] beginning of the [Aeon to come] which [has no change forever].

I am androgynous. [I am Mother (and) I am] Father since [I copulate] with myself. I [copulated] with myself [and with those who love] me, [and] it is through me alone that the All [stands firm]. I am the Womb [that gives shape] to the All by giving birth to the Light that [shines in] splendor. I am the Aeon to [come. I am] the fulfillment of the All, that is, Me[iroth]ea, the glory of the Mother. I cast [voiced] Speech into the ears of those who know me.

And I am inviting you into the exalted, perfect Light. Moreover (as for) this (Light), when you enter it you will be glorified by those [who] give glory, and those who enthrone will enthrone you. You will accept robes from those who give robes and the Baptists will baptize you and you will become gloriously glorious, the way you first were when you were <Light>.

And I hid myself in everyone and revealed [myself] within them, and every mind seeking me longed for me, for it is I who gave shape to the All when it had no form. And I transformed their forms into (other) forms until the time when a form will be given to the All. It is through me that the Voice originated and it is I who put the breath within my own. And I cast into them the eternally holy Spirit and I ascended and entered my Light. [I went up] upon my branch and sat [there among the] Sons of the [holy] Light. And [I withdrew] to their dwelling place which [. . .] become [glorious. . . . Amen].

I am [the Word] who dwells [in the] ineffable [Voice]. I dwell in undefiled [Light] and a Thought [revealed itself] perceptibly through [the great] Speech of the Mother, although it is a male off-

spring [that supports me] as my foundation. And it (the Speech) exists from the beginning in the foundations of the All.

But there is a Light [that] dwells hidden in Silence and it was first to [come] forth. Whereas she (the Mother) alone exists as Silence, I alone am the Word, ineffable, unpolluted, immeasurable, inconceivable. It (the Word) is a hidden Light, bearing a Fruit of Life, pouring forth a Living Water from the invisible, unpolluted, immeasurable Spring, that is, the unreproducible Voice of the glory of the Mother, the glory of the offspring of God; a male Virgin by virtue of a hidden Intellect, that is, the Silence hidden from the All, being unreproducible, an immeasurable Light, the source of the All, the Root of the entire Aeon. It is the Foundation that supports every movement of the Aeons that belong to the mighty Glory. It is the Foundation of every foundation. It is the Breath of the Powers. It is the Eye of the Three Permanences, which exist as Voice by virtue of Thought. And it is a Word by virtue of Speech; it was sent to illumine those who dwell in the [darkness].

Now behold [I will reveal] to you [my mysteries] since you are my fellow [brethren, and you shall] know them all [. . .]. I [told all of them about my mysteries] that exist in [the incomprehensible], inexpressible [Aeons]. I taught [them the mysteries] through the [Voice that exists] within a perfect Intellect [and I] became a foundation for the All, and [I empowered] them.

The second time I came in the [Speech] of my Voice. I gave shape to those who [took] shape until their consummation.

The third time I revealed myself to them [in] their tents as Word and I revealed myself in the likeness of their shape. And I wore everyone's garment and I hid myself within them, and [they] did not know the one who empowers me. For I dwell within all the Sovereignties and Powers and within the Angels and in every moment [that] exists in all matter. And I hid myself within them until I revealed myself to my [brethren]. And none of them (the Powers) knew me, [although] it is I who work in them. Rather [they thought] that the All was created [by them] since they are ignorant, not knowing [their] root, the place in which they grew.

[I] am the Light that illumines the All. I am the Light that rejoices [in my] brethren, for I came down to the world [of] mortals on account of the Spirit that remains [in] that which [descended] (and) came forth [from] the innocent Sophia. [I came] and I delivered [. . .] and I [went] to [. . .] which he had [formerly and I gave to him] from the Water [of Life, which strips] him of the Chaos [that is in the] uttermost [darkness] that exists [inside] the entire [abyss], that is, the thought of [the corporeal] and the psychic. All these I put on. And I stripped him of it and I put upon him a shining Light, that is, the knowledge of the Thought of the Fatherhood.

And I delivered him to those who gives robes—Yammon, Elasso, Amenai—and they [covered] him with a robe from the robes of the Light; and I delivered him to the Baptists and they baptized him—Micheus, Michar, and Mn[e]sinous—and they immersed him in the spring of the [Water] of Life. And I delivered him to those who enthrone—Bariel, Nouthan, Sabenai—and they enthroned him from the throne of glory. And I delivered him to those who glorify—Ariom, Elien, Phariel—and they glorified him with the glory of the Fatherhood. And those who snatch away snatched away—Kamaliel. [. . .]anen, Samblo, the servants of <the> great holy Luminaries—and they took him into the light-[place] of his Fa-

therhood. And [he received] the Five Seals from [the Light] of the Mother, Protennoia, and it was [granted] him [to] partake of [the mystery] of knowledge, and [he became a Light] in Light.

So, now [. . . I was] dwelling in them [in the form of each] one. [The Archons] thought [that I] was their Christ. Indeed I [dwell in] everyone. Indeed within those in whom [I revealed myself] as Light [I eluded] the Archons. I am their beloved, [for] in that place I clothed myself [as] the Son of the Archigenetor, and I was like him until the end of his decree, which is the ignorance of Chaos. And among the Angels I revealed myself in their likeness, and among the Powers as if I were one of them, but among the Sons of Man as if I were a Son of Man, even though I am Father of everyone.

I hid myself within them all until I revealed myself among my members, which are mine, and I taught them about the ineffable ordinances, and (about) the brethren. But they are inexpressible to every Sovereignty and every ruling Power except to the Sons of the Light alone, that is, the ordinances of the Father. These are the glories that are higher than every glory, that is, [the Five] Seals complete by virtue of Intellect. He who possesses the Five Seals of these particular names has stripped off <the> garments of ignorance and put on a shining Light. And nothing will appear to him that belongs to the Powers of the Archons. Within those of this sort darkness will dissolve and [ignorance] will die. And the thought of the creature which [is scattered will] present a single appearance and [dark Chaos] will dissolve and [. . .] and the [. . .] incomprehensible [. . .] within the [. . .] until I reveal myself [to all my fellow brethren] and until I gather [together] all [my fellow] brethren within my [eternal kingdom]. And I proclaimed to them the ineffable [Five Seals in order that I might] abide in them and they also might abide in me.

As for me, I put on Jesus. I bore him from the cursed wood, and established him in the dwelling places of his Father.

And those who watch over their dwelling places did not recognize me. For I, I am unrestrainable together with my Seed, and my Seed, which is mine, I shall [place] into the Holy Light within an incomprehensible Silence. Amen.

The Hymn of the Pearl

One of the most elegant compositions of early Christianity, the "Hymn of the Pearl" is embedded in the third-century Acts of Thomas (see p. 122).[1] Most scholars agree, however, that the hymn was composed by a different hand and at an earlier date. On the surface, it appears to be a simple folktale of a prince sent by his royal parents on a mission to snatch a pearl from the lair of a ravenous dragon in Egypt, only to arrive at his destination and forget his task and identity, needing a message from the royal court to be awakened from his torpor and reminded of who he is. He then seizes the pearl and returns to the glories of his father's realm.

The hymn may be something far more than a simple folk tale, however. Hints within the text itself—such as the "knowledge" (literally "gnosis") connected with the prince's heavenly garment (l. 88)—along with parallels to other literature, suggest that the story represents a Gnostic allegory of the incarnation of the soul, which enjoys a glorious heavenly existence ("my father's palace") from which it descends (to "Egypt") to become entrapped in matter ("clothed myself in garments like theirs"). Forgetting whence it came, the soul eventually relearns its true nature from a divine emissary. When it awakens to its true identity ("son of kings"), it returns to its heavenly home where it receives the full knowledge of itself.

If the "Hymn of the Pearl" was written in a Gnostic milieu, only later to be incorporated into the Acts of Thomas, it may have been composed sometime in the late second century.

1 When I was a little child, in my fa-
    ther's palace,
2 And enjoyed the wealth and luxury
    of those who nurtured me,
3 My parents equipped me with provisions and sent me out from the
    East, our homeland.
4 From the wealth of our treasury they
    gave me a great burden,

---

[1]See further Ehrman, *Lost Christianities*, 39–41.

Translation by J. K. Elliott, *Apocryphal New Testament* (Oxford: Clarendon Press, 1993) 488–91; used with permission.

5 Which was light so that I could carry it by myself:

6 Gold from the land above, silver from great treasuries,

7 And stones, chalcedonies of India and agates from Kushan.

8 And they girded me with steel,

9 And they took away from me the garment set with gems and spangled with gold
   Which they had made out of love for me

10 And the yellow robe which was made for my size,

11 And they made a covenant with me
   And wrote it in my mind that I might not forget:

12 "If you go down to Egypt and bring the one pearl

13 Which is in the land of the devouring serpent,

14 You shall put on again that garment set with stones and the robe which lies over it,

15 And with your brother, our next in command, you shall be a herald for our kingdom."

16 So I departed from the East on a difficult and frightening road led by two guides,

17 And I was very young to travel on it.

18 I passed over the borders of the Mosani, where there is the meeting-place of the merchants of the East,

19 And reached the land of the Babylonians.

20 I went down to Egypt, and my companions parted from me.

21 I went straight to the serpent and stayed near his den

22 Until he should slumber and sleep, so that I might take the pearl from him.

23 Being alone I altered my appearance and seemed an alien even to my own people,

24 But I saw one of my kinsmen there, a freeborn man from the East,

25 A youth fair and beautiful, the son of courtiers.

26 He came and kept me company.

27 And I made him my intimate friend, a comrade with whom I communicated my business.

28 Being exhorted to guard against the Egyptians and against partaking of unclean things,

29 I clothed myself in garments like theirs, so that I would not be seen as a stranger

30 And as one who had come from abroad to take the pearl,
   Lest the Egyptians might arouse the serpent against me.

31 But somehow they learned that I was not their countryman.

32 They dealt with me treacherously, and I tasted their food.

33 I no longer recognized that I was a king's son, and I served their king.

34 I forgot the pearl for which my parents had sent me.

35 And I fell into a deep sleep because of the heaviness of their food.

36 While I was suffering these things my parents were aware of it and grieved over me,

37 And a proclamation was heralded in our kingdom that all should present themselves at our doors.

38 The kings of Parthia and those in office, and the great men of the East

39 Resolved that I should not be left in Egypt.

40 So the courtiers wrote me a letter:

41 "From your father the king of kings and your mother, the mistress of the East

42 And their brothers, who are second to us, To our son in Egypt, greetings!

43 Awake, and rise from your sleep.

44 Listen to the words in this letter, Remember you are the son of kings, You have fallen beneath the yoke of slavery.

45 Remember your gold-spangled garment,

46 Recall the pearl for which you were sent to Egypt,

47 Your name has been called to the book of life,

48 Together with that of your brother whom you have received in our kingdom."

49 And the king sealed it to make it an ambassador,

50 Because of the wicked Babylonian children and the tyrannical demons of the Labyrinth.

53 I rose from sleep when I recognized its voice,

54 I took it up and kissed it and I read.

55 And what was written concerned that which was engraved on my heart.

56 And I immediately remembered that I was a son of kings and that my freedom demanded my people.

57 I remembered the pearl for which I had been sent to Egypt,

58 And the fact that I had come to snatch it from the terrifying serpent.

59 I subdued it by calling out my father's name,

61 And I snatched the pearl and turned about to go to my parents.

62 And I took off the dirty clothing and left it behind in their land.

63 And directed my way forthwith to the light of our Eastern home.

64 And on the road I found a female who lifted me up.

65 She awakened me, giving me an oracle with her voice, and guided me to the light,

66 The Royal silken garment shone before my eyes.

68 And with familial love leading me and drawing me on

69 I passed by the Labyrinth, And leaving Babylon behind on the left,

70 I reached Meson which is a great coast.

75 But I could not recall my splendor, For it had been when I was still a child and quite young that I had left it behind in my father's palace.

76 But, when suddenly I saw my garment reflected as in a mirror,

77 I perceived in it my whole self as well And through it I knew and saw myself.

78 For though we originated from the one and the same we were partially divided, Then again we were one, with a single form.

79 The treasurers too who had brought the garment

80 I saw as two beings, but there existed a single form in both, One royal symbol consisting of two halves.

81 And they had my money and wealth in their hands and gave me my reward:

82 The fine garment of glorious colors,

83 Which was embroidered with gold, precious stones, and pearls to give a good appearance.

84 It was fastened at the collar.

86 And the image of the King of Kings was all over it.

87 Stones of lapis lazuli had been skillfully fixed to the collar,

88 And I saw in turn that motions of knowledge were stirring throughout it,

89 And that it was prepared to speak.

90 Then I heard it speak:

91 "It is I who belong to the one who is stronger than all people and for

whose sake I was written about by the father himself."

92 And I took note of my stature,

93 And all the royal feelings rested on me as its energy increased.

94 Thrust out by his hand the garment hastened to me as I went to receive it,

95 And a longing aroused me to rush and meet it and to receive it.

96 And I stretched out and took it and adorned myself with the beauty of its colors.

97 And I covered myself completely with my royal robe over it.

98 When I had put it on I ascended to the land of peace and homage.

99 And I lowered my head and prostrated myself before the splendor of the father who had sent it to me.

100 For it was I who had obeyed his commands

And it was I who had also kept the promise,

101 And I mingled at the doors of his ancient royal building.

102 He took delight in me and received me in his palace.

103 All his subjects were singing hymns with harmonious voices.

104 He allowed me also to be admitted to the doors of the king himself,

105 So that with my gifts and the pearl I might appear before the king himself.

CANONICAL LISTS

Introduction

Among the many writings that still survive from early Christianity are several that discuss the issue of which books ought to be included in the canon of Scripture. These discussions provide us with our clearest indications that no set canon of the New Testament existed, even among orthodox Christians, prior to the end of the fourth century. I have included in this collection several of the fullest discussions available, all of them from forebears of orthodoxy: no "heretical" canon list survives.

Among other things, these lists show that even though the contours of the canon were still very much in flux in the early Christian centuries, there was a broad agreement in proto-orthodox circles that the canon was to include the four Gospels, the writings of Paul, and several other apostolic texts. They also reveal the criteria for canonicity that were considered in such circles: for a book to be accepted as canonical, it needed to be ancient (near the time of Jesus), apostolic (connected to one of his closest followers), catholic (used widely by like-minded churches throughout the world), and orthodox (promoting the right kind of belief rather than heresy).

It appears that of all the criteria, "orthodoxy" was primary: if a writing did not promote a perspective that was considered orthodox—so the argument went—it could not very well be apostolic. Those who made the argument found the point obvious: no apostle would support heresy. Any book, therefore, that was written in the name of an apostle, yet supported an "aberrant" perspective, was necessarily forged. These may not be the grounds scholars use today to determine the authorship of ancient texts, but the arguments proved both persuasive and powerful for the formation of the Christian canon.

The first author to list the twenty-seven books of our New Testament as *the* canonical books (these and no others) was the bishop of Alexandria, Athanasius, in 367 CE. Even then, however, debates continued, even in orthodox circles. In some parts of the Christian church, there never has been complete agreement.[1]

---

[1] See the discussion in Ehrman, *Lost Christianities*, 229–46.

The Muratorian Canon

The Muratorian Fragment is the oldest surviving New Testament canon list—that is a list of books believed to comprise the canonical New Testament—known to exist. The document is named after L. A. Muratori, the Italian scholar who discovered it in a library in Milan in the early eighteenth century. Written in ungrammatical Latin, the fragmentary text begins in mid-sentence by describing the production of an unnamed Gospel; since it continues by explicitly calling Luke the "third book of the Gospel" and John, then, the "fourth," the list evidently began with Matthew and Mark.

Twenty-two of the twenty-seven books of the New Testament canon are included here—all except Hebrews, James, 1 and 2 Peter, and 3 John. But the author also accepts as canonical the Wisdom of Solomon and the Apocalypse of Peter (see p. 280). The *Shepherd* of Hermas is accepted for reading but not as part of sacred Scripture for the church. The author explicitly rejects the Pauline Letters to Laodicea[1] and to Alexandria as forgeries made by the followers of Marcion, indicating that they are not to be accepted by the church, since "it is not fitting that gall be mixed with honey."[2] His list concludes by condemning forgeries made by various heretics, such as Valentinus, Basilides, Marcion, and the Montanists.

The time and place of composition of the Muratorian Canon are in great dispute. But since the author shows a particular concern with the false teachings of heretical teachers who lived in the middle of the second century, and knows something of the family of bishop Pius of Rome (d. 154), many scholars think he was living in the latter half of the second century, possibly in Rome. If so, then this list shows that at that time, some proto-orthodox Christians were already accepting the core of what were later to be almost universally regarded as the books of the New Testament.

---

[1]This is probably not the Letter to the Laodiceans that survives. See p. 165.   [2]On the views of Marcion, see Ehrman, *Lost Christianities*, 103–109.

Translation by Bruce M. Metzger, *The Canon of the New Testament: Its Origin, Development, and Significance* (Oxford: Clarendon Press, 1987) 305–7; used with permission.

... at which nevertheless he was present, and so he placed [them in his narrative]. 2 The third book of the Gospel is that according to Luke. 3 Luke, the well-known physician, after the ascension of Christ, 4–5 when Paul had taken him with him as one zealous for the law, 6 composed it in his own name, according to [the general] belief. Yet he himself had not 7 seen the Lord in the flesh; and therefore, as he was able to ascertain events, 8 so indeed he begins to tell the story from the birth of John. 9 The fourth of the Gospels is that of John, [one] of the disciples. 10 To his fellow disciples and bishops, who had been urging him [to write], 11 he said, "Fast with me from today for three days, and what 12 will be revealed to each one 13 let us tell it to one another." In the same night it was revealed 14 to Andrew, [one] of the apostles, 15–16 that John should write down all things in his own name while all of them should review it. And so, though various 17 elements may be taught in the individual books of the Gospels, 18 nevertheless this makes no difference to the faith of believers, since by the one sovereign Spirit all things 20 have been declared in all [the Gospels]: concerning the 21 nativity, concerning the passion, concerning the resurrection, 22 concerning life with his disciples, 23 and concerning his twofold coming; 24 the first in lowliness when he was despised, which has taken place, 25 the second glorious in royal power, 26 which is still in the future. What 27 marvel is it, then, if John so consistently 28 mentions these particular points also in his Epistles, 29 saying about himself: "What we have seen with our eyes 30 and heard with our ears and our hands 31 have handled, these things we have written to you.?"[3] 32 For in this way he professes [himself] to be not only an eye-witness and hearer, 33 but also a writer of all the marvelous deeds of the Lord, in their order. 34 Moreover, the acts of all the apostles 35 were written in one book. For "most excellent Theophilus"[4] Luke compiled 36 the individual events that took place in his presence— 37 as he plainly shows by omitting the martyrdom of Peter 38 as well as the departure of Paul from the city [of Rome] 39 when he journeyed to Spain. As for the Epistles of 40–1 Paul, they themselves make clear to those desiring to understand, which ones [they are], from what place, or for what reason they were sent. 42 First of all, to the Corinthians, prohibiting their heretical schisms; 43 next,[5] to the Galatians, against circumcision; 44–6 then to the Romans he wrote at length, explaining the order (or, plan) of the Scriptures, and also that Christ is their principle (or, main theme). It is necessary 47 for us to discuss these one by one, since the blessed 48 apostle Paul himself, following the example of his predecessor 49–50 John, writes by name to only seven churches in the following sequence: to the Corinthians 51 first, to the Ephesians second, to the Philippians third, 52 to the Colossians fourth, to the Galatians fifth, 53 to the Thessalonians sixth, to the Romans 54–5 seventh. It is true that he writes once more to the Corinthians and to the Thessalonians for the sake of admonition, 56–7, yet it is clearly recognizable that there is one Church spread throughout the whole extent of the earth. For John also in the 58 Apocalypse, though he writes to seven churches, 59–60 nevertheless speaks to all. [Paul also wrote] out of affection and love one to Philemon, one to Titus, and two to Timothy; and these are held sacred 62–3 in the

---

[3] 1 John 1: 1–3. [4] Luke 1: 3. [5] The letter "b" in the Latin text before "Galatians" may belong to "Corinthians" (πρὸς Κορινθίους β').

esteem of the Church catholic for the regulation of ecclesiastical discipline. There is current also [an epistle] to **64** the Laodiceans, [and] another to the Alex- andrians, [both] forged in Paul's **65** name to [further] the heresy of Marcion, and several others **66** which cannot be re- ceived into the catholic church **67** —for it is not fitting that gall be mixed with honey. **68** Moreover, the Epistle of Jude and two of the above-mentioned (or, bearing the name of) John are counted (or, used) in the catholic [Church],[6] and [the book of] Wisdom, **70** written by the friends of Solomon in his honor. **71** We receive only the apocalypses of John and Peter, **72** though some of us are not will- ing that the latter be read in church. **73** But Hermas wrote the *Shepherd* **74** very recently, in our times, in the city of Rome, **75** while bishop Pius, his brother, was occupying the [episcopal] chair **76** of the church of the city of Rome. **77** And therefore it ought indeed to be read; but **78** it cannot be read pub- licly to the people in church either among **79** the prophets, whose number is com- plete,[7] or among **80** the apostles, for it is after [their] time. **81** But we accept noth- ing whatever of Arsinous or Valentinus or Miltiades, **82** who also composed **83** a new book of psalms for Marcion, **84– 5** together with Basilides, the Asian founder of the Cataphrygians. . . .

---

[6]It may be, as Zahn (*Geschichte,* ii, 66) and others have supposed, that a negative has fallen out of the text here.   [7]Perhaps the Fragmentist means that there are three major Prophets and twelve minor Prophets.

The Canon of Origen of Alexandria

Origen was the most brilliant, prolific, and influential author of the first three centuries of Christianity. Born in 185 CE, he was raised by Christian parents in Alexandria, Egypt. Already as a child, Origen was recognized as a prodigy. While still a teenager, according to the church historian Eusebius, he was appointed to be head of the famous Catechetical School in Alexandria, a kind of institution of Christian higher learning. Origen soon became the leading proto-orthodox spokesperson of his day, with extensive writings that included detailed expositions of Scripture, sermons, theological treatises, defenses of the faith against its cultured despisers, and refutations of heretics. His inventive theological explorations were seen as acceptable by the proto-orthodox of his day; but he was later condemned as a heretic, largely because of the ways his views were developed by his successors. As a result of this condemnation, many of his writings were destroyed. But a good many also survive, revealing the true brilliance of Origen's mind.

None of these surviving writings provides a full listing of the books that Origen considered to belong to the New Testament canon. He does make scattered references to the canon, however, and these can help show how the canon was taking shape in the early third century in proto-orthodox circles of Alexandria. The following partial lists are drawn from Origen's Commentaries on Matthew and John and his Homilies on the Epistle to the Hebrews, as these are quoted in the writings of Eusebius (see below).

As can be seen, Origen accepted the four Gospels that were eventually agreed upon: the Pauline epistles (which he does not enumerate in this fragment), one letter of Peter, allowing for the possibility of a second, one letter of John and possibly two more, and the Apocalypse of John. In the final fragment given here, he addresses the problem posed by the book of Hebrews, accepting it as canonical, but expressing his opinion that Paul was not its actual author.

Translation by Bart D. Ehrman, based on the Greek text in Gustave Bardy, *Eusèbe de Césareé, Histoire Ecclésiastique* (SC, 41; Paris: Cerf, 1951).

Now in the first volume of his *Commentary on the Gospel of Matthew,* [Origen] defends the canon of the church, testifying that he recognizes only four Gospels. This is what he says:

> Among the four Gospels—the only ones not disputed by the church of God under heaven—I have learned from the tradition that the first written was that according to Matthew, the former tax collector and then apostle of Jesus Christ, who delivered it to believers coming out of Judaism, drawing it up in Hebrew letters. Second was that according to Mark, who recorded it as he was instructed by Peter, who acknowledges him as his son in the Catholic epistle he wrote, where he says, "The church in Babylon, chosen with you, sends you greetings, as does my son Mark," [1 Pet. 5:13]. The third was that according to Luke, the Gospel praised by Paul and made for those among the Gentile Christians. And after all these was that according to John.

And in the fifth volume of his *Expositions on the Gospel of John,* the same author [Origen] said these things concerning the apostolic epistles:

> Paul was made worthy to be a minister of the new covenant, a covenant based not on the letter but the Spirit [2 Cor. 3:6]; and he spread the gospel from Jerusalem and its vicinity, as far as Illyricum [Rom 15:19]. He did not write to all the churches he had taught; but to those he did write, he sent letters of just a few lines. But Peter, on whom the church of Christ was built and against which the gates of hell will not prevail [Matt. 16:18], left behind one letter that is acknowledged, and possibly a second, for it is disputed. And

why do we need to speak of the one who reclined on Jesus' breast, John, who left behind one Gospel, while admitting that he could produce so many that the world would not be able to contain them [John 21:25]? He also wrote the Apocalypse, after being ordered to be silent and not to write what was spoken by the voices of the seven thunders [Rev. 10:3–4]. He also left behind an epistle of a very few lines, and possibly a second and third. For not everyone agrees that these are genuine. But taken together, both do not contain a hundred lines.

In addition to these, he says the following about the letter to the Hebrews in his *Homilies* on it:

> The writing style of the epistle entitled "To the Hebrews" does not have the unskilled character of the apostle, who admitted that he was an unskilled writer [2 Cor. 11:6], at least with regard to style. The epistle is better Greek in its composition, as everyone able to evaluate differences in style will admit. At the same time, everyone who attends closely to the reading of the apostolic text will agree that the thoughts of the epistle are marvelous and in no way inferior to the acknowledged writings of the apostle.

After a few other matters he adds the following:

> But I would say that the thoughts of the epistle appear to be those of the apostle, whereas the style and composition of the letter are those of someone who had his writings in mind, and wrote down the words of his teacher at his leisure. And so any church that considers the epistle to be Paul's should be approved for their view; for the ancients had good

reason to pass it on as his. But as to who wrote the epistle, truly God knows. We have heard a report from some that it was written by Clement, who become bishop of Rome; whereas others think it was Luke, the one who wrote the Gospel and Acts. . . . . (Eusebius, *Church History,* 6. 25, 3–14).

The Canon of Eusebius

Eusebius of Caesarea is commonly known as the "Father of Church History." His famous ten-volume work, *Church History,* originally published in 311 CE, was the first full sketch of the history of the church, from the days of Jesus down to Eusebius's own time. As a result, Eusebius is an incomparable source for historians interested in the first three centuries of Christianity. For not only does he narrate events that transpired during this period and discuss its key figures, but he also quotes extensively many of the primary texts that Christians had written. A number of these texts have otherwise been lost to history, so that when Eusebius quotes them at length and accurately (which he often does), he provides us with unparalleled access to the Christian literature of the period.

Eusebius's account is, of course, told from his own perspective, with his biases affecting both his selection of material and the spin that he puts on it. Moreover, on occasion Eusebius explicitly intervenes in his historical narrative to express his own understanding of the developments he describes. One place that he does so involves his discussion of the books that he considered to be canonical Scripture. The passage is important for showing that even by his time, some 200–250 years after the earliest surviving Christian writings, there were still vibrant debates over the contours of the canon, even within orthodox circles.[1]

Eusebius's listing of books is somewhat complicated, as he indicates that the status of several books was still under dispute. In any event, he indicates that books making a claim to being canonical fall into four categories: (a) "acknowledged books," that is, those accepted as canonical by all proto-orthodox churches, (b) "disputed books," that is, those recognized by some churches but not others, (c) "spurious books," that is, orthodox books that are in fact pseudonymous and so not to be accepted, and (d) rejected books, that is, heretical forgeries.

---

[1]See further, Ehrman, *Lost Christianities,* 164–68; 172–76.

Translation by Bart D. Ehrman, based on the Greek text of Gustave Bardy, *Eusèbe de Césareé, Histoire Ecclésiastique* (SC, 41; Paris: Cerf, 1951).

Having reached this point, it is reasonable to summarize the writings already referred to as belonging to the New Testament. Among the first books must be located the holy quaternion of the Gospels, which are followed by the Acts of the Apostles. After this must be reckoned the epistles of Paul. Then to be confirmed are the first epistle bearing the name of John and likewise that of Peter. After these is to be placed, if it seems right, the Apocalypse of John; we will set forth other opinions about it at the appropriate time. These, then, are among the acknowledged books.

But among the disputed books, which are nonetheless known by many, are found the epistle of James, as it is called, that of Jude, the second epistle of Peter, and those called the second and third epistles of John, whether they come from the evangelist or from someone with the same name.

Among those that are spurious are to be placed the Acts of Paul and the book called the *Shepherd,* the Apocalypse of Peter, the surviving Epistle of Barnabas, and the book called *Teachings* [= the Didache] *of the Apostles,* and, as I have said, the Apocalypse of John, if that seems right—a book that some reject but others judge to belong to the acknowledged books. But some people also number among these the Gospel according to the Hebrews, which is particularly celebrated among those who have accepted Christ from among the Hebrews.

All these should be counted among the disputed books; but nonetheless we have felt compelled to make a list of them, distinguishing between writings that are acknowledged as true and genuine by the tradition of the church and those that are not—books that do not belong in the New Testament but are disputed, yet are known to the majority of church people. In this way we are able to know which are in that category and which are set forth by heretics in the names of the apostles, whether Gospels allegedly by Peter, Thomas, Matthias, and of some other than these, or Acts allegedly of Andrew, John, and other apostles. No one standing in the succession of the true churches ever thought it worthwhile to mention any of these in any of his treatises. And their literary character differs greatly from the style characteristically found in the apostolic writings; while the opinions they express and their choice of material clearly reveal that they are as different as possible from truly orthodox works, since they are, after all, fabrications of heretics. For that reason they should not be counted even among the spurious works, but are to be rejected in every way as absurd and godless. (Eusebius, *Church History*, 3. 25, 1–7)

The Canon of Athanasius of Alexandria

Athanasius was one of the most important figures in orthodox Christianity of the fourth century. As a young man he attended the first "ecumenical" church council, the Council of Nicea in 325 CE, called by the Emperor Constantine, in part, to resolve theological differences that were splitting the church. The creed that came out of the Council became instrumental in the formation of later Christian theology, and developed into what is now called the "Nicene Creed," still recited in churches today. Throughout the fourth century Athanasius was an outspoken proponent of the doctrinal resolutions of Nicea and wrote numerous theological treatises that explicated his views.

Athanasius became the bishop of the church of Alexandria in 328 CE. In this position, every year he wrote the churches under his jurisdiction in order to establish for them the date on which Easter was to be celebrated. He used the occasion of these letters to provide pastoral, practical, and theological instruction as well. Probably the most famous of these letters was the one he wrote in 367 CE, the thirty-ninth Festal letter, in which, among other things, he laid out for his churches the contours of the biblical canon, both Old and New Testaments. Here he indicates the books that were to be read in the churches, and indicates—both explicitly and by inference—the books that were not. "In these alone," says Athanasius of the canonical writings, "the teaching of godliness is proclaimed. Let no one add to these; let nothing be taken away from them."[1]

This is the first time—some three centuries after the earliest Christian writings were produced—that any Christian author of any kind listed as canonical the current twenty-seven books of the New Testament. It should not be thought, however, that even with Athanasius the matter was finally resolved. For other Christian leaders—including some within Athanasius's

---

[1]See further, Ehrman, *Lost Christianities,* 230–31.

Translation by Bart D. Ehrman, based on the Greek text in Daniel J. Theron, *Evidence of Tradition* (Grand Rapids: Baker Book House, 1957) 118.

own church—questioned the canonicity of several of the books he listed
(e.g., 2 Peter) and maintained that some others should be included in the
canon as well (e.g., the *Shepherd* of Hermas). Still, it was eventually the
canon promoted first by Athanasius that became the accepted list of sacred
Christian books, the New Testament.

And now without hesitation I should
again speak of the books of the New
Testament. For they are as follows. The
four Gospels according to Matthew,
Mark, Luke, and John. Then after these
the Acts of the Apostles and the seven
books by the apostles called the Catholic
Epistles: one of James, two of Peter, then
three of John, and after them one of Jude.
In addition to these are the fourteen epistles of the apostle Paul, written in the
following order: first to the Romans, then
two to the Corinthians, and after these to
the Galatians and next to the Ephesians;
then to the Philippians and to the Colossians, two to the Thessalonians and then
to the Hebrews; after these are two to
Timothy, one to Titus, and, finally, one
to Philemon. In addition is the Apocalypse of John.

But for the sake of greater accuracy I
add the following, indicating out of necessity that there are books other than
these that are not, on the one hand, included in the canon, but that have nonetheless been designated by the fathers as
books to be read to those who have recently come to the faith and wish to be
instructed in the word of piety: the Wisdom of Solomon, the Wisdom of Sirach,
Esther, Judith, Tobit, the book called the
Teaching [= Didache] *of the Apostles* and
the *Shepherd.* Nonetheless, brothers,
while the former are in the canon and the
latter are to be read, there should be no
mention at all of apocryphal books created by heretics, who write them whenever they want but try to bestow favor on
them by assigning them dates, that by
setting them forth as ancient, they can be,
on false grounds, used to deceive the
simple minded.

The Canon of the Third Synod of Carthage

The New Testament canon was never ratified by an "ecumenical" council (i.e. a meeting of bishops from around the Christian world) in the early church. But there were several smaller synods and councils that pronounced judgment on which books should be accepted as canonical Scripture. Evidently the first to ratify the twenty-seven book canon propounded by Athanasius, and accepted by most churches still today, was a Synod in Hippo, North Africa, in 393 CE, where the greatest orthodox theologian of antiquity, Augustine of Hippo, threw his weight behind Athanasius's list and pushed its acceptance. Unfortunately, we no longer have a record of the proceedings of the conference. But we do have the proceedings of the Third Synod of Carthage, held four years later, which summarized what had transpired at the earlier meeting. These latter proceedings are given here.

Even this synod's affirmation of the canon was not universally binding, as indicated in the proceedings themselves, where it is noted that the church across the sea (i.e., Rome, on the other side of the Mediterranean) was to be consulted on the matter. And, as it turns out, different churches in other parts of the world never did agree on this twenty-seven book canon, despite its overwhelming acceptance in both Western and Eastern branches of Christendom.[1]

Besides the canonical Scriptures, nothing shall be read in church under the name of divine Scriptures. Moreover, the canonical Scriptures are these: [then follows a list of Old Testament books]. The [books of the] New Testament: the Gos-

---

[1]See further Ehrman, *Lost Christianities*, 229–47.

Translation by Bruce M. Metzger, *The Canon of the New Testament: Its Origin, Development, and Significance* (Oxford: Clarendon Press, 1987) 315; used with permission.

pels, four books; the Acts of the Apostles, one book; the Epistles of Paul, thirteen; of the same to the Hebrews, one Epistle; of Peter, two; of John, apostle, three; of James, one; of Jude, one; the Revelation of John. Concerning the confirmation of this canon, the transmarine Church shall be consulted. On the anniversaries of martyrs, their acts shall also be read.